W9-BFK-022

HEROES, MONSTERS, & MESSIAHS

HEROES, MONSTERS, & MESSIAHS

Movies and Television Shows as the Mythology of American Culture

ELIZABETH C. HIRSCHMAN

Andrews McMeel Publishing

Kansas City

00 01 02 03 04 QUF 10 9 8 7 6 5 4 3 2 1

Library of Congress Cataloging-in-Publication Data

Hirschman, Elizabeth.
Heroes, monsters, and messiahs : movies and television shows as the mythology of American culture / Elizabeth Hirschman.
p. cm.
Includes bibliographical references.
ISBN 0-7407-0485-0
1. Motion pictures—United States—Plots, themes, etc.
2. Television programs—United States—Plots, themes, etc. I. Title.

PN1993.5.U6 H54 2000
791.43'0973—dc21

00-020331

This book is dedicated to

Alix, Annie, and Shannon—

my three goddesses

— CONTENTS —

Mythologies are in fact
the public dreams that
move and shape societies.

—JOSEPH CAMPBELL,
The Mythic Image

HEROES, MONSTERS, & MESSIAHS

— ONE —

MOTION PICTURES AND TELEVISION SHOWS AS MYTH

Over the course of this week, you will probably watch seven or eight television shows, perhaps catch a movie or two on cable, and then head out to the nearby cineplex on Saturday and Sunday and take in the latest blockbuster film. While we sit in the darkened theater watching Jedi knights duel with the evil Darth Maul, or we lounge on the couch in front of the television screen watching as doctors, nurses, and paramedics struggle to save a child's life on *ER,* we rarely become conscious of the fact that we are viewing mythic struggles between good and evil and life and death. Yet our inner minds do recognize the deeper forces at play in front of our eyes and cause us to feel joy, sorrow, relief, or triumph at the close of the tale.

Although we Americans like to think of ourselves as thoroughly modern and fully rational, we have much in common with our prehistoric forebears—and with the ancient Sumerians, Egyptians, Greeks, and Romans, as well. All of these cultures of the past—and ours of the present—love myth. Myth surrounds us in the form of television shows and motion pictures, novels and plays. It teaches us about the origins of the universe and the role of science and technology in our lives. Myth tells us how men and women should behave toward one another in courtship. It instructs us on how to fight to obtain our goals and overcome obstacles. Myth tells us who the bad guys and good guys are, whom to emulate and whom to condemn.

The two most popular forms of myth-telling for present-day Americans are motion pictures and television shows. As we followed the lives of the characters on *Seinfeld, Murphy Brown,* and *Cheers,* we were learning about ourselves and our society. Earlier generations of Americans watched *I Love Lucy* and *Dragnet* for the same reasons. When we go to see *Titanic* or *Terminator 2* or *Star Wars: The Phantom Menace,* we are reliving epic mythic struggles, just as prior consumers did with *The Ten Commandments, Gone with the Wind,* and *Ben Hur.*

Further, we are engaging in a human ritual that goes back as far as Mesolithic times, when our early ancestors sat around campfires and told tales of monsters and the heroes who slew them. From these prehistoric narratives up through performances of *Oedipus Rex* in the Greek outdoor theater, past Greek texts on *The Odyssey,* through Shakespearean plays like *Hamlet, Macbeth,* and *Romeo and Juliet,* the mythic impulse has always enthralled the human imagination.

The present book is a result of that same impulse to experience myth. The quest we are embarking upon is to examine the myths embedded in the most popular motion pictures and television shows in America over the last fifty years and to learn from them the values, beliefs, and spiritual dimensions that have shaped our culture. To do so, we will use the work of the anthropologist Claude Lévi-Strauss, the psychologist Carl Jung, and the mythologist Joseph Campbell.

There are two basic aspects to any myth: content and story structure. The content refers to the characters and activities in the myth; the structure to the ways in which the characters interact. According to Jung, the content elements of the myth represent cultural *archetypes*—entities embodying some significant, often primal, factor of concern to humans. For example, a bird or a spaceship may function as a divine messenger. A very tall structure may serve as a point of contact between mortals and gods, as, for example, Mount Sinai, where Moses received the Ten Commandments, or the flat-topped mountain (Devil's Tower) in Wyoming where extraterrestrials make contact with humans in Steven Spielberg's *Close Encounters of the Third Kind.*

In addition to looking at their content, we also are going to examine the structure of myths; that is, the *relationship between archetypes* depicted in the myth. Perhaps the foremost advocate of the structural analysis of myth is Lévi-Strauss.

In order to understand a myth's structure, we organize the characters according to their relationships to certain outcomes; for example, do some characters get married? do others die? do still others find fortunes? Next, we try to see if there is an overarching principle that explains why some characters are consistently led to certain outcomes, while other characters are consistently led to certain other outcomes. For example, in the popular television series *Dallas,* the character J. R. Ewing—a scheming, manipulative businessman—usually succeeds in acquiring money and power, but rarely is able to maintain his personal relationships or create family harmony.

The motion pictures and television shows whose mythology we are looking at are the most popular of all time, as evidenced by box office receipts and audience ratings. They are listed chronologically in Table 1 (motion pictures) and Table 2 (television programs).

This book devotes one or two chapters to each decade; that is, Chapter 2 covers the 1950s; Chapter 3, the 1960s; Chapter 4, the 1970s; and so forth. A summary discussion, Chapter 12, synthesizes "the meaning of it all" using the motion pictures *Titanic* and *Star Wars: Episode I* and suggests some ideas on the archetypal developments we could see in the coming decades.

To prepare us for this journey, let's now consider three motion pictures that predate our 1950 milepost, but which rank among the most popular films of all time: *Snow White and the Seven Dwarfs* (1937), *Fantasia* (1940), and *Gone with the Wind* (1939). As we shall see, they are virtual hotbeds of mythic imagery and will get us well on our way.

— TABLE I —

MOTION PICTURE CHRONOLOGY

Pre–1950

Snow White and the Seven Dwarfs	1937
Gone with the Wind	1939
Fantasia	1940

1950–1959

The Ten Commandments	1956
Ben Hur	1959
Sleeping Beauty	1959

1960–1969

101 Dalmatians	1961
Mary Poppins	1964
The Sound of Music	1965
Doctor Zhivago	1965
The Jungle Book	1967
The Graduate	1967

1970–1979

The Godfather	1972
The Exorcist	1973
Jaws	1975
Close Encounters of the Third Kind	1977
Star Wars	1977
Grease	1978
Superman	1978

1980–1989

The Empire Strikes Back	1980
Raiders of the Lost Ark	1981
E.T. the Extra-Terrestrial	1982
Tootsie	1982
Return of the Jedi	1983
Ghostbusters	1984
Beverly Hills Cop	1984
Back to the Future	1985
Batman	1989
Rain Man	1988
Indiana Jones and the Last Crusade	1989

1990–1999

Home Alone	1990
Pretty Woman	1990
Ghost	1990
Terminator 2: Judgment Day	1991
Robin Hood: Prince of Thieves	1991
Batman Returns	1992
Mrs. Doubtfire	1993
Jurassic Park	1993
The Fugitive	1993
Forrest Gump	1994
The Lion King	1994
Apollo 13	1995
Independence Day	1996
Twister	1996
Titanic	1997
Star Wars: Episode I—The Phantom Menace	1999

— TABLE 2 —

TELEVISION SHOW CHRONOLOGY

1950–1959
I Love Lucy
Dragnet
Gunsmoke
Wagon Train
Have Gun Will Travel

1960–1969
The Andy Griffith Show
Bonanza
The Beverly Hillbillies
The Dick Van Dyke Show
Bewitched
Gomer Pyle, U.S.M.C.

1970–1979
All in the Family
The Waltons
Happy Days
Laverne & Shirley
Three's Company

1980–1989
Dallas
M.A.S.H.
The Cosby Show
Magnum P.I.
Cheers
Roseanne

1990–1996
Murphy Brown
Home Improvement
Murder, She Wrote
Seinfeld
ER
Friends

Snow White and the Seven Dwarfs (1937)

Released in 1937, toward the end of the Great Depression, *Snow White* was the first in an ongoing series of Walt Disney animated films that set myths to life.[1] Both *Snow White*—and its successor, *Sleeping Beauty,* which we discuss in Chapter 2—are adaptations from the Grimm's fairy-tale collection. The Grimm's collection, itself, was constructed from long-standing Germanic mythology. Thus, the tales they tell are part and parcel of a narrative heritage that extends into the distant past and, yet, still rings true today.[2]

In the Disney version of this narrative, we are told that a vain and wicked stepmother (the Queen) has dressed Princess Snow White in rags and treats her as a servant. Daily, the Queen asks her magic mirror who is the fairest woman in the land, and repeatedly the mirror answers "You are." Snow White spends her days scrubbing the steps of a wishing well; her only friends are beautiful white doves. She sings a wishing song, asking for a prince "to find her." A prince on a white horse rides by and hears her song, but does not see her.

One day, despite her unattractive apparel and menial tasks, Snow White grows more beautiful than the Queen, and the magic mirror so informs the Queen. Enraged, the Queen sends a huntsman into the forest with Snow White, ordering him to kill Snow White and bring the princess's heart back in a box.

Already in our tale, we have encountered several archetypal figures and ample mythic imagery. The wicked Queen represents the Terrible Mother/Destructive Goddess archetype. In Freudian terms we may understand her as the evil mother who seeks to control and ultimately destroy her children. Fearful of the increasing attractiveness of her stepdaughter, Snow White, she at first attempts to control it (the rags, the chores) and then to destroy it. Snow White, in contrast, is being cast as the Good Mother/Nurturant Goddess. Significantly, she is positioned near a wishing well and surrounded by white doves. As Marija Gimbutas notes, wells are typically associated with female magic and white doves are a female symbol dating from prehistory. Significantly, also, Snow White's future mate rides a white horse, symbolic of his heroic, male status.[3]

Returning to our story, once the huntsman takes Snow White to the forest, she first sings a beautiful song, next gathers flowers, and then helps a baby bird find its parents. All three of these activities are associated with the Nurturant Goddess archetype. The huntsman, seeing Snow White's intrinsic goodness, cannot harm her and tells her to run into the forest. That night, Snow White is very fearful and tormented by the dark, ominous forest. It is filled with predatory beings, such as bats and alligators. She runs frantically, collapses, weeps, and falls asleep.

But with the morning light, the gentle forest animals—rabbits, turtles, chipmunks, raccoons, squirrels, birds, and deer—come to her aid. She sings a song with the baby bird she saved. These kind animals, which represent the beneficent aspect of nature in contrast to the dark, destructive aspect apparent during the previous night, take her to a little cottage in the woods.

Snow White sees that the cottage is very unkempt and supposes it is occupied by "untidy little children." With the animals' assistance, she cleans up the whole house, singing "Whistle While You Work." She then falls asleep across seven little beds.

Meanwhile, the seven dwarves who live in the house begin to return home from their work at a diamond mine: "Hi Ho! Hi Ho! It's home from work we go." Upon returning home, they discover Snow White. One dwarf exclaims, "She's an angel," but another warns, "She's a female with wicked wiles." (Thus, the dwarves invoke the two female archetypes: nurturant goddess versus destructive goddess.) Of course, Snow White has already displayed ample evidence of her nurturant goddess status.

Snow White promises to cook and keep house for them. When she sees how dirty and rowdy the seven dwarves always are, she gently makes them wash and clean themselves up. Here Snow White evinces the archetypal female role as not only nurturer, but civilizer. As Campbell points out, women's role in creating culture, and socializing men to accept it, dates back to Sumerian myth.

The wicked Queen has learned from her magic mirror that Snow White lives "across seven hills, over seven falls, in the house of the *seven* dwarves" and that the Queen has been given the heart of a pig, not of Snow White, by the huntsman.[4] The Queen descends into the depths of the castle where she performs black magic and transforms herself into a hag. The hag (or witch) into which the Queen makes herself is a vivid manifestation of the destructive goddess archetype. As Gimbutas (1993) notes, these figures typically have large, hooked noses (symbolizing predatory beaks) and shriveled, bony bodies, which signify desiccated corpses. Other portions of the witch's appearance confirm this: her hair is white and unkempt, her mouth toothless, and she is shrouded in a black, hooded robe. In her workshop are skeletons, skulls, and a raven—all death symbols. The transformed Queen declares that Snow White "will be buried alive" and descends into a *boat* which she poles along a black river. The boat itself is a female symbol; the river is reminiscent of the river Styx in Hades, the ancient Greek underworld of death. She carries with her a basket of ripe, red apples (a feminine fruit), one of which has been treated with a sleeping potion. Vultures, also female death symbols, accompany the hag/Queen.

Ironically, Snow White, accompanied by songbirds, is preparing a fruit pie for the dwarves when the hag/Queen arrives, accompanied by her vultures. (Here the symmetrical female good versus female evil is especially marked.) Feigning illness, the hag/Queen tricks Snow White into letting her into the cottage. Snow White bites into the poisoned apple, which the hag/Queen offers her and falls to the ground. The hag/Queen cackles, and a violent thunderstorm erupts.[5] The friendly forest animals have gone to fetch the dwarves, but they arrive too late; Snow White has collapsed. The dwarves pursue the hag/Queen to the top of a rocky mountain, where she is struck by lightning and killed. Snow White is placed into a coffin of gold and glass; the dwarves and animals mourn her passing. The dwarves keep a vigil throughout the winter (the season of death). As winter gives way to spring, flowers arise around the coffin, symbolizing the rebirth of nature. Sunlight shines upon Snow White's still body. The Prince arrives and sings to her: "My one heart, only for you" and kisses her. Snow White awakens. The dwarves and animals rejoice. Snow White kisses each dwarf goodbye; the Prince then puts her astride his white horse and leads her into the sunset. A beautiful golden castle gleams in the distance. And, the tale assures us, they "lived happily ever after."

The story of Snow White ends with the triumph of the nurturant goddess over the destructive goddess, but the victory has been obtained in a remarkably passive way. Consistent with traditional American (and European) ideology surrounding women, Snow White "wins" by being nurturant, kind, and gentle. She is an icon of the passive virtues of womanhood, unable to defend herself. The dwarves, male figures, must kill the evil Queen. Snow White is "awakened" to life and love by her prince. Curiously, there is no active role for the male hero in this tale either; the Prince does little more than ride a horse and kiss the princess. *Sleeping Beauty,* which we encounter in Chapter 2, is analogous to *Snow White,* but with a much more developed role for the prince.

Fantasia (1940)

A second early Disney animated film was also among the most popular films of all time. *Fantasia,* released in 1940, is a film of brilliant, startling originality. The basic premise of the film was to use classical music, provided by the Philadelphia Orchestra under Leopold Stokowski, to inspire Disney's animators in creating corresponding visual images. Drawing upon (both literally and figuratively) cultural mythology from various sources, the animators constructed a remarkable series of visual narratives.

In the first vignette, set to Tchaikovsky's *Nutcracker Suite,* brightly colored lights change into naked female fairies dancing in the dark and painting florescent colors across the landscape. The fairies, with their long legs and gossamer wings, dance through an enchanted forest, scattering fairy dust. These images portray the intertwined mythic themes of woman, nature, and magic.

Later, dancing mushrooms mimic Chinamen, and pink flowers fall upon dark, still water. Beautiful anemones beneath the sea become diaphanous goldfish with large eyes and petite, red mouths. All of these images, save the mushrooms, represent female beauty. The vignette closes with the earlier fairies, now in a sunlit forest. It is autumn, and they blow leaves and milkweed seeds. Later, blue fairies paint the forest with frost and skate across a frozen pond, as snowflakes fall. This vignette evokes the feminine principle in nature, that is, Mother Earth.

In the next series of scenes, Mickey Mouse appears as the apprentice in *The Sorcerer's Apprentice.* When the stern, male sorcerer (father archetype) leaves, Mickey (son archetype) dons the wizard's cap (the symbol of adult powers) and bids the broom to carry water. Mickey falls asleep in the sorcerer's chair (an ersatz throne, another symbol of paternal authority); he dreams that he can control, first, the planets, stars, and galaxies, and then the oceans, clouds, and storms. In essence, Mickey is fantasizing that he possesses adult, male powers, that he can assume his father's role. He awakens to find the castle flooded because the broom has continued to carry water during his sleep. Mickey chops up the broom, seeking to destroy it, but the broom becomes many brooms, all carrying water. Caught in a whirlpool, Mickey almost drowns, but the sorcerer returns and magically dries up the flood. He looks sternly at Mickey and swats him on the bottom with the broom. Mickey sheepishly returns to his duties.

This is a straightforward cautionary tale of the unhappy consequences resulting from unproven sons prematurely usurping their father's powers, an ancient mythic theme. On an even deeper level, it may also be read as man's ill-conceived and ill-fated efforts to usurp the powers of the gods.

The next vignette uses Stravinsky's *Rite of Spring* as a backdrop for the story of evolution. The earth is created from a ball of swirling gas; volcanoes cover its surface. As the earth cools, one-celled animals swarm in its seas and evolve into elaborate varieties of sea creatures. The fish grow legs and walk on land, where they become dinosaurs. These become increasingly complex and competitive. A Tyrannosaurus rex, our culture's iconic monster, battles and kills a stegosaurus. The sun dries up the water, causing the dinosaurs to die; their bones litter the landscape.

This vignette, although now dated somewhat in its scientific content, we must recognize as *our* creation myth. That is, it tells *a* story of how the world began.[6] Although we consider this version of events to be factual, it does serve the same cosmological function as any other culture's creation myth; that is, it tells us how the world began and where we came from.

Fantasia next presents Beethoven's Sixth Symphony to accompany what it calls "a mythological setting" (of course, all the other images have been mythological as well, just not recognized as such). Mountains and valleys are filled with childlike unicorns and colorful Pan figures playing flutes. A black father horse, white mother horse, and baby black-and-white horse course through the skies on feathered wings, like a family of Pegasuses, landing like swans on a crystal lake.

Naked female centaurs (half human, half horse) bathe in the lake attended to by cherubs. Handsome male centaurs come to view them. The females are decorated with flowers and birds (recall these female symbols from *Snow White*). After forming pairs, the centaurs gather grapes and dance on them in a vat. Drunken Bacchus, the ancient Greek god of wine, arrives on a donkey. Rain clouds form, and Zeus hurls his thunderbolts from the sky, frightening the dancers and destroying the wine vat. Zeus falls asleep in the sky and the sun comes out. Aurora, goddess of the sky, crosses the sky, creating a rainbow. Night falls and the full moon glows, as the centaurs fall asleep. This vignette pays clear homage to Greco-Roman mythology, while at the same time incorporating even earlier mythic themes concerning family formation and courtship.[7]

After a brief fantasy interlude featuring ostriches and hippos in tutus, elephants in pink toe shoes, and crocodiles in capes, the film concludes with its final vignette. Opening with Mussorgsky's *Night on Bald Mountain,* it contrasts images of the sacred with the profane. A bat-winged, horned black devil arises from his rocky mountaintop and descends to the village below. Ghosts and skeletons are summoned from their graves. The four horsemen of the apocalypse gallop through the dark night skies on skeletal horses. Human souls are tormented in the fires of hell, as the devil fans the flames. The flames turn into female figures, beasts, and lizards (no doubt, the Disney animators' views on women as sources of temptation). Suddenly, a church bell sounds. The ghosts and apparitions fly back to their graves; the devil takes refuge on his mountaintop. Schubert's "Ave Maria" becomes the musical accompaniment. A solemn procession of people carries candles across a bridge and through a row of trees. The sacred procession makes its way through an archway to a beautiful landscape of blues and pinks. The sun rises.

This last series of images is wondrously evocative of Judeo-Christian mythic motifs. In it, we glimpse visions from Dante's *Inferno* and Milton's *Paradise Lost,* combined with rural American Protestant imagery of the holiness of nature. The association of sunrise with God predates Christianity and is consistent with Egyptian and even earlier Sumerian legends, Campbell points out. Yet despite the polyglot origins of these images, they are immediately recognizable to American viewers. Indeed, *Fantasia* as a whole presents us with so many myths from so many sources that it is without parallel among American films; one is tempted to declare it a feast of multicultural mythology.

Gone with the Wind (1939)

We turn next to an American motion picture classic, one of the most popular films in U.S. history, *Gone with the Wind.* Traditionally, myths have often been set in times of great social upheaval; for example, the birth or death of a civilization, an era of cataclysmic change, or a time of radical alteration in the social order. In such settings, archetypes are most useful, because they help to signify and explain events that are beyond the control of mere individuals. *Gone with the Wind* embodies a myth of classic proportions; it is perhaps for this reason that the movie continues to be avidly consumed even sixty years after its introduction.

In a historic sense, as well as in a mythic sense, the U.S. Civil War was a cataclysmic event in American society. Symbolically and politically, it was a struggle between two ways of life, two forms of social order, two sets of values and behaviors. As we have been taught from history texts, it was a struggle in which one side of our society, the North (representing technology, industrialization, and democracy), won, while another side of our society, the South (representing nature, agrarianism, and aristocracy) was defeated. As in every major struggle of this kind, some good values of the vanquished group are lost to the civilization that emerges. Though victorious and representing the greater good, the industrial-technological culture that emerged dominant after the Civil War was seen as lacking some of the desirable social values typified by the Old South—gentility, chivalry, romantic love, harmony with nature, and even, the film's narrative instructs us, a human soul.

Visually, *Gone with the Wind* is rich with archetypal imagery. The film opens with a Tree of Life symbol in the left of the screen against a verdant, fertile background. We are informed that this is to be "the story of cavaliers and cottonfields . . . , where gallantry took its last bow. . . . The last ever to be seen of knights and their ladies fair, of master and of slave . . . a civilization gone with the wind."

We are introduced to the heroine, Scarlett O'Hara, the beautiful but manipulative daughter of a wealthy Irish plantation owner. Scarlett is significant as an archetype in several ways. First, her personality, as indicated by her name and actions, is *not* typical of the

Archive Photos

Scarlet O'Hara's exterior beauty cloaked her inner destructive nature.

reserved, feminine, genteel Southern woman (recall Snow White). On the contrary, she is highly impulsive, passionate, selfish, and dominating. Second, she does *not* quite have upper-class social status in Southern society. Her family, though affluent, is Irish Catholic, in contrast to the English Protestant aristocrats who dominated the Old South. Thus both her personality and her lineage cause her to be something of a misfit in her present surroundings. Both these characteristics, however, will permit her to emerge a successful survivor in the post-war South, when hard pragmatism and mongrel ancestry become valued characteristics. Significantly, Scarlett often dresses in green (the color of money). By the end of the story, she will declare money to be "the most important thing in the world."

The hero of the tale is Rhett Butler. Rhett (it sounds like "red") is a male version of Scarlett, both literally and figuratively. Like her, he is passionate, selfish, and competitive. As his surname (Butler) implies, he also is not a full member of the chivalrous Southern aristocracy. Rather, he survives and prospers by *serving* (as a butler does) whoever is in power: first the South, then the North, then the carpetbagger Yankees. As with Scarlett, his pragmatism and inferior status will permit him to flourish in the new order established after the war.

Rhett is immediately attracted to Scarlett, sensing in her a female manifestation of himself. However, Scarlett is infatuated with Ashley Wilkes. Ashley is archetypical of the antebellum Southern gentleman—a fairy-tale prince. He is English, blond, chivalrous, romantic, idealistic, honorable, and courageous—a knight who will not be able to survive in the coming era. Despite Scarlett's attentions, Ashley is engaged to marry his cousin,[8] Melanie Hamilton, who exemplifies the antebellum Southern gentlewoman (the nurturant goddess archetype). She is gentle, loving, compassionate, sincere, and trusting—a lady of aristocratic descent, who also will be unable to survive in the new age.

As the story develops, Southern gentlemen are discussing the impending war with the North, declaring that they must fight to defend their way of life. The Yankees are viewed as ill-bred rabble. Rhett Butler argues against war on pragmatic grounds; the Yankees will win, he believes, because they are technologically superior. Romantic ideals, he declares, cannot defeat guns and factories.

Melanie and Ashley marry. Scarlett then marries Melanie's brother, Charles, whom she does not love, in an effort to stay close to Ashley. War is declared, and both Ashley and Charles go off to fight. Rhett becomes a blockade runner for the South, earns large profits, and continues to make overtures to Scarlett. Scarlett's husband, Charles, is killed, but she does not mourn him—she still desires Ashley.

The war continues; Rhett's statement that romantic ideals will prove no match for bullets is indeed prophetic. Wave upon wave of wounded and dying Confederate men are brought into Atlanta, the heart of the Southern civilization. As General William Tecumseh Sherman marches on Atlanta, the city is burned to the ground; the civilization literally goes up in flames. Rhett heroically rescues Scarlett, Melanie, and Melanie and Ashley's newborn son from the burning ruins of Atlanta. Rhett again proposes to Scarlett, but she continues to spurn him. Scarlett returns to Tara,[9] her family's plantation, with Melanie and her baby.

The Southern civilization lies in ruins. The landscape is littered with dead bodies; barren trees and fields stretch to the horizon. Vultures hover overhead. Ashley Wilkes's plantation, Twelve Oaks, has been burned to the ground and his father killed. Tara, however, still stands, although stripped of all its elegance.[10] Scarlett's mother has died, and her father is a broken man, delirious and alcoholic. In a scene that symbolizes her death in the old civilization and resurrection in the new one, Scarlett walks from Tara into the barren fields. She finds a carrot, devours it shamelessly out of hunger, and falls to the ground. Regaining her strength from the red earth, she rises up to declare "God as my witness, they're not going to beat me; I'll never be hungry again. If I have to lie, steal, cheat, or kill, I'll never be hungry again!" The Tree of Life stands to the right of the screen, its branches bare, the landscape empty.

At this turning point, Scarlett's aggressive persona, which had always been implicit but disguised, becomes fully explicit. A new civilization driven by materialism, technology, and competition has emerged for which her character is well suited and in which it may now be *openly* exposed. Scarlett assumes control of her household; she and her sisters work in the fields. She shoots, kills, robs, and then buries an invading ex-Yankee soldier, stating, "Well, I guess I've done murder; but I won't think about that now, I'll think about it tomorrow." Ashley returns from the war. He is now an anachronism, symbolic of a lost way of life. His former princely virtues of gentility, honor, and chivalry have become deficits in a new social order that values only success and wealth, no matter how dishonorably obtained.

Scarlett lies to her sister's fiancé, Frank Kennedy, a rich merchant, convincing him to marry her and thereby cheating her own sister for money. True to her vow, she has now lied, stolen, cheated, and killed for material gain. Scarlett assumes control of Kennedy's business, becoming an extremely prosperous and highly unscrupulous businesswoman. She also carries a gun and drives her own carriage, further demonstrating her fully masculine persona. Scarlett declares that money is the most important thing in the world—a widespread credo for the modern age. Frank Kennedy, defending

Scarlett's honor in a fight, is killed; she is once again a widow from a loveless and opportunistic marriage. Another woman says to Scarlett, "You killed your husband because you acted like a man"—she emasculated him by assuming his male prerogatives.

After Frank's death, Scarlett finally agrees to marry Rhett, because he is extremely rich. She does this despite the fact that she is now very rich herself; her desire for material acquisition is insatiable. Rhett and Scarlett have a daughter, Bonnie Blue Butler, whom Rhett adores and Scarlett rejects. (She cannot feel maternal love.) To preserve her figure, Scarlett refuses to have further sexual intercourse with Rhett, but after catching her still making advances toward Ashley, Rhett rapes her. She again becomes pregnant. They have a violent argument, and she miscarries. Later, their daughter Bonnie is killed in a riding accident. Rhett and Scarlet are now humanly barren, although materially rich.

Melanie, still genteel, forgiving, and kind, comes to comfort them. Melanie's health, both as an archetype of nurturant goddess virtues and as a story character, has been weakened since the end of the war and the beginning of the materialistic era, and she dies soon after. She requests that Scarlett look after both her son and Ashley. Ashley breaks down emotionally, and Scarlett finally realizes that he is a remnant of an ideal that can no longer survive in the present social order: "I have loved something that doesn't really exist," she states, and then adds the pragmatic afterthought, "it doesn't really matter." Rhett and Scarlett part; he returns to Charleston, South Carolina, she to Tara. The Tree of Life symbol is again at the left of the scene, but its branches remain bare.

Gone with the Wind, when examined structurally with regard to the archetypes it contains and their relationship to one another, reveals some vivid and compelling propositions about our society. First, like many historic myths, it proposes that there once was a verdant, gentle, golden era in which honor, cooperation, love, and integrity were cherished virtues. This is symbolized in the movie by agrarian fruitfulness and the Old South. This golden era was defeated by the rise of a new era, driven by industrialization and technology, in which the dominant cultural characteristics were materialism, pragmatism, competition, and selfishness.

Men and women who followed the golden era values, as symbolized by Ashley and Melanie, are depicted as having *personal relationships* that are long-lasting because they are based on true, romantic love and as being *humanly fertile*; that is, their children survive. But they are *materially impoverished* and become *dependent* upon those who are materialistic, competitive, and pragmatic. That is, the gentle and kind are too weak to survive without the protection of the brutal and the strong. Conversely, we are instructed that men and women who possess the new era values of materialism, pragmatism, competition, and selfishness, characters like Rhett and Scarlett, have short-lived, *loveless relationships*, based on selfish, materialistic values and are *humanly barren*—their children die because they are not capable of nurturing them. But they are successful in obtaining *material riches*.

Some Concluding Thoughts on Archetypal Development

What have the films *Snow White, Fantasia,* and *Gone with the Wind* shown us about myth and archetypes? Six male figures predominated in the narratives (1) the Prince, (2) Ashley Wilkes, (3) Rhett Butler, (4) Mickey Mouse (the son), (5) the sorcerer (the father) and (6) the devil. It is easy to recognize that the Prince and Ashley Wilkes represent essentially the same archetype—the noble, well-bred hero whom the princess is destined to marry. Yet with the failure of Ashley Wilkes, we see an American spin put on this symbol. We are told that our heroes need more than just courage and good breeding. The figure of Rhett Butler embodies more fully an American interpretation of this archetype—a hero who is crafty, enterprising, and pragmatic. We will meet him often down the road we are traveling in this inquiry, in the likeness of Han Solo and Indiana Jones. He is not always noble or charming or even tactful. But he gets the job done. The brief appearance of the devil in *Fantasia* represents the only manifestation of male evil, the destructive god, that we have encountered thus far. But we are about to come upon a host of these images as we enter Chapter 2.

Similarly, among female characters, we have met four significant figures: (1) Snow White, (2) Melanie Wilkes, (3) Scarlett O'Hara, and (4) the evil Queen. Snow White and Melanie Wilkes are examples of the fair, kind maiden of noble birth who symbolizes the nurturant goddess archetype. Once again, we learn by comparing the more modern heroine, Melanie, with the more ancient Snow White that twentieth-century Americans may not view the princess figure with as much reverence as earlier cultures did, for Melanie, though certainly noble and kind, also comes across to us as weak and dependent. Scarlett, the female counterpart to Rhett, must save Melanie and her child. Without Scarlett's strength, drive, and sheer will to live, Melanie and her noble lineage would surely have perished.

Thus, we may distinguish Scarlett from the other female character whom she closely resembles—the wicked stepmother Queen, the destructive goddess. Scarlett shares in common with the destructive goddess archetype her vanity, selfishness, and willingness to betray family and friends to obtain her material goals.[11] Yet her competitive skills and intelligence are shown to be vital to preserving those noble persons she cares for (for example, Ashley Wilkes).

The most well developed evil character in the three films is the wicked stepmother-Queen. In her human aspect, the Queen represents the modern stereotype of the cruel, vain, domineering woman—the bitch. But her transformed self, the witch/hag, calls upon a deeper, much more ancient image, that of women's role as goddess of destruction. In this form, the desiccated hag symbolizes a supernatural bird of prey, a magical witch of the night, who is in league with the devil and uses her power to destroy life and goodness. She is a villain of the first order. But as we shall see, as we turn now to the fifties, villainy is not restricted to the female sex.

— TWO —

THE 1950s: Legends in Our Own Time

WE HAVE ARRIVED at the 1950s, a decade famous for the baby boom, Elvis Presley, Dwight D. Eisenhower, the hula hoop—and the birth of commercial television. Since our task is to document the media archetypes of the fifties and not to comment on the decade's cultural merit (thank goodness!), we will reserve comment on all of the above, save television. The Nielsen ratings, upon which our selection of the most popular television shows is based, began in 1950. From 1950 until 1959, the top-10 rated programs were the *Texaco Star Theater, Arthur Godfrey's Talent Scouts, I Love Lucy, Dragnet, The Jackie Gleason Show, The $64,000 Question, The Ed Sullivan Show, Gunsmoke, Wagon Train,* and *Have Gun Will Travel.* Because we are viewing these programs as mythology, this analysis focuses on the five shows that featured ongoing fictional narratives: *I Love Lucy, Dragnet, Gunsmoke, Wagon Train,* and *Have Gun Will Travel.* Each of these portrayed a strong central character (for example, Matt Dillon, the marshal of Dodge City in *Gunsmoke*) whose symbolic meaning could be assessed across different episodes.

However, before we examine these television series, let's first look at three motion pictures that also sprang from the 1950s and are among the most popular films of all time: *The Ten Commandments, Ben Hur,* and *Sleeping Beauty.* The first two are monumental biblical epics that take Judeo-Christian mythology and cast it upon the screen in 70mm glory, constructing several *iconic images*[1] for American culture and making a legend of the principal actor, Charlton Heston, in the process. The third, another animated masterpiece from Walt Disney, is essentially a retelling of the Snow White story with a more complex plot line, three fairies instead of seven dwarfs, and a revamped warrior-prince who, this time, actually fights for the fair maiden's hand.[2] Let's begin with the creation myth with which most of us are very familiar: the one from the Bible.

The Ten Commandments (1956)

Starring Charlton Heston as Moses and Yul Brynner as Ramses, *The Ten Commandments* has become a perennial feature on television, serving for many viewers as their most vivid source of knowledge on the biblical narrative. The story opens with material from Genesis: "And God said, 'Let there be light.'" Humans were "given dominion over the earth, but people were unaware of God's law." Ignorant of the immorality of forced servitude, the Egyptians placed the Hebrews into slavery. The Hebrews prayed to their God, Yahweh, who heard their cry and "cast his seed into the humble home of a male Hebrew child who will stand against an empire." This child's birth is proclaimed by a bright star in the sky. Egyptian astrologers note the star, and in response the reigning pharaoh declares that all newborn Hebrew boys must be killed.

Immediately, we detect a strong similarity between this birth story and that of Jesus, which we will encounter in our next film, *Ben Hur.* The motif of God (or a god) "casting his seed" into the human world is a very common one in mythology. Most often the human vessel who bears the child is a virginal woman, for example, Mary. But nonvirginal women, such as Moses' mother, are also described. As Gimbutas notes, almost always the immortal half of these pairings is male, whereas the human mate is female. This is due, Gimbutas argues, to our species' tendency to associate maleness with the ethereal world and femaleness with the material world (recall that even the term "material" springs from the Latin root *mater* for "mother"). In some American Indian myths, for example, the male Sky mates with the female Earth to produce humans.

To save the infant Moses from death, his mother puts him in a basket (ark) and places him in the Nile River, asking God/Yahweh to protect him and name him. She puts a Hebrew cloth with him as covering. The ark floats downstream, where it is discovered by pharaoh's widowed daughter, Bithia. She declares that the baby will be raised as her son—"a prince of Egypt"—and that he has been sent to her in answer to her prayers for a child. She rewraps the baby in royal Egyptian cloth, discarding his Hebrew covering. Bithia names the baby Moses, which means "drawn from the water." However, a wily slave woman secretly keeps the Hebrew cloth.

The casting of Moses upon the water by his humble family and his adoption into a royal family is another common mythical theme. In essence, the basket represents a womb, and immersion in the Nile, his rebirth. The exchange of his clothing from Hebrew to Egyptian signals his new tribe and status. But the hiding of the original cloth informs us that his new identity is but a temporary one.

Time passes, and Moses grows into a strong, handsome young man. He is the rival of the pharaoh's son, Ramses, for the hand of Nefertiri (Ann Baxter), the beautiful but vain and treacherous royal princess.[3] The man marrying Nefertiri will rule Egypt and, hence, "be" Egypt. Moses is a very capable general, conquering Ethiopia and bringing back riches to the pharaoh, Sethi. Ramses, on the other hand, has been unsuccessful at building a city to commemorate Sethi's rule, so Sethi asks Moses to build the city.

The Hebrew slaves Ramses is using to build the city are living in misery and pray for their foretold deliverer to come. Moses compassionately gives wheat to the slaves and provides them with a Sabbath day to rest from their labors. Envious, Ramses tells Sethi that Moses is a traitor. But when Sethi arrives to question Moses, he finds Moses has constructed a magnificent city in his honor. Sethi, very pleased, declares Moses his son and promises him Nefertiri. Enraged, Ramses vows revenge.

Through a series of betrayals, Ramses learns of Moses' Hebrew origins. He brings Moses in chains before Sethi and declares him to be the one "the evil star foretold, the destroyer of Egypt, the liberator of the slaves." Sethi sends Moses' adoptive mother into exile and gives Nefertiri in marriage to Ramses. Sethi declares that Moses' name be erased from all of Egypt, "erased from the memory of men for all time." At this point, Moses has "died" as an Egyptian. Significantly, his Egyptian father has rejected him and his Egyptian mate, Nefertiri, has been given to one of her own, that is, Egyptian, blood.

Ramses takes Moses to the edge of Egypt and casts him into the desert. Moses' status has now migrated from low (Hebrew birth) to high (Egyptian royal family) to low (Hebrew outcast) as he begins his journey across the desert. The desert represents the wilderness

Moses in The Ten Commandments *represents an early example of the public warrior.*

Archive Photos

he must pass through in order to find his authentic identity. Moses struggles through the desert until at last, he finds himself under a fruit-laden palm tree near a well. (Recall that fruits and wells are female symbols, associated with nature's bounty). Sephora, a shepherdess, and her sisters bring their sheep to the well and discover Moses. He valiantly helps them when goatherders attempt to drive away their flocks. Moses is attracted to Sephora, the eldest, who is the daughter of a Bedouin sheikh (king). (Moses and Sephora are of the same Semitic blood and worship the same God, two signs that the story will pair them together.)

Moses helps the Bedouin sell their wool for a good profit. When the sheikh offers him one of his daughters for a wife, Moses chooses Sephora. Here the text clearly differentiates Nefertiri from Sephora as archetypal women. Nefertiri represents the vain, glamorous beauty whereas Sephora is honest, modest, and genuine (for example, Snow White and Melanie Wilkes).

Time passes and Moses and Sephora have a son, Gershom.[4] One day Sephora discovers a stranger in the rocks; it is a Hebrew slave, Joshua. He has escaped Egypt and come to find Moses, hoping Moses will deliver the Hebrews. Moses sees a bush afire that does not burn; God speaks to him from the bush and tells him he *is* the chosen deliverer. His task is to free the Hebrews, so they can worship God and receive his commandments. Moses returns to Sephora and Joshua transfigured by his encounter; his hair is gray and his countenance beatific. He tells them he has seen "the light of Eternal Mind." (A common mythic assertion is that mind is male and body is female.)

In Egypt, Ramses has become pharaoh, taken Nefertiri as his wife, and fathered a son; thus, his life is in many ways analogous to that of Moses. Both have married within their own people, fathered sons, and become leaders. Moses arrives in Egypt and demands freedom for the Hebrews; he works a small miracle by turning his staff into a serpent that devours those of the Egyptian priests (symbolizing God's greater power); yet Ramses is unmoved. He declares the Hebrews must now make bricks without straw.

God then uses Moses to send plagues upon Egypt: the transformation of water into blood; frogs; lice; flies; sickness; and boils. However, Ramses, an atheist, claims these are due to natural causes, not to divine intervention. Moses then calls for burning hail and a solar eclipse. Pharaoh relents and decides to free the Hebrews. But Nefertiri mocks Ramses, telling him he is weak. To demonstrate his power, Ramses declares all the firstborn children of the Hebrews will be killed—beginning with Moses' son. (This repetitive theme of slaughtering children is a genocidal motif. Each mythic tribe or people seeks dominance by destroying the "seed" of its opposition.)

To protect themselves, the Hebrews mark their door posts with lamb's blood to keep away the Angel of Death. (The lamb's blood is taken from the Hebrews' ancient custom of sacrificing sheep and goats to God. Jesus later modified this ritual, declaring himself the Lamb of God, who was sacrificed to save humanity.) As Moses and his friends gather in his house that evening, they share a meal of bitter herbs, unleavened bread, and other foods. This event will come to be called Passover, because the houses of the Hebrews were passed over by death. (According to biblical myth, it was a Passover meal that Jesus celebrated with his disciples the night before his crucifixion.)

A green mist descends from the night sky and kills all those firstborn who are unprotected. The pharaoh's son falls deathly ill. Ramses, dressed in black robes of mourning, sends for Moses and tells him to take the Hebrews and leave Egypt. The Hebrews assemble with their flocks and possessions. However, once more, Nefertiri mocks her husband Ramses, telling him that she still loves Moses more than him. Ramses vows revenge and assembles his chariots to attack the Hebrews who are encamped near the Red Sea. Nefertiri, in red and black (the colors of war and death), watches his departure. God sends a pillar of fire to block the Egyptian chariots and opens a path across the sea to permit the Hebrews safe passage. When the Egyptian soldiers attempt to pursue them, they are engulfed in the waters and drowned. Ramses returns to his palace and tells Nefertiri that Moses' God *is* God. (It is interesting to note here that God used the four mythical elements to bring about the Hebrew's departure from Egypt: *Fire* blocked the chariots, while God's breath *(wind)* parted the Red Sea *(water)* permitting safe passage on dry *land.*)

When the Hebrews arrive at Mount Sinai, Moses goes up the mountain to receive God's commandments (commonly in myth, mortals interact with gods at sites that pierce the heavens). He is gone "forty days and forty nights." (A mythical number signifying a great period of time, the number 40 is commonly used in the

Middle East to mean an indefinitely long period; for example, after receiving the commandments, the Hebrews were required to wander forty years in the wilderness).[5] While Moses is upon the mountain, a traitorous Hebrew rouses the people to break God's law by constructing a golden calf (a female fertility symbol). The film, in one of the first cinematic uses of sacred/profane intercutting of scenes (we'll see more when we get to *The Godfather*), next juxtaposes images of Moses obtaining the Ten Commandments from God with images of the Hebrews drinking, singing, dancing, and fornicating with abandon.

When Moses comes down from the mountaintop, he is dismayed and furious at the Hebrews' recidivism. He calls those "who would follow God's law" to come to him, leaving the others to embrace the golden calf. The ground opens up and swallows those who embraced idolatry. Here we see the long-held archetypal notion that evildoers go "below" or "down" into the depths of the earth as punishment, whereas those who are good and righteous are elevated upward.

To punish the Hebrews for their infidelity, God forces them to wander "for forty years" in the Sinai wilderness. All of those who sinned die during this sojourn, leaving their purer descendants to enter the Promised Land beyond the Jordan River. (Rivers, a natural boundary, are often used in myth to mark transitions from one status to another.) The Hebrews[6] have now altered their status from that of a homeless people to become Israelites. To signify their obedience to God, the Israelites carry the ark with the Ten Commandments across the river to their new home. (The ark is a female enclosure—a house or uterus—for the male law. Just as an ark earlier carried Moses into the pharaoh's family so that he could become their deliverer, the Hebrews now carry God's law—obtained through Moses—into their new homeland.)

Ben Hur (1959)

Ben Hur, the motion picture, received more academy awards—eleven—than any other film in history. It is also one of the most popular movies of all time. The film extended the iconic imagery of the actor Charlton Heston, who was first established as a biblical hero in *The Ten Commandments,* and substituted the actor Stephen Boyd in Yul Brynner's role as the oppressor/villain. Both *Ben Hur* and *The Ten Commandments* closely follow Joseph Campbell's classic heroic quest pattern, a pattern that has been traced at least as far back as ancient Sumeria.[7]

Judeo-Christian religious mythology is constructed upon this same framework, and both *Ben Hur* and *The Ten Commandments* follow its structure. In essence, the myth of heroic quest requires that the protagonist (hero) leave his present status and surroundings; venture forth into a new land or wilderness where he is challenged, tempted, and tested; acquire a treasure or gift that is of benefit to mankind; and return to his home bringing the benefits of the gift. Like Prometheus, Jason, Aeneas, Ulysses, and Buddha, Moses and Ben Hur left their people, ventured into the wilderness, withstood enormous challenges, and returned home with treasure (gold, law, freedom, knowledge, enlightenment, etc.). And as we shall see, Luke Skywalker, Superman, and Indiana Jones will embark on the same quest.

Let us now take a closer look at how this pattern is constructed in *Ben Hur.* The opening titles to the film show images of God's hand touching that of Adam from Michaelangelo's painting in the Sistine Chapel. Thus we are told that the tale will concern God's acting upon the human world. Just as with *The Ten Commandments, Ben Hur* is set in a cataclysmic era. The Romans are oppressing Judea (the Promised Land the Hebrews arrived in after escaping from bondage in Egypt), and there is talk of a new deliverer. Augustus Caesar, the Roman emperor (an analog to Pharaoh) has decreed that each Judean must return to his or her place of birth to be taxed. The Judeans Joseph and Mary arrive in Bethlehem to pay their taxes. That night a special star appears over the stable where Mary gives birth. Shepherds and three wise men arrive at the stable to see the newborn boy, who is surrounded by animals. Not mentioned in the movie is the biblical text telling that the Romans had decreed that all newborn Jewish boys be killed, an effort to destroy the foretold deliverer. Mary, Jesus, and Joseph escape to Egypt to protect the infant Jesus. Already we can see that many of the same signs and symbols are used to establish Jesus' birth as a God-decreed event as have appeared in the story of Moses' birth. The Hebrews departure *from* Egypt were similarly depicted as divinely inspired.

Twenty-six years pass. Roman troops march through Nazareth, where Joseph and Jesus work as carpenters. The troops march on to Jerusalem, the capital of Judea. They are commanded by Massala (Stephen Boyd), whose father was once governor of Judea. Massala has been educated in Rome and now returns to his boyhood home as a celebrated soldier. The former commandant warns him that the Jews are very rebellious, believing that their deliverer is at hand.

Prince Judah Ben Hur (Charlton Heston), son of a wealthy Jewish family and childhood friend of Massala's, arrives to greet him. Judah is now head of his household. (No father is present; his fatherless condition makes him available as a divinely guided, or God-fathered, protagonist.) Massala is very pleased to see him, and they embrace. Massala asks Judah's help in governing Judea, but Judah argues that the Romans should leave Judea, giving the Jews their freedom. Massala responds that Rome is meant to govern the world; their emperor is divine (that is, God-on-earth), and it is their destiny to rule other peoples. (This is the same format presented in *The Ten Commandments* regarding the relative status of Egypt and the Hebrews.) Massala encourages Judah to use his influence to quiet the Jewish community, but Judah is noncommittal.

Later, Massala comes to Judah's house to visit Judah and his family. He gives Judah's mother a beautiful brooch from Libya, which his army "burned to the ground." In return, Judah gives Massala a magnificent white stallion. Massala pressures Judah to report Jewish traitors to him in exchange for favoritism, but Judah refuses. Angered, Massala leaves abruptly. Judah and his family celebrate the Jewish Sabbath (recall that Moses much earlier established this day of rest).

A caravan belonging to Judah arrives in Jerusalem carrying his employee Maimonedes and Maimonedes' beautiful daughter, Esther. Esther has been betrothed to a merchant selected by her father, and although she and Judah secretly love each other, Judah gives her permission to marry. Despite her betrothal, however, they exchange rings and kiss.

The following day, the new Roman governor arrives in Jerusalem, and as he is riding past the Ben Hur home, a tile slips from the roof and injures him. Massala seizes this as an excuse to imprison Judah's mother and sister and sends Judah to the slave galley. When Maimonedes comes to plead for their release, he too is imprisoned and tortured.

These events signal Judah's fall from grace; he has lost his family, wealth, and social standing. He must now enter the wilderness and face a series of daunting challenges.[8] Judah is marched in a slave gang through the desert. At Nazareth, he cries out to God for help, and a young man his own age (Jesus) kindly gives him water. This, of course, signals to us that Judah's life is also guided by God.

Judah is sentenced to a Roman slave galley. Like the other slaves, he is valued only for his labor; he is nameless, deprived of identity. The new ship commander, Quintas Arias (Jack Hawkins), tests Judah's strength and resolve, and they develop a grudging respect for each other. During a sea battle, Judah heroically rescues several slaves from drowning and saves Quintas Arias's life. Arias's fleet wins the battle, and he and Judah return to Rome in triumph. The Roman emperor greets them in godlike fashion, seated beneath an imperial eagle. He rewards Arias by giving him ownership of Judah.

Judah becomes immersed in Roman life—dressing well, socializing easily with the aristocracy. He excels as a charioteer and is adopted by Arias as a son. Arias gives him a golden ring signifying his new status as a Roman citizen. At this point, we recognize that the story is analogous to Moses' triumphs as an adopted son of Egypt. Just as with Moses, Judah could choose to maintain his elevated status as a successful member of this new (but oppressing) culture. But, just as with Moses, he chooses instead to return to his own people, despite the possibility of negative consequences.

Thus, Judah leaves Rome and returns, in disguise, to Judea, hoping to help his sister and mother. He is offered hospitality by an Arab sheikh, who asks Judah to drive his team of four white horses against Massala in the upcoming chariot race. The horses are named for stars, which subtly indicates their divine status (as does their white color). Balthazar, one of the three original wise men to find Jesus, is also staying with the sheikh and briefly mistakes Judah for Jesus (indicating Judah's divine purpose, as well). Recall that Moses, after being cast out of Egypt by Pharaoh, also took shelter with an Arab sheikh. Judah at first declines the sheikh's offer to race against Massala, what Campbell terms "declining the call," just as Moses several times refused to believe he was the deliverer.

Judah returns to his house, which now lies empty and in ruins. Esther has been secretly living there with her father, Maimonedes, who is now crippled as a result of Massala's beating. Judah and Esther renew their love; both still wear the other's ring. Judah tells her of his vow to punish Massala, but Esther advises him against it. She has become a follower of a new, young rabbi (Jesus) who preaches that one should love one's enemies. In essence, Judah and Esther, both Jews, now represent what many see as the moral schism between the Old and the New Testaments. Judah's vows of vengeance signify the Hebrew "eye for an eye" philosophy, while Esther's pleas to "love your enemies" signify the New Testament's Christianity.

Judah dresses in aristocratic Roman robes and goes to see Massala; he is now a full Roman citizen, equal in status to Massala. He demands to know where his mother and sister are. After Judah leaves, Massala sends guards to get the women from their cell; he finds they are afflicted with leprosy and sends them, secretly, to a leper colony. Esther discovers them there and tells them that Judah has returned. However, they are so ashamed of their hideous condition, they make her promise not to reveal that they are alive. (Here we see evidence of the cultural belief that for women their beauty and bodies are their life. A woman maimed and disfigured by leprosy is socially dead.) Thus, Esther tells Judah that his mother and sister have perished. Enraged, he goes to the sheikh and agrees to drive his horses against Massala. The sheikh places a huge wager against the Massala. Judah practices for the chariot race by gently training and praising the horses. He treats them with love and individual attention. The day of the race Judah prays that God's will be done and asks forgiveness for seeking revenge. The sheikh gives him a Star of David to wear. (Magic amulets are commonly given to heroes to help them during their quest; this one signals not only divine protection, but also the ethnic allegiance of its wearer.)

Massala's horses are black stallions; and he wears black apparel with red trim, signifying his evil and dangerous role. Judah, conversely, drives white stallions and is dressed in blue and gold (royal colors, for he is a chosen "prince"). Massala asks the pagan god Jupiter for victory. His chariot wheels are spiked to destroy his competitors, and he whips his horses brutally to drive them to win. Massala, thus, is archetypal of the destructive god; he is the male version of the wicked stepmother/Queen and equivalent to the cruel pharaoh, Ramses. He represents the dark forces of oppression and cruelty.

During the race itself, Massala destroys the chariots of several other racers and hits Judah with his whip. But on the final round, he is thrown from his chariot and trampled by horses. Judah wins the race, and the Judean spectators cheer wildly. Pontius Pilate gives him the victory wreath, saying, "You are the people's one true god—for the time being." He places the wreath on Judah's head, metaphoric of Christ's crown of thorns.

Massala lies dying; he is now disfigured, as he caused Judah's sister and mother to be, and crippled, as he caused Maimonedes to be. He has reaped the misery he had sown. With his dying words, he mockingly tells Judah his mother and sister are still alive—as lepers.

Judah goes to the Valley of the Lepers to seek his mother and sister. Judah sees Esther carrying food to them and confronts her. She tells him to not let them see him, as they will be humiliated, and reluctantly, he agrees. As Esther and Judah return to his house, they see crowds gathering to hear Jesus. Judah drinks from a stream and recalls how "a kind man [Jesus] once gave me water. . . . I am thirsty still," meaning he still seeks divine comfort. Balthazar asks him to come hear Jesus, but Judah declines (another "rejection of the call"). From afar we see Jesus in a white robe, signaling his goodness and purity, preaching to the throng.

Judah goes to see Pontius Pilate, furious that Roman rule has destroyed his family. Judah gives Pilate the signet ring bequeathed to him by Arias, symbolically breaking his ties with Rome. Full of anger and bitterness, Judah returns home. There Esther begs him to follow Jesus: "You have become like Massala, full of hate." Esther, in essence, is a sage or guide archetypal figure who gives the hero knowledge and guidance. As we shall see later, Obi-Wan Kenobi and Yoda will serve this same function for Luke Skywalker in the *Star Wars* trilogy.

Moved by Esther's words, Judah goes with her to get his mother and sister to take them to see Jesus. But when they go to Jerusalem, Jesus' trial before Pontius Pilate is under way. Jesus (in a white robe) and two other men (in brown) are condemned to death. As Jesus carries the cross through the streets, Judah suddenly recognizes him: "This is the man who gave me water!" Jesus is nailed to the cross as women weep. Judah gazes at Jesus and is transformed, just as Moses was transfigured by seeing God in the burning bush. Judah's mother and sister, too, recognize Jesus as their Redeemer. When Jesus dies, a violent storm (signifying divine power) arises to mark his passing. The divine rain falls upon Judah's mother and sister, cleansing them of their leprosy. Jesus' blood mixes with the rain and runs across the ground, similarly cleansing the earth of sin. Judah returns to his house, which also has been reborn in the divine rain. The closing scene depicts a shepherd tending his sheep beneath Calvary: metaphorically, Jesus watches over his human flock from heaven. Judah (and Jesus), both heroes in this narrative, have completed their journeys and accomplished their divinely guided missions. One has brought his people a material victory over Rome by defeating Massala; the other has provided his followers an ethereal victory over sin and death. The course of the heroic quest has been completed.

Sleeping Beauty (1959)

Just as we saw marked parallelism between *The Ten Commandments* and *Ben Hur,* our next, very popular animated motion picture largely duplicates the archetypal structure found in *Snow White,* a film that preceded it by twenty years. Disney's *Sleeping Beauty,* like *Snow White,* is drawn from the Grimm brothers' fairy-tale collection, a compilation of early German folktales.

Once more, the story opens in a royal palace, where King Stefan and his gentle wife are celebrating the birth of their daughter, Aurora (sunrise). From throughout the kingdom, people arrive to bring her gifts. A friendly neighboring king, Hubert, and his young son, Prince Philip, come, as well. Philip is betrothed to the baby princess and will one day be her husband. Their marriage will unite their two kingdoms in peace.

Three good fairies come to give magical gifts to the princess. They have deep and vivid mythical symbolism. Flora, who is green in color, gives Aurora the gift of beauty. At her touch, flowers tumble down around the baby princess. Recall that flowers are a female symbol. Fauna, who is red in color (representing the feminine animal aspect), gives Aurora the gift of song. Birds sing and fly about the princess. Recall that birds also are a feminine symbol. Merryweather, who is colored blue (for fair skies), is unable to present her gift because she is interrupted by an evil fairy—the wicked Maleficent.

Maleficent enters the palace amidst wind, lightning, thunder, and darkness. She appears first as a flame or fire. She wears a long black cape and carries a staff, upon which perches a raven. All of these attributes signal Maleficent as the destructive goddess archetype—we have met her before as the wicked Queen in Snow White.[9] Maleficent casts a magic spell upon the princess, decreeing that at age sixteen, Aurora will prick her hand on the spindle of a spinning wheel (a feminine symbol) and die. The metaphoric allusion here is to both menstrual blood and sexual intercourse. Maleficent, who is dressed in black and red, then transforms herself into black smoke and red fire and vanishes. Merryweather can counteract this spell only by transforming Maleficent's curse from death to sleep, from which Aurora can be awakened by true love's kiss.

To deter Maleficent's decree, King Stefan orders all the spinning wheels in the land burned. To further aid the baby princess, Flora, Fauna, and Merryweather turn themselves into peasant women (that is, they assume mortal status) and take Aurora to a cottage deep in the forest. They rename her Briar Rose, so she will not be aware she is a princess. This is a direct parallel with Snow White's sojourn in the forest with the seven dwarfs. However, this story is more sophisticated as indicated by the planned betrothal at the outset, the splitting of the goddess archetype into good (three fairies) and bad (Maleficent) aspects, and the high-to-low status movement of the three good fairies and the princess.

Sixteen years pass. Maleficent has yearly sent evil scouts to search for Aurora, but without success. The scouts are evil forest creatures such as bats, hawks, and alligators. One day Briar Rose goes to the forest to pick berries (berries are another female symbol; recall Snow White and the fruit pie). She sings a song about the man of her dreams; she is accompanied by an owl, birds, squirrels, and rabbits. Again, note the consistency between this and Snow White's animal friends. A young prince riding through the forest on his white horse hears her song and stops to see her. They sing "Once upon a Dream" and dance together, falling in love. But suddenly, Briar Rose remembers the fairies' warnings that she is to beware of strangers (the seven dwarfs had similar admonitions for Snow White) and runs home.

Back at the cottage, the fairies have been preparing for Briar Rose's wedding. Unable to sew her dress or bake her cake as mortals, they resort to magic. But sparks from their wands are spotted by Maleficent's raven. (The raven, here, is metaphoric for Maleficent, herself. Recall that witches and ravens can transform themselves into one another.)

Briar Rose returns to the cottage and tells the fairies she has fallen in love, but they tell her she is already betrothed. Simultaneously, Philip tells King Stefan and King Hubert that he loves a girl he met in the forest, but they remind him he is betrothed to a princess. Flora, Fauna, and Merryweather bring Briar Rose/Aurora to the palace to meet her betrothed. But before they can meet, Maleficent guides the princess to a secret spinning wheel, where the princess pricks her finger and falls into a deep sleep. To protect everyone from this sad knowledge, the three fairies put the entire castle and kingdom to sleep.

Philip, however, has gone to the woods in search of Briar Rose. Maleficent captures him and imprisons him in her castle on Forbidden Mountain. (Recall that the devil was depicted as living on a barren mountaintop in *Fantasia.* Although, generally, myths place beneficent gods atop mountains, for example, Mount Olympus, destructive gods may live there, as well.)

The fairies discover Prince Philip in Maleficent's dungeon and free him. They arm him with the shield of Virtue and the sword of Truth. Prince Philip proves his worthiness by escaping from Maleficent's henchman and then hacking through dense thorns to get into the sleeping palace. However, Maleficent bursts into flames and is transformed into a fire-breathing dragon colored black and red. The bull-head (uterus) horns are still atop her head. In this form she represents female destructive power, just as the witch/hag did in Snow White. Courageously, Philip flings his sword into the dragon's heart, slaying her. Philip mounts his horse and gallops into the palace. Gently, he kisses the princess, and the kingdom awakens. Philip and Aurora wed, uniting their two lands.

Sleeping Beauty is thus a highly elaborated version of *Snow White.* The seven dwarfs have been replaced by three fairies, the apple by a spinning wheel, and the witch by a dragon; but essentially the plot structure is the same. Perhaps the most meaningful difference is the much more developed role of the prince. In this telling, he must prove his worthiness as a leader (and mate) by battling evil. As we shall see when we next turn our attention to the most popular television shows of this same decade, heroic men were expected to continually prove their mettle in battle. However, the evil against which they struggled was not the destructive goddess, but rather mortal men who had "gone bad."

Now let's look at the archetypal content of the five most popular television programs of the 1950s. Because of similarities in their content and structure, we'll consider three shows—*Have Gun Will Travel, Gunsmoke,* and *Dragnet*—as a group. We'll then take a look at *Wagon Train* and *I Love Lucy.*

I have chosen the term "public warrior" to describe the archetypal figure depicted in *Have Gun Will Travel, Gunsmoke,* and *Dragnet.* The warrior is a well-known and ancient archetype dating back to the earliest myths. Almost always a male figure, the warrior is distinguished by his ability to engage in physical battles with various opponents—other men, dragons, sharks, dinosaurs, etc.—and emerge victorious. Warriors are not necessarily of noble blood (in contrast to princes, such as those in *Ben Hur* and *Sleeping Beauty*) and most notably, they do not necessarily end up with a female mate at the end of the story. Instead, their primary archetypal function is to challenge and defeat the forces of evil.

In the three programs to which we now turn, I have further restricted the warrior notion by terming it "public warrior," because in each case the warrior *belongs* to the public sphere; he serves the public welfare. For this reason, he is narratively *restricted* from becoming involved with women in relationships that could lead to marriage and fatherhood. For should he marry and have children, his primary duty would then be to protect *them,* instead of more broadly to protect *us.* As we shall see, our public warriors studiously avoid romantic commitments; they are first and foremost men fighting on our behalf.[10]

Have Gun Will Travel

The television series *Have Gun Will Travel* featured the actor Richard Boone in the title role as Paladin, a "gun for hire" available to any and all who need his services. *Have Gun Will Travel* remains one of the most sophisticated westerns ever produced for television. Its imagery operates on a very metaphoric level, and its story lines deal with a series of complex moral issues. The "Genesis" episode, which actually aired late in the series (September 15, 1962) provides us with Paladin's history. Paladin has returned to his San Francisco hotel room, elegantly dressed. He is assaulted by a young man. After a violent fight, which Paladin wins, the young man tells Paladin he was sent to kill him to settle a $10,000 gambling debt. Paladin replies that he has seen the young man before—in a mirror. He then relates the tale of how he, himself, was the dissolute son of a wealthy family, well-educated but degenerate. He too was told to kill a man, called Smoke, to pay a gambling debt to a man named Norge.

Paladin had ridden into the wilderness to find Smoke. Smoke was an older man, dressed entirely in black, with a consumptive cough. He captures Paladin, but instead of killing him, challenges him and teaches him to become a warrior, like himself. This story has distinct Oedipal overtones, especially since Richard Boone plays *both* roles—that of Paladin and that of Smoke. Smoke tells Paladin that he is to be "a gentleman knight in shining armor, armed with righteousness, but a mercenary. You take gold to slay the dragon." (Indeed, the name Paladin, which Smoke assigns to him, means "knight"). When his apprenticeship is over, Smoke challenges him to fight. Paladin wins, figuratively slaying himself/his father. Dying, Smoke tells him that "you think you've slain the dragon, but you've only turned him loose. I was protecting the town from Norge."

This turns out to be correct; Norge had been a terrible despot (like Ramses or Massala), whom Smoke had banished. The townspeople now are very bitter toward Paladin. Paladin, in anguish, cries out "Where is my cause?" and weeps. He vows to devote his life to "slaying dragons." In the next scene, Paladin, dressed in Smoke's black clothing and with a knight (rook chess piece) insignia on his holster, slays Norge in a gunfight. Returning to the present, Paladin tells the young man who tried to kill him that he, too, should devote himself to slaying dragons: "What a man does about his mistakes, determines what he is."

In at least three additional episodes, Paladin slays various types of dragons. Each episode begins with Paladin, elegantly dressed, at his San Francisco hotel. The hotel—a public commercial building—is a very appropriate home for him, for he has no family, other than those in need. In one episode, "Three Bells to Perdido," Paladin pursues a bandit (Jack Lord) to a small Mexican town named Perdido. Perdido equals Hell. The bandit has run off with a rich rancher's daughter, who loves him. The bandit engages in several cowardly efforts to kill Paladin, indicating that he has no honor (like Massala in the chariot race); he even attempts to kill his girlfriend to prevent Paladin's returning her to her father. Thus the theme of women as possessions of men is present here, as well. Ultimately, the girl is reunited with her father, and the bandit is jailed for trial. Somewhat ironically, given his origin, Paladin insists in this and other episodes that the *rule of law* be enforced, rejecting man-to-man frontier justice.

In another episode, "Hey Boy's Revenge," Paladin comes to the aid of his friend, Hey Boy, the hotel's Chinese bellman. This tale addresses racial prejudice against the Chinese, who are being exploited as railway workers. An oppressive railroad boss, Travis (Pernell Roberts), has killed Hey Boy's brother, faking an accident to cover up his deed. The town authorities are loathe to help out the "China boys, monkeys, and coolies." Paladin rouses the Chinese workers, speaking in fluent Chinese—he spoke excellent Spanish in the previous episode—to demand justice. When two Chinese witnesses come forward to identify Travis as the murderer, the sheriff arrests Travis and promises he will stand trial for his crime. Once again, the rule of law is upheld. Paladin and Hey Boy return to San Francisco. Paladin gives the reward money to Hey Boy's sister, Kim Lee, to prevent her from having to enter an arranged marriage with an elderly man she does not love. (Paladin only takes remuneration for his services from those wealthy enough to pay.)

Notably, Paladin leads a double life—that of a wealthy, well-bred gentleman in San Francisco and that of his "other self," the accomplished warrior dressed in black and riding a white horse. Other warriors whom we shall meet leading similar double lives include Superman and Batman.

In a final, moving episode, Paladin is hired to hunt down a condemned killer (Charles Bronson). Paladin intends to capture the man and bring him to justice (hanging in Laramie), whereas a sheriff who is also in pursuit just wants to shoot the killer. Paladin succeeds in capturing the man, Holt, who tells him he does not want to be "hung at a county fair," but rather "wants to die like a man, at the hands of a man." Holt pleads with Paladin to let him see his newborn son once before he dies, and Paladin agrees. On the way to Holt's house, Paladin falls over a cliff. Holt, after initial hesitation, saves his life. They arrive at Holt's cabin, and Holt visits with his wife and child, as Paladin waits outside. Then Holt steps outside and challenges Paladin to a gunfight. He tells Paladin he does not want to be hanged; he wants his son to know he was killed in a gunfight "like a man." Holt draws first, and Paladin kills him. Bending over Holt, Paladin says he is sorry. When Holt's wife comes out, Paladin tells her, "He wouldn't let me avoid it." The wife replies: "It was bound to come; at least he respected you." Paladin gives the reward money to the wife and child and rides off in sorrow. He has given a vanquished foe—an evil but still honorable man—a warrior's death.

Gunsmoke

This television series is introduced by John Wayne—a figure virtually synonymous in American culture with the public warrior archetype. (In his many western and war movies, Wayne's character never married.) Wayne, dressed in cowboy clothes, tells viewers that the show they are about to see is "honest, adult, and realistic." In the opening scenes, Marshal Matt Dillon draws his gun and shoots down an opponent in the streets of Dodge City. He then walks through Boot Hill, the cemetery near the city, and in a voice-over tells us that he is there to represent the law to people who draw guns. It's his job; he's a U.S. marshal. James Arness, the actor who portrays Marshal Matt Dillon, is remarkably similar in appearance and demeanor to John Wayne. We are thus instructed, both visually

Marshal Matt Dillon in Gunsmoke *is another manifestation of the public warrior archetype.*

Archive Photos

and verbally, that Dillon will be carrying on Wayne's archetypal duties on television.

In the initial episode, the sheriff from Amarillo arrives in Dodge City to warn Dillon that Dan Gratt, a ruthless killer, is coming. Matt walks over to the bar, where Kitty, a pretty bar girl, flirts with him. Like Matt, she is a "public good," serving to provide emotional nurturance to those who need it, just as Matt provides protection. Gratt challenges the Amarillo sheriff to a shoot-out and kills him. Matt goes into the street to confront him. Gratt tells him: "I can kill anybody" and shoots him. "See, Marshal. See how easy it is."

The doctor, Doc, saves Matt's life, and Kitty comes to cheer him. While Dillon is recovering, Gratt kills two more men in

Dodge City. Both Doc and Kitty plead with Matt not to confront Gratt again, fearing he will be killed. But Dillon tells them, "He's a gunman; he's got to be eliminated." Or as Paladin would have put it: He's a dragon to be slain. Dillon goes to the hotel to challenge Gratt. However, this time he keeps Gratt at a distance, realizing Gratt is a good shot only at close range. Gratt draws his gun; Dillon kills him and walks back to his office.

Significantly, Dillon, Kitty, and Doc are shown only in their places of business, which reinforces their archetypal status. Each represents his or her public function: law, nurturing, medicine. They are without homes and home-lives.

A second *Gunsmoke* episode is very similar to the first. In it, one stranger, Kriegel (Charles Bronson), kills another stranger in cold blood as they camp together. Dillon and his deputy, Chester, find the dead man's body and conclude, correctly, that the killer is a coward. Back in Dodge City, Matt and Chester go to the bar. A stranger—the killer—picks a fight with a teenager. Dillon intervenes and saves the boy. Next Kriegel makes a crude pass at Kitty, but she rebuffs him. Later, as Kitty is buying fabric for a dress, Kriegel again tries to make a crude pass at her, which she again rebuffs. This time Kriegel tries to strike her. Dillon challenges Kriegel to a gunfight but, a coward, he backs down.

Later, Doc tells Dillon that Kriegel harassed a workman into a gunfight and then shot him five times; the workman was a friend of the teenager at the bar. Doc tells Dillon that Kriegel is "crazy, kill crazy. . . . A man like that's got no right being alive." As Chester and Dillon leave Doc's office, Kriegel guns down the teenager in the street.

Dillon enters the bar where Kriegel is now drinking and challenges him to a shoot-out: "Your killing days are over; you're gonna die." Kriegel still refuses to fight, but when Dillon turns his back, Kriegel draws his gun and tries to shoot him. Chester shouts out to Dillon, who draws, turns, and kills Kriegel. Dillon walks alone back to his office.

As can be seen by these two story lines, *Gunsmoke* is a much simpler mythic narrative than *Have Gun Will Travel.* Most episodes depict a stranger—usually evil—entering Dodge City (Dillon's domain) and breaking the law (which Dillon represents), usually by killing people. Marshal Dillon then restores the law by stopping (usually killing) the lawbreaker. The archetypal message is quite plain and straightforward: Good triumphs over evil. We are also instructed that there is no place for emotion in the lawman's life. He must remain unattached and aloof in order to enforce the law.

One episode, however, does draw Matt into an emotional choice between friendship and the law. He chooses the law, but the tale is worth examining. Matt brings into Dodge City the fugitive brother of a prominent businessman. Waiting at Matt's office is an old friend who once saved his life, Hack Prine. They embrace and greet each other happily. (Recall Judah Ben Hur's youthful friendship with Massala.) When Chester locks the fugitive in jail, Hack comments that he, himself, could not tolerate being confined.

Later, as Matt walks along the street, a beggar he has helped warns him that the fugitive's rich brother, Dolph Trimble, is hiring a gunman to kill Matt. When Matt later sees Dolph and Hack at the bar, he realizes that it is Hack who has been hired to kill him. Outside the bar, Hack and Matt talk. Hack tells Matt he doesn't want to kill him, but "it's a job" and he needs the money. Matt offers to give Hack the money, instead, so that they will not have to face one another and tells Hack that the jailed man Hack is fighting for shot an unarmed man in cold blood. Matt walks away from Hack with their status still unresolved.

Later the beggar is found shot to death in Hack's hotel room; Dolph had attempted to frame Hack to force him to fight Dillon. Shots ring out from the saloon (which serves as the communal gathering place). Hack has shot Dolph Trimble for attempting to frame him. However, we learn that Hack drew first on Dolph, not in self-defense. Thus, Dillon tells him he must be arrested and stand trial. In an ending akin to that in the *Have Gun Will Travel* episode, Hack challenges Dillon to a gunfight to avoid jail. Dillon kills him; Hack says in his dying words, "You've got a job to do, and you do it pretty good." Dillon, sadly, walks down the street, back to his office.

This episode clearly asks the question, Which ideal should the public warrior hold most dear—love or law? and answers it with the same response we saw in *Have Gun Will Travel*—law.

Dragnet

The rule of law is also the central force motivating the protagonists of *Dragnet,* Sergeant Joe Friday (Jack Webb) and his partner, Bill Gannon. Friday's character, perhaps even more than Matt Dillon's, *personifies* the public warrior archetype, encasing it in a staccato armor of factual statements and the orderly reporting of the date, time, and location of events: e.g., 9:32 A.M., Saturday, April 5, crime lab. Sergeant Friday raises the dutiful commitment of the public warrior to heights not seen even in *Gunsmoke,* in which Marshal Dillon is shown drinking and chatting at the bar in almost every episode, or *Have Gun Will Travel,* in which Paladin is usually depicted reading newspapers in his hotel at the outset of each episode. In the many years that *Dragnet* ran on television, Sergeant Friday rarely took a day off, went on a date, or even went home from work! Night and day, week in and week out, he remained on duty. And, as he tells one hoodlum, for very little pay: $367 a month take-home in 1954.

We'll use the 1954 *Dragnet* pilot motion picture, directed by and starring Jack Webb, to illustrate this version of the public warrior archetype. As usual, "the names have been changed to protect the innocent." The story opens with two men walking in a field outside Los Angeles. A third man appears and guns one of them down with a shotgun. The remaining man and the shooter walk off together.

In the next scene Joe Friday introduces himself to us; he works for the Los Angeles Police Department. It is Saturday, April 9, 7:29 P.M.; he and his colleagues are working on the murder in the crime lab. They have gathered a shoe print, shotgun casings, and a fight ticket with a phone number on the back. The detectives, all white males, leaf through the records of "mob figures"; they identify five as their prime suspects. On Saturday, April 9, at 7:40 P.M., the detectives meet with their superiors and then pick up all the suspects, taking them to a hotel to interrogate them. The suspects are provided with no phone calls or lawyers. The district attorney and detectives question each subject for several hours, taping their conversations. All of the participants—cops and hoods, alike—chain-smoke cigarettes. Although one of the suspects, Max Troy, asks several times to leave, the interrogation continues. The cops note that Troy has no source of income, yet drives a Cadillac and lives in a large house. The police, conversely, make "chump change," but have a duty to protect the public. The cars of the suspects are impounded and searched. Their homes are searched too.

The detectives talk to a witness who saw the shooter leaving the scene of the crime. On Sunday, April 10, at 11:30 A.M., Sergeant Friday and his colleagues go to the Red Spot Cafe, a hangout of Max Troy's, and search it for clues. They send a policewoman—attractive and competent—to the Red Spot with a hidden tape recorder to secretly tape conversations there. However, the following day, the district attorney tells them they must release the five suspects they've been holding because of lack of evidence. Friday asks rhetorically, "Why does the law always work for the guilty?"

Friday talks to a (white male) friend of his who plays in a jazz band and obtains some useful information on the murder victim. He and his partner go to see the victim's wife; she is a crippled alcoholic living in a sparsely furnished apartment. She implicates Max Troy. Sergeant Friday and his partner next subpoena phone records for the suspects, including Max Troy. With this material and the implicating tapes obtained by the policewoman, the police go en masse to the home of Max Troy. They shine lights at his house and draw their guns. Troy comes out, unarmed, but spits on Sergeant Friday. The police again search this house and take Troy to jail.

Friday and the other detectives take their case to the grand jury, seeking an indictment against Troy. However, the eyewitness chickens out and refuses to identify the shooter (a man named Davitt). The suspects all take the Fifth Amendment; and the grand jury refuses to indict them.

In response, the police put the five suspects under twenty-four-hour surveillance, stopping and searching them several times a day, including when they are eating, talking on the phone, and out with friends. Friday and his partner follow Troy to his club, getting into a fistfight with the hoodlums there, but winning the fight.

The police wiretap the Red Spot Grill, finding valuable evidence as a result. They learn that one of the original five conspirators has been killed by Max Troy to silence him. When they inform this man's wife of this, she gives them the murder weapon and tells them Max Troy set up the original murder. With this evidence, the district attorney gives the police permission to arrest Troy. Troy has a heart attack. Sergeant Friday and his partner go to the hospital to arrest Troy, but discover he died earlier in the day on the operating table—in essence, cheating justice.

Viewed four decades after it appeared, *Dragnet* strikes our contemporary eyes as heavy-handed police work at best, an exercise in fascism at worst. Our present-day public warriors operate in a grey sea of muddled morals and confused ethics; we forget that in *Dragnet's* era, things *were* seen as either distinctly black or white, good or evil. As in *Gunsmoke* and *Have Gun Will Travel,* there was no middle ground, no room for second thoughts. The public warrior saw his duty clearly and unambiguously and carried it out. Though he might feel sorrow after killing a friend gone bad, there was no crack in his moral certitude that he had done what had to be done. Bad men were to be confronted squarely and "eliminated" from society, as Marshal Matt Dillon so plainly put it.

Also unlike today, the public warriors who enforced the law during these tales from the 1950s *were* pure, honest, and unselfish public servants. There was not even a hint of corruption in their behavior, for they not only enforced the law, they followed it to the letter. The law was their code for life, and they wanted no other.

But just as these public warriors were pure in heart and steadfast in courage, they were also remarkably narrow in their composition. From Moses to Ben Hur to Prince Philip up through Paladin, Matt Dillon, and Joe Friday, they were all portrayed by white male actors, with handsome faces and strong jaws. They embodied the white middle-class ideal of masculinity at mid-century: taciturn, forceful, pragmatic. They were men of action and, with the exception of the deeply introspective Paladin, never questioned themselves or their duty.

Wagon Train

We next encounter a program, again one of the most popular during the fifties, featuring a different archetypal figure—that of Sage, or Wise Man. According to Campbell and Jung, the sage/wise man is typically encountered by the hero of the myth as he meets with obstacles on his journey. The sage provides the hero with special knowledge or guidance, which helps him overcome the challenges he faces. In the series *Wagon Train,* this archetype is portrayed by Seth Adams (Ward Bond), the older, experienced wagon master whose job it is to guide his novice band of settlers across the great American frontier to their new homes and lives in the West.

During the fifties, a decade following a horrific world war in which familiar social patterns and ways of life were destroyed and Americans were challenged to find their way through the "wilderness" of modernity, Seth Adams no doubt served as a valuable guide and mentor. Those on his wagon train frequently were marked by losses during an earlier great war, the Civil War. The West, representing the new American society on the other side of the cataclysm, gave them a chance to start over, to reestablish themselves and restructure the moral order in keeping with their new realities.

Wagon Train used each episode to introduce fresh characters representing a given moral issue. On the course of the journey, the characters are guided and assisted on their quest by Adams. The others on the train served as surrogates for the American community, as a whole.

In "The Nels Stack Story" episode, a hot-headed former Confederate soldier, Claymore, gets into a fight with a former Yankee captain, Nels Stack. Stack refuses to fight Claymore, because he has become a pacifist since the war. Adams tells them, "This wagon train's gotta stick together." They encounter a young woman whose wagon has been burned and whose family has been killed by Indians. Stack befriends her.

A group of Souix braves rides up to the wagon train to trade horses. Claymore loudly urges the wagon train members to kill them and tries to force the woman to identify them as the killers of her family. She cries and refuses. Although Stack wants to give the Indians some horses (because the whites have run off all their buffalo), Adams sends them away empty-handed, fearing they are a raiding party. The woman and Stack discuss the war. Her father, a Virginian, had opposed it (Virginia was one of the last states to join the Confederacy). Her brother was killed during the war. Stack tells her, "The war changed a lot of people."

Clint, the wagon train scout, rides in and tells them to beware of a Souix raiding party. Their best hope is to cross an upcoming river before being attacked. Claymore complains bitterly that Stack's pacifism will keep him from fighting for the wagon train, but Adams replies, "The battles a man fights with himself are nobody's business but his own." The Indians attack before they reach the river, but are driven away. Claymore and some others want to desecrate the slain Indians' bodies and kill one who is wounded. Stack attempts to stop them. Claymore beats him, until Adams intervenes.

The wagon train is trapped against the river and cannot find a crossing. The rescued woman argues with Stack about his defense of the wounded Indian, but he replies that "killing is a contagion; you must learn to control hate." She responds, "You just fear Claymore" (that is, "You're a coward,"). Stack comments, "You may be right."

One of the wagon train's cows is stolen by an Indian. When Stack and Seth Adams track him down, they find an old Souix man, "left to die by his people." Stack wants to help him "because he's a human being." They return with him to the wagon train. Claymore wants to hang the old man; but this time Stack fights him, almost choking Claymore to death. Adams separates the men. Stack gives the old Indian a horse, so he can leave the camp: "I wish our people could be friends, but I guess that's a long time away." The rescued woman and Stack talk. He tells her that he had been a much-decorated soldier during the war, but one day he "went crazy from killing. I never wanted to kill again." The woman tells him, "You're ten times the man Claymore is."

The old Indian returns and shows them a river crossing. Because of his help, the wagon train makes it across, avoiding a deadly battle. Adams tells Claymore he should thank Stack for saving the train. The rescued woman and Stack ride together on his wagon.

Clearly, Nels Stack is the hero of this story. He has met many challenges to his ideals and successfully overcome them, bringing a gift (escape from harm) to his community, the wagon train. He is even rewarded with a desirable mate. And just as clearly, Adams is the knowledgeable wise man, keeping order, and preventing the disputing parties from damaging each other or the community.

In another similar episode, "The Colter Craven Story,"[11] the wagon train comes across a lone wagon occupied by an alcoholic doctor, Colter Craven, and his wife. In exchange for passage, the doctor offers the wagon train his services. That evening, a young boy breaks his leg and the doctor sets it expertly. Later, a pregnant woman who had previously had four stillborn children needs a cesarean, but the doctor says he is afraid to operate. The doctor's wife threatens to leave him if the woman or child dies: "You can crawl into that bottle and stay there." The doctor weeps, but his hand is clenched shut and will not open. He explains to Seth Adams that as a boy he worked at a slaughterhouse to put himself through medical school. Then he took care of the wounded during the Civil War battle of Shiloh (where there were eighteen thousand casualties). But many of his patients died, and he blames himself. Because of this tragic personal history, he is unable to operate on patients.

Adams reprimands him, saying he also was at Shiloh and virtually all the men under his command were killed. He gives the doctor coffee and tries to encourage him to abandon alcohol. While they sit at the campfire, Adams tells the doctor about a friend of his, Sam Grant, from Illinois. Sam was dismissed from the Army before the war, because of alcoholism. He returned unemployed to his wife and children and had to take a humiliating job in his father-in-law's dry goods store. When the Civil War came, Seth Adams began training a regiment of Illinois volunteers, but he was training them poorly. Sam Grant saw them from the bar in which he was drinking. Disturbed at Seth's incompetence, he slammed down his drink and went to show Seth how to do it properly. After that incident, Grant never drank again and he rejoined the Army.

The Civil War began in earnest. At the battle of Shiloh, thirty thousand people were killed or wounded. The evening after the battle, Seth again encountered Sam Grant. They embraced and Sam thanked Seth for helping him regain his sobriety in Illinois. Then a group of high-ranking officers rode up and called out to Sam—he was *Ulysses S. Grant,* the leader of the entire Union Army and future president of the United States. Seth tells the doctor: "He was able to redeem himself."

The doctor's hand becomes unclenched, and he successfully delivers the baby. The wagon train rides off into the sunrise, passing over a river, as a young colt runs ahead of it. (The colt signifies the doctor's name, Colter.) This, of course, is a tale of redemption. The doctor (hero) has "lost" himself and is in the wilderness of alcoholism. Through Seth Adams's steady hand—and excellent storytelling skills—he is "reborn" (the river crossing and the sunrise signal this) and regains his abilities as a doctor and saver of lives.

In a somewhat different tale, "The Elizabeth McQueeny Story," the narrative opens with an elegantly dressed woman, Madame Elizabeth McQueeny (Bette Davis) asking a store manager for ten sets of wagon train outfits. She is taking ten beautiful young women west to establish a finishing school.

They join the wagon train, and soon the wives of the men on the train are jealous. Seth Adams asks Madame McQueeny to please make sure her girls keep away from the men. We recognize at this point, as does Adams, that Madame McQueeny's very extravagantly furnished wagon and wardrobe signal her status as a bordello madame, or, as she puts it, "a lady of the theater," who intends to establish a palace of entertainment with dancing girls in the West. McQueeny tells Adams she is "a lot of woman" and that she and her girls "are what we want to be; someday people will progress and not curse us."

Friendly Indians bring a derelict white man riding a mule into the wagon train. He announces that he is "Count Roberto de Falconi." McQueeny takes him on to drive her wagon.[12] The women of the wagon train (representing conventional morality) are upset by McQueeny's presence. They tell Adams they want her evicted from the train. Back in McQueeny's wagon, she and the "Count" (now dressed in elegant apparel) play cards and flirt. McQueeny smokes cigarettes (a brazen habit, especially at that time). Both she and the Count are obviously flamboyant frauds, but likable nonetheless. Adams arrives and tells them regretfully that they must leave the wagon train at the next town.

That evening, one of McQueeny's girls, Roxanne, and a young man, Stanley, from the wagon train are kissing in the woods, when Stanley suddenly collapses, gravely ill. Roxanne runs to fetch McQueeny who recognizes that Stanley has yellow fever, a highly contagious disease. While she is gone, the Count sneaks off the wagon train with all of McQueeny's money.

McQueeny helps Seth Adams set up a quarantine and tirelessly tends to the sick, as do her girls. Even Adams is stricken with the fever, but McQueeny nurses him back to health. The Count also is found, stricken with the fever, and McQueeny nurses him, as well. Stanley survives, but Roxanne dies of the fever.

After the epidemic, the wagon train continues onward. McQueeny, the Count, and the girls are permitted to stay on, "tolerated but not embraced," as Adams puts it, by the others. Adams returns the money the Count had taken from McQueeny; the Count thanks him for doing so. Thus the Count has redeemed himself, as well. The story closes with Adams telling us that Madame McQueeny went on to become "one of the most legendary entertainers in the West."

Madame McQueeny of *Wagon Train* and Miss Kitty of *Gunsmoke* both represent a female archetype termed "a whore with a heart of gold." This archetype encompasses women who have "fallen" from conventional morality and typically work as mistresses, prostitutes, or strippers. (Mythically speaking, they have become impure vessels, and men do not want them as mates.) However, they retain their nurturant, caring qualities and often serve as public mothers or caregivers, extending emotional support to those unattached to a traditional family. This was certainly Miss Kitty's task on *Gunsmoke,* and it appears here again in this *Wagon Train* episode.[13]

I Love Lucy

The fifth television show we will discuss first premiered in 1952, quickly became one of the most popular programs of the decade, and has run *continuously*[14] ever since. The show is *I Love Lucy.* When viewing this show for archetypal analysis, I was stymied. It fit none of the traditional female archetypes I had encountered. Lucy was not a nurturant goddess; she was not a destructive goddess; she was not vain and materialistic, like Scarlett O'Hara; she was not a seductress or man-eater; she was certainly not a whore with a heart of gold, like Miss Kitty. What exactly *did* she signify? And, then, while I was watching one of the show's most memorable episodes, in which she and her pal Ethel try working at a candy factory—and end up stuffing their clothes and mouths with candy—her comedic kinship with Jerry Lewis and, more recently, Jim Carrey, struck me. Whatever they were, she was also. But what were they? The attributes "childish," "immature," "and "silly" came to mind. Then I glimpsed their identities: *les enfants terribles,* misbehaving children. Lucy was the first, and foremost, *female* expression of this archetype.

Lucy's persona fit comfortably within the 1950s chauvinistic mentality that viewed women as childishly silly creatures, needing close and constant supervision, unable to manage money or cope with business or political events, irrational and subject to emotional whims and excesses. After viewing the episodes again, I realized that, yes, this *was* Lucy. Remarkably, and counter to virtually every other female character on television at that time (and since), Lucy did not display those attributes associated with an *adult* woman: she was not sexy, nurturant, emotionally supportive, or even vain,

Archive Photos

I Love Lucy *typified the 1950s view that women were silly, irresponsible, and childlike.*

materialistic, or vindictive. When she cooked or cleaned or ironed, she often screwed things up—with hilarious results. She was, in essence, a little kid[15] pretending to be a woman—and Ricky was her *father,* by turns stern and indulgent, exasperated and forgiving, autocratic but affectionate.

In "The Freezer" episode, Lucy prepares Ricky's breakfast in the kitchen, popping the toast up from the toaster and catching it in midair. She tells Ricky she wants him to buy a home freezer for her because "it pays for itself." He replies that they can't afford one. Ricky leaves for work; a few moments later Ethel comes by. In conversation she tells Lucy they can go in together and get her uncle's large meat freezer for $50. They do this. Lucy then calls up the butcher and orders "two sides of beef," reasoning that this will be a little larger than two sides of bacon. The two women go out and buy expensive dresses with their "future savings" from using the freezer.

The meat delivery arrives—a huge quantity that fills Lucy's entire kitchen. To reduce the amount, Lucy and Ethel take several pieces to a nearby supermarket in a baby carriage and attempt to hawk them to housewives. They are run off by the supermarket butcher. Lucy and Ethel then laboriously put the rest of the meat (seven hundred pounds!) in their new basement freezer. That evening, Ricky and Fred return; they have learned from Ethel's uncle that "the girls" bought a freezer cheaply. Pleased, they have brought home thirty pounds of meat to stock it! Not wanting their husbands to see how much meat they have already bought, Lucy takes the new meat down to the freezer, while Ethel flatters Ricky into singing several songs. By mistake, Lucy locks herself into the freezer. When Ricky, Fred, and Ethel finally come down to the basement to put in the last thirty-pound package, they find Lucy inside frozen stiff and covered with icicles. They pry off the door and warm Lucy up by firing up the furnace. Of course, this is where Lucy hid the original meat so they end up creating a giant barbecue!

In a second episode, "Lucy Does a TV Commercial," the tale starts out with Lucy attempting to darn Ricky's socks; inadvertently she sews them shut. Ricky gets a phone call about a television commercial on his upcoming show; he needs to find a "girl" to promote the sponsor's products. Lucy begs him to let her do it, but he refuses. That night Lucy takes the picture tube out of their television set (wrecking it) and puts her face in the console to demonstrate to Ricky how good she would be. But Ricky will not relent. The next morning Lucy pouts and sticks her tongue out at Ricky. Ricky leaves for work. When the chosen actress calls during the day, Lucy tells the woman she won't be needed and goes to the television studio herself.

The product being advertised is a health tonic, Vita-meata-vegamin, which, unknown to the director and Lucy, is 23 percent alcohol. Lucy is on her "good behavior," saying "yes sir" and "no sir" to the director. She does a good reading of the script, but gags on the taste of the product, which causes her to have to read and swallow several times. Ricky comes by and sees her, giving her a reprimand; Lucy bows her head and pouts. However, the director comes to her defense, telling Ricky she is doing a good job, so Ricky permits her to continue. After several more run-throughs, Lucy gets quite drunk and begins slurring her words. On one take she swigs from the bottle, hiccups, and tells the audience: "The answer to all your problems is in thish little bottle." This scene is remarkable not only for its hilarity, but also because it plays with the cultural notion that women cannot "hold their liquor."

Ricky's show begins, and he comes onstage in a tuxedo, singing songs in Spanish. Lucy, in a drunken daze, wanders out to see him. She waves at the camera—"Hi Fred!" "Hi Ethel"—tries to sing along with Ricky, and then launches into her Vita-meata-vegamin pitch. Ricky, laughing and embarrassed, carries her off.

In a third episode, "Million Dollar Idea," Lucy, Ricky, Ethel, and Fred are eating dinner at Lucy's house. They compliment Lucy on her good-tasting salad dressing. Then Ricky begins to chastise her for overdrawing her checking account again; Lucy stuffs her mouth with pastries to avoid having to answer him. The following day, Lucy and Ethel talk about their finances; Lucy consistently "overspends her allowance" (another signal of her child status). Lucy decides she wants to make "a million dollars" (again, a child's notion of a lot of money), so she and Ethel hatch a scheme to make her special salad dressing and sell it.

The pair go on a television cooking show and hawk their new product. Back at home, the mail arrives with dozens of orders. Lucy has already bought lots of ingredients on credit. She and Ethel begin preparing the dressing and discuss what they will do with the money: "a mink coat," "a house with a swimming pool." They begin peeling onions and crying. Soon, Ricky comes in. They tell him about their plan, but he calculates that at the price they advertised, they will lose money on every jar! Lucy replies, "Yeah, but we'll make it up in volume." (Again, the story supports the proposition that woman, like children, are inept at business.) Hundreds more orders arrive in the mail.

Desperate, Lucy and Ethel go back on television to "unsell" their salad dressing. Lucy pretends to be a goofy housewife who tried the dressing and hates it. They return home. *More* orders come in—the viewers loved the commercial, viewing it as humor. Lucy and Ethel go to the store and buy hundreds of jars of salad dressing—at an expensive price—to fill their orders. They paste their own label over the store label. To save shipping and delivery charges, they load the dressing into two shopping carts and skate off behind them. Ricky calculates that they are losing "only" $600.

What to Make of the Fifties

The motion pictures and television series examined suggest that male and female archetypes of the 1950s display, in large part, the spirit of the decade. Men were depicted in (and confined to) the roles of the valiant prince (Moses, Ben Hur, Prince Philip), the public warrior (Paladin, Matt Dillon, Joe Friday), the wise sage (Seth Adams), and the father/husband (Ricky Ricardo). They were expected to be leaders, law enforcers, guides, and protectors. Women were defined according to similarly circumscribed archetypal categories, as well. They were passive princesses (Sleeping Beauty), caring wives and mothers (Sephora, Esther), evil sorceresses (Maleficent), and rowdy, pouty children (Lucy). Only two female characters that we have encountered, Miss Kitty of *Gunsmoke* and, to a lesser extent, Madame McQueeny of one *Wagon Train* episode, show competence outside the domestic sphere. And, ironically, they are both women whose employment status causes them to be viewed as unfit as traditional wives and mothers.

— THREE —

THE 1960s: Not So Turbulent

WHEN WE LOOK BACK at the decade of the sixties from our present vantage point in the new millennium, we are likely to recall it as a turbulent time. So much seemed to be happening then—the Vietnam War and its protesters, the civil rights movement, John F. Kennedy's short-lived presidency, hippies, the sexual revolution, the Beatles, the women's liberation movement, the advent of the drug culture.

What we forget, however, is how many of these significant social movements occurred during the latter, closing years of the decade. With the exception of the Kennedy assassination and the civil rights movement, which was then confined largely to the South, much of the early and mid-sixties was largely an extension of the 1950s: conservative, ordered, pro-technology, pro-capitalism, and patriarchal. Women had not yet begun to question their roles as homemakers, nor children their obedience to their parents. African Americans were still socially invisible, as were Hispanics and Asians. Divorce was unthinkable; promiscuity, by either gender, heavily stigmatized.

All of these cultural norms and values are readily apparent in the most popular television shows and motion pictures of the decade. The top TV programs were *Bonanza, The Dick Van Dyke Show, Bewitched, The Andy Griffith Show, The Beverly Hillbillies,* and *Gomer Pyle, U.S.M.C.* The most popular motion pictures were *The Jungle Book, 101 Dalmatians,* and *Mary Poppins* (three Disney productions); *The Sound of Music; Dr. Zhivago;* and *The Graduate.* Only the last two of these, *Dr. Zhivago* and *The Graduate,* released in 1965 and 1967, respectively, provide a glimpse of the epochal changes then at work in American culture. And *The Graduate* is the first truly modern myth we have encountered thus far. In it, the destructive goddess finally becomes sexualized and wreaks havoc upon the hero. Surely you remember her—Mrs. Robinson.

TELEVISION SHOWS OF THE 1960S

With that tantalizing tidbit waiting up ahead, let's now turn our attention to television. The top shows this decade are the reverse pattern found for the fifties; there, we dealt with the archetypal figures in four westerns and a situation comedy. Here in the sixties we have one western and five situation comedies.

Bonanza

As we have already seen in shows such as *Wagon Train, Gunsmoke,* and *Have Gun Will Travel,* the American West served as a metaphorical frontier for determining the boundary between law and order on the one hand and chaos and violence on the other. Characters, usually men, were placed on either side of that boundary and used to illustrate what constituted moral or ethical behavior—and what did not.

In *Bonanza,* a widower, Ben Cartwright (Lorne Green), and his three sons—Adam (Pernell Roberts), Hoss (Dan Blocker), and Little Joe (Michael Landon)—embody different types of American male heroes.[1] Ben is the patriarch—representing an almost biblical form of this archetype. Stern but reasonable, assertive yet flexible, he resembles in many ways Seth Adams, the wise wagon master on *Wagon Train.* Adam, Ben's eldest son, is rarefied, erudite, learned; always reading books and reining in his emotions, he signifies the hero-as-intellectual. Hoss, the middle son, personifies his name: he is large, gentle, and strong; he represents man-as-natural-being, acting directly, earnestly, and honestly toward others. Little Joe, the youngest son, is handsome, fiery, impulsive, and passionate. He is the hero-as-young-male-lover, full of feeling and emotion, sometimes reckless and unwise in pursuing his adventures.

Four episodes of *Bonanza* show a progression of moral development. The first, "Blood on the Land," begins with a group of sheepherders who have come to the edge of the Ponderosa, the enormous ranch on which the Cartwrights live. The boss, Jeb Drummond, urges his men to drive the sheep across it, shooting one man in the back when he refuses to do so. Jeb views himself as a Moses figure who has been shown the Ponderosa by God to claim it as his own, "even if I have to kill everything on it and burn it to the root."

The Cartwrights ride up to Drummond; Ben, the father, politely asks him to leave. Drummond then requests passage through the ranch to California, but Ben refuses. Although Drummond is a sinister and manipulative figure, Ben hesitantly permits him to camp for the night, before moving on. That evening, we learn that one of the young men helping Drummond—Billy—was rescued from a lynching by Drummond. Drummond cultivates Billy's friendship, giving him special food and bedding.

At the Ponderosa that same evening, Adam wisely counsels his father, Ben, that they need to build a public road through the Ponderosa, because many people heading west need to pass through their land. All of them cannot be turned away as Drummond was. Ben hesitates to agree to this and instead tells Adam to make sure that Drummond has left in the morning. When Adam suggests taking the sheriff with him, Ben refuses, stating, "We can take care of these things ourselves."

That morning, Drummond tells Billy he intends to take the Cartwright's land. He orders Billy and his other men to "kill any Cartwright and leave 'em to rot . . . They'd kill us, if they could . . . They got [wealth], and we ain't." Jeb moves his men and sheep to an area from which he can ambush the Cartwrights.

On his way to talk to Drummond, Adam encounters some of Drummond's men and kills one in a gunfight. Adam returns home and tells his father, once more suggesting the sheriff should be called. Ben again refuses to bring in the law, instead declaring that the land is his and he will fight for it. Adam notes that he is much like Drummond: "A law unto yourself." All four Cartwrights ride out to confront Drummond and his men. In a gunfight, Adam is taken hostage. (This is ironic because Adam was the one counseling legal adjudication of the dispute.) Drummond taunts Ben that now he can graze his sheep on Cartwright land as long as he wants, and Ben can do nothing to prevent it.

Back at the Ponderosa, Ben is torn over the two courses of action before him: (1) fighting directly for what was "his" or (2) asking legal authorities to enforce the law. He sends Little Joe to get the sheriff, while he and Hoss go to talk to Drummond. Ben offers to trade himself for Adam, but Drummond refuses. Instead, he forces Ben to sign a contract giving him the Ponderosa in exchange for Adam. While Ben is signing the document, Adam escapes and a gunfight ensues. Jeb orders Billy to kill Ben and Adam, reminding Billy that he rescued him from "those cowboys who were stringing you up for stealing those *three* horses." Suddenly, Billy realizes that Drummond was, in fact, the one who had originally stolen the horses for which Billy had been falsely blamed.[2] Billy turns his gun on Drummond and kills him, saving the Cartwrights. In the closing scenes, the Cartwrights and Billy are at the Ponderosa ranch house. They offer Billy a homestead on their land, which he gratefully accepts. Ben acknowledges that he must share his resources with others and use the law, not violence, to settle disputes.

In a later episode, "Spitfire," these lessons are put to use. The story opens with a man, Jeb Hode, setting a brush fire illegally to clear land on the Ponderosa. He is a violent man, abusive toward his teenage daughter, Willa, and has not bothered to check if anyone already owns the land he is burning. Little Joe is riding by and quickly rushes in to extinguish the fire, noting that many families' homes and livestock could be destroyed. (By this point, the Ponderosa had been opened up to other settlers. In essence, the Cartwrights serve as "benevolent dictators," bequeathing land and resources to those they deem desirable as neighbors.)

Enraged, Jeb Hode tries to shoot Little Joe in the back with a rifle, but Little Joe shoots and kills him. Willa, the daughter, is distraught and attacks Little Joe with an axe. He subdues her and takes her back to the Ponderosa. At the ranch house, the Cartwrights bury Willa's father, contact the sheriff to report what has happened, and attempt to "tame" Willa by having her bathed, having her hair combed, and getting her feminine clothes. Outwardly, at least, Willa is transformed (as in the Pygmalion story) into a beautiful young woman, although she still tends to run off, and as Hoss notes, "You have to keep her away from sharp things, like knives and hatchets."

Meanwhile, other members of her family, the Hodes, have been wreaking havoc through the countryside—killing a ranch hand at a nearby spread and shooting Adam Cartwright from his horse. (He is saved when the bullet strikes a book of poetry he was carrying.) We learn that the Hodes are an Appalachian clan from Kentucky who have been mistreated by many on their way west. Now they have become wary and violent, suspicious of all who are not their immediate kin. They are led by a strong, harsh woman, Grandma Hode, who carries a bullwhip to impose order.

The sheriff and Ben Cartwright go to talk with Grandma Hode; they tell her that her son, Dodie, who killed the cowhand must stand trial. Ben Cartwright offers her land and livestock for her family to settle on, in exchange for no longer trying to kill Little Joe. (Recall that Little Joe had killed one of her sons, Jed, when putting out the brush fire.)

While she is pondering his offer, Willa returns, and tells her about the Cartwright's kindness and sincerity. Unfortunately, just after this, Little Joe and Dodie encounter one another; Dodie attempts to shoot Little Joe in the back (apparently this is a common Hode strategy) but is outshot by Little Joe and killed. The grandmother is infuriated and vows to kill all the Cartwrights. However, her other sons and Willa tell her that in every case the Hodes have been at fault; the murdered cowhand and Little Joe were just defending themselves.

Grandma Hode, however, seems unconvinced. She calls her clan together and goes to see the Cartwrights. The Cartwrights meet them on the front porch. Grandma Hode tells them she is very upset about her sons' deaths, but that she now realizes it was not Little Joe's fault: "I can't hold no anger agin' you." She then asks to see the Cartwright's house, which Willa has told her about, and Ben happily escorts her in: "My house is your house."

The Appalachian Hodes, I believe, represent here something closely akin to Indians in enlightened westerns: they are a wild, violent tribe that remains apart from civilization, but which, at the same time, has been subjected to prejudice and abuse. At bottom, they are a moral and God-fearing people. Grandma Hode notes at one point that they "love their young'uns and pray to God, just like other folks." The Cartwrights, especially Ben, here take the path of conciliation, rather than confrontation as they did with Drummond. The Hodes were "wronged" first, and as benevolent people, the Cartwrights will attempt to make up for what others have done to them.

In a third episode, "The Fear Merchants," this lesson of inclusiveness is extended to members of another race. Hop Sing, the Cartwright's Chinese cook, arrives at the Ponderosa bloody and beaten. He has been hurt by racist whites in nearby Virginia City. After caring for him, Ben, Adam, Hoss, and Little Joe discuss prejudice against the Chinese, who have come to America to work on the railroad. The Cartwrights have befriended several Chinese and are going that evening to the birthday party for eighteen-year-old Jimmy Chang. Jimmy is bright and hardworking; he is saving money to attend college.

In Virginia City, Jimmy Chang's father attempts to buy small American flags to put on his birthday cake, but is rudely turned away by the store owner. All around town, fliers are being put up for a racist attorney, Andy Fulmer, who is running for mayor. Andy is a rabble-rouser whose motto is "America for Americans." Ben Cartwright realizes that Fulmer is responsible for stirring up the anti-Chinese sentiment and warns him not to bother Hop Sing. He also buys the flags for Jimmy Chang's birthday cake.

At the stable where Jimmy Chang works, the stable owner's pretty daughter rides in; she is harassed by a cowboy and Jimmy attempts to defend her. The cowboy knocks him down. The young woman attempts to bandage Jimmy's face when her father walks in and mistakenly thinks they are kissing. Furious, the (racist) father draws his gun and, in a struggle, fatally shoots his daughter, screaming at the girl, "You're flaunting yourself in front of a heathen." The rude cowboy comes in, and together they blame Jimmy for the shooting.

Jimmy arrives at his birthday party beaten and scared, followed by a mob of angry whites. Little Joe and Hoss, who are at the party, escort him to the jail, where he tells the sheriff what happened. Although the sheriff believes Jimmy, he keeps Jimmy in jail to protect him. Andy Fulmer uses the girl's father, Mr. Ridley, to further his racist campaign: "Our city is being overrun by these undesirables." Jimmy's father goes to the Chinese Tong (a protection society) to seek help, but they refuse him, arguing that Jimmy no longer "acts Chinese" because he wants to attend college.

At the coroner's inquest, the white witnesses lie, implicating Jimmy Chang. He is indicted for murder. Afterward, Fulmer urges the white mob to "clean" the town: "That Chinaman killed a white girl; others may hurt our wives and daughters." (This theme of ethnic cleansing and racial purity is an ancient one that continues to be invoked to the present day.)

The Cartwrights all gather at the sheriff's office and have themselves deputized to defend Jimmy, as the lynch mob gathers. Adam leaves and goes to see the slain girl's sister, Amanda. From her, he learns the truth, and he urges her to have her father clear Jimmy Chang. Amanda and her father go to see Andy Fulmer to have him call off the lynch mob, but once again Fulmer convinces Ridley to instead blame Chang: "We have to stand up for honor, decency, and the American way."

Amanda, however, finally convinces her father to tell the truth. As the lynch mob moves toward the jail, Ridley rushes out to tell the sheriff he was the one who shot his daughter, but Fulmer orders one of his cowboy supporters to shoot Ridley. Ridley is killed. Fulmer then immediately calls the cowboy "a murderer" and shoots him, neatly covering up his own complicity in Ridley's death. Amanda tells the sheriff the truth, and Jimmy Chang is saved. With three people now dead, Ben Cartwright tells the crowd that "Andy Fulmer tried to murder this town." The townspeople desert Fullmer's campaign for mayor.

This episode of Bonanza closely resembles one in *Have Gun*

Will Travel that appeared a decade earlier. In both of these, the hero sides against racial prejudice and the subversion of justice to perpetuate discrimination. In both episodes also, law is shown to be susceptible to misuse by those who are in power; right-thinking people must stand up and demand that justice be equally distributed to all.[3]

The Cartwright's support of law and respect for the justice system was perhaps most severely tested in a final episode we will consider. "The Avenger" is an extremely well-written, well-directed, and well-acted episode. Unlike the others, it begins *in medias res* ("in the middle of things") with a gallows constructed in front of the Virginia City sheriff's office. We learn that Ben and Adam Cartwright are to be hanged that evening for shooting a restaurant owner. Little Joe and Hoss ride into town with the bad news that one of two witnesses to the crime has been killed. The newspaper editor and a Cartwright friend, Barney, are attempting to have the hanging postponed, but the rest of the town's residents have deserted them, because they fear a cruel rancher named Hawkins who has vowed to take over the Ponderosa once Ben and Adam are dead.

A stranger comes riding into town and stables his horse, giving it ample food and water. He has come from a looted town in Kansas and is seeking someone. The stranger goes to the restaurant, where he meets Sally Burns, whose father was killed, allegedly by Ben and Adam. Upon hearing this, the stranger, whose father was also killed, goes to the jail to determine if Ben is the same man who killed his father. He finds Ben and Adam reading their Bible and preparing for death. Hoss and Little Joe come in to see them, and Ben warns them not to try to "save them by violence." They must follow the law and use only legal means—the newspaper and Barney's petition—to avoid hanging. The stranger realizes Ben is no killer and admires his courage and morality. He tells the Cartwrights he will back them. The stranger helps a boy bringing food to the Cartwrights, who is harassed by Hawkins's men.

Hawkins's men also terrorize Barney, preventing him from completing his petition, and destroy the newspaper printing press—essentially silencing all legitimate means of seeking justice. Night falls, the hanging time approaches, and Hawkins arrives in town.

The stranger talks to Sally Burns, the sole remaining witness against the Cartwrights. He comes to realize that Sally did not actually see her father's murder; rather she was told by Hawkins that the Cartwrights had shot him during an argument. The other, now-dead witness it seems was also "planted" by Hawkins. He urges Sally to recant her "eyewitness" account. Ben and Adam are led to the gallows. Sally runs forward and tells the sheriff she lied. Simultaneously, the stranger sees Hawkins and realizes that *he* is his father's murderer. Hawkins draws his gun, the stranger shoots him down. Ben and Adam are set free.

The stranger saddles up his horse, reloads his gun, and pays the stable owner. Sally Burns thanks him for getting her to "do the right thing." The Cartwrights thank him for his help and ask him to stay, but he tells them he must ride on—others who killed his father still remain to be punished.

As these episodes illustrate, *Bonanza* uses Ben, Adam, Hoss, and Little Joe Cartwright to explore the boundary between right and wrong, to discern what behaviors separate justice from injustice. In essence, its archetypal figures deal with large, moral issues confronting our imperfect society.

The Dick Van Dyke Show

The next two shows we will address are much smaller in scope, both thematically and metaphorically. They deal with the day-to-day issues that confront families, especially husbands and wives. *The Dick Van Dyke Show* and *Bewitched,* two extremely popular situation comedies in the early and mid-1960s, bear some strong similarities: (1) both feature attractive, stay-at-home wives who pride themselves on their housekeeping, (2) both feature husbands who work in glamorous professions—Rob Petrie is a comedy show writer; Darrin is an advertising agency creative director[4]—and (3) both are set in the suburbs of a major city, an attempt to represent the white, suburban, middle-class lifestyle to which most of America aspired.

In the pilot episode of the *Dick Van Dyke Show* (October 3, 1961) the story opens with Laura Petrie (Mary Tyler Moore) in her kitchen. Her son, Richie, has come home with a slight fever. She frets that he is not eating his after-school treats—a cupcake and milk. Rob returns from the office and announces that they've been invited that night to a big party at his boss's house; several important network executives will be there. Laura tells Rob they can't go—she expects Richie to become sick and doesn't want to leave him with a sitter. The situation to be resolved is the commonplace family conflict between parenting and career advancement. After much comedic interplay, Laura finally agrees to go, but she emotionally warns Rob that her *woman's intuition* is telling her that something terrible will happen. She tells Rob she will go, but "I won't let myself enjoy it" (the mother-as-martyr archetype!).

At the party, Rob and his colleagues entertain the guests with comedy routines and are a big success. Laura finally manages to drag Rob away, and they return home to find their neighbors and a doctor at their house talking about blood. Both parents panic, assuming something terrible has befallen Richie, but humorously, it turns out that the baby-sitter hit her head, requiring stitches. Rob tells Laura that next time he'll respect her woman's intuition.

The same woman's intuition theme is played upon in a later episode (February 20, 1963). Rob, a novice skier, is going on a weekend ski trip with his next-door neighbor, Jerry, an expert skier. Once again, Laura has become fretful over Rob's safety. She tells Rob that she had a dream the night before that he was very seriously injured in a ski accident. He acknowledges her "womanly intuition," but assures her he will be fine, and leaves with Jerry. Laura continues to fret, and when the phone rings, but stops before she can answer it, she fears Rob has had an accident.

Up at the ski lodge, Rob *has* had an accident—there was a pile-up on the slopes caused by an errant goat. He is taken to the hospital and taped up from head to foot. He tells Jerry not to reveal this to Laura for fear she will say "I told you so." Then, he believes, he will "be at the mercy of woman's intuition for the rest of my life."

Rob plans to make Laura mad when he arrives home, reasoning that this way she won't sleep with him and detect his injuries. When he comes in the door, Laura greets him in a sexy black negligée. She believes that she was wrong; Rob didn't have an accident and wants to make up with him. To keep her from finding out the truth, Rob is gruff with her, causing her to cry and run into the bedroom. However, she comes out again as he is slowly and painfully undressing in the living room and discovers the truth. He admits that she was right; she makes him a hot chocolate. They kiss.

Both these shows, as well as several others, develop the theme that women have special powers of insight and foresight that men lack. This notion, of course, harks back to prehistoric times in which women were seen as linked to nature and the life forces—the Fates of Greek mythology, who spun out men's lives on their looms, were female. Laura Petrie also represents, of course, the Good Mother/Nurturant Goddess archetype, here weakened and modernized sufficiently to be placed in a suburban ranch house. But still the stories warn us that men ignore her intuition at their peril.

A more hidden theme running through the *Dick Van Dyke Show* is that such extraordinary powers, and the women who possess them, are best left at home, confined to the domestic sphere. During the early sixties, just as in the fifties, very few women were permitted to venture beyond their domestic boundaries, and when they did so, trouble often followed. A story line of another episode very much resembles some found on the *I Love Lucy* show: A woman out of the house can be a dangerous thing.

In the September 15, 1965, episode, Laura and her friend Millie are guests on a game show. (Rob has used his industry contacts to get them tickets.) Laura is chosen as a contestant by the mean-spirited talk-show host; she tactfully dodges several embarrassing questions and wins several prizes (a hair dryer, vacuum cleaner, and rotisserie). Richie sees her on television and calls up his dad, Rob, at the office to tell him. Rob and his colleagues, together with his boss, Alan Brady, watch Laura's skillful performance. She even manages to get in several compliments regarding Alan Brady, prompting him to tell Rob, "She did good. Didn't lose your job for you." They turn off the show and go to lunch. However, as the game show ends, the host tricks Laura into admitting that Alan Brady is bald and wears a toupee! Laura is horrified at her disclosure. When Rob returns home that evening, she tells him what has happened. She apologizes profusely, and Rob is more sad than angry.

The next day at the office one of Rob's coworkers ribs him about the gaffe, kidding him that Alan will fire him. Unbeknownst to Rob,

Laura has gone to Alan's office to apologize. She finds Alan talking forlornly to all his wigs, which sit atop Styrofoam heads. Alan tells them: "Look, it's the little lady who put you boys [wigs] out of business." Her voice quivering, Laura tells him how sorry she is, but that she also truly believes that Alan looks better without a hairpiece: "More mature, nicer, natural." Alan admits that his wife, accountant, and lawyer have told him the same thing. He tells Laura he has decided to give away all the wigs to "needy bald people."

Just then, Rob bursts in the door, determined to protect Laura from Alan's wrath. Here, of course, he is the archetypal prince coming to rescue the "damsel in distress." But Alan tells Rob not to worry; he's decided Laura has actually done him a service; he no longer needs to hide his baldness; he can be "himself."

In this instance, unlike in the *I Love Lucy* show, Laura's activities outside the home are shown to have a positive outcome. Her husband does not have to rescue her financially; his boss is led to adopt a more honest lifestyle, and Laura herself takes responsibility for her mistake. This is a long way from the juvenile world of Lucy.

Bewitched

The superstitious notion of woman's intuition is expanded to much larger proportions in a second mid-decade situation comedy, *Bewitched.* The pilot episode for this series appeared September 17, 1964, and told the story of a "typical American girl" who is blond and pretty, Samantha (Elizabeth Montgomery), and "a typical, red-blooded, American boy," Darrin (Dick York), "who have a romance." They have "a typical courtship, a typical wedding, a typical honeymoon, except . . . this girl is a witch." The story then picks up on their honeymoon night, when Endora, Samantha's witch mother, shows up to talk her out of "marrying a mere mortal." Samantha refuses and discloses her secret to Darrin: she is a "house-haunting, broom-flying, cauldron-stirring witch." When Darrin does not believe her, Samantha performs some simple magic—moving ashtrays, creating drinks—to convince him. Darrin is somewhat shaken by this news. He discusses the fact that he "is married to a real witch" with his friend at a bar, his doctor, and a bartender—all three take the term "witch" to mean a difficult woman. After thinking it over, Darrin decides he loves Samantha so much, he couldn't part with her, but he makes her promise to perform no more witchcraft. Samantha promises to be "the best suburban housewife—just like everyone else."

The couple is soon invited to a dinner party by one of Darrin's old girlfriends, Sheilah. Sheilah is the more common type of "witch"—a manipulative, tricky woman—and makes the dinner party miserable for Samantha while she (Sheilah) flirts openly with Darrin. In retaliation, Samantha uses her genuine magic to muss up Sheilah's hair, move her food, unzip her dress, and make her sneeze. And in a mythic gesture, as Sheilah hobbles upstairs to repair her appearance, a violent wind bursts open the front door and blows off her wig. (Witches control the good and evil forces of nature, including wind.)[5] Darrin understands why Samantha acted as she did, but makes her promise "no more witchcraft." Samantha agrees, but back at their own home as Darrin goes upstairs to bed, she magically cleans up their messy kitchen.

What are we to make of this? On the most simple, metaphorical level, this is a show that plays with the cultural distinction between good, attractive women (beguiling, entrancing, under their spell) to whom men are drawn—Samantha—versus the mean, crafty women (Sheilah) who may seduce men with their wiles. On a somewhat deeper metaphorical level, we can imagine that the notion of having magical powers with which to attract men and clean up houses was a particularly happy fantasy for many 1960s–era housewives, when their own personal reality was not nearly so enticing. However, on an even deeper level we see lurking here the very ancient notion that women do embody magical, supernatural powers; powers that may be used for good or evil. Samantha and Sheilah are modern evocations of the nurturant goddess and destructive goddess, respectively. Samantha, being truly magical, is analogous to Flora, Fauna, and Merryweather in *Sleeping Beauty,* whereas Sheilah is more akin to other manipulative female mortals, such as Scarlett O'Hara and Nefertiri.

Although presented in a humorous context, Samantha's powers do lead us into some deep cultural waters. In an episode that aired October 1, 1964, Samantha is preparing an elaborate dinner party for Darrin's coworkers and some important clients. (Entertaining her husband's work associates was a large part of the suburban housewife's role.) At the office, Darrin is talking to Rex Barker, a potential, lucrative client. Barker is a very aggressive man, but Darrin holds his ground. Darrin's boss comments that he hopes Darrin's wife is preparing a "marvelous culinary experience" for this client.

That evening at the party, Barker drinks heavily and flirts crudely with Samantha, who is doing an excellent job as hostess. Darrin pressures Samantha to "be nice" to Barker, as it will help him get a large account. Barker lures Samantha to the backyard and begins to make explicit sexual advances. Samantha turns him into a small, furry dog. The party ends and the dog is left behind. Samantha tells Darrin what she has done. Darrin is very upset with her; his main concern is losing the account, not in recognizing Barker's abhorrent behavior: Darrin tells Samantha, "You're just a wife; he's a livelihood." Rightly angry, Samantha makes Darrin sleep on the couch.

The dog escapes and Samantha goes to retrieve him. She changes Barker (pun obviously intended!) back into a man, but he immediately begins to harass her again, so she changes him back to his dog form. Samantha takes the dog back to her house. Darrin apologizes, but she still will not forgive him.

The next day, Samantha takes the dog to the veterinarian, because he'd been scratched by a cat.[6] There he is given a tetanus shot, a bath, and a poodle clip. Samantha then takes him to Darrin's advertising agency and turns him back into a man. Barker, apparently unaware of all that has happened to himself, begins talking to Darrin about the account, but decides he needs a drink. He goes into Darrin's office bar to get one and sees Samantha sitting there. Once again, he begins harassing her. However, this time, Darrin witnesses his behavior and punches him—Darrin is now being the prince archetype. When the boss is upset about not getting the account, Darrin tells him, "In that case, I quit."

The story ends happily, however. Barker comes to Darrin's house, apologizes, and awards the agency his account. We learn that fortunately, he also lives in a distant city and won't be by to visit very often. To celebrate, Darrin takes Samantha to dinner; as they leave, she magically lifts his hat onto his head.

This tale, like one of the *Dick Van Dyke Show* episodes, presents a modern predicament: the wife's behavior affects her husband's career, either positively or negatively. Very often, as we have seen, this was a source of great anxiety for both members of the couple, usually causing the husband to act (at least initially) in a less-than-princely way. Indeed, both Rob Petrie and Darrin Stevens are not princely characters; they often appear to be anxious, insecure, self-centered men. Perhaps this portrayal is closer to the reality of human behavior than those of the gallant princes in *Snow White* and *Sleeping Beauty,* but it is also less inspiring or admirable.

Ironically, given the mid-sixties date of *Bewitched,* Samantha-the-suburban-housewife is shown to be the one who is truly empowered. Not fettered by corporate pressures to make a living, she is free to act on the basis of morality and "rightness." She is unfettered by another central mortal concern as well. In an episode that aired February 25, 1965, as Endora, Samantha, and Darrin explore an antiques store, Endora moves a painting toward Darrin's view. The painting shows Samantha as one of the Salem witches in 1682, looking only slightly younger than she does now.

Back at their house, Darrin asks Samantha how old she is. Samantha hedges, but finally admits that she will only age very slowly (over centuries), whereas Darrin will age in decades. He realizes that this is the curse of his mortality; he will age and die while Samantha is virtually immortal. Over the next few days, Endora plays several mean tricks on Darrin which heighten his sense of aging and oncoming senility. Darrin goes to see his usual retinue of confidantes to discuss his problem: his boss, the friend at the bar, the bartender, his doctor—none of whom understand the problem. Finally, he goes to a park (a natural site) to think things over.[7] Samantha discovers where he is and flies to see him. They realize their love is very strong "and that's all that matters."

Although this story ended on a positive note, it is very bittersweet. Indeed, the human desire for immortality is possibly what gave rise to ancient notions of gods and goddesses who did not die, but rather lived forever. As a culture, we still treasure this possibility and project it into our present-day myths.

The Andy Griffith Show

We now turn to a set of three situation comedies of a different sort. The Hode family from the "Spitfire" episode of *Bonanza,* in most respects, represented the most negative stereotype of southern, Appalachian folk: They were violent, uncivil, unclean, and dirt-poor, in short, *primitive.* But as Jung instructs us, for every archetypal image, there is a shadow image—its opposite. Our culture, similarly, has two simultaneous, yet diametrically opposed, views of rural, mountain folk. The Hodes embody the negative image, but the shows to which we now turn illustrate the positive archetype: mountain people as naturally virtuous, honest, resourceful, and insightful. It is likely that this beneficent view springs from a Marxist or populist undercurrent in American society. Rural people are deemed "close to the land," that is, nature, which serves to purify them and enhance their spirituality. Conversely, city dwellers are often portrayed as corrupted, secularized, and negatively materialistic.

The *Andy Griffith Show* first aired in the very early 1960s and featured Andy Griffith in the title role as Andy Taylor, sheriff of rural Mayberry, North Carolina.[8] Andy is a widower with a young son named Opie (Ron Howard). They live with an elderly Aunt Bea. Significantly, Aunt Bea is a maternal, nurturant figure, but one having no sexual relationship with Andy. Thus, he is free to be the husband/father figure for the entire community, unlike Rob Petrie and Darrin Stevens, who are "tied" to their wives and homes. Indeed, we most often see Andy at the jail, like Matt Dillon, rather than at home with Aunt Bea.

In an episode entitled "Dogs, Dogs, Dogs" (April 1963), the notion of rural goodness toward the less fortunate is illustrated. The story opens with Andy providing a delicious breakfast and special hangover remedy, which he and Aunt Bea have prepared, to a drunk man who has spent the night in the Mayberry jail. The man recovers and Andy releases him, sending him home with the admonition "be nice to your wife."

Opie, Andy's son, arrives at the jail with a little dog on a rope, begging to keep him. Andy feeds the dog some snacks from the lunch bag of his deputy, Barney Fife. Barney warns Opie and Andy that the state jail inspector is coming that day to look over the Mayberry jail for possible funding. Andy tells Opie to take the dog home. However, the dog—with five canine friends—returns shortly to the jail. Barney convinces the released drunk, Otis, to take them with him when he leaves, and Otis does so.

Soon, however, the dogs have run away from Otis and returned to the jail with five more of their friends. Opie wants to keep all of them, but Andy tells him there are too many. Barney suggests the dog pound, but Otis whispers to Opie that "they'll be gassed at the pound." So, while Andy and Opie are gone briefly, Barney, still worrying about the jail inspector, drives the dogs to the countryside in his patrol car and releases them. When Opie and Andy return, Barney tells them the dogs are now leading a joyous life in the countryside, "running, jumping, and playing." Opie is skeptical.

A violent thunderstorm comes up, and Barney, Opie, and Andy all become concerned about the dogs' welfare. They drive together and retrieve all twelve dogs, bringing them back to the jail. Opie and the dogs hide in the back room. Andy tells Barney: "You did a cardinal act of mercy." At that moment, the jail inspector arrives in a suit and hat with a very precise and conservative manner. Moments later, Opie and the pack of dogs burst in. Chaos reigns. However, the inspector, instead of being furious, is delighted: "What a fine bunch of dogs," he remarks. It turns out he is a dog fancier and completely in sympathy with their desire to help these animals. He gives them more funds than they had originally requested. As he leaves, Barney comments to Andy, "You were right: 'the quality of mercy is not strained'"—a biblical quote regarding God's love for all creatures. In the closing scene, a farmer arrives looking for his lost dogs, and they all happily return home with him. This is a simple but effective country parable—you reap what you sow. Andy, Opie, and Barney's generosity toward the dogs, even at peril to their own welfare, resulted in generosity being extended to them.

An October 1, 1962, episode, "Mr. McBeevee," tested the notion of a parent's faith in his or her child. At the outset, Opie and Andy are in the backyard pretending that Opie is a cowboy with a horse named Blackie. Barney arrives and mistakenly believes Opie really has a horse; he is humiliated when he learns the truth and warns Andy not to let Opie play make-believe. Later that day, Opie comes to the sheriff's office and tells Andy and Barney that he is on his way to the woods to see "Mr. McBeevee, who walks in the trees and has a silver hat." Barney and Andy both assume that McBeevee is imaginary.

Opie returns with a hatchet, which he says Mr. McBeevee gave him. Andy is concerned about Opie's tale and instructs him to return the hatchet to wherever it came from. Opie sadly walks to the woods where, to our astonishment, there *is* a Mr. McBeevee—a telephone linesman who "walks in the trees" and "wears a silver hat." Mr. McBeevee takes back the hatchet he had given Opie, but gives him twenty-five cents, because Opie kindly had brought him water and apples the day before.

Opie returns to the sheriff's office with the quarter, again telling Andy and Barney that Mr. McBeevee gave it to him. Andy is upset, believing that Opie may have stolen the quarter. He accompanies Opie to the woods to see Mr. McBeevee and is even more disappointed in Opie when no one is there. McBeevee had left on an errand, and Opie has no other explanation for the twenty-five cents.

Andy and Opie return home, and Andy sends him upstairs. He tells Opie that he must spank him unless Opie admits that Mr. McBeevee is make-believe: "If you don't tell me the truth, I'll have to whip you." This is a genuinely heart-rending scene, as the boy is in a tragic quandary between pleasing his father and lying. Opie tearfully declares that Mr. McBeevee "*is real*—don't you believe me?" Andy relents and goes downstairs where he tells Bea and Barney he "has to have faith in Opie."

Andy goes for a walk in the woods; in frustration he calls out "Mr. McBeevee, where are you?" only to hear a jovial man's voice answer "I'm up here. What do you want?" In disbelief, Andy looks upward as McBeevee, silver hat and all, descends from the trees. Andy exclaims: "Mr. McBeevee, I am so glad to meet you!" Andy invites him to dinner, hopelessly confusing Barney, who still does not think he exists. This beautiful story had a magical quality to it. It instructs us not only to have faith in the honesty of children, but also to recall the occasional truthfulness of fantasy.

Gomer Pyle, U.S.M.C.

Gomer Pyle, U.S.M.C., another extremely popular show during the 1960s, was also one of the first television programs to be spun off from an earlier series. The character of Gomer Pyle (played by Jim Nabors) originated on *The Andy Griffith Show* and then was transferred out to another setting—a Marine boot camp, where Gomer must contend with the complexities of modern life, most notably in the personality of his drill sergeant (Frank Sutton).

Gomer represents a uniquely American archetype that we have encountered before only very briefly in the character of Hoss Cartwright. He is a large, powerful man physically, but has the gentle, simple, honest nature of a small child or animal.[9] Typically, these characters are not sexualized as men, nor do they often use their physical strength against others. In fact, their trusting nature frequently may be taken advantage of by crafty, manipulative characters with evil intentions. Yet, in most stories their basic, innate goodness triumphs. It is my belief that they represent, at their most basic level, an incorporation of what humans most admire about animals into a human figure: animals are believed to have an essential honesty, purity, and inherent incorruptibility that humans often see their own species as lacking. Thus, we construct human characters in our myths to embody these traits. Gomer Pyle and Hoss Cartwright are two such figures.

Two episodes illustrate these principles. In the first, Gomer has been told by his girlfriend, Lou Ann, that she must work late, because they are taking inventory at her store. Lou Ann is a very sweet, blond, Southern woman. Gomer is quite understanding, but Sergeant Carter tells him he is "stupid" to "trust any broad; they all lie." However, Gomer does not believe the sergeant is correct; he does trust Lou Ann.

After taking inventory, the new store owner quite innocently asks Lou Ann to dinner to thank her for helping out. But at the restaurant, Sergeant Carter and his girlfriend, Bunny, see Lou Ann with the "new man." Despite Bunny's admonitions to "stay out of it," Sergeant Carter insists on telling Gomer what he saw, giving it the worst possible interpretation. Gomer is confused, but so honest and trusting in Lou Ann that he believes the sergeant must be mistaken.

Sergeant Carter drags him back to the same restaurant, where Lou Ann again is having dinner with the new store owner, again quite innocently, to celebrate finishing the inventory. Seeing her and the man together, along with Sergeant Carter's whispering "see, she's two-timing you" in his ear, makes Gomer disconsolate. Carter tells Pyle, "She's a conniving dame, and you're a sucker."

When Gomer decides to simply call Lou Ann and ask for an explanation, the sergeant stops him. Instead, the sergeant arranges a fake double date with himself, Gomer, and two sexy-looking women. The foursome arrives at the restaurant, where Lou Ann sees them. When Lou Ann calls Gomer at the Marine base to ask what is happening, Sergeant Carter tells Gomer several abusive things to say to her. He does so and she hangs up; Gomer feels terrible.

The next day, Sergeant Carter drags Gomer to confront Lou Ann and her new man to prove to them that "he doesn't care about her." When they arrive, they discover that the new store owner is married with children and has no personal interest in Lou Ann, nor she in him. Gomer is elated; the next night Gomer and Lou Ann have dinner with the store owner and his family. Meanwhile, Bunny, Carter's girlfriend, has learned of Sergeant Carter's date and is angry at him. Carter calls her pleading on the phone, while Gomer tells him *kind* things to say.

In a second episode, Lou Ann and Gomer have been dating for a year, and he has decided to get her a friendship ring to celebrate. He goes to a nice jewelry store to buy the ring, but discovers they are all too expensive. After apologizing to the jewelry store clerk for not buying anything, he runs into a sidewalk salesman, Friendly Freddy, outside the store. Freddy sells him a "genuine pearl and gold" ring for $12 (all the money Gomer has), and Gomer is elated. That evening, he gives the ring to Lou Ann, and she is very happy, promising never to take it off.

At a bar, Friendly Freddy is talking to his supplier and discovers he has mistakenly sold Gomer a real pearl ring worth $500. Freddy goes to see Gomer the next day and tries to trade rings with him, telling him the earlier ring is "worthless." Gomer says he and Lou Ann don't care; they are very happy with the ring as it is: "Lou Ann would never take it off." In desperation, Freddy goes to see Sergeant Carter; he gives Carter five "pearl" rings to give to Gomer as a trade.

That evening at a restaurant, Lou Ann and Gomer are dancing when Freddy and his girlfriend, Stella, come in. Freddy enlists Stella and the cigarette girl to help him get the ring back. Stella, Freddy, and the cigarette girl all pretend that Gomer has given many girls similar pearl rings. Their case is strengthened when Sergeant Carter dances by, with Bunny, and drops the five "pearl" rings on Gomer and Lou Ann's table saying, "These are for you, Gomer." Lou Ann is very upset, but can't get the ring off her hand to give it back to Gomer as Freddy was hoping.

At this moment a police detective comes in and gets Freddy. It seems his supplier had scammed even Freddy—*none* of the rings is genuine—and they want Freddy to testify against him. Gomer and Lou Ann don't care, as they believed the ring was worth only $12 anyway. The next day, however, they visit the nice jewelry store, and the ring is appraised for $25—more than twice what Gomer paid. On their way down the sidewalk, they encounter Friendly Freddy and thank him for giving them "such a great deal."

The central moral of both these stories is that *innocence is its own reward.* Gomer and Lou Ann, because of their genuineness, goodness, and honesty, reap happiness and well-being; whereas those who attempt to abuse them inevitably end up damaging themselves. It is significant that culturally we often portray such characters as *Southerners,* that is, as coming from rural, Southern origins. I believe this is because the rural South is seen as more pristine, natural, and primitive and hence as more likely to give rise to such men.[10] In the 1990s we encounter the epitome of this archetypal character. Like Gomer Pyle he is simple and Southern and has an awkward name: Forrest Gump.

The Beverly Hillbillies

Now let's consider what happens when an entire family of rural Southerners is placed into contact with the modern (1960s) world—*The Beverly Hillbillies,* of course. *The Beverly Hillbillies* debuted on September 26, 1962, only a few years after *The Andy*

Griffith Show and prior to *Gomer Pyle, U.S.M.C.* In the opening episode, a rural family, the Clampetts (again, missing the mother), are shown in their natural habitat: a log cabin with a wood-burning stove and fireplace, no telephone or electricity, a water pump, and an outhouse. They farm with mules and raise chickens, pigs, and cattle for food. The Clampett family, dressed in hillbilly attire, consists of the father Jed (Buddy Ebsen); grandmother (Irene Ryan); daughter Ellie Mae (Donna Douglas); and cousin Jethro (Max Baer). They are a happy family, resourceful, self-sufficient, and physically robust—all of the members engage in difficult physical labor, such as hunting, making lye soap, churning butter, chopping wood, fetching water, gardening, and washing clothes. Grandma Clampett also operates a still.

Their lives change dramatically when oil is discovered on their property and they receive a windfall of $25 million. At first Jed does not want to move or change his lifestyle: "A man'd be a dang fool to leave all this!" but his cousin Pearl tells him that Beverly Hills, California, has much warmer winters, so he agrees to try it. Pearl loans him her truck and her son Jethro to help with the move west. The Clampetts load all of their possessions onto the decrepit truck (recall the Hodes in *Bonanza*) and head for California. Meanwhile, in Beverly Hills, Mr. Drysdale, their banker, has bought them a palatial estate next to his own and assigned Miss Hathaway, an elite secretary, to assist with their transition. The first episode ends with the Clampetts mistaking their huge, walled estate for a prison and running off.

In the next episode (October 3, 1962) Mr. Drysdale and Miss Hathaway begin the task of civilizing the Clampetts to late-twentieth-century consumption behaviors, but their efforts are frequently thwarted. The Clampetts good-naturedly resist the modern fascination with time-saving conveniences. They continue to try to farm their lawn, chop wood (telephone poles), fetch water (from the swimming pool), and cook their own food (by putting wood in the electric stove). Unlike the Drysdale family, which is estranged, the Clampetts are emotionally close and supportive. In one scene, Jed tells Ellie Mae she must "tame her wild ways" and become more ladylike now that she is growing up. He hugs her and tells her he will always love her because "you're just like your ma."

Archive Photos

In The Beverly Hillbillies, *the Clampetts arrive in Hollywood: Traditional, pioneer America encounters the modern world.*

What *The Beverly Hillbillies* is playing with is the underlying cultural tension between modernity and traditionalism in American society. Although it is humorous to see the Clampetts' confusion with their "new-fangled" lifestyle, we also admire them for their common sense, practicality, and resourcefulness. They never shrink from doing a tough chore or ask for a handout. They are unfailingly appreciative to those who are trying to assist them (for example, Miss Hathaway) and always look for ways to repay the favor. In many ways, they embody the traditional strengths that Americans believe they possess as a people.

It is likely also that on a more abstract metaphorical level, they represent the cultural anxiety that many Americans felt at the outset of the 1960s, a time during which life seemed to begin moving too quickly and the pace of technological innovation grew more and more rapid. "New-fangled" machines, possibilities, and demands probably made many people feel like the Clampetts: awash in a confusing sea of social change and novel technology.

The competition between nature and science as sources of knowledge in American culture is dealt with explicitly in an episode that aired March 25, 1964, and titled appropriately "Granny versus the Weather Bureau." Jethro is watching a pretty weather girl give the local forecast on television. Grandma Clampett watches the forecast too, but gets upset because she believes it is incorrect. When Ellie Mae asks her why, Grandma tells her to come along with her and learn how to tell weather according to natural signs. Significantly, given the mythological linkage between women and nature, Grandma tells Ellie Mae that because Ellie Mae is female, she needs to learn how to read nature; in other words, this is a skill that is passed through the female line. She then shows Ellie Mae several natural weather indicators: bobcats licking their fur; roosters crowing; cats sneezing; the activities of wolves, frogs, ladybugs, beetles, ants, dogs, and tree leaves—all have import for predicting weather. Knowing how to interpret them is "what separates girls from grannies."[11]

Grandma Clampett scoffs at the "weather girl on TV who gets her weather from the government." To set things straight, Grandma goes to see the principal forecaster, a conservative man dressed in a dark suit, at the U.S. Weather Bureau who shows her the elaborate technology used to predict the weather: space satellites, elaborate radar systems, weather balloons, computers, barometers—"all the latest in scientific data gathering." But Grandma disputes the accuracy of this knowledge, saying she would rather depend upon natural signs to forecast the weather. She tells the forecaster that it will rain hard that night; but he disregards her, predicting a clear evening.

Back home, Granny warns several people about the upcoming heavy rain, including Jethro, Miss Hathaway and Mr. Drysdale, but they all ignore her, preferring to believe the scientific government forecast. To further convince Granny that she is wrong, the forecaster—accompanied by Drysdale and Hathaway—brings a movie over to the Clampetts' house to instruct Granny about how weather is predicted. They tell her definitively: it won't rain tonight. Minutes later, an enormous storm erupts, sending down torrents of rain. The story closes with the forecaster now using Granny's "signs" to predict the weather. Here, clearly, the old tried-and-true methods of gaining knowledge are being favored over reliance on technology.

MOVIES OF THE 1960s

We now want to shift our focus to the six motion pictures that were most popular during the 1960s. Happily, they fall into three sets of pairs in terms of thematic content. The first pair consists of two animal-and-human tales from the Disney Company—*101 Dalmatians* and *The Jungle Book.* Next are two stories about a nurturant goddess figure who comes into a family and helps it become closer and happier—*Mary Poppins* and *The Sound of Music.* Finally, we have two, more modern films that deal with marital infidelity and its aftermath: *Dr. Zhivago* and *The Graduate.* As we shall see, these last two films present very different versions of what befalls those who stray from their marital bonds.

101 Dalmatians (1961)

This animated Disney film was released in 1961, but in many ways is a timeless story.[12] *101 Dalmatians* is representative of a large group of animal-human films that inform us about family formation and parenting responsibilities (others include *Beethoven, Turner and Hooch, Bingo, Homeward Bound,* and *Lady and the Tramp*).

Pongo, a male Dalmatian, and Roger Radcliffe, his human owner, are leading leisurely, bachelor lives, when one day Pongo sees a very pretty female Dalmatian, Perdy, and her attractive owner, Anita, out their window. Pongo gets Roger to take him for a walk so they can meet. In the park (a natural setting), Perdy and Pongo manage to tie their owners together with their leashes and dunk them both in a pond (all of which signals rebirth and a change in status). Naturally, Roger and Anita get married, uniting Pongo and Perdy, as well. Thus, we have two families being formed, one animal and one human.

Cruella Deville (her name implies "cruel," and "devil"; this is the destructive goddess archetype), a college friend of Anita's, comes by and tells Roger and Anita she wants to buy some puppies when the dogs produce a litter. Cruella is a vivid archetypal figure: she has black and white haggard hair, wears a fur (dead animal) coat, smokes cigarettes (fire), wears heavy perfume and a fashionable dress (vanity), and has long bony fingers with talonlike nails (the bird-of-prey image).

Assisted by Anita, Perdita has a litter of fifteen puppies, as Roger and Pongo wait outside in a scene reminiscent of old motion picture delivery-room scenes. Cruella appears again and offers to buy the entire litter, but Roger and Anita refuse her offer. The puppies lead a happy existence at the house, chewing on the furniture, lounging on the couch, and watching *Top Dog* on television. One day while Pongo and Perdy are out for a stroll with Roger and Anita, two crooks (hired by Cruella, of course) break into the house and steal all the puppies. Roger immediately calls the police.

The puppies' parents, Pongo and Perdy, also go into action, searching the countryside for their lost children. The entire canine community assists their search by barking the news from one house to another. A bloodhound and goose living near Hell Hall hear the message. They've heard strange noises coming from the deserted, decrepit mansion (similar to Maleficent's evil castle in *Sleeping Beauty*). A cat and sheepdog who patrol the area go to Hell Hall to investigate. Note here that the animals are assisting in the search *across species;* this is an admirable trait and no doubt is intended to suggest the value of interracial cooperative efforts to the human audience.

Inside the mansion, the cat and sheepdog discover ninety-nine Dalmatian puppies watching television, guarded by a drunk crook. Pongo and Perdy have also learned where the puppies are located through the animal grapevine, and they head for Hell Hall as well. Cruella arrives at the mansion and tells the two crooks to begin skinning the puppies (yuk!) so she can make a coat from them.[13] But the cat has been organizing the puppies to make their escape. Just as the last of the puppies is sneaking out the door, the crooks discover their absence. Fortunately, Pongo and Perdy have arrived on the scene and attack the crooks. Very interestingly, both the male *and female* parent attack the crooks, whereas in most human dramas only the male figure is the warrior. It is intriguing that as a culture we are more able to acknowledge female animals' fighting propensities than female humans'. Perhaps this is because female humans—as the primary sources of civilizing behavior for the species—are metaphorically viewed as unable to engage in or inappropriate for physical conflict. Conversely, female animals, still belonging to the wild realm, are permitted to engage in combat, despite their gender.

The cat leads the entire group of puppies to a horse stable, where Pongo and Perdy join them. The crooks pursue them, but are kicked by the horses, another instance of interspecies cooperation. This time, the puppies and their parents make their way through deep snow to a barn, where cows furnish them with milk (interspecies cooperation again).

The next morning, they leave the safety of the barn to begin making their way back home. However, Cruella and her two henchman are pursuing them in her huge limousine (another sign of her vanity). The dogs and puppies hide in a coal bin, where they cover themselves with coal dust to look like Labrador retrievers; they then board a truck bound for London and home. Unfortunately, water drops fall on the last few puppies, revealing their true color, and once again Cruella is in hot pursuit. During a desperate and dangerous car chase, the crook's jalopy crashes into Cruella's limousine, killing, we infer, all on board. Finally, the dogs and puppies make their way back home, where Anita and Roger carefully clean them all off—all 101 of them. Roger, a musician, plays a happy song on the piano, as the story ends.

101 Dalmatians uses an animal family to illustrate several behaviors that humans admire: courage, perseverance, intelligence, and resourcefulness. Although Anita and Roger are good humans, it is the dogs Pongo and Perdy—together with several other animal allies—who save the day and the puppies. Roger's call to the police had no apparent impact on the outcome of the story, whereas Pongo and Perdy's immediate decision to go in search of their puppies resulted in their salvation.

This represents *anthropomorphism*—the projection of human traits onto nonhuman characters—in its most distinctive form.

Like human heroes, Pongo and Perdy inspire us to follow their admirable example.

The Jungle Book (1967)

In 1964, following the great success of *101 Dalmatians,* Disney released a second animal-human motion picture, *The Jungle Book,* which also became one of the most popular films of all time. Based loosely on the writings of Rudyard Kipling, *The Jungle Book* begins with Bagheera, a black panther, discovering a human baby ("man cub") in a basket aboard a broken boat in a jungle river. This origin scene recalls Moses, who was set adrift in a basket and ended up in the royal Egyptian household, heir to an alien kingdom. Mowgli, the baby in this basket, is analogous to Moses—he has drifted into the animal kingdom and now must grow up in this alien household. Bagheera brings the baby Mowgli to a family of wolves, who raise him as their own. Wolves are the most anthropomorphized of all wild animals and are often mythically depicted as rearing human children, as in the story of Romulus and Remus. Ten years pass, and Mowgli is happy with his wolf parents and siblings.

However, one day Shere Khan, the man-hating tiger, learns of Mowgli's existence and vows to kill him and all who help him. The wolf pack collectively decides that Mowgli must leave them, and Bagheera plans to take him to a human village. Riding reluctantly on Bagheera's back, Mowgli sets off through the jungle to join a people he has never known. While Bagheera and Mowgli are sleeping in a tree, a boa constrictor hypnotizes Mowgli and intends to eat him. Fortunately, Bagheera awakes in time to rescue Mowgli, but warns him: "You must go to the human village; you are not safe here in the jungle."

As Bagheera and Mowgli continue their journey, they encounter a friendly herd of elephants and a big, happy bear named Baloo, who promises to teach Mowgli how to forage in the jungle. Mowgli finds Baloo to be a delightful friend and believes if he can act like a bear (that is, become *that* species), he will not have to go to the human village.

Bagheera warns Mowgli and Baloo that Shere Khan the tiger is nearby, but they pay him no mind. While Mowgli and Baloo are swimming, a band of raucous monkeys kidnap Mowgli. Bahgeera and Baloo go together to the monkey king's headquarters in a ruined city. The monkey king asks Mowgli how to *make fire,* but Mowgli does not know about this human practice. Note that at this point, Mowgli has been trying on different animal identities—wolf, panther, elephant, bear, and monkey—but none of them fit perfectly. The *use of fire,* as we soon see, is the demarcation point between humans and other animals and is a key to Mowgli's discovering his true identity.

Through a series of funny tricks, Mowgli, Bagheera, and Baloo escape the monkeys. Mowgli, exhausted, falls asleep on a bed of leaves. While he sleeps, Bagheera convinces Baloo that Mowgli cannot be a bear and that if Baloo really loves him, he will send Mowgli to live with humans. Baloo realizes this is true, but when he talks to Mowgli, Mowgli runs away.

The boa constrictor (who sees Mowgli as *food*) follows him and coils around Mowgli; but Shere Khan, the tiger, also has been tracking the boy. Shere Khan and the snake fight and Mowgli escapes. He runs and runs until he reaches a riverbank where a group of friendly vultures is gathered.[14] Suddenly, Shere Khan appears and confronts Mowgli. Remarkably, Mowgli is not afraid of the tiger; instead of running away (as prey), he grabs a tree limb (the human use of a weapon or tool) and whacks Shere Khan.

Just as the tiger springs to eat Mowgli, Baloo arrives and grabs the tiger's tale, permitting Mowgli to run to safety. The tiger turns his anger on Baloo and is injuring the bear, when lightning strikes a nearby tree, causing it to burst into flames. The other animals fear the fire, but Mowgli grabs a burning stick and ties it to Shere Khan's tail. The tiger runs off—never to be seen again, and Baloo's life is saved. Mowgli has mastered the human use of tools and fire. He is now ready to join his own kind.

The next day, Mowgli, Baloo, and Bagheera go to the river's edge near a human village. Baloo tries to play with Mowgli, but Mowgli hears a beautiful sound, unlike anything he has heard before. It is a beautiful girl singing a wonderful song. This is a lovely use of the female siren image—it calls to Mowgli and lures him to live with his own kind. In a deeper sense, the image also evokes women's mythic roles as the civilizers of men. Indeed, one of the very earliest human myths (Sumerian) tells of a wild man being tamed by a beautiful woman, who teaches him to live as a man and not a beast. The girl fills her water jug (a female symbol if there ever was one!) and Mowgli carries it back to the village for her.[15] The animals return to the jungle without him.

This wonderful tale is rich in mythic imagery. As Levi-Strauss would note, it delineates the boundary between nature and culture, and as Freud would observe, between boyhood and manhood. Mythically, women draw men into both civilization and procreation. In an even more modern metaphorical sense, we may read Mowgli's journey as roughly paralleling the standard story of human evolution. According to this, humans evolved from living in trees (Mowgli and Bagheera) to foraging for food on the ground (Mowgli and Baloo); they then discovered *tools* (the tree branch) and later *fire* (the burning stick), and then began living in human *groups* (villages). Mowgli's narrative traces this same pattern for us in a disguised form.

We turn now to a pair of 1960s films featuring nurturant goddess archetypes as their central figures. Released one year apart, *Mary Poppins* (1964) and *The Sound of Music* (1965) were both live-action musicals featuring Julie Andrews.

Mary Poppins (1964)

Mary Poppins is set in the London of 1910, a wealthy, patriarchal Victorian time. We see an overhead shot of the city at twilight, its lights glittering like stars. Above it, Mary Poppins sits on a cloud in her nanny uniform, powdering her nose and packing her suitcase. She is going on a trip, literally heaven-sent, to assist a dysfunctional British family, the Banks, who live at 17 Cherry Tree Lane. Our narrator is Burt (Dick Van Dyke), a magical character who works as a poet, one-man-band, sidewalk artist, and chimney sweep. Burt notes that the wind has shifted to the east, signaling "something about to begin." (Goddesses of both good and evil mien travel with the wind.)

At the Banks' home the situation is in disarray. George, the father, is an affluent banker, so busy with his job that he has no time for his family; Mrs. Banks is a suffragette so busy attending demonstrations she has no time for her children; and the children themselves (Jane and Michael) have grown so wild that a series of nannies have quit after only a few days. This particular evening, George has returned home from work, had his glass of sherry, his slippers, and his pipe, and expects his children to be put to bed promptly. Unfortunately, the nanny has quit and a policeman returns Jane and Michael, who had run away. George berates his wife for being unable to hire a suitable nanny and composes his own newspaper ad seeking someone who is "firm, commanding, disciplined and precise." The children, meanwhile, have composed their own ad requesting a nanny who is "sweet, happy, fun, plays games, gives treats, sings songs."

George tears up their ad and calls his into the newspaper. However, the pieces of torn-up paper rise up the chimney, like Santa Claus, and into the sky (heaven), where they are received by Mary Poppins. A strong wind blows away all the stern nanny applicants who arrive at the Banks' door. Mary Poppins descends from the sky with her open umbrella, enters the Banks' home, and is hired by the befuddled George Banks. She slides magically up the stair banister to the children's nursery. In the nursery, she magically helps the children clean up, singing all the while, and produces several large items from her small carpet bag—a hat stand, mirror, plant, light, shoes, and tape measure.

The next day, Mary and the children go to the park to meet Burt. Today he is a sidewalk artist and has drawn several fanciful scenes. Burt, Mary, Michael, and Jane go on a "jolly holiday" by imaginatively entering the various scenes, which are filled with flowers, sunshine, birds, butterflies, and animals, all in bright colors. Unfortunately, a rain storm arises, washing away the pictures; the children and Mary return home. She tucks them into bed and sings them a lullaby.

The next morning, Mrs. Banks sets off for another suffragette rally; she notes that with Mary there, the whole house seems happier—a bird is even singing at the window (nurturant goddess symbol). George becomes cross at everyone else's good spirits. This day, Mary takes the children on a walk. She speaks to a dog (recall that goddesses can communicate with animals) and goes with Burt and the children to see a delightful man named Uncle Albert, who is having a tea party on the ceiling. Albert teaches Jane and Michael how to laugh and tell jokes, something they had not done at home. That night, when George arrives home, the children are very happy. George reprimands them, saying they must learn "seriousness, precision, tradition, practicality, discipline, and rules." They must stop engaging in "slipshod, sugary, female thinking." Mary somehow manages to get George to take the children with him to the bank the next day; he has never taken them anywhere before.

The next morning, George marches his children to the bank. On the way they see a bird-feeding woman Mary had told them about. She sits on the steps of the cathedral selling bags of crumbs for the birds. This scene is full of sacred, female imagery—the birds, the cathedral, the very old woman, and her song. Michael decides he wants to use his money—a tuppence—to feed the birds, rather than investing it in the bank, as his father had intended. At the bank, a cache of old male bankers, dressed in dark suits, confronts Michael and encourages him to invest his money: "You'll have a sense of conquest as your affluence expands . . . do as propriety demands." But Michael refuses to give up his tuppence to them.

A struggle ensues and the other bank customers panic, withdrawing their money. Michael and Jane run away. They become lost in a decrepit part of London, but fortunately are discovered by Burt, now working as a chimney sweep, who takes them home. When they arrive home, it is Mary's day off and their mother is off to another rally. Mrs. Banks asks Burt to look after them, so he shows them how to clean the chimney. Mary arrives back at the house, and the four are all swept magically up the chimney to the rooftop. From here they glimpse a wonderful view of London. They dance with a group of chimney sweeps who then march happily with them into the Banks' home. Unfortunately, the gaiety is halted when George receives an ominous phone call from the bank president telling him to come to the bank at nine o'clock that evening. Burt reminds George that he is the children's father and should care for them more than his job. Jane and Michael apologize for the disruption at the bank and give him the tuppence.

At the bank that evening, George is escorted to the boardroom where a group of grey-haired old men condemn him: they tear up his boutonniere, reverse his umbrella, and break his hat (all symbols of his "office"). George, however, begins laughing wildly at the absurdity of it all, gives the tuppence to the bank president, and dances out of the bank. The bank president, a doddering old fool, begins laughing too and floats to the ceiling.

The wind shifts to the west, indicating that Mary's job is done. She gathers up her belongings and puts them back in her magic bag. George arrives home singing, embraces his wife, and takes the entire household out to fly a kite. The kite symbolizes an upward link to heaven; the family has been transformed by Mary. Burt is now making kites; and soon the elderly bankers arrive and begin to fly kites as well. They inform George that he has just been made a new partner in the firm. Mary unfolds her umbrella and ascends up to the sky—her mission as nurturant goddess fulfilled.

In addition to presenting us with a fine archetypal figure in the form of Mary Poppins, the story line of the movie also sets up and explores some interesting cultural juxtapositions between the sacred and the secular. With the sacred are allied Mary Poppins, Burt, the bird woman, the cathedral, the home, animals, nature, Jane and Michael Banks, kites, singing birds, flowers, butterflies, laughter, and spontaneity (one could call this "naturalness"). Conversely, with the secular are allied George Banks, the bank and its bankers, money, the city, formality, precision, practicality, sobriety, and order.

George's shortcoming is not that he works at a bank *per se,* but rather that he attempts to impose the rigid, masculine rules of the bank upon his home life and children—driving out spontaneity, fun, familial bonding, and happiness in the process. At the end of the narrative, George *chooses* his children and home and, because of this, wins back his job. This ending is very similar to two of the *Dick Van Dyke* and *Bewitched* episodes discussed earlier. Making a sacred choice results in both spiritual (happy home) and secular (money) rewards.

The Sound of Music (1965)

We are now going to visit another household where the same kind of rigidity is being forced upon a family by its father. Once again, Julie Andrews is going to appear—this time in the sacred figure of a

Twentieth Century Fox/Archive Photos

Julie Andrews in The Sound of Music *represents the nurturant goddess archetype.*

nun—and serve as a nurturant goddess who breathes new life into the home. *The Sound of Music* is a Rogers and Hammerstein musical set in the late 1930s in Salzburg, Austria. It is a fictionalized account of the Von Trapp family, an aristocratic Austrian family of singers who escape the Nazi regime in a daring trip across the Alps. But the more human aspects of the story focus upon a blossoming love affair between Captain Von Trapp (Christopher Plummer) and an *ex novicia* nun named Maria (Julie Andrews).

The story opens with Maria, not in habit, singing happily in a sun-filled mountain meadow—a natural, spiritual setting. A peeling church bell calls her back to her more formal religious responsibilities as a novitiate nun. When she arrives, the Reverend Mother gently but firmly tells Maria that she needs to try life outside the convent; she is not convinced that Maria has the right disposition to join the order. Reluctantly, Maria goes to become a governess for widower Captain Von Trapp and his seven children. On her way to the Von Trapp estate, Maria sings and dances joyfully—she is a free spirit embarking on an important journey.

Von Trapp, an extremely stern, formal man, informs Maria that she is their twelfth governess (recall the Banks' family!) and he expects her to impose order on his seven children. The children are all dressed in identical, military style uniforms, and march in lock step as their father blows a whistle. Maria is startled by his demeanor and demands; the household seems more a barracks than a home. She befriends the children and ignores their initial attempts to scare her off with pranks. That evening, a big thunderstorm arises, scaring the children; one by one they creep into Maria's bed to sleep with her. Captain Von Trapp is angered when he hears this, viewing it as a breach of discipline. He is on his way to Vienna to spend several days with a countess he is courting.

The next day, Maria dresses the children in flowery, individual outfits and takes them to the village. They buy food for a picnic and hike up to a beautiful mountain meadow. She begins teaching them to sing: metaphorically, of course, she is showing them how to enjoy life. Over the next several days, Maria opens up the children's world, teaching them songs, taking them on bike rides and in a horse carriage.

Captain Von Trapp, the countess, and his uncle Max, a music promoter, drive into the Von Trapp estate. The countess is blond, elegant, and very sophisticated. The children and Maria arrive by rowboat at the back of the house, singing loudly; while docking, the boat capsizes and they all fall laughing into the water. The captain is not amused. He blows his whistle sharply and orders them to stand at attention before Countess Schrader. The captain then takes Maria aside and fires her. However, from afar he hears the children singing a song Maria has taught them and serenading the countess. He begins singing too and embraces his children. He thanks Maria "for bringing music back into our house" and asks her to please stay. Later, the children and Maria entertain them with a puppet show.

In honor of the countess, Captain Von Trapp hosts an elegant party, complete with an orchestra. Maria is beautiful in a simple white dress (her naturalness and virginity stand in stark contrast to the appearance of the urbane and experienced countess). Von Trapp dances a traditional folk dance with her, and they fall in love. The countess sees them and becomes jealous. After Maria and the children sing a song to the delighted guests, several of them ask Maria to join the party after the children go to bed. The countess goes to Maria's room, ostensibly to help her select a dress to wear, but instead shames her into leaving the house and returning to the nunnery.

Days later, the countess is attempting to take Maria's place in the family by playing games with the children, but she has no natural knack for mothering. She tells Uncle Max that as soon as she and Captain Von Trapp are married, she plans to ship the children off to boarding school. The children, meanwhile, have gone to the abbey to plead for Maria's return. They are unable to see her, but the Mother Superior hears of their visit and talks to Maria. She learns that Maria loves Von Trapp and encourages Maria to return to the family. Maria rejoins the family, and the children are joyous.

A few days later, Countess Schrader realizes that the captain and Maria are in love; she graciously releases him from their engagement. The captain and Maria meet that evening in the garden, beneath the trees and stars (all early symbols of nature and sacredness); they agree to marry each other. In a magnificent ceremony held at the abbey, Maria and Captain Von Trapp marry. Bells make heavenly music. Maria wears a white (virginal) gown and a garland of green leaves in her hair. (Here the purity of white and the symbolic spirituality of nature are intermingled.)

The happy couple depart on their honeymoon leaving Uncle Max to prepare the children for the Salzburg music festival. Meanwhile, on a much larger scale, the Germans have annexed Austria and Nazis now are in control of the country. Von Trapp and Maria return home to find a Swastika flag in front of their estate. Von Trapp, an Austrian patriot, destroys it.

Because Von Trapp is a significant Austrian figure, the Nazis want to make an example of him: he is given the choice of serving in the German military or being jailed. The family attempts to sneak out of Austria one evening, but is prevented by the Nazis;

they are, however, permitted to perform at the Salzburg Festival, because it is considered a Nazi showcase. They sing beautifully, including a moving patriotic anthem, "Edelweiss," and manage to sneak out secretly while the prizes are being awarded. They seek refuge in the abbey, but the Nazis pursue them even there. With the nuns' help, they obtain a car and escape to the mountains. The family hikes over the Alps to freedom.

Representationally, *The Sound of Music* is a love story set during a war; the basic archetypal forces are those dealing with parenting and child rearing. Von Trapp is a father who has lost his ability to parent since the death of his wife. He and his children have come to interact as a military unit, with himself as commander and the children as soldiers. Two women, Maria and the Countess Schrader, enter the narrative as competing mother figures. The countess has beauty, charm, and wealth, and there is no doubt she loves Von Trapp. She is a slightly milder version of Nefertiri in *The Ten Commandments* or Scarlett in *Gone with the Wind.* Maria, conversely, represents the Good Mother archetype in its virtually sanctified form—a singing virgin, gentle, loving, honest, nurturant; she is a Madonna-like figure. The narrative instructs us that a Good Father will select the Good Mother to bear and raise his children, and pass the seductress by.

Doctor Zhivago (1965)

Doctor Zhivago[16] is a mediating[17] narrative in the sense implied by the anthropologist Claude Lévi-Strauss; that is, its story line and archetypal figures contain elements of prior texts we have discussed and yet it also bears within it the seeds of modernism. I will argue when we reach *The Graduate* (1967) that that film serves as the first truly modern story we have yet encountered and represents a watershed in American motion picture and television archetypal development. Yet *Dr. Zhivago* contains the nascent elements that emerge full-blown two years later in *The Graduate.*

The story opens in post-revolutionary Russia (about 1935). A high-ranking army officer, General Zhivago (Alec Guinness), has come to a large hydroelectric plant in search of his young niece,

Tonya Komorova, whom he has never seen. The young woman is brought before him, and he shows her a photograph of her mother, Lara, and father, Yuri Zhivago, who was a doctor and also a very revered poet, now deceased. However, Tonya does not recognize the names or faces he shows her.

The narrative then shifts back to a time in the past when young Yuri Zhivago, a boy of only four or five, attends his mother's funeral in a remote area of Russia. An aristocratic and kind couple, the Gromykcos, come for Yuri to take him to Moscow; his only inheritance is a balalaika.

The time then shifts forward approximately twenty years.[18] Yuri (Omar Sharif) is now in medical school. He has grown into a handsome, gentle young man, very well bred, but not arrogant or elitist. We are also introduced to a beautiful young blond woman, Lara (Julie Christie), seventeen, whose mother works as a dressmaker. Yuri and Lara thus represent bipolar levels of Russian society—Yuri the aristocracy, Lara the proletariat. Lara's mother is the mistress of a well-connected politician, Andre Komorov (Rod Steiger); that evening she is to go to an elegant party with him, but falls ill. At her mother's request, Lara is taken to the party by Komorov instead.

A young Marxist, Pascha Antipov, who is engaged to Lara, is leading a political demonstration that same evening. While Lara and Komorov are riding home after dinner that evening, Komorov sexually assaults Lara, as Czarist cavalry cut through the unarmed demonstrators, leaving them dying on the frozen streets. The metaphor here is that the powerful exploit the weak—taking what they wish without permission. Pascha, Lara's fiancé, is cut on the face by a saber, leaving him scarred—both literally and metaphorically—for life.

Yuri rushes down from the balcony of his aristocratic residence into the streets below and begins tending to the wounded and dying. Soldiers stop him and order him to leave. He is ready to defy them, but his adoptive father pulls him away, reminding him that their daughter Tonya, his fiancé, is arriving from Paris in the morning. Here we see vividly the role Zhivago is to play in this narrative. Although by birth and upbringing a member of the Russian aristocracy, his soul and sensibility lie with the plight of the common people. As we shall see, his two great loves, Tonya and Lara, represent these two aspects of the Russian culture, and he is torn continuously between them.

The next day Tonya (Geraldine Chaplin) arrives on the train. She is beautiful and radiant, and has brought many suitcases full of lovely clothes and accessories. (In essence, Tonya represents the best aspects of the upper class: beauty, gentility, graciousness.) Yuri and Tonya, although to some extent a "brother" and "sister,"[19] are in love and plan to marry with her parent's blessing. Paralleling their reunion, Pascha, cut and bleeding, comes to Lara's house; he tells her he is now fully committed to the revolution.

Lara realizes that she is sexually attracted to Komorov, and they begin an ongoing affair. She meets him at discreet salons, where other important men are seeing their mistresses. She has become highly sexualized, dressing in red and black, her hair swept up, her hands in elbow-length black gloves. Komorov is physically and verbally abusive to her. However, despite the sordidness of the relationship, Lara is unable to leave it.

After suffering additional abuse by Komorov, Lara takes a gun that Pascha has left at her home (symbolically, the gun is now an instrument of the revolution) and goes to the elegant party where Moscow's upper class has gathered to light the Christmas tree. Just as the hostess is announcing the engagement of Yuri and Tonya, Lara shoots Komorov, wounding him. This event is deeply symbolic on two levels. First, it signals the coming of the class revolution in Russia—the exploited proletariat strikes back against the exploitative ruling class. Second, it signals Lara's entry as a disruptive force into Yuri and Tonya's marriage, for just as her action interrupted the announcement of their engagement, her continued presence will later interrupt their marriage. Ironically, it is Yuri who—as a doctor—now mends Komorov's injured arm.

The following day, World War I begins. Yuri's Bolshevik brother—our narrator, General Zhivago—joins the army to help organize the Communist revolution. Pascha and Lara marry and have a daughter; he leaves her to enlist in the army (as a Communist organizer) and Yuri Zhivago begins tending to the mounting casualties. As the war draws to a close, the soldiers begin to return home, bitter and disillusioned with their leaders. The Communist organizers among them have successfully sown class discontent, and the officers are murdered by the enlisted men: the revolution has begun.

Lara and Yuri Zhivago find themselves in the same field hospital tending the wounded. Yuri falls in love with Lara, but Lara urges him to be loyal to his wife. When the hospital closes, they go their separate ways. Yuri returns to find Moscow in ruins and a new social order in place. His former home is now occupied by several families. Tonya works hard to help Yuri adjust to the new realities; she is resourceful, loving, and protective toward him and their son, Sasha.

One evening, Yuri arrives home early to discover the heat is off and Sasha is ill. Tonya tearfully tells him that there is no fuel for the stove; she had been trying to hide these unhappy things from him. Upset, Yuri goes out and pulls some sticks from an old fence, a forbidden act. His brother, the Bolshevik officer and our narrator, observes him but decides to help, rather than prosecute him. Yuri is thrilled to meet his brother after so many years. His brother warns Yuri that he must leave Moscow; he arranges for transport papers for Yuri and his family. The Zhivago family is transported to the rural countryside aboard a freight train. Besides the clothes on their backs, the family's only possession is the balalaika.

The Zhivagos disembark at a small village near the city of Muriatin. In pre-revolutionary times they owned a large estate there. They discover it has now been boarded up by the Bolsheviks, so they settle into the vacant caretaker's cottage nearby. (The Zhivago family has now made the perilous political and physical journey into the new Russia intact. They have survived the social upheaval, although losing their former elevated status.) Yuri begins a garden behind their house, and soon the family is growing its own food. Tonya, although pregnant with their second child, happily accommodates herself to their new lifestyle, ironing, drawing water, and cooking on a woodstove.

The family endures a long and oppressive winter; Yuri daydreams of Lara. Spring arrives; yellow daffodils cover the meadows and new leaves appear on the birches; life is reborn. Yuri ventures into Muriatin, where, by chance, he encounters Lara. They are joyous at seeing each other. They talk and walk through the town, again falling in love. Yuri goes with Lara to her apartment, which is laden with flowers (symbolic of her nurturant goddess role). He hangs his key on the hook by the front door, symbolic of his entry into her life. They spontaneously make love. Afterward, Lara asks him about Tonya and Sasha; both she and Yuri are torn between their passion and their guilt.

Yuri begins making regular trips to Muriatin to see Lara. Her daughter, Katya, has come to know and like him. In essence, he is now serving both families as a husband and father. Tonya is near the end of her pregnancy. One day, feeling his child move within her, Yuri is overcome by guilt. He rides to Muriatin and breaks off his relationship with Lara. On his way back to Verichino, Yuri is kidnapped by a Red Guard regiment that needs a doctor; he never makes it back to Verichino. (This represents the narrative's punishment of Yuri's infidelity; his wife and children are taken from him, because he has already deserted them.)

Another brutal winter arrives, and Yuri tends to the wounded after each miserable skirmish. Summer comes, and Yuri's duties continue. In the grey sky, Yuri catches a glimpse of the sun, which reminds him of Lara. He deserts his post and walks toward Muriatin. Like Moses and Ben Hur before him, he endures incredible isolation and physical torment until, finally, he stumbles into Muriatin. Here he learns that his family has departed for an unknown destination. He finds a note and door key from Lara; deliriously happy, he enters her apartment. A glance in the mirror reveals Yuri to be a bleak and haggard man—a ghost or zombie of his former self. He collapses on the floor thinking that Tonya and his son may be lost in the snow. He awakens to see Lara's beautiful face smiling at him.

This series of events resembles in many ways the penance and purification of Moses in *The Ten Commandments.* His true identity discovered by Ramses, Moses is cast out of Egypt and endures a brutal, lonely journey through the Sinai desert. He collapses at a well (female symbol of renewal) and awakens to see the face of Sephora, who becomes his wife after he has lost his first love, Nefertiri. Similarly, in *Zhivago,* Yuri does penance by spending two years at the front tending to his slaughtered countrymen; his earlier aristocratic life and marital infidelity must be purged from him. He then embarks on a lonely, treacherous quest in which he loses one woman he loves (the aristocratic Tonya) and gains the love of a second woman (the commoner Lara). For Yuri, his existential journey from Russian aristocrat to purified common man is now complete.

Tonya has left Yuri's beloved balalaika with Lara, signaling her recognition that *Yuri* now belongs with Lara. Tonya, although certainly a humane and kind person, is at her core an aristocrat. As such, she is unable to make the transition to the new Russian culture.[20] So instead she departs for an aristocratic haven, Paris, taking the aristocratic portion of Yuri with her in the form of their two children. This part of Yuri will now live on, apart from the new Russia.

Lara, Yuri, and Katya continue living at Muriatin. One snowy evening, drunken Komorov stumbles in, offering to help them escape Russia. He is now Minister of Justice (a great irony) for the Bolsheviks. He warns Lara that she and Katya are in danger because of the renegade actions of her revolutionary husband. For their safety, Yuri, Lara, and Katya decide to leave Muriatin and enter the Zhivago's abandoned estate. There they find some rooms that are still habitable, as well as a writing desk with sheaves of paper and ink. Yuri begins to write a series of poems for Lara.

In the evenings, wolves howl outside the house, evoking the larger, dangerous forces afoot in the land. One morning Komorov arrives and, once again, offers to help them leave Russia. He tells Yuri that soldiers will soon arrive to execute Lara and Katya; reluctantly, they agree to go with Komorov. Komorov, Lara, and Katya make it safely to the train, while Yuri chooses instead to remain behind in Russia. Lara is carrying Yuri's child, the child who will later become Tonya "Komorovsky."

At this moment, the narrator, General Zhivago, tells us (and Tonya Komorovsky) what became of Yuri and Lara. The general helped Yuri obtain a medical position in Moscow after the war. One day Yuri saw Lara walking along the sidewalk. He ran after her, but before reaching her, was felled by a fatal heart attack—his dreams always just beyond his grasp. Many came to Yuri's funeral; his poetry had become much loved through all of Russia. Even Lara attended; she introduced herself to General Zhivago, who agreed to help her locate her young daughter, Tonya. Shortly thereafter, Lara, herself, became lost.

The story returns to the present. Tonya Komorovsky tells General Zhivago that all she recalls of her childhood is running from soldiers and her "father letting go of her hand." General Zhivago replies that it was not her father (Yuri) who let go of her hand, but rather Komorov, who was always more interested in saving himself. General Zhivago tells her he wants to help her, as she is his only living relative, "the carrier of all that goodness." Tonya thanks him and tells him she will think about what he has told her. Her boyfriend, a bright young engineer, comes to get her. As she walks away, the general sees she is carrying a balalaika. He calls out to ask if she plays. Her boyfriend calls back to him: "She taught herself to play—she's like an artist." General Zhivago smiles to himself; he knows he has indeed found his niece. The camera pulls back to reveal a rainbow in the mist created by the hydroelectric dam. It represents the power and vitality of the new society, and the river of life gushes over it.

To me, one of the most significant aspects of *Dr. Zhivago* is its archetypal pattern of mating and parenting. It does not contain any villains per se; there are no thoroughly evil characters and no supernatural events. The closest we come to an evil man is Victor Komorov, who indeed represents the worst aspects of Machiavellian dominance and manipulation. Yet it is Komorov who safely extracts Lara and Katya from Russia, ensuring their survival. The film also gives us a traditional moral message, as well: Although good men may be fruitful with both their wives and mistresses, they are punished for their infidelity by not being able to live with either one. Yuri Zhivago dies alone, as does, we assume, Lara. Illicit love may be fertile, but it does not result in a long-lived relationship, we are instructed.

The Graduate (1967)

We now turn to the watershed film that ended the decade. *The Graduate* was released in 1967 and quickly became one of the most popular movies of all time, launching the career of Dustin Hoffman. It opens with the young Benjamin Braddock (Hoffman) arriving at the Los Angeles airport, home from his college graduation. He wears a suit and a confused, vacant expression as he rides the conveyor belt through the airport, signifying his passive entry into formal adulthood. The soundtrack plays Simon and

Garfunkel's "The Sounds of Silence," lamenting the emptiness of American culture.

At home Ben sits disconsolately in his bedroom looking at his aquarium, another example of a self-contained, artificial society. His parents are dressed in party clothes and are throwing a festive dinner in his honor; all of *their* friends are in attendance. They want to display Ben, who graduated with honors, as a trophy of their success. Ben is forced to come to the party, where his father's drunken law partner, Mr. Robinson, tells him to pursue "plastics" as a career.[21] Ben hastily retreats back to his room.

Mrs. Robinson (Ann Bancroft) enters Ben's room. She is the height of 1960s sophistication: fortyish, streaked blond hair, glamorously dressed, smoking a cigarette. She asks Ben to drive her home in his new car, a red convertible; Ben very reluctantly agrees. When they arrive, Mrs. Robinson, a truly predatory female, asks him into her house, feigning fear or vulnerability. Benjamin hesitantly enters and is given a bourbon to drink by Mrs. Robinson, who then puts sensual, Latin music on the stereo. Mrs. Robinson

UA/Embassy/Archive Photos

The prince is tempted by a sexualized destructive goddess: Benjamin Braddock and Mrs. Robinson in The Graduate.

(she is *always* called Mrs. Robinson throughout the movie) asks Ben if he finds her attractive. She tells him she is an alcoholic and that her husband won't be home for several hours. She cocks her legs upon a barstool, opening her crotch. When Benjamin accuses her of trying to seduce him, she denies it; Benjamin becomes embarrassed and apologizes.

Mrs. Robinson then entices Ben upstairs to see her daughter Elaine's new portrait. Once Ben is in Elaine's bedroom, Mrs. Robinson asks him to help unzip her black dress; underneath is a leopard-print half-slip and brassiere. The color black and the leopard print strongly signal Mrs. Robinson's status as a predatory female archetype—the man-eater; Benjamin is her prey. Benjamin retreats downstairs, but she makes him bring up her purse (symbolically, her vagina) and stands before him nude. Benjamin runs out of the bedroom, just as Mr. Robinson comes in the front door.

One evening, Ben calls Mrs. Robinson from the Taft Hotel. He is dressed in a suit and tie, smoking a cigarette and drinking a bourbon, all the accoutrements of adulthood. He asks her to meet him at the hotel, and she agrees, arriving in a leopard coat with a black dress. Benjamin registers himself as Mr. Gladstone (happy genitals!) and takes his toothbrush up to the room.

Mrs. Robinson is cool and calculating; Ben is inept and insecure. He tells her "I think you're the most attractive of all my parents' friends." A virgin, he almost chickens out, but is shamed into having sex by Mrs. Robinson. The next scene shows him floating passively in the family pool, wearing sunglasses. This is intercut with scenes of Benjamin and Mrs. Robinson in their hotel room having *dis*passionate sex. Ben says of himself, "I'm just drifting." His life is purposeless.

One evening at the hotel he learns that the Robinsons (Mr. and Mrs.) have separate bedrooms. Theirs is a marriage of convenience, originated when Mrs. Robinson became pregnant with Elaine while dating Mr. Robinson. Once a promising art student, she is now a forty-year-old alcoholic woman having an affair with a twenty-one-year-old college graduate. When Benjamin jokingly tells her he is going to go out with the Robinson's daughter, Elaine, as Mr. Robinson keeps suggesting, she becomes infuriated: "Don't you go near Elaine!" Benjamin promises he will not. They argue. He tells her, "I'm not proud I spend my time with a broken-down alcoholic. . . . This whole thing is sick and perverted." He tells her he is leaving; but when Mrs. Robinson begins dressing in her sensual way, Benjamin changes his mind: "I like you. . . . It's the only thing I have to look forward to." He promises not to see Elaine.

Soon afterward, Ben's parents pressure him to take Elaine, who is coming home for the summer from Berkeley, out to dinner. Benjamin agrees to do so. Ben goes to pick Elaine up and finds Mrs. Robinson in the family room, smoking and drinking heavily, obviously furious that he has broken his promise. Elaine comes downstairs; she is a beautiful, long-haired brunette dressed in a simple white suit, evoking female characters we have met before—Snow White, Sleeping Beauty, Melanie Hamilton, that is, the virginal princess.

On their date, Benjamin treats her abysmally, hoping she won't like him. But when Elaine breaks down in tears, Benjamin goes after her apologizing profusely. They then go out for hamburgers, talk, laugh, and fall in love. Ben tells her, "My whole life has been such a waste." Elaine, sensing something deeper, asks if he is having an affair. Ben tells her yes, with a married woman, but "it's all over now." They agree to go out the next day.

The following day, a hard rain is falling—portentous of events to follow. When Ben arrives at the Robinson's house to pick up Elaine, Mrs. Robinson jumps into his car—she is wet, haggard, dressed in black (now symbolizing death). She tells Ben *not* to try to see Elaine or she will tell Elaine of their affair. Ben runs into the house calling for Elaine, but her mother blocks the way. Suddenly, Elaine comprehends the truth; she screams at Ben to get out. Mrs. Robinson resembling a hag from hell, hovers in the corner of the hallway. She shrieks out to him: "Good-bye Benjamin."

The next few days, Ben forlornly spies on the Robinson household, while Elaine is taken back to Berkeley. Benjamin announces to his parents that he is "going to marry Elaine Robinson." They are thrilled until they realize that none of the Robinsons have agreed to this. Ben leaves his house and drives his red car (like a white horse) to Berkeley in search of Elaine. Here we have our heroic prince off on a quest to find his virginal princess, who has been sent away by the evil (step)mother/witch/hag. (Notably, although Ben's quest seemed pure and noble by 1960s standards—and certainly by fairytale analogs—it would represent stalking behavior during the 1990s.)

Ben takes a room at a Berkeley boarding house, where he is questioned by the landlord about being an "outside agitator." The Berkeley campus of the University of California was the birthplace of the free speech movement and remains an icon of the youth revolution of the late 1960s. Thus, Elaine's placement here is clearly no accident. We are being told that she and Benjamin represent that generation's overthrow of the corrupt, inauthentic "false consciousness" of their parents' generation.

Ben follows Elaine to the zoo, where she is meeting a blond, preppie medical student. He is her fiancé and has been selected as her mate by her parents. We sense, of course, that if she marries him, her life will be as miserable as that of her parents. Thus the threat facing Elaine is a loveless marriage, from which Ben must save her. Here we must address a subtle subtext of the story. Benjamin is clearly of Jewish ethnicity—although this is *never* touched upon overtly in the text. Elaine's fiancé—the blond, preppie medical student—is clearly WASP. Representationally, the film is casting Benjamin as the "radical, Jewish, ethnic element" that is so much associated with the social unrest of the sixties, for example, Jerry Rubin, Abbie Hoffman. In contrast, the blond WASP fiancé, who in past tales would have been Prince Charming, or at least Ashley Wilkes, is here cast as the Establishment. He is everything in American culture that looks good from the outside, but is in fact internally corrupt and inauthentic.

Ben learns that Elaine and her fiancé are to be married that weekend in Los Angeles. He runs from the boarding house to his car (horse) and drives all night determined to stop the wedding. He charges into the Robinsons' house, where Mrs. Robinson, dressed in black with a leopard coat, coolly calls the police, reporting him as a prowler. Ben jumps back in his car and heads for San Diego, where the wedding is being held at the First Presbyterian Church. Ben's car runs out of gas, and he must run the rest of the distance on foot. He dashes into the church and screams "Elaine! Elaine!" from the balcony, which is behind a glass partition, signaling his outsider status. Elaine goes to him, drawn by that mystical force, true love, screaming, "Ben! Ben!" The father and fiancé attempt to separate the pair, but are not successful. Mrs. Robinson (in black and leopard) screams at Elaine, "It's too late"; but Elaine responds "Not for me, Mother!" and, with Ben, runs out of the church in her full wedding regalia. Ben pins the door shut with a metal cross, trapping the parents, fiancé, and attendees inside. (When I first saw this in 1967, I thought the scene had strong religious connotations—a Jew versus the Protestants. It still does!) Ben and Elaine jump aboard a municipal bus, a markedly proletarian form of transport, and make their way to the backseat, the spot reserved for Negroes until early that decade, and sit there, happily. They have abandoned their parents' affluent (but hopelessly shallow and corrupt) lifestyle for the purity and innocence of true love.

The Graduate has much the same core archetypal content as *Snow White* and, especially, *Sleeping Beauty:* the prince, the princess, and the destructive goddess. However, in this modernized retelling, two of the archetypal figures have been substantially modified in character. First, the prince (Benjamin Braddock/Dustin Hoffman) is subtly a member of an ethnic minority. Even more significantly, he is shown to be corrupted through sex, alcohol, and cigarettes by the destructive goddess. He must make pilgrimages to several shrines (Berkeley, the Robinson's house, the church) and engage in several battles in order to purify himself to win the fair maiden's hand. The fair maiden, it must be said, is remarkably true to form—a passive, virginal princess who seems willing to let her parents, fiancé, and Benjamin struggle to determine the outcome of her life. Feminism clearly has not yet penetrated this narrative.

This is especially apparent when we examine more closely the character of Mrs. Robinson. When I first saw this film in 1967, I was terrified by the specter of this woman. She seemed all too real—a country club version of the fairy-tale witch, oozing predatory sexuality, alcohol, and cigarette smoke, draped in expensive lingerie. However, now in my forties and with feminist eyes, I look at Mrs. Robinson quite differently. She is to me a pathetic figure and probably a misogynistic cultural stereotype as well.

As the sociologist Norman Denzin notes, American films consistently portray alcoholism in women as more degrading than this same condition in men, and further, Mrs. Robinson does not *act* like an alcoholic. She is never drunk, out-of-control, or confused.

Rather, she is a sexual, predatory person, who drinks and smokes. I think what the moviemakers did in this case was to play with American cultural fears of *powerful* women, that is, the man-eaters, and attempt, quite successfully, to construct a witch out of these misogynistic fears. The cigarette smoke is Mrs. Robinson's witch's fire; the liquor, her magic potion; the sensual lingerie and erotic body, her means of entrapping and corrupting poor Benjamin.

However, let us not forget that it is Benjamin who calls up Mrs. Robinson from the hotel, arranging their first date. It is Benjamin who regularly has sex with this woman, and it is Benjamin who dumps her immediately after spending one hamburger date with her daughter, Elaine, the girl he had promised not to see. As a teenager, I despised and feared Mrs. Robinson; as a forty-year-old woman, I see in her a host of failed dreams, a patriarchal system that told women of her generation that they had to "marry well" and stay married in order to have any identity in the world, a woman who hadn't had sex with her husband for the past twenty years and who therefore sublimated her frustrations in liquor, cigarettes, and the pursuit of young men. In short, I no longer see Mrs. Robinson as the villain, but rather in many ways as the victim, and in many ways more ill-used than either Benjamin or Elaine.

— FOUR —

THE 1970s IN MOTION PICTURES

THE OPENING YEARS of the decade were a continuation, and in many ways a culmination, of the social changes underway during the latter part of the 1960s: women's demands for equality, the civil rights movement, youth unrest with established authority, and the antiwar movement. In April 1974, the Watergate scandal erupted. Six months later, the U.S. president resigned, and a cynical malaise regarding politics, from which the country has yet to fully recover, infiltrated popular culture.

One of the most critically lauded films of this time period remains among the most popular of all time. The first truly tragic film we have yet encountered, it traces with metaphoric eloquence the hero's loss of innocence, documenting with graphic violence and body-blow emotional force the notion that even good intentions may be fatally corrupted by evil means. Like the Vietnam War, it is the story of an initially valiant effort that evolved into spiritual decay.

The Godfather (1972)

Francis Ford Coppola's epic paean to his ethnic roots and American culture featured a cast of extraordinary performers: Marlon Brando as Don Vito Corleone, Al Pacino as Michael, James Caan as Sonny, Robert Duvall as Tom Hagen, Diane Keaton as Kay Adams, and Talia Shire as Connie Corleone. The film earned Brando an Oscar for Best Actor, as well as itself taking Best Picture honors, and made stars of Pacino, Duvall, Caan, and Shire. Like *The Graduate,* which finally sexualized the destructive goddess, *The Godfather* also stands as a watershed narrative in American archetypal development, for it is the first popular film to show its hero's descent from good into evil. Over the course of the story, Michael Corleone—always with good, even noble, intentions—trades away bits of his soul until, finally, there is nothing left.[1]

The story begins in June 1945. In the opening scenes of the film, an Italian undertaker is asking a favor of Don Corleone, the godfather (head) of a mafia crime family. The undertaker's conversation with the Don is a business transaction in which the undertaker swears allegiance to the Corleone family in exchange for revenge upon two American boys who have beaten his daughter. Don Corleone, the undertaker, and the others present in the room are all dressed in tuxedoes, for it is Connie Corleone's wedding day. Outside the heavily shaded windows, the sun shines brilliantly upon a festive wedding: the bride radiant in white, old people singing songs with the band, children running on the lawn, young people eating and drinking. Thus, immediately we see the contrast being presented to us, the dichotomy between the profane world of violence and business and the sacred world of family and love. By the end of the film, this very marriage will have been destroyed by those who now celebrate it.

Michael Corleone, the youngest and smallest of the three sons of the Don, has brought his girlfriend, Kay Adams, a WASP from New Hampshire, to the wedding. She is aghast when Michael tells her his father once helped Johnny Fontaine's career by threatening to kill a recalcitrant band leader. Michael reassures Kay: "That's my family; that's not me." And indeed Michael is the family's bright hope for the future: a college graduate and a war hero, he is on his way to becoming a "legitimate" American.

The Don's other sons, Fredo and Sonny, are involved in the family business, as is a surrogate brother, Tom Hagen, the family's legal counselor. Tom suggests to the Don that Carlo, Connie's new husband, should be given an important job in the business, but the Don replies that "Carlo will be given a living, but that's all; he's not part of the family." As we shall see, this purposeful exclusion sets in motion a course of events that will ultimately destroy the family.

Tom informs the Don that a narcotics gangster, Salazzo, wants to do business with the Corleone family. This would add drugs to the family businesses, which presently include unions and gambling. Don Corleone meets with Salazzo, but politely declines his offer, reasoning that drug pushing will scare off the judges and politicians who now support his interests. The Don, a few days

Archive Photos

Michael and Vito Corleone in The Godfather, *an American fable about the corruption of the prince.*

later, sends a trusted associate, Luca Brazzi, to check up on Salazzo. Luca is brutally strangled; and Don Corleone, himself, is gunned down at a fruit stand. Salazzo then takes Tom Hagen hostage in order to negotiate with Sonny, the oldest son and heir apparent.

Michael and Kay are out Christmas shopping while all this is transpiring; Kay glances at an evening newspaper and reads that Vito Corleone has been shot. Michael rushes to a phone booth and, locking Kay outside, calls up Sonny to find out the fate of their father. This is a key scene in a symbolic sense; the camera is inside the phone booth where we see and hear Michael talking with Sonny. From this point forward, Michael keeps Kay distant from him emotionally.

Mike goes to visit his father at the hospital, only to find all of the guards gone. He realizes rival gangsters will soon arrive to kill his father, so he and a nurse move his father to another room. He then courageously stands with another man outside the hospital to act as a guard, saving his father's life. Glancing at his hands, Michael realizes they are not shaking; he is a calm, steel-nerved strategist. A corrupt police captain, McCluskey, arrives and hits Michael in the face, breaking his jaw.

Back at the Corleone home, Sonny, an out-of-control hothead, vows revenge for the assaults upon his family. Tom counsels him to cool off. Mike, in a master stroke of strategy, wants to arrange to have both Salazzo and McCluskey meet him at a restaurant to "make peace." In this key scene, Michael is sitting in the center of his family living room, Tom and Sonny are at either side and other business associates flank them. Michael has deftly become the new head of the group. The dinner with Salazzo and McCluskey is arranged. During it, Michael shoots both men and calmly walks out.

Michael goes to Sicily to escape the gang war in New York, and Don Corleone returns home from the hospital, where he is kissed by his many grandchildren. Tom tells the Don what Michael has done and where he is. The Don cries, realizing that Michael's purity has been lost.

While in Sicily, Michael encounters a beautiful young woman; they court in the very traditional Italian manner and are married there in a rustic ceremony. Back in New York, Sonny beats Connie's husband Carlo for hitting Connie. Connie, quite pregnant, is beaten again by Carlo and calls Sonny for help. Sonny drives to help her, but is gunned down in an ambush. Carlo, having been emasculated by the Corleone family, has obtained revenge by setting up Sonny's murder with a rival family, the Barzinis. Unfortunately, the violence has now spread back to Sicily, as well. A bomb meant for Michael explodes, killing his wife instead. Finally, Don Corleone meets with the heads of the other New York crime families, and a truce is called. Michael marries Kay Adams, telling her, "I need you, I love you; it's important that we marry and have children."[2]

Michael is now head of the Corleone family; he uses his position to extend the family's illicit business into Las Vegas. As the Corleone's criminal activities expand, the old Don himself enjoys a peaceful retirement, dying of a heart attack in his vegetable garden. A career criminal, he is fortunate to have his life end so peacefully, amidst nature. Many others have not been so lucky.

At the Don's funeral, Michael is seated as the head of the family; mafiosi from many families come to pay their respects—and make deals. One of the Corleones' trusted soldiers sets up a meeting to betray Michael to his arch foe, Barzini. Michael learns of this and plans to revenge himself on all the family's enemies. To provide himself an alibi, he agrees to serve as godfather to Connie and Carlo's son. While the ceremony is being conducted and Michael is pledging "to renounce Satan and all his works," a series of murders is underway. Four of Michael's enemies are shot down, leaving him the dominant criminal in New York and Las Vegas.

Immediately after the ceremony, still dressed in his formal apparel, Michael takes Carlo back to the house and tricks him into admitting he helped engineer Sonny's death. Michael then has Carlo strangled to death. Ironically, only hours before he had been instituted as godfather to Carlo and Connie's infant son. Michael's appearance has changed, no doubt because of the burden of evil he now carries. He appears heavy, slow, beaten down, and emotionless.

Later that same afternoon, Connie learns of her husband's murder and bursts into the house screaming at Michael, "Murderer, murderer . . . you lousy, cold-hearted bastard." Kay looks beseechingly at Michael and asks him if it is true. Michael looks her directly in the eye and lies, "No, I didn't do it." When Kay leaves the room for a moment, one of Michael's henchmen closes the door, shutting her out. The narrative ends with men kissing Michael's hand in oaths of allegiance.

The Godfather is an authentic tragedy in that its central figure, Michael Corleone, had heroic qualities at the outset. He was brave, intelligent, loyal, and a brilliant strategist. However, he chose to immerse himself in his family's business, which was inherently corrupt, and hence his original nobility was lost. By the end, all familial bonds have been shattered by a series of violent actions ironically intended to preserve the family.

The central issue here is the forcing together of two bipolar oppositions—sacred family life with profane, criminal business. Indeed the entire narrative plays these two oppositions against one another over and over again. From the opening sacrament of marriage to the closing sacrament of baptism, each rite of passage within the family is contaminated by its proximity to money, greed, violence, and corruption. The two become so intermingled and interwoven that ultimately the entire fabric of the family has become hopelessly soiled. The moral is clear: No good end is ever achieved by evil means.[3]

The Exorcist (1973)

While the evil in *The Godfather* is clearly man-made and not due to supernatural forces, the next film we consider calls upon demonic possession to set up a confrontation between science and religion as two alternative means for dealing with evil. *The Exorcist* was released in 1973, a year after *The Godfather,* and continued its tradition of graphic violence. As we shall see, the story line also plays with the archetypal notion of the virgin princess, but in truly horrifying ways.

An archaeologist-priest, Father Merritt, is on a research dig in northern Iraq. He finds a small silver Christian religious medallion and a black devil's head carving. The wind whips up a sandstorm around a large devil statue with an erect penis, as two male dogs tear at each other. The priest is shown in profile against the sun facing the devil statue. Thus, the text informs us, the power of religion will be set against the power of the devil.

The story shifts abruptly to the Georgetown section of Washington, D.C. A woman, Chris McNeil (Ellen Burstyn), who is an actress filming a movie on location there, hears noises in her attic. She enters her sleeping twelve-year-old daughter's room and finds the window wide open and the room freezing cold; unknown to her, an evil spirit has entered the house. The next day the woman goes to the movie set and films a scene as a young priest, Damien Karras, looks on. On the way back to her rented house, she passes two nuns (representing religion) and a group of Halloween trick-or-treaters (representing supernatural evil). Her daughter, Regan, is happy to see her; she is spirited and playful. Concurrently, Father Damien Karras has gone to see his aged mother in a squalid section of Brooklyn, New York. He bandages her leg, which is injured, and begs her to move to a better neighborhood.

That evening, McNeil awakens to find Regan in bed with her; Regan says her own bed was shaking. The rattling in the attic continues. A priest carrying flowers into a nearby church discovers a statue of the Virgin Mary desecrated with sexual markings, a foreshadowing of the fate awaiting Regan. Father Karras's mother grows ill and is taken to a state-run mental hospital. She is confused and upset, asking him, "Why did you do this to me?'"

The next evening, McNeil hosts an elegant dinner party at her Georgetown house. Regan comes down to the party in her nightgown and urinates uncontrollably on the floor. She tells the guests: "We're all going to die here." Her mother calmly excuses her and then later gently bathes her. Regan asks her desperately, "What's wrong with me?" A doctor prescribes tranquilizers for what they believe is a case of "nerves." This is the first attempted intervention by medical science. However, by the next evening Regan's bed is jumping off the floor, and she is terrified.

Chris takes Regan to a psychiatric clinic. Regan is now possessed by evil—speaking in a man's voice, yelling out profanity and obscenity. The doctors give Chris a medical explanation for Regan's condition—a brain lesion. They put the girl through a series of excruciating tests using elaborate equipment, but the results are negative. Later, the doctors are called to the house to see Regan; she is having violent seizures on her bed and growling. She strikes one of the doctors, screaming "Fuck me! Fuck me!" The doctors sedate her heavily, refusing to believe anything unnatural is occurring.

Regan is taken back to the clinic and put through even more extensive medical testing; the results are still negative. The doctors advise Chris, her mother, to get a psychiatrist.

Chris returns home to find the lights in the house flickering. The telephone rings, but no one is there. (The house is becoming increasingly haunted.) Once again the window in Regan's room is wide open, and the room is freezing. A family friend, Burke, was supposed to be watching her. A friend arrives at the door and tells Chris that Burke was found outside the house with a broken neck, dead.

A psychiatrist hypnotizes Regan, causing the devil personality to emerge and growl; she grabs the psychiatrist's testicles. We realize that Regan, a virgin girl, is becoming increasingly sexualized as a result of the demonic possession. In our culture, prepubescent females are deemed the most pure, sacred form of humanity. Thus, the greatest evil is one which would despoil such purity. A detective investigating Burke's death discusses the case with Father Karras. He believes Karras may know of a priest who is practicing "black magic"; it seems that Burke's head was turned completely around—a sign of satanic worship.

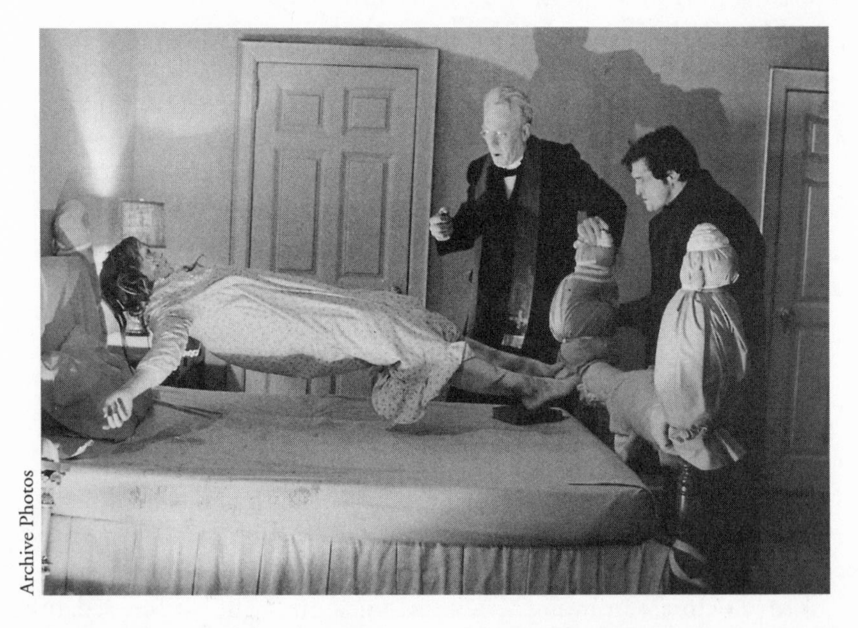

Archive Photos

A virginal princess becomes infected with evil in The Exorcist.

A team of psychologists recommend to Chris that they try exorcism for Regan. They do not believe she is actually possessed by a demon, but they believe that an exorcism may help Regan rid herself of "whatever guilt is causing the symptoms." Regan is brought home under heavy sedation. The detective arrives to question Chris about Burke's death, telling her about Burke's neck. The mother now realizes that Regan is responsible for killing Burke, but keeps this knowledge to herself. She goes up to see Regan, who is spinning furniture around the room violently. Regan begins stabbing herself in the leg with a crucifix; she then stabs her mother and hits her with a chest of drawers.

In desperation, Chris goes to see Father Karras and asks him to perform an exorcism. The priest finds Regan strapped down, her bed padded to prevent injury. Regan's face has been completely transformed to that of an ugly hag. She speaks in French and Latin and vomits green bile on his vestments. Chris tells the priest, "That thing up there is not my daughter." The next day, Father Karras visits Regan again. She moves furniture around the room and speaks in various languages, cursing the priest in his mother's voice. The priest talks with Regan's mother, and she confides in him that she believes Regan killed Burke. Father Karras is called back to the McNeils' house again that night. Regan's stomach now has the words "Help me" inscribed on it. Karras approaches his Monsignor about conducting an exorcism. They decide to use Father Merritt, the archaeologist priest we met at the outset of the story, who has conducted exorcisms before, in Africa.

Father Merritt decides to do the exorcism immediately; he and Father Karras enter Regan's ice cold room. Regan assaults them both with obscenity and phlegm. They begin the ceremony. The bed vibrates violently as they implore God to "strike terror into the beast and cast him out." Regan's tongue darts like that of a lizard; she howls like an animal; the shutters on the window bang; the ceiling and door crack; her head rotates around completely; she floats up to the ceiling. The priests continue chanting: "The power of Christ commands you!" and throw holy water upon her. She knocks Karras across the room. A thunderbolt sounds, and the image of the devil appears behind her.

Father Merritt sends Karras downstairs and continues the ceremony alone. After a short while, Father Karras returns and finds the older priest dead; Regan is giggling. Father Karras attacks Regan, beating and strangling her, and for a brief moment the devil enters him, leaving Regan. Thus possessed, Father Karras leaps from the open window, killing himself (and the devil). Regan is transformed to her former self, recalling none of what has happened to her. On the sidewalk outside the house, another priest holds Father Karras's broken body and administers the last rites.

There are two streams of archetypal meaning that we want to consider in *The Exorcist.* The first has to do with Regan's saviors—the priests Karras and Merritt. These two men both represent the force of God/good on earth. They are set as holy warriors against the force of the devil/evil who has taken human form in Regan's female body. Their rescue of Regan from the devil differs in two highly significant ways from that of other earthly warriors who have rescued princesses (in *Snow White* and *Sleeping Beauty*). First, they do not intend to marry Regan, that is, to save her so they can mate with her and produce children. To the contrary, they are saving her from the premature and craven sexuality with which the devil has infested her. Importantly, these two men, as priests, have foresworn their own sexuality to better serve as God's representatives. This springs from the very ancient association of femaleness with human and animal sexuality and earthly (material) pleasure, in opposition to the association of maleness with ethereal, ascetic religion, which denies the cravings of the flesh. Thus, these two men act not to acquire Regan's sexuality for themselves, as all our prior princes have done, but rather to preserve her chastity and virginity, which the devil is attempting to corrupt.

A second significant point of difference between the outcome of this story and all the previous hero tales we have discussed is that the two priests perish in fulfilling their mission. That is, to save the spiritual life of the girl, they must sacrifice their material life as men. In essence, they die in her stead. This, of course, is entirely consistent with the Christian dogma that Jesus Christ died as a sacrifice for all mankind's sins. If we metaphorically view Regan as representing mankind's innocence, which has become corrupted by the devil, then we can view the priests' deaths as a vivid reenactment of Christ's expiring as a mortal to bring about human salvation. Thus *The Exorcist* portrays a much more Christian archetypal pattern than anything we have encountered previously.

The second stream of archetypal thought we need to consider in regard to this film is its presentation of the beast or monster. We have not before encountered a beast, in the archetypal sense. Beasts/monsters represent that part of human experience that is violent, chaotic, and dangerous. Often they are portrayed as strange, unnatural creatures (cyclops, dragons, dinosaurs) or wild animals (lions, bears, snakes, whales) that attack and devour humans. Because the devil often represents that part of human experience which is violent and destructive, especially to the religious and moral order, the devil is often portrayed as a monster or termed a beast. Indeed, the exorcism ritual recited by the priests in the film refers to the devil as the "Beast."

When Regan is taken over by the devil, she develops qualities completely opposite those she normally displays: she becomes violent; she spews forth bile and phlegm; she becomes precociously sexualized; she destroys objects and people. In short, she goes on a beastly rampage; she becomes a monster. What is so symbolically shocking about Regan's transformation is that young, virginal girls are deemed the least likely members of human society capable of becoming monsters. The most likely candidates are typically large, adult men, whom we visualize as being capable of monstrous crimes. We think of such persons as being beasts, of being taken over by the devil. In these cases, it is the beast lurking within mankind that we fear. We turn next to a film which features a beast outside ourselves, a monster in the form of a great white shark.

Jaws (1975)

From issues of supernatural evil and sacred sacrifice, let us now consider a myth about primordial human fears. Insatiable, man-eating monsters lurking in the darkness of the forest or the depths of the sea have been a central archetype in myth since prehistory. The huge, carnivorous great white shark in *Jaws* depicts exactly this archetype.

It has been proposed by many mythologists that monsters such as sea serpents, dragons, giant snakes, whales, and similar beasts do

Fotos International/Archive Photos

The id (hunter), ego (scientist), and superego (sheriff) encounter the monster in Jaws.

not represent death and evil per se, although destruction often occurs to men who encounter them. Rather, a more sophisticated interpretation is that they represent a wild, primal life force that has remained outside of civilization and beyond the rule of law and the social code. In Freudian terms, such beasts represent the untamed and extremely potent force of the id, which has been driven back into the wild places, but never truly defeated, by the civilizing influences of science and technology (ego) and law and moral order (superego).

In many historic myths, the beast lies in wait outside the peaceful, settled village, until some mortal strays within its grasp and is devoured. In Freudian terms, one could say that the beast lies dormant in each of us, waiting for reason and conscience to lapse, and then overcomes us—leading to brutal, violent behavior. Thus, the monster "out there" is also the monster "within" and can only be kept at bay by our conscience and will.

Jaws opens with a group of young, happy teenagers gathered around a campfire on the beach—an iconic image of the settled community, the village. A girl and boy leave the security of the group and venture toward the ocean. The boy, drunk, passes out. The girl swims into the sea—the lair of the beast—and is brutally devoured. The scene shifts to a man (Roy Scheider) and a woman in their house. The man is the new sheriff; he is responsible for law and order on Amity Island, the peaceful village. The fact that Amity is an island surrounded by the ocean is further indication of the precarious nature of this, or any, bit of civilization, similar to the image of a small settlement surrounded by jungle, cited by anthropologist Bronislaw Malinowski.

Despite the girl's death by shark attack, the town council pressures the sheriff to leave the beaches open so that profits can be obtained from vacationers to Amity, and he reluctantly agrees. People return to the beach and go floating out into the ocean on little rubber raft "islands." A dog and a child are devoured by the beast below. A town meeting is held at which three actions are taken: (1) the sheriff closes the beaches for twenty-four hours, that is, attempts to reassert law and order (the Freudian superego) by protecting the boundaries of the village; (2) the sheriff sends for shark experts on the mainland, that is, attempts to conquer the beast (the Freudian id) by enlarging the amount of reasoning power (the Freudian ego); and (3) a mysterious outsider named Quint (Robert Shaw) appears and promises to kill the shark violently, that is, a human id will be sent to battle the primordial id.

The expert (Richard Dreyfus) from the mainland arrives; he is well educated (reason) and wealthy (material resources of civilization), and he possesses elaborate scientific and technological equipment. Science is viewed in our culture as the primary means to control nature. Meanwhile, the shark continues to attack Amity residents, to devour civilization. When the sheriff's son is almost killed, the sheriff realizes that he himself must go into the ocean, the wilderness, and battle the beast. The sheriff, the scientist, and the hunter (Quint) venture after the shark in Quint's boat. Quint has excellent intuitions about the shark and is able to hook it; being id-driven himself, he can understand similarly id-driven entities. However, the shark is much too large for their boat and equipment; the beast's power exceeds that of their small bit of civilization.

When the shark begins attacking their boat, the *sheriff* attempts to call the Coast Guard for help (to acquire more law and order), but the hunter destroys the boat's radio. Instead of relying on moral force, he wants to match his own wild force directly against that of the shark. They tie the shark's line to the boat and attempt to draw it back to shore; but the shark is too powerful. It shatters the boat, rupturing their island. The *scientist* then attempts to use elaborate technology to defeat the beast, but is thrown out of the boat; science and technology fail. Quint, symbolic of the human id, attempts to battle the shark, but instead is devoured, indicating that the primal id is much more powerful than that still residing in man. Finally, only the sheriff is left. With the boat sinking (civilization on the wane), he climbs to the top of the tower and shoots at a gas canister that the shark has caught in its teeth. The shark explodes. The sheriff, by conquering his own fears of water, death, and the beast, has reestablished law and order; the primal id has been suppressed. The scientist resurfaces (he was alive, but impotent); and together, the sheriff and the scientist swim back to the island on the remnants of the hunter's ship.

What do we know about American culture from *Jaws*?

First, although we have an advanced modern society characterized by sophisticated technology and a complex system of law, we still fear its destruction by some primal force. No matter how far society has come from its primitive origins, we still dread the unknown beast that lies just beyond our control. This beast may rise up at any time and devour us. Second, three heroes were sent to conquer the beast: the violent hunter Quint, who represents our own primal force; the educated scientist, who represents the reason and technology we have developed within civilization; and the sheriff, who represents law, order, and the moral code. Of these three, we learned, only law could conquer the beast. Thus the primary component of civilization is law. Third, we must consider why science did not defeat the beast in this story. Science is manmade reasoning applied first to understanding and then to controlling nature. However, we are taught in *Jaws* that science is less powerful than nature, where nature represents that primal creative and destructive force that remains outside civilization. The real factor that separates man and civilization from that primal, wild force is law. Without law, any civilization, no matter how scientifically advanced, can be destroyed.

Jaws was the debut of a twenty-seven-year-old film director named Steven Spielberg. Spielberg demonstrated vividly his ability to evoke mythic imagery in this film and would continue to do so. His next effort, *Close Encounters of the Third Kind,* appeared only two years later and dealt with a theme he would develop again in the early 1980s: the relationship between God and man.

Close Encounters of the Third Kind (1977)

The story opens with the present-day discovery of three 1945-vintage airplanes in the Sonora Desert of Mexico. An old man tells investigators that the "sun came out last night and played music"; his face is sunburned. That evening, two pilots report seeing an unidentified flying object (UFO) as they are flying over Indiana. At a farmhouse near Muncie, Indiana, a little boy and his mother are startled when his toys "come alive." The little boy runs into the yard laughing. That same evening, a electrical company worker (Richard Dreyfus) is playing with his children; he is trying to talk them into seeing Pinocchio.[4] He gets a call that there is a power outage and goes to repair it. While he is waiting at a train crossing, a UFO circles above his truck and wreaks havoc with the electrical circuitry; he sees the UFO disappear into the night sky. A while later, the electrical worker and two police cars chase three small UFOs down the road and through a toll booth. As the UFOs ascend to the sky, lightning flashes and thunder rolls. Here Spielberg is mixing science fiction imagery with supernatural and spiritual imagery; as we shall see, this is the gist of his message, that space aliens are gods, sent to provide us with advanced knowledge.

The electrical worker rushes home and gathers up his wife and children to witness this wondrous sight; but it is gone. He is left only with a sunburned face as evidence of his encounter. Symbolically, he is now a "marked" man; the aliens have chosen him. In the Gobi Desert in Mongolia, a convoy of United Nations trucks and helicopters discovers a huge freighter in the desert. Thus, inexplicable phenomena are occurring around the world.

Back in the Indiana heartland, Roy, the electrical worker, is fired from his job. Apparently his boss does not believe what hap-

Fotos International/Archive Photos

The arrival of the gods in Spielberg's Close Encounters of the Third Kind.

pened to him. His wife and children too are skeptical and concerned about him. In northern India, a French investigator, La Combe (François Truffaut) is recording a musical chant the inhabitants claim they "heard from the sky." He takes the recording back to a scientific conference and demonstrates that it is a sign language set of harmonic tones; it is a purposeful communication.

The next evening, Roy, his family, and several other residents wait on the road to see if the UFOs will reappear. Instead, a group of government helicopters fly overhead to frighten them. The suggestion here is that it is U.S. governmental policy to deceive the public about the existence of UFOs. Government technicians, however, have translated a set of coordinates transmitted by the UFOs and discovered it proposes a rendezvous at Devil's Tower in Wyoming. The Devil's Tower meeting place is quite mythic in that it is a rock platform jutting upward toward heaven—an ideal meeting place for contact between men and gods.

Back at the Indiana farmhouse, the little boy plunks out the harmonic signal on his xylophone, as his mother, an artist, draws pictures of Devil's Tower; neither understands why they are compelled to do this. The sky clouds up and thunder rumbles—gods are approaching. Lights glow in the night sky, and a red beam enters their house. All electrical gadgets turn on. The boy runs out of the house and is taken up into the sky, his mother screams hysterically.

The government prepares for the meeting with the UFO by selecting military volunteers and creating a cover story to deceive the public. All civilians are evacuated from the Devil's Tower area. Roy's marriage collapses after he attempts to construct a Devil's Tower out of mashed potatoes during dinner. His wife and children leave, and he begins constructing a huge, mud version of the structure in his living room. A newscast about the "livestock epidemic" cover story in Wyoming comes on television, and Roy experiences an epiphany—there in the background is the image in his head, Devil's Tower.

He jumps into the family station wagon and begins driving to Wyoming, to his destiny. Near the site, he is stopped by military personnel who are evacuating the area. He sees the little boy's mother who has also been "called." They embrace, sensing their common fate, and pair up, driving Roy's car through fences, past various barriers, until they reach the mountain. There they are captured again by military personnel. Roy is taken to see La Combe, who shows him photos of others who were similarly "called." La Combe argues with the military officers to permit this set of people meet the aliens, sensing that they are a *chosen* people, a special group called for this purpose, but the officers refuse.

Roy, Jillian (the mother), and another man, Larry, escape from the government authorities and begin climbing up the mountain. They support one another on their arduous trek (actually a pilgrimage to find God), but Larry is doused by a sleeping gas sprayed from army helicopters. Roy and Jillian make it to the summit and see before them the enormous landing pad set up by the military and scientists. Multitudinous forms of technological equipment are set up to record the encounter. Three small spacecraft fly down to the landing strip, and the humans play the five-tone harmonic pattern suggested by aliens. The spacecraft respond with music and leave. Everyone applauds, thinking the visit is over.

However, a huge cloud-head forms above them, and from it emerges an enormous space station. Lightning and thunder explode above them as the station descends. This scene is quite reminiscent of God's encounter with Moses in *The Ten Commandments.* Roy sneaks down to see the spacecraft, as do the military and scientific personnel. More harmonic music is played. The space station opens, and several missing U.S. pilots emerge—they had been taken aboard UFO ships years earlier. Other people and children also come out, including the little Indiana boy who runs to his mother, Jillian. The craft reopens and a spidery, manlike figure can be seen. The figure raises his arms in a Christ-like gesture of greeting. Smaller, child-size aliens emerge; Jillian takes snapshots of them.

Roy has now been dressed as one of the military volunteers by the government authorities, who have come to accept his role. As the volunteers line up, the small aliens select only Roy and take him aboard. He joyfully enters the craft and finds it filled with golden, glowing lights; he figuratively has entered heaven. An alien signals good-bye to La Combe and the others, and the spacecraft ascends back to the sky.

Close Encounters is a tale about being chosen by a supernatural force and embarking on a quest to reach that force. The film instructs us that even the most humble people may be chosen for such a mission: a child, a single mother, an electrical serviceman. Once called, an overwhelming impulse takes over one's life, and the journey toward contact begins. Manmade and physical barriers are overcome, and ultimately, our stalwart protagonist reaches his goal. Sadly, however, Roy has left several responsibilities and commitments behind, most notably, his wife and children. The film suggests that these are beyond Roy's pervue, he has been selected for a greater God-directed purpose, much as Moses was called away from his family by God. Although not portrayed explicitly, it is likely that Roy is being taken on a voyage of learning and knowledge-seeking by these alien beings. Someday perhaps he will return to Earth (as a savior or messiah) and share the gifts he has gained with the rest of humanity. Human affairs here are depicted as less important than the overall plan of the universe.

We turn next to motion picture that tells essentially a reverse-trajectory story. Instead of a man leaving Earth and going away with gods, let us consider a man who is sent from a distant planet to Earth by gods—Superman.

Superman (1978)

On the planet Krypton in a distant galaxy is a civilization thousands of years in advance of ours. A prosecutor, Jor-el, has presented a case against three traitors; they are condemned by the council to banishment. The three are embedded in a shimmering screen and sent to outer space. Jor-el (Marlon Brando) next turns his attention to Krypton, itself, which has changed orbit. He warns the council that the planet soon will disintegrate, but they disagree with him and forbid anyone to leave. Jor-el secretly has constructed a small, crystal-laden spacecraft in which he places his baby son, Kal-el. As the planet explodes, Kal-el is carried into space in his tiny craft, evoking the images of Moses in the ark in *The Ten Commandments* and Mowgli in the canoe in *The Jungle Book*. His glowing, godlike parents perish, but Kal-el is carried toward the new home his father has selected for him, Earth. On his journey, his father's voice and image instill all the facts of the universe in Kal-el. He is told that he will have extraordinary powers on Earth—flight, X-ray vision, and great strength.

Kal-el survives the arduous trip to Earth; his starlike craft crashes to ground in a Kansas wheat field, the American heartland—a sacred, rural place, where he is found by a kindly, childless farming couple, the Kents. Mrs. Kent had long prayed for a son and believes that the boy is a divine gift. When the boy lifts up the car to help Mr. Kent change a flat tire, they realize he is truly "not of this world." The Kents raise him as their son, calling him Clark, in the rural community of Smallville. Clark looks very much like other Midwest American boys: he is clean-cut and handsome, and he has their normal feelings. Yet he is always aware that he is different. He has special powers; his adoptive father tells him he is sure Clark was sent to Earth for a special purpose.

When Clark is around eighteen, his father dies of a heart attack; this is his second loss of a father. Clark mourns his father and is angry that even with his special abilities, he was unable to save him. Shortly after his father's death, Clark is awakened early in the morning by a mysterious urge. Going into the barn, he finds a glowing, green crystal shaft (male, phallic) which was part of his Krypton spacecraft. He bids good-bye to his mother in a field of ripening wheat; like the wheat, he is now mature and ready for "harvest." Nourished by his rural upbringing, he embarks on his quest.

Clark treks to the North Pole—a frigid, lonely, barren place akin to the Sinai desert, where Moses walked. He casts the glowing green crystal upon the ice, and it grows into a huge crystalline structure: "my father's house," a bequest from his father Jor-el. The image and voice of his father appear before him. Jor-el instructs him to meditate about spiritual matters, to consider the notion of life and immortality. He helps Clark comprehend his great powers and his purpose on Earth: "I have sent you, my only son, to be a light to humanity; to show them the way to goodness." All of this is strongly evocative of Christian religious tradition. Clark emerges from the crystal house in his adult Superman (Christopher Reeve) form; he has metamorphisized from man to god. He flies to Metropolis (New York City, the headquarters of human culture) and dons street clothes to become a reporter with the *Daily Planet,* a prominent newspaper.

While working as mild-mannered Clark Kent at the paper, Clark meets Lois Lane (Margot Kidder). Lois is a modern career woman—assertive, ambitious, decisive (a fairy-tale princess she is not!). Clark likes her immediately. One day Clark and Lois are walking when a gunman threatens them. Without Lois's awareness, Clark stops a bullet aimed at her, saving her life. This is his first adult "miracle." Meanwhile, several hundred feet *below* Grand Central Station, the evil criminal mastermind Lex Luthor (Gene Hackman) is planning to blow up California. His two accomplices are a blond bimbo (Valerie Perrine) and a bumbling stooge (Ned Beattie). Lex's location underground and in a public, commercial building help to signify his devil-inspired, profane objectives.

Back at the Daily Planet building, Clark asks Lois out for a date. She declines because she is on her way to the airport to interview the president. On the way, her helicopter crashes. Clark sees this and quickly changes himself to Superman, rescuing Lois and the helicopter pilot. Onlookers and Lois are thrilled as Superman flies—like a god—through the air. Unleashed, Superman sets off around the city foiling criminals and saving lives. In essence, rescuing Lois has cued him to his life-long task of aiding humanity; each act is a miracle. Superman, thus, is much like Jesus: mortal in his thoughts and feelings, godlike in his knowledge and powers to perform miracles. All Metropolis is abuzz with the news of Superman. Perry White, editor of the *Daily Planet* challenges his reporters to interview Superman, telling them it will be "the most important interview since God talked to Moses."

Lois receives a mysterious note from Superman asking for a date that evening. She waits on her high-rise terrace in a beautiful, flowing dress. Superman arrives and flirts with her as she attempts to interview him. She learns he is six feet four, weighs 225 pounds, and can see through matter (except lead). Lois asks him "Why are you here?" and he responds "To fight for truth, justice, and the American way."

Superman takes Lois flying through the night sky—a wonderfully magical, romantic adventure; they are falling in love. Lois says to herself "I'm holding hands with a god . . . you can fly . . . you belong to the sky . . . If you need a friend, if you need to be loved, here I am." When he flies away, she calls him Superman. Clark then arrives to see Lois. He tries to tell her his real identity, but can't bring himself to do it. The next day, Lois gets the lead story in the *Daily Planet.*

Lex Luthor, reading the paper, learns that Kryptonite is dangerous to Superman and obtains some. He also continues his master plot of stealing nuclear bombs and using them to activate the San Andreas fault in California. Meanwhile, Lois and another reporter, Jimmy Olsen, have been sent to cover a story in California. Lex tricks Superman into coming to his headquarters, where he poisons him with Kryptonite. At the last minute, the blond bimbo rescues him. Superman then flies off to save the world (or at least California!). Superman succeeds in stopping one missile, but the other one strikes the San Andreas fault and sets off a cataclysmic earthquake. Superman flies through the molten rock to mend the fissure. He is like the Greek mythological character Atlas, who held the world on his shoulders. Superman rescues a school bus trapped on a bridge, and a train on broken tracks; he blocks a flood and saves Jimmy Olsen from drowning.

But while he is doing this, Lois Lane's car slides into a fissure and she is suffocated. Superman arrives too late to save her. Once again he is confronted with the loss of a loved one; he cries and

Superman represents the Americanized warrior-savior archetype.

Archive Photos

holds her lifeless body for several hours. He kisses her cold lips, but the princess does not awaken. Superman flies into the sky, toward heaven, and streaks backward in time, reversing history. He arrives (this time) just before Lois's car is buried and finds her still alive. They are about to kiss when Jimmy Olsen arrives. In the closing scenes, Superman takes Lex Luthor and his stooge, to prison; then streaks upward into the stratosphere.

Superman is an Americanized version of the messiah myth from Christian theology, combining the ideals of both goodness and physical power that our culture holds dear. Clearly, he is a godlike figure from the outset of the narrative, sent to Earth from the heavens. In contrast to Jesus, however, he is not born of mortal woman, but rather adopted, intact, by a farming couple, the Kents. The

Kents are an American iconic representation of Mary and Joseph. Like this earlier couple, they are humble and common, raising their heavenly son in the sacred values of the Protestant heartland. And, just as Jesus did, young Clark early on demonstrates he has powers far beyond those of mortals. Instructed by his heavenly father, Jor-el, at age eighteen young Clark is called to his larger role as Superman and makes his pilgrimage to Metropolis (Jerusalem), the center of sinful American culture.

Quickly he discovers that there is ample work for him to do here—arresting bandits, foiling crimes, and staving off manmade disasters. Unlike Jesus—but much more in keeping with American tastes—this savior is *active*; he *does* feats of spectacular courage and strength. Thus, he combines the messianic and public warrior roles in one being.

Also in keeping with American preferences, this messiah/warrior is permitted at least the beginnings of a sex life. Although Superman and Lois Lane do not manage to consummate their attraction for each other, we are provided with sufficient evidence to recognize—to our comfort—that Superman is indeed a *man-god,* with appropriate natural passions. Jesus, with his gentleness and passivity, is not as desirable to many in our culture.

Star Wars (1977)

Star Wars opens with an explicitly mythic format.[5] We are informed that these events occurred "a long time ago, in a galaxy far, far away" or in what Malinowski (and the aborigines of Australia) would call "the Dream Time," that time in which gods, demons, and heroes battled to establish the social order. As is typical of such mythic sagas throughout history, the principal archetypal forces are presented early on. A war is under way (the classic struggle for social dominance); a chosen person of royal descent, who is blessed by the gods and necessary to the fulfillment of some destiny, Princess Leia (Carrie Fisher), is in peril. She possesses a magic secret crucial to the survival of the forces of goodness, but is pursued by a dark, evil figure—Lord Darth Vader—bent on destroying her and preserving the oppressive regime of the evil Galactic Empire. The evil empire is analogous to the Egyptians in *The Ten Commandments* and the Romans in *Ben Hur.* To further reinforce the gothic nature of the story, the characters are clothed in medieval apparel: Princess Leia wears a white, flowing, floor-length gown, her hair in an English braid; Darth Vader is clothed in a voluminous black robe, armor, and helmet.

On a dusty, farming planet, we are introduced to Luke Skywalker (Mark Hamill). A pure archetype of the savior hero, Luke is blond with blue eyes and dressed in all white, peasant-type apparel. His name suggests a noble or holy birth (soon to be revealed) that belies his current humble circumstances. Luke resides on a farm (as did the young Clark Kent) with his aunt and uncle; his father and mother have disappeared under mysterious circumstances. Luke encounters an older, prophetic man, Obi-Wan Kenobi, who possesses magical powers. Obi-Wan tells Luke of a secret order to which Luke is destined to belong, the Jedi knights, who were once guardians of peace and justice. They were defeated by the evil Galactic Empire after one of their leaders, Lord Darth Vader, was seduced by the desire for power—"the dark side of the Force"—and betrayed them.

Obi-Wan reveals to Luke that Luke's father was a Jedi knight and presents Luke with a magic light sword. He counsels Luke on how to "feel" the Force (a transcendent power that emanates throughout the universe) and to become a member of that ancient sect. Luke agrees to becomes a Jedi knight and joins Obi-Wan Kenobi in an effort to rescue Princess Leia. En route, they meet Han Solo (Harrison Ford), archetypal of the rogue-hero. As his name suggests (Han Solo means One Alone), Han is highly self-sufficient and not prone to establish emotional relationships. He possesses many of the characteristics we saw earlier in Rhett Butler—materialism, pragmatism, profiteering, and selfishness, coupled with courage and cleverness. To *some extent,* then, we should note that Luke Skywalker and Han Solo represent archetypal reincarnations of Ashley Wilkes and Rhett Butler. American culture appears to revere two types of heroes—the chivalrous, idealistic knight of noble or aristocratic birth and the adventurous, buccaneer rogue with a courageous heart. They evoke two sides of our nature and two dialectic sets of ideals.

Han, Luke, and Obi-Wan Kenobi sneak aboard the Death Star spaceship that is the headquarters of the evil empire. Although he agrees to help rescue Princess Leia, Han does so only on the condition that he be paid handsomely for his efforts. Luke, on the other hand, wishes to rescue Leia because he loves her and it is the "right" (selfless, noble) thing to do. Both Luke and Han exhibit great courage in rescuing Princess Leia. However, it is Luke who actually finds and saves her.

Obi-Wan Kenobi and Darth Vader pair off for a duel to the death with light swords. Obi-Wan was formerly Darth's mentor and so was most dishonored by Darth's betrayal of the Jedi knights. Obi-Wan permits Darth to slay him, pointing his sword toward heaven in a martyred pose, knowing that Darth's damningly destructive act (patricide, essentially) will free sufficient Force to enable Luke to ultimately destroy Darth.

Luke, Princess Leia, and Han Solo escape to the rebel base, occupied by those who support the Jedi knights. The rebel base is located on a very beautiful, green, fertile planet, dense with life and nature. The Death Star spaceship moves in to destroy this last remnant of goodness in the universe. Han Solo collects his reward money and declines to help save the rebel base. In sharp contrast, Luke sets out with a small band of rebel fighter pilots to attack the Death Star. Darth Vader himself pursues the rebel fighter pilots, shooting down each one until only Luke's is left. Directed by Obi-Wan's disembodied voice, Luke switches off his elaborate technological guidance system, closes his eyes, and relies on the Force (spiritual faith) to guide him. Luke succeeds in destroying the Death Star, but Han assists him by shooting down Darth Vader, who escapes. Luke and Han Solo are both rewarded in a special ceremony by Princess Leia at the close of the tale.

As before, the archetypes in *Star Wars* and the relationships among them present several powerful cultural propositions. First, the two heroic archetypes, Luke Skywalker and Han Solo, have been discussed to some extent already; however, let us reiterate their roles more explicitly. Noble, self-sacrificing heroes, like Luke Skywalker (and Ashley Wilkes), represent spiritual purity (sacredness) for whom virtue is its own reward. Conversely, opportunistic, materialistic heroes, like Han Solo and Rhett Butler, represent secular success (worldliness), and their courage is rewarded by material gain (money, riches). The centrality of both these types of heroic figures to our, and many other, cultures is signaled by the fact that in the present story they must *both work together* to achieve what each desires and to secure the good.

Darth Vader we recognize as an explicitly evil archetype, but his role as a symbol is complex and requires elaboration. Most prominently, Darth Vader represents the "fallen angel" who, having once occupied a position of leadership among the sacred or royal—the good—was tempted to betray this fellowship by the promise of even greater power within the evil congregation. Milton's poem of Satan's rebellion against God and subsequent expulsion from heaven, *Paradise Lost*, deals with exactly this issue. The desire for power can corrupt even those who were once noble—any of us can be seduced by its spell and be transformed from good into evil (as was Michael Corleone in *The Godfather*).

On a somewhat more abstract level, Darth Vader represents the coupling of religion or magic with technology to create enormous destructive force. The notion that a universal force could somehow be harnessed by evil humans is a widespread fear and emerges in such related notions as black magic, sorcery, alchemy, the evil scientist, Frankenstein's monster, and so forth.

In a more Freudian sense, we may also interpret Darth Vader as an evil, destructive, and potent father figure (Darth Vader equals Death Father), who must be overcome by his son, Luke Skywalker, to permit the good destiny to occur. The father-son Oedipal conflict between Luke and Darth is only hinted at in *Star Wars*, but becomes increasingly explicit in *The Empire Strikes Back*. Finally, as we shall see in *Return of the Jedi*, the Oedipal symbolization becomes explicit, as Luke's paternity is revealed and he and Darth duel to the death with light swords (potency versus potency). Luke's ultimate triumph is one that echoes back over millennia of myth-making, as it is based upon a continuing, fundamental human struggle.

A third, more subtle, but pervasive proposition to arise from *Star Wars* is the relationship of spirituality and religion to science and technology. In this case, and as we have already seen in *The Exorcist* and as will be reiterated in *Raiders of the Lost Ark* and *E.T. the Extraterrestrial*, in American culture, spirituality and religion are aligned with the gods, *moral* order, and the good destiny. Conversely, technology and science are often shown to be impotent against supernatural evil—recall *Jaws* and *The Exorcist.* A telling moment is when Luke, the chosen one destined to reinstate the moral order, turns off his technological guidance system and relies on the wisdom and power of the Force to guide his spaceship on its mission.

We turn now to the final motion picture from the 1970s that was among the top fifty most popular of all time. Up to now the films we have considered have dealt with the relationship between good and evil, God and man, and/or science and religion, that is, issues of a cosmological or moral nature. We turn now to a simpler archetypal tale, one we have seen before in fairy tales such as *Snow White* and *Sleeping Beauty*—a tale of courtship between a young man and a young woman. What challenges will true love confront at the close of the 1970s? Let's take a look at *Grease* and see.

Grease (1978)

The two central characters, Danny (John Travolta) and Sandy (Olivia Newton-John), meet one summer on a beach where, we learn later, he rescues her from drowning. They fall in love, but must part before learning anything more about each other. The story then shifts to Rydell High on the opening day of school. Rydell is archetypical of the family or community (as was Amity in *Jaws*); its principal is a woman who has "mothered" the students while they are still in children's roles. We learn that Danny is the second in command, lieutenant, of a boys' gang called the T-Birds. A girls' gang, the Pink Ladies, is also present at the high school, led by an Italian girl named Betty Rizzo. Both gangs are composed of students from the lower social classes.

Sandy, the blond, virginal heroine, is a foreign transfer student to Rydell High. She is, by her appearance and actions, from a higher social class than the T-Birds and the Pink Ladies. Sandy, as is typical for her social position, tries out for the cheerleader squad and begins dating a football player. All of the central characters, it should be noted, are *seniors.* Hence, this is the year they must make the transition to adult roles and responsibilities. Thus, this is a classic rite of passage situation that young people in U.S. society must confront.

Sandy and Danny meet again. She is friendly to him, but he rebuffs her because his friends are present. Social class bonds still exert a stronger pull on Danny than his affection for Sandy. Sandy, being from another social class, is viewed by Danny's friends as an inappropriate mate for him: not one of their "kind." Thus Danny, as a potential prince and hero, fails his first challenge. Sandy, desiring to regain Danny's affection, goes to a slumber party with the Pink Ladies, who tempt her to drink liquor, smoke cigarettes, pierce her ears, and engage in sexual activities with the T-Birds. Sandy, a virgin in every sense, can cope with none of these activities. Hence she, as a modern heroine, fails in her first challenge.[6]

Betty, the leader of the Pink Ladies, likes Danny, but he rebuffs her advances. To retaliate, she has sex with the leader of the T-Birds and believes that she is pregnant. Meanwhile, Danny has fallen in love with Sandy, an inappropriate mate for his social class, and has rejected Betty, an appropriate mate for his social class, which suggests he must now attempt to alter his social class. He does this by trying to become an athlete (baseball, basketball, and wrestling) to win Sandy away from the football player. He fails however, because his gang norms lead him to use *violence* to win, rather than to play by the *rules* of the game. Hence, he fails his second challenge as a prince/hero.

Danny makes a third attempt to regain Sandy by taking her to a dance contest. They are doing well when a sexy Hispanic girl, one of his former lower-class lovers, breaks in to dance with Danny. He dances with her, dropping Sandy, and together they win the contest using a very sensual dance. Once again our hero, Danny, has been lured back to the norms of his own social class, this time by its hedonic pleasures. Danny again pursues Sandy, this time offering her his ring "to go steady." Having made this overt commitment, he expects to become sexually intimate with her. Sandy, still unable to renounce her upper-status virginity, refuses. In this test, *she* is unable to make an overt commitment and fails.

After some other acts of genuine heroism by Danny,[7] which evidence his courage and dependability, we come to the graduation scene at Rydell High, where the following elements point to a resolution: (1) The woman principal (nurturant goddess archetype) encourages all of the graduating seniors to succeed in their new lives. (2) The leader of the T-Birds (male archetype of the lower class) agrees to marry Betty (female archetype of the lower class). Recall that she has already had sex with him; thus, this myth serves to reiterate the prevailing social order that "like should mate with like" and the middle-class viewpoint that lower-status persons' lives are largely controlled by their carnal impulses. (3) Danny appears at the graduation ceremony wearing *upper*-status apparel (a preppy suit and tie), while Sandy appears wearing *lower*-status apparel (black, tight leather and teased hair). This signals that each is prepared to compromise social class norms in order to attain a more important personal goal: the love of the other person.

Although following a relatively simple story line, *Grease* introduces two archetypal innovations vis à vis the other films we have examined. First, Danny is a prince/hero drawn from the *lower* classes, while Sandy, the princess, is clearly upper middle class. This is one of the first instances we have encountered in which the two lovers are not from comparable social backgrounds. In *Snow White* and *Sleeping Beauty* the princess and prince were both royal; Rhett and Scarlett were both nouveau riche; in *The Ten Commandments* Moses was raised an Egyptian prince and marries the daughter of an important Arab sheikh; Yuri Zhivago marries a fellow aristocrat; in *The Graduate* Benjamin marries the daughter of his father's law partner, and so forth. The only exception to this pattern has been Judah Ben Hur, who was paired with a former slave girl, but this occurs after he himself has served time as a slave.

Although Danny and Sandy's social class discrepancy seems novel, it actually signaled the loosening of social class mobility constraints that occurred during the late 1960s and early 1970s. Upward mobility became more possible in America than it had been in the past, and Danny, as an "ethnic" Italian-American, is symbolic of this greater social freedom. One of the sub-themes in *The Godfather* was the continuing prejudice against Italians and other ethnic minorities that prevailed in the United States well after World War II. Think back over the films and television shows discussed so far, and you will see the paucity of appearances by Italian, Irish, Asian, Slavic, Latino, and black characters.

The second innovation in archetypical content featured in *Grease* is Sandy's willingness to "come down off her pedestal" and adopt the sexually explicit, assertive behaviors of the Pink Ladies. Up until this point, all of the princesses have guarded their virginity and virtue like a treasure, always waiting patiently for the hero/prince to "awaken" them after a suitable courtship and proposal. Only Sandy drops this stance and presents herself, publicly, as a "sexually liberated woman." The abandonment of virginity and passivity as the ultimate in female desirability was a major shift in the popular culture of the 1970s. As we shall see in the coming two decades, women were never the same, at least on film and videotape, after this point.

— FIVE —

TELEVISION AND THE 1970s

THE EARLY 1970S were a particularly turbulent time in American culture. Of the decade's most popular motion pictures, those at the beginning of the decade, *The Godfather* and *The Exorcist,* portrayed metaphorically the political and sexual upheavals tearing at American society: the resignation of Richard Nixon; the Vietnam War; Watergate; the deaths of Janis Joplin, Jimi Hendrix, and Jim Morrison; promiscuous sexuality; the rocketing divorce rate; and the continuing ghettoization and repression of minorities created a potent mixture of cynicism and rebellion.

Television series attempted to deal with these issues head-on; Norman Lear's brilliant *All in the Family* presented American audiences with readily recognizable archetypes that embodied the spirit of the period perfectly. However, the waning years of the decade (1976–1979), perhaps rendered intellectually vegetative by the onslaught of "disco," culminated in *Three's Company*—a monument to the decline of Western culture that is sadly recorded for all eternity on videotape.

All in the Family

The iconic highlight of the early 1970s is undoubtedly the character of Archie Bunker (Carroll O'Connor) in the enormously popular series *All in the Family.* Archie was a patriarch/father figure like none Americans had ever seen before: domineering, self-centered, bigoted, scapegoating, narrow-minded, loud, abrasive, abusive, patriotic, and blissfully ignorant. In the same household with Archie, Norman Lear placed other vividly recognizable icons of current Americana: the devoted "dingbat" wife, Edith (Jean Stapleton), the earnestly liberal, highly emotional daughter, Gloria (Sally Struthers), and the actively liberal, "meathead" son-in-law, Michael (Rob Reiner). The neighborhood—working-class Brooklyn, New York—is populated by a variegated mix of Jews, Italians, Irish,

An archetypal dysfunctional American family: All in the Family.

Fotos International/Archive Photos

blacks, and Hispanics, about whom Archie and the other family members are in constant ideological contention. Through working out these political and social disputes "in the family," the series assisted Americans in at least recognizing and making visible these same issues in our larger cultural family.

Each show in the series opened with Edith and Archie seated at the piano in their living room happily belting out "Those Were the Days," a song that nicely encapsulated Archie's racist, sexist ideology: "Didn't have no welfare state, everybody pulled his weight . . . Men like me, we had it made, girls were girls and men were men; those were the days!" Let's take a look at some episodes and see how Archie's ideology plays out when confronted by the younger generation's liberalness, as represented by his daughter and son-in-law.

A January 19, 1971, episode opens with Archie mistakenly sampling "soup," which is actually one of son-in-law Michael's shirts, which Edith is boiling to remove a harsh chemical finish (the finish had given Michael a rash). Later, Michael argues with Archie over television programming: Michael wants to watch a special show on pollution; Archie wants the football highlights. After a brief attempt at discussion, Archie unilaterally declares they will watch football. He then settles in front of the set and yells at "dingbat" Edith to bring him a can of beer. Archie comments to Michael that "those spooks [blacks] can really run the football . . . even if they do have funny names."

Gloria returns home after stopping by a health food store to purchase organic cereal for the family. Archie turns up his nose at it and demands his "sweet, crunchy cereal." When Gloria and Michael ask to watch the pollution television special, Archie silences both of them. He informs then that the last special he watched was "Sing Out Sweet Land" hosted by John Wayne, which "talked about what's good for America."

Michael then announces he's written a letter to President Nixon protesting the Vietnam War, racial inequality, and pollution. Archie, in response, decides to write his own letter. He orders Edith to find his fancy stationery, puts on a suit, washes his hands, smokes a cigar, dons his American flag pin, and sits down to compose a letter: "Dear Mister President, Your Honor, Sir." Unable to spell "constituency," Archie orders Edith to write as he dictates.

When a nun comes by soliciting money for an orphanage, Archie requests her help in spelling and then has Edith give her a fifty-cent donation: "If you give 'em [Catholics] money, they'll just spend it on golden candlesticks." Archie then daydreams that Nixon reads his letter on television, as the family looks on in awe, and calls Archie "one great American." Archie leads Edith, Gloria, and Michael out the door to mail their two opposing letters. They return from the mailbox visibly moved by their sacred act of citizenship: "It feels good being a citizen!" declares Gloria.

An October 30, 1971, episode has a similar ideological theme. Gloria and Michael are supporting a liberal female candidate, Claire Packer, for a local office. Archie complains about her and some other ethnic candidates who are running for offices: "Salvatore, an Italian, he's gonna keep an eye on crooks?" "Feldman, a Jew, he'll be good for treasurer" and "Nelson, a real American, he can help with p.r. [public relations], TV." Archie intends to vote for Al Lundy, a conservative pro-war candidate opposed to school busing, welfare, and feminism.

Edith arrives home from the supermarket and tells the family that Claire Packer helped "crack the code" so that now consumers can tell the freshness date of the products. Claire is coming over to their house to meet with Gloria and Michael. Archie calls Claire the "queen of the liberals" and informs her that "politics and women don't mix." Claire, Gloria, and Michael are all "progressive, pinko liberals." Meanwhile, Edith is fetching his beer, chips, and footstool. When Archie complains about blacks receiving welfare, Claire rejoinders with federal subsidies to huge corporations. Gloria, Michael, and Claire leave to go campaign. A gay man and a lesbian woman arrive at the door and ask for support for homosexual rights. Archie calls them "Tutti and Fruiti" and slams the door. Edith, by contrast, supports "two consenting adults doing as they please."

Later that day, the entire family goes en masse to the polls to cast their respective ballots. There it is discovered that Archie is not even registered to vote, having not voted in the past two elections! He tries to browbeat Edith into voting for his conservative candidate ("*We've* got to share *your* vote"), but she claims to believe in a secret ballot. At the story's end, the family sits in front of the television set, watching the election returns. Edith lets it slip that she voted for Claire Packer.

In a third episode (November 4, 1972), Archie and Michael enter the house arguing over money. Archie is complaining that Michael, a college student, pays no money for room and board. Michael rejoinders that Gloria works to help pay for food and that Michael has agreed to pay Archie back once he graduates and obtains a job. Then, Michael receives an inheritance of $275 and decides to give $80 of it to Gloria to buy a new winter coat and the rest to George McGovern's presidential campaign. Some of the money (it was originally $500) has already been deducted for taxes. Michael says he doesn't mind it going for taxes as long as the taxes are used to help people, but he fears Nixon will use it to "burn another Vietnamese village." Archie replies, "That's good; it'll keep the gooks out of the country."

Archie becomes furious that Michael is giving the money to McGovern (who represents "commie crapola") and not to him for rent. Archie, Gloria, and Michael all get into a screaming frenzy as Edith tries to serve dinner. Archie tells Edith she is no longer to give food to Michael, so Gloria says she will prepare Michael's food. After a few weeks, conditions in the household deteriorate. Edith and Gloria have begun arguing over which food items belong to whom and the use of various kitchen utensils. Michael is coming home late every night and argues with Gloria; he is secretly working at a night job to pay Archie. The family is filled with internal strife over bills, responsibilities, and resources.

Secretly, Mike shows Gloria the $150 he has made so far to repay Archie, but only moments later another rift erupts between Michael and Archie with Gloria caught in the middle. Edith enters the room and tells the combatants: "A house divided against itself falls down." Michael gives Archie the $150 he made pumping gas. Archie feigns smugness, but actually is pleased; he relents. The house settles back down to what passes for normal.

All in the Family brought to the fore thoughts, beliefs, prejudices, and attitudes that had previously been taboo topics for television. It dared to speak openly of racial prejudice, political unrest, ethnic stereotypes, and patriarchal oppression—topics which prior to its appearance had been part of our national denial system. The show also, in its own crazy way, provided various segments of American society with their own representative archetypes: the devoted old-style wife, the patriarchal father and husband, the liberated young wife, and the liberal young husband. Yet Archie was not a complete fool, nor were Gloria, Michael, and Edith consistently good guys or archetypal paragons. Michael was financially supported by Archie—his bigoted, but employed, father-in-law. Thus, radical youth was instructed to examine its own free ride at its parents' expense.

Gloria, liberated to work at a menial job, still lives with her parents and eats meals prepared by her mother. It is also clear that Michael is still the male head of their impoverished household; it is, after all, *his* education and career that everyone else is supporting. And Edith, though doused with what now would be viewed as continuous verbal abuse by Archie, continues to respond eagerly to his every whim and command, a stellar example of the "battered wife syndrome." Remarkably, as miraculous an event as *All in the Family* was—and still is—we look at it twenty-five years hence and see ourselves still bound up in invisible chains, especially those of gender.

The Waltons

The Waltons first appeared on air in 1971 and became highly popular during the 1973–1974 season, coming in second place to *All in the Family.*[1] In some ways, *The Waltons* represents an ideological response to the political dissension found in *All in the Family,* for it mythologized the American family and reaffirmed basic cultural virtues such as self-sufficiency, productivity, and Christianity. Yet it was a family show very much influenced by the 1970s prevailing political climate of social change and equal opportunity. Set during the Great Depression in rural Virginia, the series told the retrospective story of John-Boy Walton's (Richard Thomas) childhood and adolescence growing up on his family's farm. The Walton family itself was an archetypal representation of white, Anglo-Saxon Protestant America's version—and vision—of its pioneer ideology.

The family of two grandparents, two parents, and seven children lives and works on a farm whose land has been in the Walton family since Colonial times. In one episode, John-Boy even takes a girlfriend to the top of Walton's mountain, where the family first settled in the 1600s. Here they find a rock chimney and hearth, tangible evidence of the family's, and country's, origins.

The Walton family is placed in a sacred, natural setting (rural Virginia), earns its living working the land, and is itself a hearty, warm, communal group. The father and mother are placed on equal intellectual and moral footing; the children respect their parents—and in turn are accorded respect for their own individuality and dreams. Indeed, the oldest son, John-Boy, aspires to be a writer with his parents' blessing, despite their agricultural heritage. The episodes follow a common pattern, one that we have seen before in *Have Gun Will Travel, Gunsmoke, Wagon Train,* and *Bonanza*—other television series which were designed to instruct the viewer about moral choices and the preservation of community. Basically, this pattern shows an outsider or stranger entering the community or family. The stranger carries a set of problems or challenges to which the community must respond. It is in *choosing* what type of response to make that the community defines its moral values. An episode airing September 16, 1972, titled "The Foundling" illustrates this pattern well.

A young woman places her six-year-old daughter on the Walton's doorstep early one morning. The family finds her and takes her in, where she is fed and bathed. They discover she cannot speak or hear. Mother and Father Walton take her to town to the sheriff, who tells them he must take her to the county orphanage. Mother Walton, however, wants first to have her examined by a doctor, despite the expense. The doctor confirms that the child is deaf and tells them that she very likely will get no assistance in the orphanage. He refuses money for examining her and instead gives the Waltons a sign language chart to teach her to use words. Concurrently, at the local high school, John-Boy is reading a poem he composed to his girlfriend, but she is unable to grasp the metaphor it contains, "Your soul is to me a heady wine."

The Waltons bring the deaf girl back home to await the sheriff's coming to get her; their children are all befriending her. By the time the sheriff arrives, Mr. Walton has relented and decided the family will keep her. They begin trying to teach her to read, spell, and sign, but like John-Boy's girlfriend, she cannot grasp the metaphor.

The Walton brood, barefoot because it is summer, walks to the general store to buy licorice. On the way home, they pass an abandoned house where the deaf child's mother has been hiding, but do not see her. After they pass, the child's father drives up and discovers the mother. We learn that she and the girl ran away to prevent the father from putting the girl in the county orphanage. He believes she is mentally retarded, and they cannot care for her, as they are quite poor.

That evening, the Walton family is listening to the radio, their link to the larger world, laughing at the Charlie McCarthy show. Polly, the deaf child, becomes frustrated and runs upstairs. John-Boy goes to comfort her. He begins talking and signing to her, and in an epiphany, Polly grasps the meaning. Polly and John-Boy show the family what has happened, and everyone rejoices. The next day, John-Boy tries kissing his girlfriend, instead of reading her a poem, and she too is much more responsive.

The Walton kids and Polly again visit the store. When one of the boys buys a toy for Polly, Elizabeth, the Walton daughter of the same age, becomes envious. Later, Polly tries to placate Elizabeth by offering her the toy, but Elizabeth refuses to accept it. She runs off to the abandoned house, and Polly follows her. Elizabeth tries hiding from Polly in an old trunk, but the lid slams shut and she is unable to escape. Polly is running to get help, when her father drives by and grabs her. Unable to understand her frantic gestures, he continues driving.

Concurrently, Polly's mother has finally come forward and told the Waltons she feared her daughter's being sent to the orphanage and chose instead to abandon her with their family. Mrs. Walton explains to Polly's mother that she is quite bright, just deaf, and now able to use sign language. Two Walton children suddenly rush in and report Elizabeth and Polly are missing. Mr. Walton and the children jump in the truck and begin searching for them. They learn from the store owner that Polly's father had recently driven by with Polly, crying, in his truck. Believing he has kidnapped both girls, the Waltons pursue him. They catch up to them, and Polly frantically signs that Elizabeth is trapped in the old trunk. Elizabeth is rescued, and Polly is the hero. Polly's father realizes she is intelligent and able to communicate; he and his wife embrace Polly. As they depart, John-Boy finds a gingerbread cake left on the porch for him by his girlfriend. The note reads "Love is as sweet as gingerbread." She too has grasped the metaphor.

The Waltons is structured to teach the same lesson in two planes of meaning. It purposely creates a redundancy within the storyline, so that the mythic message is clear. Let's take a look at "The Boy from the C.C.C.," which aired on November 2, 1972. John-Boy, his oldest sister, Mary Ellen, and youngest sister, Elizabeth, are walking barefoot down a country road; it is late spring. Their dog begins chasing a sick raccoon; they run after it and come upon a teenaged boy who is about to kill the raccoon. The boy is quite hostile and arrogant, pulling a knife on John-Boy. When the boy falls and hurts his leg, the Walton children gently befriend him. We learn his name is Gino, and he is a runaway from New York City. The Walton's bring both Gino and the sick raccoon, who Elizabeth has adopted and named Pete, back home. Here we are being shown the parallel between the hurt, wild raccoon and the hurt, wild boy.

Back at the Walton farmhouse, Gino still acts in a hostile and suspicious manner. The family does not fully trust him, but feels it cannot turn him away either. John-Boy makes him a warm hay bed in the barn loft. At dinner, the family holds hands and says grace, but Gino begins gobbling down his food. Elizabeth asks her father to build Pete, the raccoon, a safe cage, and he agrees. The grandmother advises her though that "it's not good to bring wild things into the house; it hurts both the house and the wild thing." That night, John-Boy writes in his journal about the "wild things" outside the house, that is, Pete in his cage and Gino in the barn.

The next morning Gino comes in with some chicken eggs he's found, but at first he refuses to share them with the family. Later, when Gino talks to Elizabeth we learn that both his parents are dead and that he has a younger sister who is in an orphanage. Gino also talks to John-Boy, and we learn that he is from Hell's Kitchen, a very tough area of New York. John-Boy fantasizes about one day going to New York and seeing plays he has read. We learn that Gino was sent to work at a C.C.C. (Civilian Conservation Corps) camp in northern Virginia constructing a national park, but he has run away.

Mr. Walton tells the family he is going to train a wealthy man's bird dog for $5 to put in the family's winter shoe fund. John-Boy and Gino help Elizabeth with Pete, who is getting increasingly ill.

Mrs. Walton puts a blanket into Pete's cage. That night after dinner, Gino spies through the darkened window to see where the Waltons keep their money. A violent thunderstorm, signaling evil spirits afoot, rages. He breaks into the house and pockets their savings. But Mr. Walton, holding a rifle, stops him. The next morning, Mr. Walton and John-Boy send for the sheriff and guard Gino in the barn. The father tells Gino he is very disappointed in his "repayment" of their hospitality.

Pete's condition continues to worsen. Gino asks John-Boy why the Waltons care about him (Gino). John-Boy responds, "We care about life." Gino passes up a chance to escape and instead helps the father and John-Boy tend Pete. Despite their efforts, the raccoon dies. The family buries Pete, holding a simple funeral ceremony complete with a song and prayer. Elizabeth is very angry at her father that the raccoon is dead, believing that not enough was done to help him. She runs to the barn and Gino follows, comforting her. He tells Elizabeth his own father was shot down by gangsters in New York. After that he lived on the streets and stole food, while his sister was placed in an orphanage. When the sheriff arrives, Mr. Walton does not tell him about Gino, but instead invites the sheriff to go quail hunting. Gino returns to the C.C.C. camp, helping to construct a beautiful national park and continues to keep in touch with the family. The story closes with Elizabeth placing stones on Pete's grave.

The Waltons contrasts sharply with *All in the Family,* for while the Bunker family usually seethes with internal dissension created by the generation gap, the Walton family is consistently harmonious and well balanced. Indeed, although *The Waltons* undoubtedly glorifies and mythologizes family values, it does not do so in a way that is maudlin or saccharin. What is notable about the show's characters is their distinct individuality and mutual respect for one another's differences. Character, in the WASP sense of the word, is constructed out of guidance and kindness, rather than power and punishment.

In short, *The Waltons* represent not just a "nice family" in the banal sense of shows such as *The Brady Bunch,* but the archetypal Good Family in the sense of narratives we have discussed previously, such as *The Andy Griffith Show* and *Bonanza.* The central moral of each episode is that all manner of problems—disabilities, death, abuse—can be dealt with within the context of a loving, respecting family or community.

Happy Days

Our next series was enormously popular during the latter half of the 1970s, yet is set during the late 1950s. As with *The Waltons,* it focuses upon a family, this time the middle-class, suburban Cunninghams. The ethos of the show recalls those innocent times when records were 45s, and teenagers drove hot rods, dined at hamburger drive-ins, and wore blue jeans and bobby socks. Of course, those innocent times also had their share of juvenile crime, drinking, and teenage pregnancy (*Grease*), but this has been largely sanitized away in *Happy Days.* Indeed, even the proverbial hood in a black leather jacket riding a motorcycle has been refashioned into a good guy—the Fonz (Henry Winkler).

Richie Cunningham (Ron Howard, formerly of *The Andy Griffith Show*) lives at home with his parents and sister in Milwaukee, Wisconsin, and attends a local college. His sister, Joanie, is in high school; his dad works at a local store and his mom is a housewife. In one episode, Richie is running for sophomore class president. He carefully practices his overlong speech in front of his family and his friend Fonzie. During the actual debate the following day, Richie bores the students and appears likely to lose the election to his more pragmatic opponent, whose sole campaign promise is to introduce beer to their campus.

That evening, Fonzie joins Richie and his family for dinner. Two of Richie's college buddies arrive with a camera and a child's baby doll to take his photo kissing the baby. Richie is nervous and irritable and refuses to cooperate. To calm him, Fonzie takes him to a local, legitimate massage parlor. But while Richie is being massaged by the beautiful blond attendant, his opponent and a pal rush in and snap his picture. Richie and his two college friends decide to break into the opponent's fraternity room and steal the film. Wearing stocking masks with their letterman jackets, they sneak in through a window and search for the film; instead they find a girlie magazine. Fonzie comes in through the window and counsels them against taking anything: "This is breaking and entering . . . two wrongs don't make a right." After some thought, they agree and leave the room undisturbed.

The next evening Richie laments his presumed loss; the photo of him with the masseuse is on the front page of the college paper. His two friends arrive and tell him he has actually *won;* the students thought the photo was terrific! Fonzie arrives and brings him a framed version of the photo. Richie offers to buy sodas for everyone and is carried triumphantly out the front door. In this episode we see Fonzie playing the archetypal role of wise counselor (like Obi-Wan Kenobi in *Star Wars*); he serves as a moral and spiritual guide for Richie and his friends.

Another episode follows this same pattern. Fonzie is having a hamburger at the malt shop. Richie sits down with him and confides that he is taking over the local newspaper's advice column, Dear Aunt Fannie, for two weeks. Richie rhapsodizes that this could be his big break into becoming a national television talk-show host. After Richie leaves, two of his friends who are college roommates sit down with Fonzie and describe how much difficulty they are having getting along together. Fonzie advises them to write to Aunt Fannie. They do so, and Richie (as Fannie), not realizing their identity, jokingly recommends that they put a line through the middle of their room. They follow Aunt Fannie's advice and soon are fighting constantly about use of the bathroom, refrigerator, door, oven, and television set, all of which are on different sides of the room. This problem is reminiscent of the *All in the Family* episode where Gloria and Edith had to cook separate meals for Michael and Archie. Separating their jointly owned possessions has made each one selfish, petty, and Machiavellian.

Fonzie learns of the combative situation and goes to Richie's house to tell him the identity of the couple and that he needs to straighten out the mess. Richie goes to see his two friends, who are still arguing, and has them stand with him on the white line: neutral territory. He is beginning to hesitate about revealing his role, when Fonzie enters and asks, "Did you tell them you're Aunt Fannie, yet?" Richie, embarrassed, apologizes profusely for giving such poor advice. The Fonz advises the two feuding roommates to be more sensitive to each other's feelings and to talk out their problems, rather than fight and yell; the story ends peacefully.

In both these episodes, the Fonz stands above the fray and dispenses useful wisdom. However, in other episodes he becomes a rival of Richie's for a beautiful girl's affections. One such story line takes the entire Cunningham family out to Colorado, where they have gone to help Mrs. Cunningham's uncle Ben operate his dude ranch, the Bar A. Uncle Ben has fallen ill, and unless he can raise money to pay off a bank loan, he will forfeit the ranch. The Fonz, Richie's two college pals, and the Cunninghams all venture out to run the ranch. (This story line clearly has aspects of the heroic quest myth discussed by Joseph Campbell. The entire group is being called on a journey to a distant land where they will face difficult challenges and have the opportunity to prove their mettle.) The group encounters two novel people once they arrive: a rich, mean rancher, H.R. Buchanan, who is trying to foreclose on Uncle Ben's ranch, even if that requires skullduggery, and Thunder, a beautiful, Annie Oakley–like young blond woman, to whom Richie and the Fonz are both attracted.

As guests begin arriving at the ranch, the Cunningham clan, Fonzie, the college pals, and Thunder all pitch in to make them comfortable. It is a fine communal effort, worthy of *The Waltons;* they even decide to hold a rodeo. Richie's sister Joanie flirts with a cute young cowboy and excels in trick riding during the rodeo. The Fonz likes Thunder, but when she spends time with Richie, he hangs out with a bevy of beautiful young women. (The Fonz is depicted as enormously attractive to pretty girls.) Fonzie assists the Cunninghams by routing Buchanan and his bad guys away from the ranch; later, however, the Fonz and Richie compete with one another during a square dance contest. Thus, their relationship is shown to be a mixture of competition (over women) and cooperation (to save the ranch).

Buchanan retaliates against the Cunninghams by spooking a team of horses Joanie is driving. As the wagon careens down the road, Thunder on horseback and the Fonz and Richie on Fonzie's motorcycle chase after her. Richie manages to jump on the horses and bring them to a halt: he has saved his sister and proven himself a hero. Fonzie's courageous efforts in bringing his motorcycle alongside the runaway wagon are overlooked in the fuss over Richie. However, later that evening, as Richie is feted, he calls Fonzie up and publicly thanks him. Richie realizes that he and Thunder have been flirting and begins to feel guilty, recalling his steady girlfriend back in Milwaukee. He tells Thunder about his steady, but she is unfazed. It turns out she had liked the Fonz all along.

At the close of the summer, the Cunninghams realize they are still $1,017 short in repaying the bank loan; Buchanan still is aggressively seeking ownership of the ranch. Fonzie pledges to ride the killer bull, Diablo, whom no one has ever ridden, in order to win $1,000, and save the ranch. As Fonzie mounts the bull, Thunder gives him her scarf (a magic amulet). Fonzie successfully stays aboard the bucking bull, but is then tossed off inside the ring. Richie courageously rushes to his aid by flagging the bull with a blanket, permitting the Fonz to escape. The rest of the family and friends pitch in the remaining $17, and the ranch is saved. Thunder, Fonzie, and Richie ride off on horseback together—all rivalries resolved and friendships restored.

Happy Days is a simplified (and also perhaps simplistic) version of stories we have encountered before: a young man approaching adulthood faces challenges of varying levels of difficulty. Sometimes they involve questions of moral judgment (stealing the film), other times they involve physical courage (saving Joanie from the runaway horses), and sometimes they require admitting mistakes and errors of judgment (being Aunt Fannie, flirting with Thunder). These are the challenges, both big and small, that all of us must wrestle with in constructing our lives. Along the way, *Happy Days* informs us, we would do well to attend to the sage advice of the wise guides we encounter (Fonzie) and not to let our desire to win a competition obscure the larger goal of community harmony.

Laverne & Shirley

Only a year or so after the appearance of *Happy Days*, its creator, Garry Marshall, had developed another series, also a situation comedy set in Milwaukee.[2] *Laverne & Shirley* was also situated in the late 1950s/early 1960s and featured Garry's sister (Penny Marshall)

Archive Photos

Sisterhood comes to television: Laverne & Shirley.

and Cindy Williams in the title roles. Laverne and Shirley are two single, working-class women who share a basement apartment and work at a local brewery. As we shall see, part of the appeal of *Laverne & Shirley* is its transference of a 1970s women's liberation mentality to the relative safety and sexual conservatism of the 1950s. Just as with *Happy Days,* the repressive aspects of the 1950s (endogenous racism and sexism) have been sanitized away, and the era is represented as a mythical time of innocence and purity. Despite this, however, the show exudes a wonderful aura of sisterhood and sense of community that is refreshing. The community archetype developed in *Laverne & Shirley* consists of their families and work buddies, Lenny and Squiggy (note that the L & S naming pattern is carried forward).

In one episode, Laverne and Shirley have gone bowling with Lenny and Squiggy. While they are at the bowling alley, a sumptuous blond woman escorted by a handsome, preppie man (Bart) arrives.

When his blond date is not looking, Bart asks Shirley for a date by reading her palm. She excitedly agrees. The next day, Shirley and Laverne are working as waitresses at a diner, when Bart walks in. Not seeing Shirley, who is in the kitchen, he begins flirting with Laverne and asks *her* out for the following night. Laverne declines, noting that he is supposed to be seeing Shirley. Shirley enters the scene, oblivious to what has just occurred, and introduces Bart to Laverne.

Back at the apartment building, Laverne asks an older woman for advice on whether or not to tell Shirley of Bart's advances. She decides not to, believing it would only hurt Shirley. Shirley bounces in, delighted that Bart has asked her to accompany him on a weekend trip. Laverne says nothing, but then, while Shirley is in packing for the trip, the phone rings. It is Bart, and again he asks Laverne on a date! Laverne tells Shirley that Bart has been making advances. However, Shirley does not believe her and instead accuses Laverne of throwing herself at Bart.

Laverne is deeply hurt and offended; she and Shirley argue angrily. Bart arrives to take Shirley away for the weekend; but when she goes out of the room for a moment, he again flirts with Laverne, asking her out for the following week. This time, however, Shirley overhears his overture. Shirley tells Bart she has decided to go out with someone else for the weekend. Laverne, who has consistently resisted Bart's overtures, pours beer into his cap and escorts him to the door. After Bart has departed, Shirley apologizes to Laverne. They make a pact as friends never to "fight over a guy again" and shake hands.

As simple as this tale is, it is important to credit it for recognizing and dealing in a positive way with a classic source of conflict among single women, that is, competing for desirable men. Bart was, at least on the surface, a good catch—handsome, well mannered, nicely dressed, and successful. It would have been quite understandable if Laverne had become as besotted by his charms as Shirley had and had eagerly dumped her friend for a chance at marrying well and escaping her blue-collar existence. That the show, instead, chose to depict two women who opted for friendship above marriage (to a cad) is an archetypal step forward. Recall that in virtually all the other texts we have examined in which two women have battled over a desirable man (*Gone with the Wind, The Ten Commandments, Bewitched, The Graduate*), they have usually resorted to seduction and deceit to obtain an advantage. Genuine friendship among single women was out of the realm of possibility. It was during the feminism of the 1970s that the social idea arose that women should view one another as *allies,* rather than competitors. This story line depicts that proposition put into practice.

This theme is expanded in a subsequent episode in which Laverne and Shirley find they *both* must choose between desirable men and maintaining their sexual virtue. At a chance "people on the street" encounter, Laverne and Shirley meet two handsome, unmarried male medical students—again, highly desirable mates for them given their blue-collar occupations and incomes. The two medical students invite them up to Oshkosh for a date, and the girls eagerly accept. On the bus trip to Oshkosh, both Laverne and Shirley fantasize about the possibility of marrying the two young men. They are wearing their prettiest dresses and practicing their best manners in order to show them that they are "classy ladies," suitable as future wives for medical school princes.

But, as soon as Laverne and Shirley arrive at the station in Oshkosh, the young men try to get them to come to their apartment "for a drink and fun." The young women demure and request to be taken to lunch at a restaurant, as they were promised. The two students pretend to agree, but then sneak off, stranding Laverne and Shirley at the bus station. With no money for a hotel room and the next bus going back to Milwaukee not leaving until ten the next morning, the two young women must sleep, uncomfortably, on the depot benches. When the male ticket agent offers to give them money for a hotel room in exchange for sex, they whack him with their handbags. Finally, at one o'clock in the morning, Lenny and Squiggy, their two blue-collar male friends, arrive in their jalopy and rescue them. In this case, the working classes are clearly depicted as the true princes and princesses; the upper classes, revealed as crass opportunists. The earlier episode in which Bart almost lured the two women into forsaking their friendship for the chance at an upper-class marriage had the same theme.

In a third episode the rewards of authentic friendship and genuine community are played upon again. Laverne and Shirley are in the commissary of the beer factory talking with Squiggy and Lenny. Squiggy has just received notification from the factory, where he works as a truck driver, that he failed his written driving test. He is to be retested, and if he fails again, he'll be fired. Later, at the apartment building where all four friends live, Lenny comes to tell Laverne that he is making little progress in helping Squiggy study—could she come help? Laverne gamely tries to help him, but Squiggy lapses into inattention. Laverne becomes frustrated and calls upon Shirley, who also gives it a good try and gives up in frustration. Fearing Squiggy will never pass the test and therefore forfeit his job, Laverne and Shirley each turn to family members to try to obtain a job for Squiggy. Laverne's father, who runs a pizza parlor, asks Squiggy to be his assistant; Shirley's boyfriend, Carmine, has a dance studio and offers to let Squiggy become an instructor. Squiggy turns both of them down; he likes neither pizza nor dancing! Squiggy runs from their apartment in a despondent state: "I'm just too dumb!"

Lenny discovers him in the apartment that Lenny and Squiggy share very drunk and dressed in a tiger-skin jacket with spangled lapels. Squiggy drunkenly tells Lenny, "I'm going to become a priest," to which Lenny replies, "You can't. You're a Lutheran!" Squiggy becomes even more disconsolate: "I'm worthless; nobody wants me." Lenny sits Squiggy down and gives him a heartfelt pep talk, reminding Squiggy of what an excellent driver he is and telling him how much he would miss Squiggy if he left. Squiggy vows to do his best on the test; they hug. A few days later, Laverne, Shirley, Lenny, and Squiggy are gathered in the boys' apartment. The mail has arrived; Lenny carefully opens the letter containing Squiggy's results: he has passed. They all cheer.

Laverne & Shirley is not a politically ascerbic show like *All in the Family,* nor is it a deeply metaphoric morality tale such as *The Waltons.* But what the series does model quite effectively is the nature of genuine friendship. It shows us how two women, two men, and, ultimately, four people can provide one another with support and companionship. It is perhaps indicative of the tenor of the times, the late 1970s, that both this show and *Happy Days* were set two decades earlier—in the mythical 1950s, when life was ostensibly more simple and genuine. This suggests that the 1970s were *not* seen by those actually living them, or producing television programming for them, as representative of these same values.

How did the 1970s appear to those actually viewing and producing television during that time period? I think a pretty close approximation can be found in the program that closed out the decade as the top-rated series[3]: *Three's Company.* This show represented a dramatic departure from the communal/familial programs that dominated the 1970s. While the bulk of the other top-rated shows were espousing the value of committed relationships, sexual modesty, and/or platonic love, *Three's Company* reveled in one-night stands, breast-and-pickle humor, disco, gold neck chains, flared polyester pants, chest hair, and swinging singles.

Unlike the modest locales of the other shows of the decade—Brooklyn, Milwaukee, Walton's Mountain in Virginia—*Three's Company* is set in Santa Monica, California, which permits its characters to spend ample time on the beach, bicycling, roller skating, jogging, dancing, and wearing bathing suits and short-shorts. It is truly archetypal in content, but not in the senses we have encountered before. There are no cosmological or metaphysical questions being posed or answered. And even the sociological and psychological pickings are slim. But the series does capture one aspect of the 1970s spirit quite well: *its narcissism,* its concern for the presentation of a fashionable, swinging public persona, and its overwhelming preoccupation with the activities of dating and mating. Let's take a look at the three central characters—Jack Tripper (John Ritter), Chrissy (Suzanne Sommers), and Janet (Janice De Witt)—as they portray young American singles dwelling in a garden apartment.

In one episode, Jack has been taking cooking lessons so he can meet attractive young single women. He has encountered one he likes, Debbie, and they are planning to cook lasagna together. But first, Jack must get his two pretty female roommates to leave the apartment for the afternoon, fearing Debbie will misunderstand their platonic living arrangement. Chrissy and Janet leave; Debbie arrives; and she and Jack begin cooking in the kitchen. However, the two young women mistakenly return before the lasagna is finished and hide behind the couch to escape detection. Jack lures Debbie onto the couch and begins kissing her. When he discovers Chrissy and Janet behind the couch, he makes up a silly excuse to get Debbie out of the house before she discovers the two girls. Jack explains to Chrissy and Janet that Debbie is an old-fashioned girl and would never understand their living arrangement.

Debbie returns to her apartment, which she shares with two young single *male* roommates. She warns them that *they* must leave before Jack comes over, because he is very old-fashioned and would never understand their living arrangement. When Jack arrives, the same joke is encountered. Debbie must engage in silly machinations to keep her roommates' identity a secret; this is difficult as Jack keeps finding men's apparel around the room. Jack returns to his own apartment, where Chrissy and Janet are vacuuming and dusting, while wearing very short shorts and tight knit tops. When Debbie unexpectedly arrives at the door, Janet and Chrissy pretend that they are maids cleaning Jack's apartment. However, their ruse falls apart when their two dates arrive to pick them up. Jack tries to continue the deceit, but finally confesses to Debbie that Chrissy and Janet are his roommates. Debbie, in turn, admits to Jack that she has two male roommates. Jack is shocked, not believing it is possible for single men and women to cohabit without "getting it on." But he then realizes his hypocrisy and apologizes.

In a second episode, the story opens in the apartment of the Roper family, a husband and wife who manage the apartment complex. Mrs. Roper wants to have fun, excitement, and sex, but Mr. Roper is always too tired. Mr. Roper decides to throw a surprise party for his wife. He calls up Jack, Chrissy, and Janet and invites them to the party. Chrissy volunteers to come over early and teach Mr. Roper to dance. Before she goes, she dances around Jack to show off her new pants; when she asks Jack how "they" look, he stares at her breasts and says "Great!"

Mr. Roper sends his wife away on errands so he can secretly learn to dance to surprise her. However, as Chrissy comes in to Mr. Roper's house with her record player (and tight pants), the next-door neighbor sees her and assumes she is there to have sex. Chrissy and Mr. Roper begin dancing very sexily; Janet arrives after a jog and tells Mr. Roper she must shower because she is sweaty. The neighbor looks in and sees Mr. Roper and Chrissy dancing and Janet in a towel, nude. He spills water on his pants, a sexual innuendo, and takes them off. Mrs. Roper returns from her shopping trip, and the neighbor runs out in his underwear and grabs her shouting: "There's something I want to show you!"

Meanwhile, Janet and Chrissy have departed; Mr. Roper hears a commotion outside and sees the neighbor talking to his wife in his underwear. He calls the neighbor a pervert and takes his wife inside. Jack arrives with the party supplies, and Mr. Roper sends him next door to the same neighbor's house to hide. Jack stumbles and breaks a jar of pickles, spilling pickle juice down his leg. Jack invites the neighbor's wife and her husband to the surprise party. The wife stumbles and falls into Jack's arms just as her husband comes in the door. They must explain that everything is "innocent."

Later that evening, the party is in full swing, but Mrs. Roper has not yet arrived; finally she comes in. We learn she had locked herself in a gas station rest room and just got out. Her husband kisses her, and everyone applauds. (Yes, folks, it's hard to believe, but this show was actually watched by millions of people on a weekly basis!) Let's take a look at another episode.

Jack finds an expensive gift that Chrissy and Janet have hidden in their bedroom and thinks it is for him; but he is broke and has no money to get a gift for them. Jack's friend, Larry, who is very "seventies"—chest hair, gold chain, flared pants—comes by and tells Jack that he sometimes works as a professional escort for $100 a night. He gives Jack a two-night job to escort a woman named Lana. Jack very reluctantly takes it, because he needs the money. Larry tells him to "do the best you can with what little you've got." Jack escorts Lana to an elegant restaurant; she is very attractive, thirtyish, three times divorced, and a successful career woman. She is also very sexually rapacious (dressed in a tight black suit) and immediately begins pursuing Jack. Chrissy and Janet show up at the same restaurant and Jack tries to hide under the table and in the dessert cart to prevent them from seeing him. He fears having to explain that he is a paid escort.

Lana spills a drink on Jack so they will have to go back to his apartment for new clothes; while there, she tries to seduce him. When Larry comes in, Jack embraces him and pretends to be gay; however, Lana views this as a sexual challenge and promises to keep after Jack. After Lana leaves, Chrissy and Janet return from their dinner; they ask Jack who Lana is and why he is dating an "older woman." Larry, in secret, tells Chrissy and Janet that it is because Jack feels insecure and unloved. He encourages them to be more physically affectionate to Jack; they agree.

The next night, Jack and Lana again go out to dinner (recall that it was a two-night escort date). Lana is seductively dressed in a revealing red-and-black outfit. She tells Jack she expects him to have sex with her. Jack refuses, leaves the restaurant, and returns home. Chrissy, in her skimpy nightgown, beckons him to the couch and begins kissing him; but Lana barges in carrying a bottle of champagne. Jack then spills the beans—telling Lana he is not gay and admitting to Chrissy and Janet that he is Lana's paid escort. Lana leaves. Jack tells Chrissy and Janet he went out with her to get money for a gift for them. They laugh, telling him their gift is not for *him,* but rather for a couple celebrating their wedding anniversary. Jack laments, "I'm so ashamed. I sold myself for nothing."

What are we to make of *Three's Company*? Despite its shallowness of intellect and humor, the show represented the contemporaneous cultural struggle with gender roles and sexuality. In this way, the show recalls Rod Stewart's big disco hit of the same time period, "Do You Think I'm Sexy?" whose opening lyrics were "If you want my body, and you think I'm sexy, c'mon sugar, let me know." Both women and men were working at jobs that paid them enough to permit partying on weekends. Women no longer felt tied to the sexual conservatism of earlier generations. There was ample knowledge and availability of birth control—and, as yet, no knowledge or widespread presence of herpes and AIDS. As a result, sexual mores were perhaps the most liberal and unconstrained that they ever had been in American society. Further, by the end of the decade, political and social unrest had calmed considerably. The Vietnam War was over, the leaders of the radical left and black power movements were dead, in jail, or retired, and the students who had been marching in the streets and occupying university administration buildings now had graduated and were working at the very jobs and engaging in the same dating and mating behaviors depicted in *Three's Company.* As Pogo once keenly observed: "I have met the enemy and it is us!"

So perhaps it is fitting that we must own up to, if not enthusiastically embrace, this not-so-flattering image of ourselves as we tread onward to the 1980s.

— SIX —

MOTION PICTURES OF THE 1980s

After the halcyon disco and party years of the late 1970s, American culture began settling down to do business in the early 1980s. A benevolent, paternal icon, Ronald Reagan, occupied the White House, the baby boomers had finally decided to get serious about their careers, and capitalism was in full flower. In short, it was a back-to-basics time: time to reassert basic cultural categories of good and evil, male and female, and God and man. But with a twist. As we shall see, our society's tumultuous passage through the 1960s and 1970s had left its mark on us . . . and on our archetypes. The decade produced some genuinely brilliant motion pictures and brought us mythic tales and characters that have become embedded in our culture: E.T., Indiana Jones, Batman, and Axel Foley.

Tootsie (1982)

Our first film, *Tootsie,* made good on Archie Bunker's lament at the beginning of the 1970s that girls were no longer girls and men no longer men. A decade later, sex roles were in great flux; women had entered the work force in large numbers, spawning fears of female masculinization. While men, especially those following in the footsteps of Dustin Hoffman's character, Benjamin, in *The Graduate,* were trying to find greater depth of emotion and meaning in their lives.

It was truly ironic, therefore, that one of the first enormously popular films of the decade would again star Dustin Hoffman representing the pathos-filled search of American men for their sexual identity. Jungian psychology, from which the notion of archetypes is drawn, describes a feminine nature (anima) and a masculine nature (animus) present in every person, irrespective of gender. We are not complete human beings, Jung posits, unless both our anima and animus are fully developed and integrated. There are two ways of accomplishing this. The traditional way has been for women to develop only their anima and for men to develop only their animus; unity and integration are achieved when the fully feminine woman and the fully masculine man unite to form a completed couple.

Fotos International/Archive Photos

The anima and the animus on display in Tootsie.

However, an alternative path to completion is for an individual man or woman to develop *both* the anima and animus internally; such people would be termed "androgynous" in current sex role terminology, according to Spence and Helmreich, and would appropriately mate (unite) with other complete individuals. The plot of *Tootsie* concerns itself with exactly these issues.

Michael Dorsey (Dustin Hoffman) is an out-of-work *actor* (a profession that suggests he frequently takes on a variety of temporary personal roles). His lack of success as an actor stems from the fact that he rebels against conventional stereotypes; he is a social misfit. However, despite his searching for the right role, in life and in his career, he is entirely an animus figure. He is very domineering and aggressive and is attracted to highly feminine women. In a rebellious effort to prove his talent as an actor, Michael tries out for the role of a woman in a television soap opera. To get the part, Michael adopts the apparel, hairstyle, and voice inflection of a woman. He inverts his name (reflecting his new gender) to "Dorothy Michaels."

Once he has been cast in the role of Dorothy, Michael begins to see life as if he were a woman. In short, his anima, long dormant, begins to develop. While playing the female role of Dorothy, Michael falls in love with Julie (Jessica Lange), an actress on the soap opera. Julie is in many ways a budding inversion of the traditional woman. She has had a child out of wedlock (the father is never mentioned). Further, she is independent and working to support herself, all of which suggests that she is in the process of developing her animus. However, she has not fully achieved this status, as she is still involved with the show's producer, a domineering, abusive (animus) man. Thus, we are presented with a man developing his anima and a woman developing her animus, who are being drawn emotionally to each other.

The myth embodied in *Tootsie*, however, addresses some further subtleties and social mores. One subtlety is that Julie's anima has fallen in love with the masculine (animus) side of Dorothy, whom she trusts and is able to fully love because she believes him to be a woman. She wants friendship with the masculine side of a woman, so that she can develop her own animus and free herself from dependence upon masculine men. Ironically, Dorothy's newly developed anima falls in love with Julie's animus. He, as a woman, is now able to feel feminine attachment and romantic love for the first time and to *admire* Julie's independence. Drawing strength from Dorothy/Michael's animus, Julie is able to break off her relationship with the abusive producer and become fully independent; that is, to complete her own animus.

A second subtlety of the story is that Julie's widower father, a self-described "old-fashioned" (animus) man, falls in love with Dorothy whom he, like Julie, believes to be a woman. However, unlike his daughter, who is attracted by Dorothy's animus, the father is drawn to the now fully developed anima of Dorothy. Dorothy is, in his eyes, very feminine and, hence, desirable. Julie's father proposes marriage to Dorothy.

At this juncture, Dorothy/Michael realizes he has no choice but to reveal his true biological sex. In a dramatic live scene on the soap opera (itself a parody of the unreal nature of reality), Dorothy removes his wig and makeup to reveal the man underneath. However, the man underneath is now psychologically a very different person from the original masculine male who had assumed the role of Dorothy. Michael is now a *completed* person, one whose anima and animus are fully developed and integrated. His character of Dorothy announces to the nationwide television audience that although he is actually a man and not Dorothy, he is as "proud to be a woman as she ever was, and lucky to be the woman who was the best part of my manhood, the best part of myself."

Julie, shocked to discover that her best friend, Dorothy, is actually a man, at first rebuffs Michael. She is a fully integrated woman now, one who does not need or trust a traditional man. She tells Michael that she misses Dorothy and wishes he *were* Dorothy. Michael responds that Julie doesn't have to miss Dorothy; that Dorothy is now inside of him and "she" misses Julie. Michael then makes a final statement to Julie regarding his transformation, which clearly expresses the anima/animus notion: "I was a better man with you as a woman, than I ever was with any woman as a man. . . . We're already good friends. . . . That's a great beginning." Julie recognizes the validity of this, and as equals, they reunite.

Tootsie thus represents three propositions regarding the newly constructed masculine/feminine gender identities of the 1980s.

First, persons who seek to complete themselves by developing only their gender-consistent psychological component (anima-woman, animus-man) and then finding a complementary partner of the opposite gender will fail. It has become culturally inappropriate to be an all-animus man or all-anima woman and to seek completion by coupling with one's opposite. Michael's all-anima girlfriend (Sandy) and all-animus boyfriend (Julie's father), and Julie's all-animus boyfriend (the producer) were rejected because they were now viewed as *incomplete* and *underdeveloped.* Second, persons who first complete themselves by developing *both* their anima and animus, regardless of gender, will then be able to successfully develop a relationship with a similarly developed "full" person. Thus, in the 1980s two half people cannot form a couple; two whole people can. Thus, what Archie Bunker bemoaned and *Grease* hinted at during the 1970s came to pass in the 1980s: to be fully human, one must have both feminine and masculine qualities; androgyny triumphs.

We now turn to a series of films addressing what was to be *the* central mythic issue of the decade: the relationship between spirituality and science or, said differently, between God and man. Joseph Campbell viewed this juxtaposition as being the *cosmological* function of myth. Perhaps this deeper, existential questioning came about as a result of the gender turmoil cited above. With self-identity guidelines falling by the wayside, it is likely that America's bedrock belief in the virtue of science and notions of humankind's inexorable progress toward ultimate knowledge and control of the universe became similarly weakened. "Who are we and where are we going?" became central social issues. Let's take a look at how our mythology responded.

E.T. the Extra-Terrestrial (1982)

Five years after the success of *Close Encounters* and seven years after the extraordinary *Jaws,* Steven Spielberg—a man with an instinctual genius for archetype—directed his third film: *E.T. the Extra-Terrestrial,* which was destined to become one of the most popular and enchanting films of all time. The advertising for *E.T.* showed an outline of *E.T.*'s hand stretched downward from a starry sky touching a human hand that extended upward from Earth. Purposely reminiscent of Michelangelo's Sistine Chapel fresco depicting the hand of God extended toward the hand of Adam (*Ben Hur* also made use of this image), the advertisement foreshadowed the many references to Judeo-Christian mythology contained in the movie.

The central archetypal image conveyed in *E.T.* is that of messianic visitation. Indeed, there are so many references to traditional Christian imagery contained within the film—E.T.'s glowing red heart, his heavenly origins, his working of miracles, his earthly death and resurrection—that this conclusion is unmistakable. Yet *E.T.* contains additional messages not central to Christian ideology, but which reflect our cultural character, fears, and aspirations. The twelve disciples have become neighborhood children; the Roman centurions have become modern-day scientists and policemen; and the messiah takes the form of a small, squat spaceman.

E.T. opens with a view of the starry, moonlit sky; a spaceship rests in a misty, magical forest clearing—a supernatural event is occurring. Small humanlike figures outside the spacecraft are gathering plant samples. One of the figures (E.T.) wanders into the forest. Trucks drive toward the spacecraft, and men get out; they are searching for the aliens. E.T. is separated from his comrades and abandoned when the spacecraft is forced to depart. The most prominent scientist wears several keys attached to his belt—a symbol that is repeated several times throughout the movie; the keys are metaphors for man's control of technology and profane (manmade) knowledge.

The story shifts to several boys talking in a suburban kitchen. The youngest, Eliot, hears something in the backyard shed and goes to investigate. The shed is made of latticework wood, has a straw floor, and is brightly lit from within—much resembling Christmas card scenes of the stable in which Jesus was born. E.T. and Eliot encounter each other, both scream from fright, and run off. We sense that they are destined to be together, however, as "Eliot" and "E.T." are synonymous.

The next day Eliot lays a trail of candy in the woods (the now-famous Reese's Pieces) hoping to attract E.T. Eliot's family will not believe he has actually encountered E.T.—prophets traditionally encounter skepticism—and say that if E.T. does exist they will "call someone to take him away." Eliot worries that if E.T. falls into the hands of the authorities, that is, scientists, they will "cut him up and do experiments on him."

The next night, E.T. returns to the shed; Eliot lures him into his bedroom. E.T. at first imitates Eliot's actions and then puts Eliot to sleep, the first demonstration of his supernatural powers. Eliot shows E.T. to his previously skeptical sister and brother. Seeing is believing, and they too become converted to believing in E.T.'s existence. The three vow not to tell any adults about E.T.'s presence, because they fear he would be harmed. An interesting parallel can be drawn here between the movie's story and Christian theology. Jesus' first converts were little children, fishermen, and other plain folk, the least powerful members of society. E.T.'s disciples are children, also powerless as compared to adults and the least corrupted by technological norms.

E.T. demonstrates to Eliot and his siblings that he is from a distant galaxy by levitating several objects, a miracle in which supernatural knowledge is demonstrated. He also revives a dying flower, a miracle in which a mortal life is restored. Later, during a frog dissection lesson in school, Eliot leads a children's revolt against the authority of the teacher. The archetypal imagery here is straightforward. Eliot has adopted E.T.'s doctrine of compassion for all life and rebels against the teacher's attempts, representing modern technological norms, to indoctrinate him into a culture that values scientific knowledge (anatomy and dissection) above the sacred life of another being: the frogs must be murdered before they can be studied. With E.T.'s guidance, Eliot demonstrates that there is a sacredness to humans, as well, if they transcend the urge to destroy life in order to acquire scientific knowledge. Recall that this theme was also present in *Star Wars,* and we shall see it again in *Raiders of the Lost Ark.*

E.T. has been weakening; he is homesick and also senses that the human scientists are searching for him and will destroy him. He and Eliot have become spiritually joined; what one feels the other feels. Eliot pricks his finger and E.T. says "Oh!" E.T. cures Eliot's injured finger, the miracle of healing. On Halloween night, a traditionally supernatural time (recall that the devil entered Regan on Halloween eve in *The Exorcist*), E.T. and Eliot fly into the forest on

Eliot's bicycle, another miracle, to set up a machine that will allow E.T. to "phone home." Spielberg appropriately sets this scene in a forest full of spruce trees, whose conical shapes all are archetypal markers pointing from the Earth toward heaven. Eliot and E.T. direct their quaint machine toward heaven and wait for an answer. E.T. causes Eliot to fall asleep; the next morning E.T. is gone.

Eliot's older brother, Mike, goes in search of E.T. and finds him, dying, in the forest. He takes E.T. back to the house. Scientists, their human features completely masked by technological equipment (like Darth Vader), converge on the house, covering the entire household in *plastic* (recall *The Graduate*), symbolizing manmade technological dominance over its habitants. Eliot and E.T. both become very sick.

A scientist says, "Eliot thinks E.T.'s thoughts," but Mike corrects him: "No, he *feels* E.T.'s *feelings*." Thus, the essence of life is proposed to be love, not reason. The scientists, who do not understand this, are unable to comprehend E.T. or to save him. Their technological cures are impotent against a spiritual ailment. E.T. dies; the flower he revived wilts to signal his passing. The scientists pack his body in ice, assigning a number to his death—fifteen hours, thirty-six minutes—as if quantification will permit them some measure of control over the outcome.

Eliot's sister and mother (recall Jesus' mother, Mary, and the convert, Mary Magdalene) wish for E.T. to "come back to life," that is, be resurrected, as E.T. is packed into a dry-ice tomb. Eliot says, "Look what they've done to you. You must be dead, because now I don't know how to feel." As Eliot prepares to leave, however, he notices that the flowers have revived.[1] He opens up E.T.'s tomb. E.T.'s heart is glowing red; he is again alive. E.T. says his "phone home" has been responded to: God has answered his prayers. Eliot and his brother Mike drive off with E.T. in an ambulance to escape the scientists. They are joined by four of Mike's friends. In a playground, E.T. opens the back door of the ambulance and shows himself to these four other children. A resurrected messiah, he is dressed in a flowing white robe and his red heart is glowing. He stretches his right hand outward toward these new disciples.

Eliot, Mike, and the four neighborhood boys carry E.T. away on their bicycles. They are pursued by scientists, policemen, and

Fotos International/Archive Photos

The new messiah—E.T. is resurrected.

other authority figures armed with guns. Almost captured, they are saved when E.T. levitates all of them back to the forest, his final miracle. Darkness falls and a spaceship descends for E.T. Eliot's mother, sister, brother, the four other children, and a humane scientist are present. E.T. touches Eliot's forehead with his glowing finger and says "I'll always be right here." Carrying the revived flowers, E.T. boards the spaceship and ascends to heaven. A rainbow is left in the sky. (Like the moon and sun, the rainbow is a pre-Christian spiritual symbol.)

The archetypes in *E.T.* and their relationships to one another convey several ideas of a cosmological and metaphysical nature. First, we are told that it is the innocent, the powerless, and the uncorrupted among us who are best able to recognize and respond to God-sent messages. Eliot is the least powerful and the most sensitive even among his young peers, and it is to him that E.T. first makes his presence known. Second, the story proposes that divine knowledge which is given to man may be misunderstood, and even destroyed, by man's insistence on creating and using only secular, scientific knowledge.

Third, divine beings, such as E.T., who die in our secular society, or are killed by our culture, can be brought back to life by divine intervention. The failure of modern technology to save E.T. and his subsequent resurrection by supernatural forces was used to demonstrate that only sacred power can overcome death; man and science cannot. Those who recognize and believe in the sacred power, as Eliot does, can communicate directly with it at any time and, the story's ending suggests, could be revived from mortal death if the divine being chose to intervene. If these ideas sound remarkably familiar, it is because to persons raised in a Judeo-Christian culture they *are* familiar. The traditional archetypes of Christian theology have been translated into modern-day icons, and the propositions about love, death, faith, and rebirth encoded in *E.T.* continue to exercise a powerful influence on our hearts and minds.

Straddling the release of *E.T.* in 1982 were the second and third episodes of the *Star Wars* trilogy: *The Empire Strikes Back* in 1980 and *Return of the Jedi* in 1983. These films, as well, went on to become among the most popular of the decade. And, having been re-released in early 1997, they have now earned sufficient income at the box office to be ranked the most successful film series of all time.

The Empire Strikes Back (1980)

The Empire Strikes Back appeared three years after *Star Wars* and continued the saga of Luke Skywalker, Princess Leia, and Han Solo. Once again, the story opens with a mythic narrative scrolling across the screen; the setting is again space ("the last frontier," as *Star Trek*'s Gene Roddenberry so insightfully observed), and archetypal forces of good and evil are in conflict for dominance in the universe.

Luke, Leia, Han Solo, and the band of brave rebels are holed up on an ice-covered planet at the far reaches of the evil Galactic Empire. Here they are gathering strength and forming strategy to combat the Rome-like oppression enforced by the empire. Han and Leia are increasingly drawn to each other, but each remains wary of commitment and rejection. And indeed, Han is planning to leave the rebel base soon to make amends with an evil criminal to whom he owes a large sum of money, Jabba the Hutt. Also present are Han's half-animal/half-human sidekick, Chewbacca, and the anthropomorphized robots who have become a central part of the *Star Wars* team: R2-D2 and C-3P0. Like the rebels themselves, who come from a diverse set of species, the presence of Chewbacca and the robots represents the concept of respect for life across all its diverse forms. Further, while one of the central tenets of the *Star Wars* trilogy is to oppose *oppressive* technology, the use of "humanized" technology in the series (the friendly robots and the Millennium Falcon) makes it clear that machines per se are not evil; it is their use to destroy or inhibit freedom that is to be feared.

Han, Luke, and Leia have all matured psychologically since we last met them. Han has abandoned his fully selfish personality and is now about halfway between sharing with and caring for others and pursuing his own goals. Leia has evolved into a decisive, intelligent leader of the rebel forces. Indeed, archetypically she is the *first female leader* we have encountered in all the films and television shows analyzed. As noted in our discussion of *Tootsie,* the early 1980s were a watershed time for women's, and men's, gender identities. And Luke is gaining patience and self-control—two attributes he must acquire to reach manhood and become a Jedi knight.

These new statuses are evident at the outset of the film. Luke is patrolling the icy area around the camp when he is attacked by an ice monster and hung up in its lair for a late supper. By concentrating, Luke is able to telepathically retrieve his light saber and free himself, escaping into a heavy blizzard. Han, who had been planning to depart that day, learns that Luke has not returned from patrol and, heroically and unselfishly, ventures into the blizzard to rescue him. When the pair does not return that evening (Han has constructed a snow shelter for himself and Luke in which they ride out the storm), Leia must seal the entry doors to the rebel base to conserve heat, knowing she may be sentencing two men she dearly loves to death in order to preserve her larger responsibility to the rebel forces. Of course, Han and Luke survive (otherwise it would have been a ten-minute movie), but each of the three has proven his or her mettle.

At the space station of the evil empire, Darth Vader is preparing his troops to locate and annihilate the rebel forces. The archetypal dimensions of the evil empire have become more clearly visible to us. Its locale is always shown to be in a technological setting—a space station—populated by plastic armored troops, uniform-clad officers, and the black-caped, plastic-and-metal covered Darth Vader, whose "voice" itself is machine-generated. Quite significantly, there are *no* females or children present, *no* plants or animals present, and *no* positive emotions present. It is an entirely male, military, and technological social system.

The Galactic Empire succeeds in locating the rebel base and sends an army of huge, elephant-like robots armed with guns to destroy it. Luke heroically pilots his small fighter plane, calmly working with and directing the other rebel pilots, and destroys several of the "beast-machines." Most of the rebels escape the attack. Luke, directed by his mentor, Obi-Wan Kenobi, then flies with R2-D2 to a distant planet to seek the mysterious Yoda. Han Solo rescues Princess Leia, and with Chewbacca and C-3P0 they jump aboard the "hot-rod" Millennium Falcon and fly off with enemy troopers in hot pursuit. Han cleverly evades the troopers, first, by hiding the plane in an asteroid field and, second, by pretending the plane is a piece of debris when the Empire's huge Death Star satellite jettisons garbage.

Concurrent with this, Luke is on a personal quest. Following Obi-Wan Kenobi's telepathic instructions he flies to a primitive, swampy, misty planet covered in rain forest. This clearly represents nature in its most essential form—the primordial ooze from which all life sprang. In essence it is the extreme female complement to the evil empire's technological "planet," the Death Star. Luke is symbolically immersed (reborn) in the swampy water when he lands, preparing him to meet his second mystical guide to adulthood, Yoda. When Yoda appears—a small, troll-like creature, green in color with big ears and dressed in soft brown robes—Luke does not recognize him. No doubt Luke expected a strong, tall, powerful warrior figure to be his guide.

The emperor of the evil empire appears in vision form to Darth Vader, expressing concern that Luke Skywalker has become "a new force [for good] in the universe." He tells Darth to destroy Luke. Darth responds that instead he will convert Luke to the Dark Side, transforming him into a powerful servant of the emperor. Meanwhile, Luke has been taken into Yoda's diminutive house. Yoda informs Luke that he knew Luke's father, Anakin Skywalker, a brave Jedi knight, who died mysteriously. Yoda begins training Luke to be patient, humble, and focused. He sends Luke into a dark cave (a death tomb/womb), where he is attacked by an image of Darth Vader. In the ensuing fight, Luke severs Darth's right hand (a symbolic castration); but when Darth collapses, his face is revealed to be that of Luke. This is a symbolically complex scene. In part, it prefigures the upcoming real battle between Luke and Darth; but metaphorically it represents the Oedipal struggle between patricide (killing one's father) and the castration anxiety male children feel toward their fathers.

After cleverly escaping from the Galactic Empire's Death Star station, Han, Leia, Chewbacca, and C-3P0 venture to an outlaw mining colony run by a former crony of Han's, named Lando (Billy Dee Williams). Han and Leia have, by this time, admitted their feelings for each other. Lando is a scoundrel much like Han once was; to protect his own economic interests, he sells out Leia, Han, and the others to Darth Vader, who intends to use them as bait to attract Luke. Just as Vader calculated, Luke leaves his still incomplete training with Yoda and flies to the mining colony to rescue his friends, having sensed their danger intuitively through the Force. Luke arrives like a young god or angel through clouded skies. Even as he arrives, however, his friend, Han, is being "carbonized" into suspended animation by Darth Vader. Luke enters the outlaw town, gun drawn, like an avenging gunfighter (such as Paladin) with his faithful robot sidekick, R2-D2. Lando, deeply regretting his earlier act of betrayal, has rallied his men to free Leia, Han, and the others. Darth locates Luke, his primary intention all along, and challenges him to a duel for supremacy. The blade of Darth's light saber is red (violence, death); that of Luke is blue (purity, truth). Han's carbonized body is sold to bounty hunters for sale to Jabba the Hutt. Lando rescues Chewbacca, Leia, and C-3P0, and they escape in the Millennium Falcon.

Meanwhile, Luke and Darth continue to duel. Darth severs Luke's right hand (again, an act of castration) and tells him that to survive, Luke must join him in serving the emperor and the Dark Side. Darth tells Luke *he* is his father; Luke, realizing this is true, cries out in torment. He refuses to join his father in serving evil. Severely injured and clinging perilously to a building structure at the edge of oblivion, Luke cries out to Obi-Wan Kenobi, his spiritual father, and to Leia. Leia telepathically hears his cry (it will soon be revealed that she is his sister) and tells Lando they must fly back and rescue him. Courageously, they save Luke and, with R2-D2's technological expertise, escape the pursuing empire troopers. As they depart, Darth calls out telepathically to Luke "you are my son." During their voyage of escape, Luke's hand is replaced with an artificial prosthesis. He and Leia are both dressed in white, biblical-era robes, signifying their sacred status.

Thus, at the end of this second episode of the *Star Wars* series, we find our three heroes in transitional status. Luke has learned the true, and awful, identity of his father. He has acted bravely to save his friends, and he has suffered serious losses—his right hand, his friend Han Solo. His road to mature manhood is well under way, yet not fully realized. Leia and Han have found—and lost—each other. Han's criminal past and Leia's responsibility as a person of royal descent have both operated to prevent the culmination of their love for each other. Additionally, the team of Good People, which includes Han, Leia, Luke, Chewbacca, Lando, C-3P0, and R2-D2, has become a more tightly integrated community. Each now contributes to the common welfare to the full extent of his or her or its abilities, which is necessary, of course, for the forces of darkness still hold sway in the universe. What will happen next?

Return of the Jedi (1983)

George Lucas's finale to his *Star Wars* trilogy opens with the evil Galactic Empire massing its forces for one, conclusive assault upon the good rebels.[2] To this end, Darth Vader and his minions are constructing an enormous mass of destructive machinery, termed a Death Star. This is, in effect, a huge technological colony floating in space whose only purpose is to destroy other life forms. The color spectrum aboard the Death Star ranges across shades of black, white, and grey. Here we may read colors as emotions; the evil empire is colorless, that is, without emotion or soul.

The scene shifts to R2-D2 and C-3P0, who are walking across a hot, arid planet; they arrive at an enormous armored door constructed on the side of a mountain, the lair of Jabba the Hutt. Jabba is a tremendously ugly creature resembling an amphibian or fish. (His appearance plays into American cultural disgust with fat, slimy beings.) Jabba dwells in a dark underground cavern; after all, he is an "underworld" criminal, surrounded by a coterie of unattractive sycophants. A carbonized Han Solo hangs from the wall. We are quickly clued in to Jabba's sadistic personality when he sends a chained dancing girl to her death and devours live animals for lunch. A bounty hunter arrives with Chewbacca as captive and bargains shrewdly with Jabba for a handsome payment. The clever bounty hunter turns out to be Leia, who then secretly decarbonizes Han. Unfortunately, Jabba discovers this and has Han and Chewbacca thrown into a cell and forces Leia to be his replacement dancing girl.

Another stranger arrives shrouded in mysterious monklike robes. This turns out to be Luke, who can now use the powers of the Force to disarm Jabba's guards. Jabba, however, drops Luke into a grisly pit with a flesh-eating monster much like the Cretan minotaur. Luke, through cleverness and bravery, kills the monster. Angered, Jabba sends Luke, Han, and Chewbacca to be devoured by an enormous sand worm. Fortunately, Lando arrives and with R2-D2's help saves Han, Luke, and Chewbacca from being eaten alive. (This is a common "terrible" death in myth: recall the shark devouring Quint in *Jaws.*) Leia, still garbed as a dancing girl, strangles Jabba with her chain. The entire troupe then makes its escape.

Back at the Death Star, the evil emperor has arrived. He is a forbidding figure of deformed and disfigured humanity, with a scarred, bloodless face, metal teeth, and a crippled gait, covered in a full-length black cloak. Darth bows to him, calling the emperor "Master." Concurrently, Luke has returned to the sacred planet inhabited by Yoda. Yoda, now nine hundred years old, tells Luke his training is complete; his only remaining task is to confront Darth Vader. Yoda warns Luke that although Darth is his father, Luke must never underestimate the power of the Dark Side, which "feeds upon anger, fear, and oppression." He tells Luke that there is still another member of the Skywalker family in whom the Force runs, as well; Luke correctly guesses that it is Leia, his sister. Yoda then lies down and dies; thunder booms to mark his passing.

Obi-Wan Kenobi appears telepathically to Luke and assures him that he and Yoda will always "be with you." He also provides more information to Luke about his father. His father's name once was Anakin Skywalker, a brilliant Jedi knight, who was "seduced by the Dark Side." Now, as Darth Vader, he is "more machine, than man." Luke and his sister, Leia, were hidden from their father at birth for fear he would slay them. Despite his father's horrific history, Luke tells Obi-Wan he cannot kill him; instead, Luke hopes to turn his father away from the Dark Side.

Back at rebel headquarters, an array of species prepares to do battle with the Death Star. Lando will command the rebel pilots, while Luke, Leia, Han, Chewbacca, R2-D2, and C-3P0 land on a nearby planet to disarm the force field protecting the Death Star. The planet upon which they land is verdant and fertile, filled with sumptuous vegetation and populated by "primitive" teddy bear–like creatures called Ewoks. The Ewoks are analogous to Rousseau's noble savages—pure, brave, and simple, living in harmony with nature; they represent the symbolic opposition of the hi-tech, plastic-covered empire troopers. Leia, Luke, Han, and C-3P0 are kidnapped by the Ewoks after landing on their planet, but soon become members of their tribe and enlist their support against the empire. That evening, on a misty forest bridge (signifying a new relationship) Luke tells Leia they are brother and sister and that he intends to try to turn their father, Darth, from his evil ways. Luke journeys to the Death Star to confront his father, as Han, Leia, Chewbacca, the robots (C-3P0, R2-D2), and the Ewoks attempt to gain control of the trooper bunker protecting the Death Star.

Luke battles Darth, as the emperor encourages them to slay each other, thus releasing even more evil into the universe. On the forest planet below, the empire's ostrichlike killing machines stalk the Ewoks and rebels. Here, as in the elephant-like killing machines we saw in the previous episode, destructive technology is given an animal-like form. This contrasts with the animals and robots of the good forces, who are anthropomorphized.

Luke, refusing at first to mortally battle his father, attempts to slay him in earnest when his father learns telepathically of Leia's existence and threatens to harm her. Luke succeeds in severing Darth's right hand, revealing it to be machinery. The emperor is happy at this horrific event. Luke, realizing he cannot kill his father without corrupting his own goodness, casts away his light saber. The emperor retaliates by tormenting Luke with lightning bolts from his hands—a long-running mythic image of a destructive god's power. Luke pleads to Darth to help him; finally, Darth picks up the emperor and destroys him. Darth begins dying, as well, the evil force that had supported him now gone. Luke cradles his dying father in his arms; Darth asks that Luke remove his mask "so that I can look upon you with my own eyes." Luke, crying, tells his father, "I want to save you." His father replies, "You already have" and expires.

The Death Star is blown to pieces by the rebel forces, just as Luke escapes it in a small plane. Revelry erupts on the forest planet below; Leia and Han embrace and kiss. That night, Luke burns his father's body on a wooden funeral pyre, freeing his spirit to return to goodness. A communal festival is under way in which rebel pilots, Ewoks, robots, Luke, Leia, Lando, Chewbacca, and Han all rejoice. Smiling down upon this happy scene are the ghosts of Yoda, Obi-Wan and Anakin Skywalker, clothed in biblical white robes. The universe has been saved!

To enter our next trio of films, the Indiana Jones series, the reader need only retain his/her mental image of the archetypic rogue-hero, Han Solo, together with the actor who portrayed him, Harrison Ford, and step back two years to 1981. Steven Spielberg has replaced George Lucas as our film's director, and we are going to concern ourselves with a different juxtaposition of good and evil. In this series, our intrepid hero, Indiana Jones, must learn to overcome his own too-zealous search for knowledge and learn to respect the important demarcation between the sacred and the profane.

Raiders of the Lost Ark (1981)

Our story opens in the South American jungle in 1936—a wilderness setting appropriate for facing heroic challenges. The central figure is an adventurer-archaeologist, Indiana Jones, whose name suggests an American Everyman. After exhibiting cleverness and courage to obtain a golden idol, Jones loses it to a sinister figure, identified as Bellock. Jones returns from the jungle to his university post as an archaeology professor. We are informed that he is an expert in both archaeology and the occult. Thus Jones is a complex heroic archetype—a rogue adventurer who is also a member of the scientific-technical elite, which is both revered and feared in our culture.

Government officials inform Jones that Hitler is gathering up magical antiquities to obtain their power for the Nazis. In particular, Hitler seeks the Ark of the Covenant, which is rumored to be buried in Egypt. Jones agrees to help the government locate the ark, but primarily because it will further his academic career and permit him to obtain "forbidden" knowledge. The symbolism here is subtle, but powerful. Hitler and Nazism are the most compelling evil archetypes of our era, in both a mythic and a historical sense. In the present story, the Nazis seek to obtain the power of our culture's God and to use it to overthrow all that is good and moral. Even more ironic and chilling, they are focusing upon a religious relic sacred to the Jews, a people they seek to obliterate from the Earth.

Jones flies to Nepal, another wilderness, where he enlists the aid of a former lover, Marianne. Marianne, we gather, was jilted earlier by Jones, as a result of his selfishness and overriding concern for his career. She has become quite masculine and independent; she wears a tie and pants, runs a bar, and wins a drinking contest—all animus-oriented activities. The Germans arrive in Nepal and attempt to steal a clue to the ark's location from Marianne. In the ensuing gunfight she and Jones both save each other's lives. Hence they are shown to be equally potent as heroes.

They fly together to Cairo, yet another wilderness, where Bellock, the sinister archaeologist, is helping the Germans excavate the ark. Bellock tells Jones that "archaeology is our religion. . . . I am a shadowy reflection of you." Bellock is a Faust-like character; a scientist whose desire for knowledge is indifferent to both moral and sacred restrictions. He will help even the most evil of causes, if it will further his quest for knowledge. As Bellock notes, "the ark is a transmitter for speaking to God," the key to universal truth, the source of all sacred knowledge. Like Faust, he has sold his soul to the devil in order to enrich his mind. Although this is a different kind of sacred-profane conflict from that encountered in the *Star Wars* trilogy, it reflects a similar underlying mythic theme in our culture. The quest for secular gain and profane knowledge must not tread upon that knowledge which God controls. Any man who tries to manipulate God or to alter destiny by subversion of God's power does so at great peril.

Using cleverness and heroism, Jones is able to discover the correct location of the ark, but before he can unearth it, Marianne is kidnapped by the Nazis. If Jones chooses to rescue her—fulfill the moral good—he will be unable to obtain the ark, that is, acquire forbidden knowledge. Significantly, he chooses to obtain the ark, thus valuing forbidden knowledge above human welfare. As Jones retrieves it from its earthly tomb/womb, a violent storm erupts, quite unusual in that this is the Egyptian *desert.* Lightning, thunder, and wind warn Jones that he is disturbing the resting place of a sacred object and that God is not pleased with his actions. As a result, in the next sequence he again, significantly, loses the ark to Bellock and the Nazis, and he and Marianne are cast into a dark pit filled with snakes (the biblical serpents of temptation) and the skeletons of other mortals who sought forbidden knowledge.

Marianne and Jones, again through cleverness, escape their tomb and then once more save each other's lives in a fight with Nazi soldiers. As the ark is being driven off by the Nazis, Jones dressed in his cowboy gear rides after it, on a white horse, naturally, and heroically rescues it. Marianne, Jones, and the ark set sail for England, but a German submarine intercepts their ship. Bellock recaptures Marianne and the ark, while Jones sneaks aboard the submarine. When the submarine arrives at a secret island, Jones again has the opportunity to rescue Marianne by destroying the ark,[3] which would prevent the Nazis from subverting its power. But he once again fails, choosing the ark's knowledge over the value of Marianne's and even his own life.

That evening, Bellock, dressed in Hebrew religious regalia, chants incantations and opens the ark, thereby exposing his profane mind to its sacred knowledge. As a result, he is destroyed by a violent wind and horrific spirit images who melt those who looked upon the ark, and all the surrounding Nazis who hoped to subvert sacred knowledge to their own profane purposes are also destroyed.

Jones, having *finally* comprehended the moral lesson, instructs Marianne to "keep your eyes closed," as he does himself while this is occurring. They do not look upon the sacred knowledge that their mortal eyes were not meant to see and, hence, are spared. God reseals the ark. It is transported back to Washington, where it is effectively reburied among piles of nameless crates in a nameless warehouse.[4]

Raiders, even more explicitly than the *Star Wars* trilogy, deals directly with man's relationship to the gods. What do we learn from it? First, although Jones is the hero and Bellock the villain in the story, both represent science and the desire for knowledge. Jones *survives* not only because he is a hero, that is, courageous and clever, but more importantly because he learns to place human welfare above the desire for knowledge and to not seek knowledge that is forbidden to mortals—*sacred knowledge.* This reflects a deep cultural metaphysical belief that there are some things that we, as humans, must not tamper with, must not seek to know, but rather must leave solely in the hands and minds of the gods. Bellock *dies* not merely because he is evil, but because he has placed the desire for knowledge above all other priorities. He permits his research to be sponsored by immoral and evil forces. Further, he is willing to use his scientific skills to put sacred knowledge in the hands of those who would use it to destroy moral goodness. The myth also proposes that there is a larger sacred power than the power of both good and evil mortals. This power is controlled only by the gods, and mortals will never come to know it or control it; if they attempt to do either, they will be destroyed.

Spielberg returned to the sacred knowledge/evil scientist theme in the last episode of the Indiana Jones trilogy, *Indiana Jones and the Last Crusade,* to which we now go.

Indiana Jones and the Last Crusade (1989)

This film provides us with valuable clues to Indiana Jones's adult character by providing a window to his youth. In the opening segment of the story, young Indiana Jones (River Phoenix) is on a Boy Scout field trip in the American Southwest. He and a fellow scout come across a renegade archaeologist, who eerily resembles Jones as an adult, ransacking a Spanish trove. The young Jones foils the theft, but is pursued by the archaeologist and his henchmen who want to sell the gold Coronado cross Jones has rescued. After mounting his horse (he misses in an attempt to jump on the horse from a rock, indicating his still-novice rogue-adventurer status), the young Jones rides to a train. The bad guys chase him through several train cars, which, as luck and a great script would have it, are occupied by a circus, thus initiating Jones's first contact with the crocodiles, snakes, lions, and rhinoceroses he will encounter frequently as an adult.

Jones finally eludes his pursuers and makes it home to show his archaeologist father (Sean Connery) the cross he has saved. His father is largely oblivious to his effort, being buried in his own research on the Holy Grail. When the (bribed) sheriff arrives, he takes the cross from Jones and gives it to the crooked archaeologist, who in turn sells it to a rich, businessman collector. Recognizing the courage of young Jones's efforts, however, the archaeologist places his weathered hat on the boy's head, "crowning" him and very likely starting Jones on his archetypal road to manhood.

The time moves to 1935. The adult Indiana Jones (Harrison Ford), now a professor, is in his university classroom lecturing students on the fact that "archaeology does not consist of discovering the golden cities mentioned in mythology; most archeological research is done in the library." This, of course, is true in a real-life sense, but humorously and blatantly false, as we the audience know, in the case of our hero, Indiana Jones, who is always out engaging in mythic adventures in exotic locations—and is, indeed, about to embark on another one.

Sure enough, Jones sneaks out the window of his office to escape clamoring students[5] and is intercepted by Walter Donovan, a wealthy museum donor. Donovan takes him to his luxurious home and shows Jones a priceless tablet with a clue to the location of the Holy Grail, the cup from which Christ drank at the last supper. Symbolically, the grail is the Christian equivalent of the Jewish Ark of the Covenant sought by Jones in *Raiders.* Donovan, dressed in a dinner jacket and sipping champagne, wants to enlist Jones's help in finding the grail. He also tells Jones that Jones's father,

Henry Jones Sr., *was* assisting him on the project, but has mysteriously disappeared while looking for religious clues in Venice, Italy. Thus, Indiana Jones sets out to find two treasures—the grail and his father.

The Holy Grail diary his father had been keeping for thirty years arrives in the mail for Indiana Jones. Jones goes to his father's house and finds it ransacked. He asks his good friend Marcus if Marcus believes in the grail; Marcus replies, "The search for the grail is the search for the divine in all of us." Marcus and Jones travel to Venice, where they are met by the very beautiful, very blond, very Aryan Elsa Schneider, an archaeologist working with Donovan. She takes them to an ancient library, formerly a church, where she had been working with Jones's father, before his disappearance. Using clues in a stained-glass window there, Indiana and Elsa venture below the church/library, through a labyrinth of dark, wet, rat-infested tunnels to find the tomb of one of the knights who once guarded the Holy Grail. In his coffin lies a second tablet giving a portion of the grail's location. After emerging from the tomb, Indiana and Elsa are pursued by a group of dark men wearing Turkish fezzes. These men belong to an ancient order sworn to protect the grail from profane usage. They ask Indiana: "Why do you seek the cup of Christ? for your glory or his?" When Indiana tells them his main desire is to locate his father, they tell him he is being held by the Nazis in a castle on the Austro-Hungarian border. Indiana sets off with Elsa to rescue his father.

Indiana succeeds in finding his father, only to be betrayed to the Nazis by Elsa. It turns out she was archetypal of the blond seductress/destructive goddess. The Joneses also discover to their chagrin that Donovan, as well, is in league with the Nazis. He and Elsa are analogous to the Bellock character in *Raiders*. They intend to use sacred knowledge and power for profane purposes. Indiana and his father escape from the Nazis, but must next venture to Berlin to regain Henry's grail diary. They arrive during a nighttime rally of goose-stepping Nazi troops. Henry tells his son: "We're pilgrims in an unholy land." Indiana locates Elsa at the rally and takes the diary from her; Adolf Hitler passes by and signs the diary, thinking Jones wants his autograph. This is a vivid archetypal juxtaposition of secular evil and sacred good.

Indiana and Henry board a dirigible in Berlin to fly out of Germany. For the first time in their lives, as father and son, they talk about their relationship to each other; it has never been close. Indiana's mother died when he was young, and his father seems to have taken emotional refuge in his scholarly research. Suddenly, they realize the Nazi authorities are investigating the dirigible, and they escape using a small biplane.

Meanwhile, Donovan and his Nazi accomplices are making a deal with a Middle Eastern despot to gain access to the grail site. As the Nazi entourage approaches the holy site, men from the ancient Grail Guardian Order attack them, but their feeble guns prove no match for the Nazis superior destructive technology. Their dying leader tells Indiana, "For the unrighteous, the cup of God holds everlasting damnation." Indiana, now an accomplished horseman, jumps on a black Arabian stallion owned by one of the dead guardians and rides up to the Nazi tank that holds his father and friend Marcus, who have been taken prisoner. As Indiana struggles with the tank commander, their vehicle goes over a cliff, seeming to kill Indiana. His father, Marcus, and an Egyptian friend gaze over the edge in sorrow. Henry Jones, in tears, declares, "I never told him anything," that is, "I never shared myself with him." Indiana crawls up from a ledge, and they all embrace and rejoice. Although treated somewhat humorously, it is clear that both father and son have made a wonderful discovery—their love for each other.

Indiana, Henry, Marcus, and their Egyptian crony mount up on horses and seek the grail. They discover an extraordinary temple carved in a cliff face in which the grail is housed. As they enter, they find Donovan, Elsa, and the Nazis are already present. They have sacrificed several soldiers already trying to penetrate the inner chamber. Donovan captures them and then purposely shoots Henry in the abdomen, forcing Indiana to obtain the grail to save his father's life (drinking from the grail provides eternal life).

Carefully following the clues in Henry's diary, Indiana risks his own life entering the chamber. By relying upon his father's wisdom and his own courage, he crosses the various hazards, finally crawling through a narrow tunnel (sacred vagina) to the inner sanctum (holy womb) in which the grail resides. An ancient knight greets him, saying "you don't *look* like a knight" and informs Indiana that *he* is now guardian of the grail. Donovan and Elsa, who have been following Jones, enter the holy chamber. Donovan instructs Elsa to select the correct chalice for him. There are around a hundred cups on display, meant to confuse unsanctified claimants. She knowingly picks a false cup—a very ornate, jewel-encrusted chalice. (Elsa has redirected her loyalty to Indiana and his father.) Donovan dips the cup in a sacred well (a goddess symbol) and drinks. In seconds, he horribly disintegrates and turns to dust—a just punishment for his materialism.

Elsa and Indiana choose a plain clay cup[6] and fill it from the holy spring. Indiana sips from it to test whether it is destructive or not, again risking his own life for that of his father. When it has no ill effects, he hurriedly carries it to his father and pours the sacred water into his father's mouth and upon his wound. Miraculously, Henry recovers.[7] Elsa clutches the grail and attempts to walk from the temple with it. As she does so, an earthquake, God's power, opens up a chasm, which swallows Elsa and the chalice. (Recall God's wrath also swallowed up the disbelieving Israelites in *The Ten Commandments.*) Indiana, too, attempts to recover it; but his father gently yet firmly tells him: "Indiana, *let it go*" and pulls him back from the abyss. Here Henry is symbolically rescuing Indiana from his baser ambitions. The ancient knight waves farewell to them as an internal rock slide seals the entrance to the temple for all time. Indiana asks Henry "What did you find, Dad?" to which his father replies, "Illumination." The foursome remount their horses and gallop into the sunset and cultural immortality.

As the reader has no doubt discerned, the archetypal structure of *Crusade* closely follows that of *Raiders.* The exceptions are that the woman's role (Elsa) has been made somewhat more negative and complex. Elsa Schneider resembles Bellock (*Raiders*) in that she herself is a scientist seeking knowledge and is willing to use evil sources of support (the Nazis) to further her goals in this regard. However, she displays some kindness to Indiana Jones and his father by returning the grail diary in Berlin and purposely choosing the wrong chalice for Donovan, causing his death. Thus, she is a *mediating* archetype, one who displays both good and evil characteristics simultaneously.

The biggest change in plot pattern, however, between *Crusade* and *Raiders* is the introduction of Henry Jones. Among all the rogue-adventurer heroes we have discussed, from Rhett Butler to Han Solo, none have been depicted as having fathers. Indeed, most of the examples of this archetypal category have no family members present in the narrative. Further, what makes the father-son presence of even more interest to us is that it is shown to evolve into a positive, mutually supportive relationship in which Henry and Indiana both instruct and save each other repeatedly.

This positive father-son bond stands in stark contrast to the vast human mythic heritage that focuses instead upon destructive and rivalrous relationships between father and son. From Oedipus to Jack-and-the-Beanstalk through Darth Vader and Luke Skywalker, most mythic tales of father and son have dwelled upon the son's fear of death/castration at the hands of the father and the father's fear of sexual competition[8] with his son. Here, at long last, are two characters who evolve past these hazards and become good friends.

The same, positive message is presented in a contemporaneous tale, *Back to the Future.*

Back to the Future (1985)

Back to the Future was released four years prior to *Crusade* and may well have influenced Lucas and Spielberg's inclusion of the father-son reconciliation theme in their closing episode of the Indiana Jones trilogy. *Back to the Future* develops the themes of father-son cooperation and conflict in a very different and more detailed manner than we have encountered in previous works.

It also is very significant in its presentation of the good/beneficial scientist archetype. As the reader will no doubt recall, up to now many of the scientist characters (such as Bellock) have been Faust-like personas, in league with dark forces to obtain forbidden power and knowledge. In contrast, the scientist in *Back to the Future,* Dr. Emmett Brown (Christopher Lloyd), is an ethical, brilliant man with an endearing whimsical nature; he represents the funny "mad scientist." The archetypal lineage of both the good and evil versions of the scientist extends back into prehistory to ancient notions of a wizard, sorcerer, magician, or shaman, who had access to knowledge, be it medicines, potions, or spells, which others in the community did not. Memorable examples of this archetype include not only Dr. Faustus, but also Merlin of Arthurian legend and Mary Shelley's Dr. Frankenstein. Our own century has experienced the same profound ambivalence regarding these figures as have previous generations. On the one hand, we revere the genius of Albert Einstein (who, not coincidentally, is alluded to often in *Back to the Future*), but we greatly fear the destructive scientists who may blow up the world, as in *Dr. Strangelove,* or conduct horrifying experiments upon us, for example, Dr. Mengele, the Nazi concentration camp surgeon.

It is because scientists possess such superhuman knowledge that we both worship and dread them. Their ability to do *either* good or evil at their own choosing provides them with enormous power to help or damage us. As we shall see, in the present film the scientist does a great deal of good.

The story opens at the home of Dr. Emmett Brown. It is eight o'clock in the morning, and a multitude of time pieces ranging from cuckoo clocks to elaborate chronometers are signaling the hour. And signaling, as well, our mortal entrapment within a tiny time span. We can neither revisit the past nor take ourselves ahead to the future. Dr. Brown is not home, but his teenaged friend, Marty Mc*Fly* (Michael J. Fox) has come by to see him. While at the house, Marty receives a cryptic message from Brown to meet him that night at the local shopping mall for a surprise. Marty continues on his way to Hill Valley High School, where he is auditioning his rock band to play for the upcoming dance. After school he meets with his girlfriend, Jennifer, to plan for their weekend date. A woman gives them a flyer about the local clock tower, which the town is considering refurbishing; it was struck by lightning thirty years ago and has not worked since. Marty rides his skateboard home to find his father, George McFly, once again being bullied by his boss, Biff, who has borrowed and crashed George's new car. George is a classic wuss or nerd—submissive, with greasy hair, pocket protector, white shirt, skinny tie (that is, small penis), and glasses. Biff refuses to pay for the car damage and reminds George he must hurry up and finish Biff's work, so Biff can turn it in as his own.

The rest of Marty's family is similarly unattractive. His mother is heavy and plain, his sister is overweight and plain, his brother works full-time at Burger King, and his uncle Joey is in jail. Even Marty's home is plain, common, and unattractive. Marty's mother, Lorraine, and father recall how they first met each other: Lorraine's father accidentally hit George McFly on the street with his car. George subsequently asked Lorraine to the big high school dance, where they fell in love. All this occurred thirty years ago, the night lightning struck the Hill Valley clock.

That evening, Marty goes to meet Dr. Brown in the Twin Pines Mall; it is a dark night, the magical time. Dr. Brown takes a gleaming silver (spaceship) DeLorean automobile out of a truck. Mist pervades the scene: Dr. Brown's wild, white hair (similar to Einstein's) and white radiation suit give him a ethereal quality. He and Marty send Dr. Brown's dog, Einstein, one minute into the future by placing him in the DeLorean and racing the special engine, powered by "magical" fuel (plutonium), to 88 miles an hour. With a lightning bolt and a burst of fire and smoke, the car disappears with the dog and then reappears one minute later.

Dr. Brown shows Marty how the time machine works and sets the dial for November 5, 1955, the day Dr. Brown first conceived of time travel and a special device to produce it. Just then, a van pulls up filled with terrorists intent on stealing the plutonium; they shoot and kill Dr. Brown. Marty jumps into the DeLorean and attempts to escape. When the car hits 88 miles an hour, he disappears with a lightning crack, leaving behind a trail of smoke. Marty has unwittingly transported himself to 1955. Slowly he realizes what has happened and hides the car behind a sign for his yet-to-be-built suburb. Marty walks into Hill Valley, circa 1955, and finds the world of the 1950s. Everything is clean and new; "Davy Crockett" plays on the radio; service station attendants wear crisp uniforms; there are no diet colas; and the town hall clock is still working.

Marty enters a restaurant and sits down; soon afterward, the young George McFly enters and is bullied by the young Biff and his buddies. Marty decides to walk George home to try to get him to stand up to Biff, and on the way, *Marty* is struck by Lorraine's father's car. Of course, this event was supposed to happen to George, starting him on the road to marrying Lorraine. Marty is taken into Lorraine's home, where Lorraine tends to him, even undressing and caressing him. Here we have the quintessential unconscious Oedipal desire of every teenage boy: Mommy loves me more than she loves Daddy and wants to have sex with me. Marty joins the family for dinner, but decides to leave abruptly after Lorraine begins flirting with him.

Marty flees to the young Dr. Brown's mansion and tells him that he, Dr. Brown, in the future invents a time machine and sends Marty, not yet born, back in time by mistake; and here he is. Emmett Brown at first doesn't believe him. Marty shows him his 1985 driver's license and tells him actor Ronald Reagan is now president. Brown now really doesn't believe him! But Marty convinces him by telling Brown about the time travel device he developed that very morning (November 7, 1955). Now Brown believes him. It is a wild and windy night; Marty takes Brown to see the hidden DeLorean. Brown tells Marty he fears he cannot send him back to the future, because he does not have access to plutonium in 1955: "By 1985, it'll probably be on every supermarket shelf," he speculates.

The next day, Marty goes to Hill Valley High School and attempts to get George together with Lorraine. He learns that his father, George, wrote creative fiction at this time and that Biff made frequent sexual overtures to Lorraine. However, George is still too shy to approach Lorraine. That night, Marty dresses up in his radiation suit and helmet (from the DeLorean) and enters George's bedroom, pretending to be a space invader. He tells George his name is Darth Vader and that he is from the planet Vulcan and orders George to ask Lorraine to the dance. George agrees.

The next day at the malt shop, George approaches Lorraine but is again foiled by Biff. Marty, to protect George, punches Biff, making Lorraine even more attracted to Marty. Here again, we see a disguised version of the Oedipal fantasy: "I'm more manly than my father, and Mom knows it." As a result, Lorraine asks Marty to the dance: "I think a man should be strong, and stand up for himself, and protect the woman he loves." Marty agrees to go with her, because he has hatched a plot with George to let George pretend to save Lorraine, when he (Marty) gets fresh with her at the dance. In the meantime, Marty and Dr. Brown have devised a plan to use the lightning strike on the town hall clock to generate the energy (magical fuel) to transport Marty back to 1985.

That Saturday night, Marty drives Lorraine to the dance. To Marty's amazement, Lorraine is wearing a breast-revealing dress, smokes a cigarette, and has brought an alcohol flask! (And we all thought our moms were so good!) Lorraine indicates she would like to make out with him. Marty is extremely uncomfortable with this, but when Lorraine actually kisses him, it is *Lorraine* who recoils: "There's something wrong with this!" she declares. Just then, Biff and his pals show up and drag Marty from the car; they rough him up and lock him in the trunk of the car belonging to the black dance band. Biff begins to rape Lorraine; at this moment, George appears, believing he is going to "rescue" Lorraine from Marty. (Here George is being *genuinely* tested.) At first, George shies away when he sees Biff, but then summons authentic courage and knocks him out. The surrounding high school students are amazed.

It is time for Marty to depart back to the future, but one of the black band members has become injured. Unless they play at the dance, Lorraine and George will never dance and kiss, or so the tale goes. To ensure his parents' mating and his own conception, Marty must play at the big dance, his fantasy come true. Marty does a wonderful job as a guitar icon, akin to Chuck Berry and Pete Townsend. As he departs to meet with Dr. Brown, George and Lorraine thank him and ask, "Will we ever see you again?" to which Marty replies "yep."

Dr. Brown awaits Marty on the courthouse steps. He has rigged up a wire to harness the lightning's energy and transfer it to the car. Marty gives Dr. Brown a letter describing the doctor's death in 1985—the terrorist shooting—and imploring the doctor to do what is necessary to avoid it. But Dr. Brown rips up the letter, refusing to read it. He tells Marty he does not want to do anything that might disturb future events, believing to do so would be tampering with the divine plan. An enormous storm erupts: wind, rain, thunder, lightning—all signs of supernatural power are present. The crucial lightning bolt strikes and powers the car; Marty and his magical vehicle disappear; only fiery tracks remain. Marty arrives back in 1985. He has reset the clock by ten minutes to permit him time to save Dr. Brown from the terrorists' fatal shots. But the car stalls, and he must run to the mall on foot. Shots ring out, but miraculously Dr. Brown does not die. He had pieced together the letter Marty left for him and worn a bullet-proof vest. Thus, future events had been tampered with, but in a beneficial way.

Marty goes home to bed. He awakens the next morning to find his life magically, and wonderfully, transformed. His parents' home looks different: prettier and more colorful. His sister and brother are competent, confident, and attractive. His mother and father, Lorraine and George, return from a morning tennis game looking fit, handsome, and happy. A FedEx man arrives with a copy of the latest science fiction best-seller George has just written. Biff, the bully, is now out in the driveway washing George's new sportscar. And there is a new 4x4 truck that Marty had always dreamed of owning in the garage. It is his. His girlfriend, Jennifer, shows up for their date, and Marty remarks to himself: "Everything is great!" As the narrative closes, Dr. Brown drives up in the DeLorean and invites Jennifer and Marty to go with him to the future. They hop in and off they go. . . .

Back to the Future is mythic narrative directly counter to the primary themes of *E.T., Star Wars* and *Indiana Jones.* These contemporaneous stories featured evil scientists and evil fathers (although the father-son conflicts are ultimately resolved) with whom the protagonists had to struggle to bring about goodness. In contrast, *Back to the Future* begins from a much more optimistic premise: Science can be a boon to those persons willing to place faith in it, and fathers can turn out to be good men, if they are just given some assistance by their sons. And certainly, the romp through Oedipal territory presented in *Future* is a good deal more refreshing and inspiring than the Dark Side version usually depicted. Two years after *Back to the Future,* another whimsical myth appeared on screen—a comedic version of the "evil invaders" tale. As we shall see, the scientists are here again presented as heroes, albeit zany ones, much as Dr. Emmett Brown was depicted.

Ghostbusters (1984)

Our first clue that something is amiss in this tale is when a very proper librarian at the New York Public Library, the center of human culture and knowledge, is spooked by a slimy, green phantasm. Two paranormal psychologists—"scientific cranks"—at Columbia University, Dr. Venkman (Bill Murray) and Dr. Ferber (Dan Akroyd), learn of the event and go to investigate. They find green slime everywhere; it is ectoplasmic residue—mucus! They then encounter a horrific apparition and run. Upon returning to Columbia University, they learn that the scientific grant funding their research has been terminated because their paranormal experiments were largely hoaxes. Now in the "private sector" (meaning they must actually *work* to make a living), they decide to go into the ghostbusting business; that is, they will rid dwellings of their supernatural presences. They mortgage Akroyd's house and set up shop in a decrepit firehouse, using an old hearse as a ghostbustermobile.

Meanwhile, a beautiful musician,[9] Dana Barrett (Sigourney Weaver), returns to her apartment in an elegant building in New York. Her nerdy next-door neighbor, Louis, an accountant, flirts with her in an awkward way. She enters her apartment and sees her television is already on; the Ghostbusters ad is playing. When she enters her kitchen, several bizarre events occur: eggs hop onto the counter and fry, a growling monster is in her refrigerator, and there is a vision of a temple with the god's name uttered, Zoule.

Dana rushes over to Ghostbusters headquarters, where the skirt-chasing, charlatan scientist Venkman quickly latches on to her. He accompanies her to her apartment, flirting constantly. Venkman finds nothing abnormal in her apartment, but he pledges to save her from any monsters, should they return. Venkman returns to Ghostbusters headquarters, where reports of ghost, gremlin, and ghoul attacks are beginning to pour in. They are called to several buildings to catch the nasty creatures, which they then carry back to their office and deposit in a huge bin. The Ghostbusters become media celebrities and soon have more business than they can handle. They hire a black man, Winston Sedmore, to be a third partner.[10]

Venkman and Akroyd have located a mythic reference to Zoule, the monster that threatened Dana; he is a demigod in the Hittite and Sumerian pantheon. Venkman tells Dana this and then again asks her for a date. Meanwhile, storm clouds have been collecting around Dana's building. Lightning (supernatural power) strikes one of the demonic gargoyles atop the building, causing it to come to life. The gargoyle enters Dana's apartment and kidnaps her. The monster gargoyle next enters Louis's apartment next door, where his party is in full swing. It chases Louis into Central Park (a wild place) and attacks him; Louis is transformed into a persona termed the Keymaster, a male demigod.

When Venkman arrives at Dana's apartment a short while later to take her on a date, he finds her completely transformed into a seductive goddess, called the Gatekeeper. (This is a funny and clever way to set up a mythological date between Louis and Dana. Only when the Keymaster inserts his key into the Gatekeeper's gate can Zoule enter the world!) When Venkman answers that *he* is the Keymaster, Dana lies back on her bed and spreads her legs; she is "possessed" by carnal sexuality. Her voice is that of the demon (like Regan's in *The Exorcist*), and she growls and floats in the air. Venkman doses her with Thorazine, rather than having sex with her.

Akroyd and Winston examine the blueprints to Dana's building and discover it was designed as an entry point for evil destruction on Judgment Day, which is apparently rapidly approaching in New York City. When a pesky Environmental Protection Agency inspector shows up at Ghostbuster headquarters, he releases all the caged goblins and all hell breaks loose. Carried by violent winds, the bad spirits spread across New York; the mayor, in desperation, sends for the Ghostbusters to save the city. Dana awaits Louis in her elevated bed. He arrives; they make love, bringing forth Zoule into the world.

The mayor, convinced that Judgment Day has indeed arrived, sends the Ghostbusters forth to battle the spirit of evil. They jump in the Ghostbuster-mobile and race toward Dana's building; people of all faiths pray for their success. An enormous storm has gathered over the building, the building itself is heaving, and the pavement around it buckles and erupts. The Ghostbusters climb the stairs to the top of the structure, the contact point between gods and humans (as in *Close Encounters*). Blue lightning illuminates the top. Dana and Louis turn into a pair of monstrous dogs; a pyramidal temple rests atop the building.

Zoule arrives and is depicted to be a female, Amazon-like creature; the destructive goddess is still very much with us in the 1980s. She has a deep, demonic voice and shoots lightning from her fingers at the Ghostbusters. Here we have a confluence of iconic conventions drawn from prior cinematic depictions such as *Exorcist* and *Star Wars.* The Ghostbusters confront Zoule, pointing their stick weapons (symbolic penises) at her. The building begins to quake, and a voice instructs them: "Choose the form of the Destructor." Akroyd inadvertently brings to mind the Staypuft Marshmallow Man. This causes a huge Staypuft figure to begin walking through the town, panicking the populace. The Ghostbusters train their electron beams on him, exploding Mr. Staypuft and the entire top of the building in a huge burst of flame and melted marshmallow. The Ghostbusters triumph; they find Louis and Dana encrusted in demon-dog statues, but otherwise unharmed. They exit the building and are embraced by the cheering throng. They have saved the world, or at least New York.

Ghostbusters was a wonderful, mythical romp, featuring ghosts, demons, ancient gods, and modern special effects. Toward the end of the 1980s, however, darker clouds loomed on our cultural horizon. The stock market crashed (October 6, 1987), taking with it much societal optimism. We turned our attention toward much more material, and materialistic, villains. We now examine three films which dealt with this form of evil, albeit in widely disparate ways: *Batman, Beverly Hills Cop,* and *Rain Man.*

Batman (1989)

Batman opens with director Tim Burton's apocalyptic vision of American capitalism in the late 1980s. The city, Gotham, is dark, cold, and dismal; its inhabitants grim and cynical. Crime is rampant and there is no sign of salvation. A mother, father, and young son search for a cab along deserted streets. They are confronted by two hoodlums who terrorize the family and steal all their valuables. Later, however, as the two criminals look over their loot in an alleyway a strange apparition appears before them: A huge bat-man with a voluminous black cape and black body armor (like Darth Vader). The bat-man terrorizes *them* and warns them to tell their cronies that he is now on guard in Gotham. Batman, as we shall see, is a dark warrior for a dark time.

A Machiavellian criminal, Jack Napier (Jack Nicholson) tells his blond girlfriend, whom he has stolen from crime lord Boss Grisham (Jack Palance), that he intends to take over "the action" in Gotham. He is envious of the media attention Batman is receiving; and indeed, two reporters are hot on the trail of Batman. One of them, Vicky Vale (Kim Bassinger), is also blond and beautiful. The next evening two critical events occur. First, Bruce Wayne (alias Batman, alias Michael Keaton) hosts an elegant fund-raiser at his enormous estate outside town. Bruce is an orphan; his parents were slain by a vicious hold-up man when he was a young boy. In fact, the opening scenes of the mother, father, and child being accosted in Gotham's dark streets exactly duplicate his own experience—except his mother and father were slain, because there was no one to come to their aid. As we shall find out, their killer was none other than Jack Napier. Vickie Vale is attending Wayne's charity fete and catches his eye; they flirt with each other as Vale looks over Wayne's large and varied collection of warrior costumes (for example, samurai, knight costumes) on display at his home. Wayne is being shown to us as someone fascinated by the warrior role.

That same evening, Boss Grisham and a fat, dirty, crooked police lieutenant have set up Jack Napier's death. Jack has been sent by Grisham to Axis Chemicals, a mob-run industry, ostensibly to secure some records. While there, he is to be shot by crooked police. Wayne/Batman discovers the break-in and arrives before Napier is killed; however, as he is pursuing Napier, the crook falls into a vat of chemicals. When he recovers, he has been transformed into the Joker, a hideous and cruel man whose face always wears a false smile. A few days later, Bruce Wayne invites Vicky Vale to dinner at his estate. They begin the evening in the mansion's huge dining room, but soon move to the more cozy and intimate kitchen, where Alfred, Wayne's butler and surrogate parent, regales them with stories of Bruce's childhood exploits. Bruce and Vicky are smitten with each other and go to bed; she wears a white bathrobe, he a black robe. Late that night, she awakens to see him hanging upside down, batlike, from a chinning bar in the bedroom.

Jack Napier/Joker visits Boss Grisham and shoots him to death, laughing wildly all the while. The Joker then gathers together the other crime lords and tells them he is the new overlord. When one resists, Jack electrocutes him; he has become completely insane. A few days later, the Joker invites the remaining crime lords to a news conference and arranges to have them all killed. He is now the dominant evil force in Gotham; he rails against Batman's fame and media attention. Back at Axis Chemicals, the company where the vat of chemicals transformed him into the Joker, Jack Napier begins manufacturing cosmetics that poison their users. The Joker/Napier inserts himself into television broadcasts and challenges Batman to fight him.

Pretending to be Bruce Wayne, the Joker sets up a date with Vicky Vale at an art museum. He then poisons everyone there, except Vale; he has disfigured and killed his own blond mistress and intends to make Vale his next girlfriend. Batman learns of the scheme and rescues Vicky, taking her to the Batmobile. After some more skirmishes with the Joker's henchmen, Batman takes Vale through the dark night into a secret tunnel in a mountain. He has carried her to his inner sanctum, his lair, but still does not reveal his true identity; he gives Vale a dossier of information he has collected on the Joker's deeds, which she is to publish in the newspaper.

Alfred urges Bruce to tell Vicky the truth about himself, to permit himself a genuine relationship with a woman. (Like most public warrior archetypes, Bruce Wayne/Batman shies away from romantic entanglements. In service to their mythic function, they must remain unattached, so they are free to fight for all of us, not just their personal family.) Bruce goes to Vicky's house intending to finally tell her the truth. Just before he reveals himself, the Joker enters the apartment and guns down Bruce; he is not killed, however, having put a silver tray under his shirt. Before shooting Bruce, the Joker taunts him by saying, "Did you ever dance with the devil in the pale moonlight?" the same taunt he had made to Bruce's parents many years ago before killing them. Thus the Joker and Batman have been predestined to confront each other; they are on a mutually destructive trajectory.

That night, the Joker announces he will give away $20,000,000 to Gotham residents who attend a midnight (the witching hour) parade he is sponsoring. Meanwhile, Alfred has fetched Vicky Vale, dressed in a beautiful white dress, and brought her to Wayne, all in black, in the Bat Cave. Wayne's true persona is revealed; Vicky vows to love and support him. Wayne loves her, but is called to his warrior role. He races to blow up Axis Chemicals, but the Joker is still at large. That evening, the Joker's bizarre parade gets under way through the darkened streets of Gotham. The Joker's black-garbed henchmen throw money to the groveling throngs. Vicky Vale and other news journalists are there. Suddenly, a sickly green gas begins shooting from the garish parade floats (recall the green cloud of death in *The Ten Commandments*); the gas is a poison intended to kill the crowd.

Batman arrives, flying overhead in his Batplane. He snatches up the poisonous balloons and carries them out to the edge of the stratosphere, saving the city. The Joker positions himself in the middle of the street, pulling a huge, long gun (penis) from his pants. Amazingly, he shoots down the Batplane, causing it to crash. (He is obviously a very potent opponent!) The Joker then kidnaps Vicky Vale and hauls her to the top of Gotham Cathedral. Once again we have a high structure representing a contact point between gods and humans or, in this case, good and evil. Batman follows them upward on foot, that is, on equal footing, with the Joker;

Fotos International/Archive Photos

Batman, the archetypal public warrior.

both are mortals, albeit very unusual ones. At the top of the tower, the Joker has secreted several thugs whom he sends to fight Batman, while he waltzes with Vicky Vale. Vicky is still in her white, virgin-bride dress. Batman finally reaches the Joker, and they fight—each accusing the other of causing him to be as he is: "You made me. You dropped me into those chemicals," "No, you killed my parents; you made me first." During the struggle, all three dangle perilously over the edge of the cathedral. The Joker falls to his death on the dark, mean streets below. After pulling himself and Vicky Vale to safety, Batman stands triumphant atop the tower against the night sky.

Batman is a dark, nighttime hero, qualitatively different from heroes we have encountered before. This can be seen most vividly by comparing Batman to his purer, daytime counterpart, Superman. Superman is a superhuman, godlike figure. Like Jesus and E.T., Superman came from the heavens and brought a higher moral code and sacred knowledge to mortal humans. Superman also, like E.T. and Jesus, possesses special powers with which he can work miracles, like bringing the dead back to life, and he is himself immortal.[11] Bruce Wayne/Batman, however, is a mortal man, like ourselves, who does remarkable feats, like Indiana Jones or Han Solo, but, at least as far as the narrative reveals to us, is not divinely inspired or directed. Both Ben Hur and Moses were also "mere mortals," but were depicted as acting through divine providence. Similarly, Luke Skywalker also appears to be a divinely inspired mortal; the Force that guides and empowers Luke is mythically equivalent to the biblical concept of God/Yahweh.

Bruce Wayne/Batman also was created by a significantly different process than Superman. Recall that Superman, like Jesus, was raised in a loving, humble family. He left these humble origins as manhood approached and sought out his supernatural birthright; Clark Kent became transformed into Superman. Similarly, Jesus left his origins as a carpenter's son and became the Christ, the savior of mankind. Thus, both Superman and Jesus emerged from pure, untroubled origins to assume their adult status as messiah or savior. Batman/Bruce Wayne, conversely, was created from a horrific tragedy—the murder of his parents. Further, rather than coming from simple, humble surroundings, Bruce Wayne was born into a family of enormous wealth and privilege. His tragic past, coupled with his ready access to unlimited funds for creating his Batman weapons and persona—the Batmobile, the Batplane, the dark caverns filled with technological gadgetry—provide him with a different mission and method of operation. Batman does not *enlighten* mankind, so much as he battles darkness. His own inner self is very dark, filled with unhappiness and isolationism. In eliminating tangible, external demons, such as the Joker, he seeks to exorcise his own invisible, internal demons. Thus, while Clark Kent makes friends and forms relationships and even works at a bustling "day job," Bruce Wayne spends most of his time locked away, alone in his castle, brooding.

Interestingly, both these characters have very similar lovers: Superman and Lois Lane, Batman and Vicky Vale. Besides the fact that Lois and Vicky both share duplicating initials, they also both work as highly competent, inquisitive, assertive *newspaper reporters,* a remarkable coincidence! I think this occupation was chosen for both women because it places them in positions of protecting the public interest. In essence, they are women whose job it is to be truth-tellers. That is, the press functions to inform the public and to expose crime and corruption. Batman and Superman function to battle crime and corruption.

Further, because both Batman and Superman are representatives of the public warrior archetype, they are permitted to have girlfriends (like Matt Dillon and Kitty in *Gunsmoke*) but not to marry and father children. For to do so would privatize their protective powers and make them less available to us, the public, as warriors against evil. Finally, I must add that Batman/Bruce Wayne, to me, most closely represents Paladin of all the warrior icons we have encountered previously. Both have a dark, melancholic quality, both rely on state-of-the-art technology to fight criminals, and both originated in very wealthy families. Indeed, of all the heroes we have discussed, only Paladin and Batman *dress* in black.

Beverly Hills Cop (1984)

Above we have been using the term "black" in a metaphoric sense. In American culture, blackness and darkness have negative associations; we speak, for example, of black moods or dark clouds to describe unhappiness or misfortune. Often, villains or evil persons are garbed or cloaked in black, for example, Darth Vader and the Star Wars emperor. Yet on occasion our cultural storytellers will play against this convention, placing good men in black costume, for example, Paladin, Batman, and Zorro. Also in our society, black skin has also been all too frequently cast in a negative metaphorical light. Black and dark-skinned persons are treated derisively, viewed as dangerous outlaws, or seen as unworthy and unheroic. This cultural bias has carried over into and been transmitted by our myths, including those on television and in motion picture theaters. In our analysis, we have now reached the epochal year of 1989, and still no person of color has been presented to us as a heroic archetype.[12] And then along comes Eddie Murphy and *Beverly Hills Cop.*

What is particularly notable about this film is its direct manner of acknowledging and addressing American culture's deep prejudices against and fears of young, black men. In the film, Eddie Murphy's character, Axel Foley, is not cleaned up or sanitized. He is not purified for white audiences. In short, he is *not* an Oreo. Further, as we shall see, the film makes excellent symbolic use of playing an honest, poor black man against a crooked, wealthy white man, exposing the inherent corruption of smug, white capitalism, whose very victims are most often black laborers.

At the outset, two sets of archetypes are set into oppositional play, the cities of Detroit and Beverly Hills and the characters of Axel Foley and Victor Maitland. The story opens in Detroit, depicted as a decrepit, poor, industrial-era carcass, afflicted by rusted-out cars, abandoned buildings, closed factories, and unemployed black residents. This is the dark side of American capitalism, the detritus, discards, and despair. Axel Foley functions in this environment as an undercover cop. He is courageous, clever, and resourceful, but seldom follows the rules. This pattern has caused his (also black) police chief to view him as a talented pain in the ass. The Detroit Police Department itself mirrors the city it protects and serves. It is overcrowded, run-down, low-tech, and underfunded.

Axel drives home to his run-down apartment in his "crappy old blue Chevy Nova." Here he finds his best friend, Mikey Tandino, ensconced in the kitchen eating leftovers; Mikey has a prison record, having taken a stolen car rap for Axel several years ago, and is out on probation. Already Mikey has gotten into trouble again by stealing a bagful of bearer bonds from Victor Maitland, his wealthy employer in Beverly Hills. Hoodlums employed by Maitland ambush Axel and Mikey, taking back the stolen bonds and killing Mikey. The Detroit police arrive, and the chief, sensing trouble, warns Axel *not* to pursue the case himself. Axel, of course, feigns acquiescence and then uses his vacation time to travel to Beverly Hills in search of Mikey's killers.

Axel drives his decrepit car to Beverly Hills, where the contrast between his home city and that of this mecca of white affluence is shocking. He marvels at the palm trees, mansions, boulevards, exclusive stores, and elegant hotels. Still, he remains his clever, resourceful, wise-ass self. Arriving at a posh hotel, he pretends to be a writer for *Rolling Stone* magazine. When told that no rooms are available, he plays upon white, liberal guilt by complaining, loudly, that he is being rejected because of his race: "No niggers are allowed in the Beverly Palms Hotel." The blond, WASP staff rushes quickly to assuage him by offering up a suite of rooms. After ensconcing himself in the hotel, Axel goes to visit Jenny, a pretty, young, blond childhood friend of his and Mikey's. She works as a receptionist at Victor Maitland's art gallery and had gotten Mikey his job there. Jenny is shocked to learn of Mikey's murder.

Axel, pretending to be a flower delivery boy, obtains access to Maitland's office. Victor is blond, European, highly cultivated, well dressed, and extremely wealthy. After first pretending to be solicitous of Axel, his manner changes quickly and he has several bodyguards toss him out of the entrance to the building. There, two white, blond, uniformed Los Angeles police officers immediately pull their guns on Axel, cuff him, and read him his Miranda rights. They then transport Axel to the enormous, beautiful, spotless, high-tech Beverly Hills Police Department. Sergeant Taggart and Detective Rosewood encounter Foley; Taggart gets into a fight with him. At this point, the blond, white police lieutenant makes Taggart apologize to Foley. Foley is now fully aware that "Beverly Hills is not like Detroit."

Jenny picks up Axel and takes him back to his hotel, followed by Taggart and Rosewood, who are to make sure Foley gets into no further mischief. Axel foils them, however, by first sending food out to their surveillance car and then stuffing a banana into their tail pipe (a homosexual innuendo). Axel and Jenny visit Maitland's large art warehouse, where Axel discovers coffee grounds, suggesting that Maitland is actually smuggling cocaine. Here the implication is that the most seemingly respectable and elite people may actually be crooked scum; appearances can be deceiving. They next visit a customs inspection warehouse where Foley, after browbeating all the white security personnel ("How could you let someone who looks like me sneak into a place like this!"), obtains records indicating Maitland's shipments are indeed being smuggled past customs.

Axel befriends Taggart and Rosewood—they are, after all, fellow cops—and takes them to a strip bar. When two armed robbers arrive, Axel foils them, but gives the credit to Taggart and Rosewood. However, the two officers tell their superior the truth,

Archive Photos

Eddie Murphy as Axel Foley in Beverly Hills Cop *expands our cultural notion of the warrior.*

that Axel was the hero. Axel follows Maitland and his primary bodyguard to an exclusive men's club. Pretending to be the gay lover of Maitland, Axel enters the club and confronts Victor, accusing him of smuggling cocaine and killing Michael Tandino. Maitland's bodyguard lunges at Axel, who tosses him across the buffet table. Once again, a pair of blond Beverly Hills cops arrive and arrest Axel.

Once again taken to the police station, Axel tells the police lieutenant, as well as Taggart and Rosewood, that he suspects Maitland of drug smuggling and murder. They are sympathetic, but the old white male police chief enters the room and orders Foley escorted to the city limits. However, on the way out of town, Axel convinces Rosewood to get Jenny to let them give Maitland's warehouse one last search. Within the warehouse, Axel and Jenny discover a huge cache of cocaine; however, Maitland and his men discover *them.* Jenny is taken to Maitland's house while Foley is beaten. Courageously, Rosewood enters the warehouse and rescues Axel. The pair race to Maitland's house to rescue Jenny, where Taggart joins them; unable to wait for a search warrant, the three jump the wall to the estate. The estate itself is well guarded and monitored by video surveillance. Characteristically, Axel, dressed in jeans and a sweatshirt, is much more adept at sneaking up on the house than are Taggart and Rosewood, both attired in suits and hampered by their more formal personas.

Axel enters the house to locate Jenny, killing the cruel bodyguard who had executed Mikey Tandino; but Victor Maitland shoots Axel in the arm. A swarm of police cars converge on the estate, surrounding it. Maitland holds Jenny hostage, but she bravely breaks free. Axel and the Beverly Hills police lieutenant both shoot at and kill Maitland. When the chief of police arrives demanding an official explanation, the lieutenant creates an elaborate cover story, exonerating Taggart, Rosewood, and Foley of any misconduct. He has learned the lesson that sometimes the gaining of genuine justice requires the breaking of formal rules. In the closing scene, Axel checks out of the posh Beverly Palm Hotel for his trip back to Detroit. Taggart and Rosewood arrive to escort him to the city limits and pay for his room at the department's expense. Axel gives them each a luxurious Beverly Palm bathrobe, having already taken one for himself.

Beverly Hills Cop is a parable of opposites and contrasts. It tells us that it is better to bend small rules in the pursuit of justice than to observe every etiquette while engaging in criminally corrupt acts. Axel Foley, a black man from Detroit, is not well bred, cultured, or polite; yet he exemplifies the heroic qualities of courage, loyalty, and goodness. Victor Maitland is a white man from Beverly Hills, elegant, tasteful, aristocratic, and ever so proper. Yet beneath his glittering surface lies a cruel, sadistic, selfish, and conscienceless brute. We are asked to judge which is the "better" man.

Rain Man (1989)

Batman and Axel Foley, each in his own distinctive way, showed Americans how to overcome the destructive aspects of greed and power-seeking. We next take a look at a hero who teaches the same lesson, but in a much gentler way. There are two paths to treating corruption of the spirit and soul. One is to root it out violently, destroying the host who is carrying the corruption in the process. The Joker and Victor Maitland were both destroyed, and their tales advise us that the world is a better place for their absence. But the path less taken, particularly in rough-tough American culture, is one of passivity, simplicity, and purity. Every once in a while, one person simply bumbling through life in an innocent, childlike way can serve to remind the rest of us, who are busy carrying our selfish grudges, corrupting ourselves with resentment and bitterness, and treating others like means to our ends, that life can be serene and meaningful, if we just permit it to be so.

Rain Man is just such a story. It opens with Charles Babbitt (Tom Cruise), a young, cool L.A. hustler who imports expensive sports cars for a living. It is not coincidental that he has been given Sinclair Lewis's fictional surname "Babbitt," for Charlie Babbitt is a materialistic, self-serving, manipulative wheeler-dealer, a young Victor Maitland in the making. His Italian girlfriend, Susannah, and friend Vince both work for him, and he treats them abusively. Charlie's father dies, and he and Susannah attend the funeral; Charlie remains standing at some distance from the ceremony.

The will is read, and Charlie learns his father has left him only a Buick Roadmaster convertible, which he had once driven without permission, infuriating his father. The rest of the estate, $3,000,000 has been placed in trust for an unknown beneficiary. Charlie is consumed with bitterness; he drives to the bank and, through flattery and manipulation, learns that the beneficiary is a home for retarded adults, the Wallbrook Institute. Charlie storms into Wallbrook and demands of Dr. Bruner, the head of the institute, an explanation as to why "his" inheritance has ended up there. While they are talking, a middle-aged autistic man, Raymond (Dustin Hoffman), climbs into the Buick with Susannah, telling her it is his father's car. Charlie returns with Bruner and demands to know "Who is this guy?" whereupon Bruner replies, "He's your brother, Raymond."

Charlie is astonished. "I never knew I had a brother." He learns that Raymond is a high-functioning autistic savant who dwells largely in a world of his own construction. Ray has some extraordinary mental gifts including an eidetic (photographic) memory and remarkable mathematical talent. Charlie walks Ray to the end of the long institute drive and puts him in their father's car with Susannah and drives him away, essentially kidnapping him.

There is some rich symbolism here, much of it ironic, that we need to attend to before proceeding further. First, the *car* is a critical metaphor. Charlie makes his living importing and selling "special" cars. Yet, ironically, it was using his father's "special" car without permission that drove him away from his father. Now returned, he is again driving the car, this time with his dead father's permission, and has used it to discover his lost brother, Raymond. Charlie and Raymond are now together, for the first time, in this same car and are driving off to a new relationship. In essence, the car is the catalyst and vehicle for their relationship as brothers.

That night, Charlie and Susannah learn just how ordered Ray's life must be; he has food habits, sleeping habits, bathing habits, and television viewing habits. Charlie gives him the phone book to read. Late in the evening Ray wanders in on Charlie and Susannah making love. Charlie becomes enraged at him, calling Ray an idiot; Susannah, by now disgusted with Charlie's selfishness, leaves him: "You need nobody; you use everybody."

The next morning, Charlie and Ray eat at a small diner. Charlie is astonished when some of Ray's mental gifts emerge. He remembers the waitress's phone number from reading the phone book the night before and is also able to calculate correctly the number of toothpicks accidentally spilled on the floor. However, Charlie continues being abusive and cruel to him. Charlie calls Dr. Burner from the diner and tells him for $1.5 million (half the inheritance), he will return Ray to the institute, but Bruner refuses. Charlie drives to the airport, intending to take Ray to Los Angeles. But Ray balks and begins screaming hysterically at the sight of the airplane. Charlie relents; they will drive to Los Angeles in the Buick.

Ray proves to be a troublesome passenger. They cannot use the interstate highways, because he fears an accident. They cannot drive when it is raining, because he does not like rain. Every afternoon at five o'clock, they must stop so that Ray can watch his favorite television program, *People's Court.* When Ray insists on locating a Kmart at which to purchase boxer shorts, Charlie realizes he has no grasp of what is going on in Ray's mind. He drives to a small-town clinic and, finding no psychiatrist, asks the local doctor for help. The doctor is a gentle soul and explains what autism is, and that Ray requires a structured, stable environment. He tells Charlie to just "take a break" if Ray gets on his nerves, rather than lashing out at him in frustration and anger.

The brothers continue their journey through the vast wilderness of the West, where many others have gone to find themselves. Charlie's money is running out; but he does not burden Ray with this, realizing that he is Ray's caregiver. As they stop at a cheap roadside motel, he carefully places Ray's bed by the window, puts out his pens and papers, and furnishes him with his cheese balls, apple juice, and tartar control toothpaste. Charlie is learning to love. Ray shows Charlie a picture of the two of them: Charlie is a toddler, Ray about twenty. Charlie recalls that Raymond (Rain Man) would sing and comfort him when he was scared. Ray was sent away when Charlie was a little over two, because he accidentally burned Charlie with hot water.

This is epiphanic for Charlie; he realizes now that Ray was institutionalized to protect Charlie's well-being. Charlie's bitterness toward his own bad luck begins to look very meager compared to the limited, narrow life his brother has led. Charlie gently helps Ray get into bed, carefully placing his slippers nearby. He calls Susannah and tells her he very much wants to continue their relationship; he is learning how to form bonds and make emotional commitments, two areas in which Charlie had long been "disabled."

Charlie and Ray hit the road again; Charlie has bought Ray a small, battery-powered television set so he can watch his favorite programs. Charlie learns that his imported cars have been impounded in Los Angeles; his business closed. Charlie is angry; however, his anger is due to fear that he will lose custody of Ray, if he has no income. Ray is no longer an "inheritance" to him; he is a brother. When the pair stops at a Nevada diner and Ray memorizes the entire jukebox selection in minutes, Charlie gets a brainstorm. He shows Ray a deck of cards and within seconds, Ray has memorized their numbers and order. They hop in the Buick and head for Las Vegas.

Once there, Charlie pawns his Rolex watch, the last material possession of his former life, to obtain gambling funds. He and Ray purchase new suits, shoes, and haircuts; thus transformed, they hit the casinos. They win big and are given a huge, lavish room designated for high rollers. Charlie moves Ray's bed near the window, where he likes it. He teaches Ray how to dance, but when he spontaneously embraces Ray, Ray screams and cringes. Ironically, Charlie is now willing and able to give more love than Ray can accept. Thankfully, Susannah arrives at their door, willing to give her relationship with Charlie a second chance, and Charlie embraces her.

The next day, Charlie and Susannah ride as passengers, while Ray drives the Buick around the cascading fountains at the hotel. The soundtrack plays "You can't take that away from me." Charlie and Susannah have provided Ray with experiences he would never have encountered in the institute; they have broadened his boundaries.

But there are limits. The three drive on to Los Angeles and find that Dr. Bruner is also there to seek custody of Ray; that evening Charlie and Bruner talk. Bruner offers Charlie $25,000 to relinquish custody of Ray, but Charlie refuses; he no longer wants to trade his brother for money. The next morning, there is a custody hearing. Ray wakes up early and accidentally sets off the smoke detector in the kitchen. The sound makes him hysterical and he bangs himself against the door. Charlie rescues him but realizes that Ray cannot live in an unsupervised place. They arrive at the hearing in the Buick that has served so well as their vehicle of self-discovery and brotherhood. Charlie admits he was wrong to "steal" Ray; but also insists that, "I don't want to give him up; this is my family." However, when Ray grows increasingly confused and humiliated trying to choose between Charlie and Dr. Bruner, Charlie, displaying true love—and the wisdom of Solomon—agrees to give up full-time custody of Ray in exchange for open visitation rights. He tells Ray, "Dr. Bruner really likes you and will take good care of you; I like having you for my brother." Ray rests his head on Charlie's shoulder: "I like having you for a brother." The next morning, Charlie brings Ray to the Amtrak station and puts him on the train to Cincinnati with Dr. Bruner; Charlie gives him a backpack filled with his favorite items and tells Ray he will come to see him in two weeks. Ray replies, "That's 20,160 minutes."

As the astute reader has no doubt already noted, we are closing the decade of the 1980s as we opened it: with a brilliant portrayal of humanity by actor Dustin Hoffman. As Dorothy Michaels, Hoffman instructed us on transforming ourselves into gender-balanced, androgynous, whole people, capable of loving deeply and empowering ourselves simultaneously. This was a lesson men and women struggling with the sexual legacy of the 1970s needed to learn. As we leave the 1980s, a decade more renowned for its greed and material vulgarity than for spirituality or kindness, we once again have a deeply etched performance by Hoffman to ponder. Raymond Babbitt is a man with many limitations, narrow boundaries, and low ceilings. Yet, ironically, he is brilliant at numbers—the iconic currency of the decade. And as the tale teaches us, he is even more brilliant at illuminating the value of love, caring, and commitment—the very items no amount of money can buy.

— SEVEN —

TELEVISION SHOWS IN THE 1980s

THE LATE 1970S blended almost imperceptibly into the early 1980s. Ronald Reagan, a Hollywood actor of lesser rank, assumed the presidency; peace and prosperity dominated the domestic landscape. The nation grew simultaneously more conservative politically, yet more liberal in finance. We were headed toward a cultural obsession with materialism; we worshipped Wall Street, business, power, status, and, most of all, *money* and all the things it could buy. Michael Milken, Carl Icahn, Ivan Boesky, and Donald Trump were cultural icons. Tom Wolfe wrote *The Bonfire of the Vanities* in 1987, capturing the spirit of the era perfectly. Six television shows both reflected the spirit of the era and also contested it. They present archetypes of greed and villainy—and also generosity and community. They are *Dallas, M.A.S.H., Magnum P.I., Cheers, The Cosby Show,* and *Roseanne.*

Dallas

One particular show, in the view of many, encapsulated the ideology of the late 1970s through 1987: *Dallas. Dallas* is the saga of the Ewing family of Texas. Founded by John Ross "Jock" Ewing (Jim Davis), the family consists of Jock's wife, Miss Ellie (Barbara Bel Geddes); oldest son, J. R. Ewing Jr. (Larry Hagman); J. R.'s wife, Sue Ellen (Linda Gray), who is a former Miss Texas; a middle son, Gary, who was alcoholic and ended up in California on *Knot's Landing;* his teenaged daughter, Lucy (Charlene Tilton); and a third son, Bobby (Patrick Duffy), who has married Pamela Barnes (Victoria Principal), the daughter of the oil prospector Jock cheated to become rich—Digger Barnes. Opposing the Ewings is Digger's son, Cliff (Ken Kercheval), an attorney and politician whose avowed goal is the destruction of Ewing Oil.

Perhaps the major reason *Dallas* so dominated the late 1970s and early and mid 1980s is that it carried within its narrative framework such a rich mixture of archetypal figures. There were good mothers (Miss Ellie), teenage sirens (Lucy), trophy wives a là Tom Wolfe (Sue Ellen), and good wives (Pam) among the women. And among the men there were rogue adventurers (Jock Ewing), good warriors (Bobby Ewing), and greedy villains (J. R. Ewing).[1] Further, the show juxtaposed two ideological value systems that were currently dueling for dominance within American society: (1) the communal, populist, cooperative ideology espoused during the 1960s and 1970s by the hippies (and for decades by union workers) versus (2) the hierarchical, elitist, competitive, get-rich-at-any-cost ethic represented by Wall Street and the junk bond kings, such as Henry Kravis and Michael Milken. Indeed, within the Ewing family itself, Miss Ellie with her family background in cattle ranching, her generous spirit, and her Mother Earth personality represented an oppositional ideology to that of her husband, Jock, who had gotten rich by sucking oil out of the land and cheating his partner.

Each episode of *Dallas* begins with images that show the ideological contrast discussed above: scenes of cowboys (the "workingman" in a Marxist sense), cattle, and land are juxtaposed with oil rigs, freeways, and the gleaming office towers of Dallas, Texas.

These represent the two cultures of America: the rural and agricultural versus the urban and technological. As we learn from the series, goodness lies in the humble countryside; corruption and power are centered in the city.

The Ewings themselves live in a baronial ranch house—virtually a contradiction in terms—a large, white, elegant house that happens to be located in the middle of a cattle ranch. Oil money and business prowess built the house; the ranch land came from Miss Ellie's family, where it has been used to raise cattle for generations. Thus, the rural/urban dichotomy is carried consistently through the props of the narrative. In one of the first episodes, Bobby Ewing is driving with his new wife, Pamela Barnes Ewing, to South Fork Ranch. They are casually dressed and very much in love. Because they've married on impulse, this is Pam's first trip to the Ewing Ranch as Bobby's wife.

Concurrently, Pam's brother, Cliff, is leading an investigation into Ewing Oil's crooked business dealings. Pam and Cliff are the children of Digger Barnes, an oil prospector cheated by Jock Ewing decades before. Ewing Oil Company is headquartered in an enormous (phallic) skyscraper at the center of Dallas. Founded by Jock, it is now run by his eldest son, J. R. J. R. is crafty, competitive, and crooked. He wears handsome, well-tailored suits and short-cropped hair—the 1970s–1980s icon of a slick businessman. Jock telephones J. R. and directs him to "call in his markers" by pressuring state politicians under Ewing control to derail Cliff's investigation.

Jock next goes to talk with Ray Krebs. Recalling that Ray used to date Pam Barnes (and not yet knowing of Bobby and Pam's marriage), he pressures Ray to have her stop Cliff from pursuing his vendetta. Unknown to Jock and the Ewing family, Ray and Lucy Ewing (age sixteen) have been conducting a daily dalliance in the barn. Lucy, as we shall learn, is something of a teenage tramp: beautiful, blond, breasty, and bored. Bobby and Pam drive through the South Fork gate and up to the main house. Miss Ellie is incredulous that they have married; she is polite to Pam, but calls Jock and J. R. at the office and tells them to come home quickly. J. R. inquires if Bobby's new wife is "anybody," implying that marriages should be made for social and/or business reasons, not for love. This is why he married his own wife, Sue Ellen, a former Miss Texas. That evening, the Ewings gather in their living room eyeing Pam and deciding what to make of the situation. Their home is traditionally elegant, not ostentatious like their office building, representing the difference in character between Miss Ellie's authentic gentility and Jock's more crass new money.

The next morning, J. R. offers Pam money to "end this sham of a marriage"; Pam is insulted and refuses. That evening J. R. tells Jock of his failed payoff attempt, and Jock gives J. R. some sage advice: "You need to learn the art of subtlety; a lack of it turns competitors into enemies and enemies into fanatics." Jock tells J. R. that he, actually, is in favor of the marriage: "Pam's teaching Bobby to settle down and get serious about working in the business." J. R., of course, fears exactly this—he wants sole control of the company. Hearing Pam and Bobby laughing in their upstairs bedroom, J. R. further fears they will produce a child before he and Sue Ellen do.

J. R. Ewing of Dallas *epitomizes the fascination with greed, money, and power of the 1980s.*

Archive Photos

With Ray Krebs, who is also jealous of Pam and Bobby, J. R. plans to break up their marriage.

J. R. takes Bobby for a drive to Austin, while Pam is taken up in a helicopter for a tour of South Fork Ranch by Ray. Ray lands the helicopter near a lakeside cabin and playfully pushes Pam into the water, forcing her to disrobe and dry off in the cabin. J. R. then drives up with Bobby, attempting to trick him into thinking Ray and Pam are having an affair. Fortunately, Bobby sees through the ruse and, instead, learns to develop a wise suspicion of his older brother's intentions.

Pam's love for Bobby is genuine; despite being the daughter of an enemy, she is representative of the nurturant goddess archetype. In the next episode she exhibits behaviors consistent with this meaning. It is now winter at South Fork Ranch. Lucy—ever the "bad girl"—rides her horse daily to the mailbox, where she intercepts and burns letters from the school principal complaining of her consistent truancy. She prefers to stay home each day and have sex in the hayloft with Ray. However, Jock has now decided that Lucy must attend school. Miss Ellie tells Pam that she is concerned about Lucy's well-being: "She's spoiled; we just can't control her."

Pam gets a call from Lucy's school saying she is again absent. Pam marches to the barn, calls Ray and Lucy down from their hayloft, and loads Lucy in her car to take her to school. She uses a "gentle" form of blackmail, warning the pair that Lucy must attend school or she (Pam) will tell the Ewings of their illicit couplings. Once at school, Pam talks to Lucy's guidance counselor, a kind man named Mr. Miller, who promises to help Lucy catch up. While Lucy is in school, Pam purchases her several new, more modest outfits (Lucy had worn a red, skin-tight pants suit). Pam drives her home and, once again, warns Ray to leave Lucy alone.

The next day, Lucy visits Mr. Miller's office and, ripping her own blouse, fakes a sexual assault. (A young male student sees it but keeps mum.) Pam accuses Lucy of faking the incident and tells her it could cost Mr. Miller his job, but Lucy is unmoved. That night, the male student calls Lucy and forces her into a date, making it clear he expects to have sex with her in exchange for his silence about the phony assault. Lucy and the student go to a disco, where Bobby, Pam, and Ray Krebs and his date also happen to be. Lucy at first makes sexual advances toward Ray in an attempt to get him to help her dump the student. Bobby sees this and punches Ray. Pam, however, senses the deeper problem and accuses the student of blackmailing Lucy. The student confesses, and Lucy agrees to clear Mr. Miller's name the next day. Lucy has learned that Pam is strict, but genuinely cares about her welfare.

A third episode sharply contrasts Bobby and Pam's marriage and personal character with that of J. R. and Sue Ellen. The offices at Ewing Oil are noisy because of construction. To escape the noise, Bobby brings home some sensitive business files at lunch. He and Pam make love, and he accidentally leaves the files on the couch. J. R. also comes home early at lunchtime. Sue Ellen is delighted to see him; she has bought a new, silky black negligee, but J. R. coldly rejects her: "You're not acting like a lady . . . Put your clothes back on!" She pleads with him: "We never talk; we don't make love anymore." He yells at her and leaves, slamming the door.

J. R. returns to Dallas where he spends the evening with his beautiful secretary, Julie. Julie is J. R.'s "sexual comforter," a former girlfriend who was not of sufficient social or financial status to become his wife. Now, she serves as his assistant at work and bedmate upon request. Julie tells J. R. that he should go home to Sue Ellen; Sue Ellen loves him, and she, Julie, needs to move on with her life. J. R. has, once again, forgotten Julie's birthday; she realizes she is essentially a sexual service provider and will never be his wife or partner. J. R., however, seduces her once more, leaving as soon as the act is consummated and draping a $100 bill on her shoulder. (In essence, reducing her to a prostitute, whose sexual services are purchased.) Julie seeks revenge by calling up Cliff Barnes; she offers to take Cliff to dinner (using the $100 bill).

Meanwhile, at Ewing Oil, Jock, J. R., and Bobby discover that Bobby has left some potentially damaging information at home in the files he dropped on the couch. Bobby calls Pam and asks her to bring the files to town, which she does, placing them on Julie's desk. Julie reads the files and, sensing they could be helpful to Cliff's investigation—and damaging to J. R.—makes a copy. Cliff and Julie have a wonderful evening; she gives the documents to him as a gift. Cliff calls a press conference and uses the documents to discredit a legislator loyal to the Ewings. J. R. is furious, believing

Pam to be the source of the "leak." He denounces Pam as a spy and traitor in front of the family; no one—except Bobby—rises to her defense. Bobby, deeply angry at his family's suspicion of Pam, takes the two of them to a hotel.

Pam confronts Cliff, furious that his actions have come between her and her husband's family. In essence, Cliff has placed his own selfish political aspirations above her marriage—the same pattern J. R. has followed. Pam and Bobby discover Cliff's unlisted phone number in Julie's desk. Bobby informs J. R. that Julie, not Pam, is the culprit and that she acted out of emotional rejection caused by J. R.'s abusive behavior. That night, Bobby and Pam rejoin the Ewing household. Without revealing J. R.'s sexual indiscretions with Julie (which would injure Sue Ellen), Bobby informs the family that Julie, not Pam, was the traitor. He calls upon his family to apologize to Pam. They do so sheepishly. Pam is generous toward them, acknowledging the historic basis for their fears and distrust.

The narrative pattern of these three episodes, replayed innumerable times over a decade, constituted the moral conflict of *Dallas.* J. R., always attempting to consolidate his power and control over others, manipulating people as if they were chess pieces and satisfying his own carnal and ego needs, continuously creates an atmosphere of mistrust, betrayal, suspicion, and disappointment. In contrast, Bobby and Pam—and to some extent, Miss Ellie—just as ardently struggle to do the right thing, honor familial bonds, strengthen emotional relationships, and act honestly. At basis, it is the ancient tale of good versus evil cast in the modern-day context of America's struggle to define itself as an agrarian, communal culture or an urban, competitive culture.

M.A.S.H.

The series *M.A.S.H.* has several archetypal features setting it in opposition to *Dallas.* In contrast to *Dallas*'s stateside formula of capitalism and competition, *M.A.S.H.* portrays the plight of a community of American servicemen and -women stationed in Korea during the 1950s military conflict there. Metaphorically, it represents the ideological opposition to the Vietnam War, only recently fought by America at a great loss in lives, honor, and spirit.

Using humor, *M.A.S.H.* decries the inherent stupidity and impotence of war. "M.A.S.H." stands for "Mobile Army Surgical Hospital," and each episode presents a stream of emotional and/or physical casualties who stream into and out of the hospital's community. As with *Dallas, M.A.S.H.* juxtaposes opposing ideologies by embodying them in various characters. In the early episodes, opposition to the war and the military is represented by Benjamin "Hawkeye" Pierce (Alan Alda). Colonel Blake (McLean Stevenson), and Captain John McIntyre (Wayne Rogers), whereas law and order, patriotism and military power are supported by Major Frank Burns and Major Margaret "Hot Lips" Houlihan (Loretta Switt). The two primary iconoclasts, Drs. Blake and Pierce, display their radical ideology using biting wit and off-kilter apparel. Blake sports a fly-fishing hat, while Pierce favors Hawaiian shirts and khaki shorts. Conversely, Burns and Houlihan—surgeon and nurse, respectively—are always in full military regalia and continuously utter piously patriotic platitudes. Despite their militarism, the latter two characters display a lack of moral fiber. They engage in a daily romantic affair, despite Burns's marriage. (Thus, the series hints at their underlying hypocrisy.)

In the first episode, Houlihan expresses shock and disgust when Blake and Pierce bring a porno flick onto the base; yet she beds down with Major Burns that very evening. And, should the point be missed, Pierce states the obvious: "War is an even bigger obscenity." Angered by this, and by Burns's inability to make a commitment to her, Houlihan decides to transfer out of the unit. This is announced by Pierce over the loudspeaker with promises of a celebration banquet of wine and ice cream. However, when Houlihan stops by their tent to say good-bye, Pierce and McIntyre relent and offer her a drink from their homemade still. Houlihan drinks and then comes again to their tent to return Burns's possessions (he also lives in the tent with Pierce and McIntyre): love letters and a stuffed dog. She again imbibes from the still.

Now drunk, Houlihan goes to see Colonel Blake, telling him she still wishes to transfer out—but would also appreciate a drink from his extensive liquor cabinet. Just then a planeload of incoming casualties arrives. Houlihan knows she must stay and assist the surgeons; Pierce and McIntyre escort her to a cold shower—fully clothed—and thence to the operating tent, where she performs well. The next morning Houlihan is hung over, but has decided not to leave. She gets into her usual squabble with Burns and Pierce. Blake comments to McIntyre: "It's good to have the children all together again." Indeed, this is quite accurate, for *M.A.S.H.* is the story of a "family." We shall see this again in *Cheers, Friends, Murphy Brown,* and *Seinfeld.*)

In another episode, Houlihan makes several errors during an operation, unable to concentrate because a famous Army nurse, Colonel Reese, is due to arrive that evening. When Hawkeye humorously reprimands her sloppiness, Houlihan demands that Frank (her married lover) defend her honor. Frank berates Hawkeye, who then punches him. Frank then demands a court-martial against Hawkeye. Hawkeye is ordered confined to his tent. Colonel Reese arrives; she is a large, unattractive, and sex-starved woman. She quickly sizes up the men available: "I'm back in the saddle again." Hawkeye enjoys dinner in his tent; he's set up an elaborate repast complete with linen and crystal. The chaplain brings him by a steak and a P.O.W. care package.

The next day, Colonel Reese instructs Houlihan in correct surgical procedures and flirts with the doctors. That evening, the entire camp gathers in Hawkeye's tent to watch a Jean Tierney film. Colonel Blake gropes as many nurses as possible. Frank leaves the tent and goes to Houlihan's tent in search of love; he finds, instead, the amorous Colonel Reese in a red silk kimono. She offers him brandy and massages his shoulders, promising him career advancement in exchange for sex. But when Houlihan enters the tent, Reese screams "rape" and pretends Frank attacked her. Although the charge is not taken seriously, Frank is confined to his tent, and Hawkeye released.

We need to take an aside here and consider this story line a bit more deeply. By the late 1970s and early 1980s, women's sexuality had become more public—and publicized. Men feared the newly "liberated" sexual mores that permitted women greater latitude in approaching sexual partners, and a backlash got under way. Men believed that women might both aggressively seek out sex and then cry "rape," if they did not like what they got. Hence, in *Dallas* we have sexually active Lucy Ewing feigning a sexual attack to damage a teacher, and in *M.A.S.H.* the sexually aggressive Colonel Reese screaming "rape" to cover up her own philandering.

A final episode of *M.A.S.H.* brings us face-to-face with the true sense of community. An aid station in the combat zone is shelled, and the surgeon and nurse are killed. M.A.S.H. receives a request to replace them for a short time until new military medical personnel can be found. Houlihan immediately volunteers, and Hawkeye and Corporal Klinger (a man who cross-dresses to try to get an army discharge) are chosen by lot to go to the front. They say their farewells to their comrades at the hospital and set off in a jeep. On the way, live shells explode around them and a tire goes flat. Houlihan changes it herself to spare Hawkeye's (the surgeon's) hands.

The trio arrives at the aid station to find it totally decimated; they are confronted by the brutal chaos of war and death. Hawkeye immediately begins organizing the site, initiating triage and setting up operating equipment. Houlihan and Klinger also display admirable courage, resourcefulness, and cooperativeness. Operations are conducted under the most primitive of conditions, as bombs explode yards away. These scenes of heroism and commitment are contrasted with Dr. Burns complaining bitterly about the "horrendous" conditions he must operate under back at M.A.S.H., where supplies and sterilization are ample. Colonel Blake, McIntyre, and others gather in Hawkeye's tent that evening and hold a quiet vigil for their missing friends. At the front, Hawkeye, Klinger, and Houlihan share their army rations and huddle together under blankets—a community of necessity. The next day, the group successfully returns to M.A.S.H. Hawkeye, normally sarcastic to Houlihan, kisses her gently on the cheek: "Houlihan, you're my favorite officer."

Cheers

A similar type of community, albeit in a different setting, is found in *Cheers.* Cheers is a Boston bar—metaphorically, a communal watering hole—where a variety of different types of people come to drink and share experiences. The owner and primary bartender, Sam Malone (Ted Danson), is a recovering alcoholic and former baseball pitcher for the Boston Red Sox. His assistant bartender is a former baseball coach, and there are two waitresses, Carla (Rhea Perlman) and Diane Chambers (Shelley Long). The primary archetypal opposition within the program is between Sam, who represents masculine sexuality, athleticism, and earthiness, and Diane, who exemplifies feminine prissiness, intellectualism, and ethereality. The shows works by playing off Diane's efforts to civilize and tame Sam's wild, primitive persona, while Sam, just as earnestly, is intent on bedding Diane—arousing her animal passions. We are going to take a look at three of the earliest episodes.

Diane, a twentyish, blond, erudite, prim-and-proper English lit graduate student, arrives at Cheers, where she is to meet her beloved—a middle-aged professor—and fly off to Barbados to get married. The bar phone rings, and Diane answers it; it is a woman named Vicky looking for a man named Sam (the bartender). Sam has Diane pretend he is not there; Vicky tells Diane to thank Sam for being "a magnificent pagan beast" in bed. The professor, Sumner Sloane, comes in and tells Diane he must first get her engagement ring from his ex-wife; then they can fly to Barbados. She agrees to wait. Diane then settles in and reads a book at the bar. Norm, a heavyset accountant, enters the bar; he's a regular, and begins a sports conversation with Sam and Coach, the bartenders. Carla, a waitress, arrives for work. She is short, dark, loud, and ethnic—the opposite of Diane. Despite Diane's pleas that Sam not tell anyone why she is there, he does so while she is in the bathroom. When she returns, a loud cheer and shouts of congratulations ring out.

Time passes and Professor Sloane has not yet returned. The others at the bar discuss which movie was the "sweatiest": *Ben Hur* or *Cool Hand Luke,* which disgusts Diane's more refined sensibilities. Finally, Professor Sloane returns, only to announce he's confused; he's discovered he still has feelings for his ex-wife. However, after seeing Diane, he decides to attempt once more to retrieve the ring and go with Diane to Barbados to marry. Hours pass; it is closing time, and Professor Sloane is nowhere to be found. Norm, the accountant, has passed out on the bar; Diane is desolate. She begins to pour out her life story to Sam, who attempts to cheer her up by demeaning Professor Sloane. Diane springs to his defense: "He's urbane, well bred, educated—everything you're not." But when Diane calls the airline to alter their reservations, she discovers Sloane and his ex-wife have flown off to Barbados together! Sam offers Diane a job, since she now has none. She haughtily refuses his offer: "Somewhere there's a job perfect for me. This isn't it!" But, a few seconds later when Carla calls out a very complex drink order to Sam and he cannot remember it, Diane recites it perfectly. She takes the job.

This tale is what is termed an "origin story." It tells how things came to be as they are. Here we learn how Diane "came to be" at Cheers. We also see the rough outlines of the community or family, into which she has been adopted. It is a rough and coarse—but also loving and supportive—community. She adds elegance and erudition to it; it provides her with emotional support and a social home. In the next episode, Diane has begun work as a barmaid. The regulars—Carla, Norm, the Coach, and Sam—are all in their accustomed places. A beautiful buxom blond, named Brandee, waltzes in and sets the place atwitter. The men all gape and rush to light her cigarette; Sam asks her out. Diane, meanwhile, has sized her up (correctly) as an airhead and tells Sam as much.

Sam is upset with Diane's haughtiness and takes her to the back room to reprimand her. While they quibble with each other, Brandee leaves with another man. Diane retorts: "See!" Sam, however, is stung by Diane's criticism of his consistently dating women with fabulous bodies and a low I.Q. Determined to prove he can date intelligent women, Sam brings in Debra to the bar. A very pretty redhead, Debra and Sam describe to Diane how they have just returned from a classical music concert. Diane, however, notices that the concert program they are waving at her is *two years old*! (They actually went to see *The Return of the Jedi.*)

Once again Sam takes Diane to the back room to talk things over. He is embarrassed that he "only dates dumb women," but tells Diane she must "stop being such a snob." They each apologize to each other. Diane informs him that *she* would never fall for him, because *she* could see "his line of bull coming from a mile away." Sam bets her that she wouldn't. They return to the bar. A few moments later, Sam makes a lovely and poignant comparison between Diane's blue eyes and the sky above a mountain range in Stowe, Vermont; Diane is very moved. Then Sam retorts: "But an intelligent woman could see through that right away, right?" Thus, we learn that Sam is a more talented flirt than he generally lets on.

In a third episode, Harry, a hustler, arrives at the bar set to fleece customers, and Sam throws him out; Diane and Norm arrive to work and drink, respectively. A local Boston television sportscaster, Dave Richards, comes in and asks Sam for an interview. It is to be a retrospective on Sam's glory days as a baseball relief pitcher. Diane beckons Sam to the back room (their private space) and asks him not to do the interview. She finds "where are they now" stories depressing. Sam, however, wants to do the interview and tells Dave to go get his news crew. Carla talks to Dave as they wait and learns that Sam was near the bottom of the list for Dave to interview; several other sports celebrities had backed out or were out of town. Despite this, Carla is proud of Sam and helps him primp for the interview.

The news crew arrives, and all of the bar patrons try to get within camera range. Sam launches into an exciting story of a close game during the World Series; but Dave's assistant rushes in and tells him John McEnroe is now available for an interview. Dave immediately dumps Sam and dashes out the door with his crew; Sam is depressed. He retreats to the back room to throw darts. Diane enters to console him, telling him to "express his feelings" and assorted psycho-babble; Sam yells at her to get out. Diane then tells him about a humiliating experience of her own and tells Sam he has "a great deal to look back on with pride and a lot of hope for the future." Sam impulsively grabs her and kisses her. Diane instinctively slams him onto the pool table using karate. She then declares (much like Iago in *Othello*) that she and Sam would "never, never, never" be right for each other. Diane then asks Sam to tell *her* his baseball story, which he does. Harry, the flimflam man, returns to the bar; life in the *Cheers* community goes on.

Cheers and *M.A.S.H.* represented a new type of situation comedy in American television. If we look back to the 1950s, 1960s, and 1970s, we see that virtually all of the very successful situation comedies were set at home: *I Love Lucy, The Dick Van Dyke Show, The Beverly Hillbillies, All in the Family.* Indeed, *Gomer Pyle, U.S.M.C.* was the first situation comedy we encountered set outside the home. The community of *Gomer Pyle,* however, was almost entirely a masculine one, set on a Marine Corps base.

It was perhaps a direct result of the women's movement during the 1970s that we got two women living and working together (*Laverne & Shirley*) and then, a decade later, mixed-gender work settings such as we have seen on *Cheers* and *M.A.S.H.* Yet even in these series, men are the dominant characters: Sam Malone *owns* the bar; Diane only works there as a waitress. Analogously, Dr. "Hawkeye" Pierce is a *surgeon,* while "Hotlips" Houlihan is a *nurse* on *M.A.S.H.* We will have to wait until the 1990s and *Murphy Brown* before we encounter a top-rated, work-based situation comedy in which a woman is the dominant character (both in terms of personality and job status). The work-based, mixed-gender sitcom, however, represents a major cultural shift in America's views of men and women. Women and men are now portrayed no longer as merely living together (as wife and husband), but also as working together as professionals. This represented a watershed shift in our cultural notion of male and female roles.

Magnum P.I.

The 1980s were also notable for the return of an archetype missing for three decades from television's top-rated shows: the public warrior. Recall the law and order heroes of the 1950s: Palladin, Matt Dillon, and Sergeant Joe Friday. It had been a long time since men such as these had appeared on television. *Magnum, P.I.,* starring Tom Selleck in the title role, once again presented us with a public warrior, but with a decidedly 1980s flavor. The good guys of the 1950s represented the ideals of their era, a time when justice and morality were viewed as black-and-white issues and treated with enormous seriousness. However, by the 1980s (post-Watergate, post-Vietnam, post-women's lib) American culture had become markedly more cynical and more "hip." Iconoclasts were trusted more than duly-vested authorities; the bad guys were just as likely to be found lurking in the military or the White House as in "crime families," and the populace was simultaneously fascinated by and fearful of material wealth as manifested in sports cars and walled estates.

Still, we needed our heroes and—spoiled by the 1970s emphasis on beautiful bodies—we wanted them to be handsome, big, and sexy. And of course, it would also be great if they dressed well and drove a hot car, so long as they weren't "rich." Enter Tom Selleck and *Magnum P.I.,* a miraculous blend of chaste sexuality, impoverished luxury, intelligent athleticism, and down-to-earth sophistication,[2] in other words, an enormously successful oxymoron, or combination of opposites. The pilot episode of *Magnum P.I.* provides us with several insights into "who" he is. We learn that Thomas Magnum is a much-decorated, heroic lieutenant commander in the Special Forces. He served on dangerous "special-ops" in Vietnam and is deeply loyal to his former military comrades. However, he resigned his commission after the war in a dispute with a corrupt commanding officer. Now he works as a private investigator and security consultant in Hawaii. On one of those jobs, Magnum was hired by a famous, wealthy writer, Robin Masters, to check security on his luxurious estate outside Honolulu. As a part of that assignment, Magnum lives "permanently" in the guest house on the estate and has full use of the owner's red Ferrari convertible.

Also living on the estate is British Major Higgins, a retired military man, who represents the pomposity, elitism, and stuffiness of the Old Guard (literally and figuratively). One of the primary levers of humorous tension in the series is the conflict between Higgins's refined sense of order and decorum and Magnum's earthy pragmatism. Further, as we shall see, several beautiful women are consistently woven into the narrative, but are just as consistently woven out by the episode's end.

Let's take a look at three representative episodes. In the first, titled "Thank Heaven for Little Girls," it is Christmas Eve and Higgins is proudly placing Robin Masters's newest acquisition—a Gauguin painting—over the mantel. A Christmas tree stands in the living room; outside the climate is Hawaiian tropic.

Some young boarding-school girls (ages eight to twelve) from Vermont call up Magnum and report their teacher missing. They tell him that she has run off with a Hawaiian beach bum and abandoned them. Sympathetic to their plight, Magnum takes them back to the estate, leaves them with Higgins, and goes to search for their teacher. Unbeknownst to either Magnum or Higgins is the fact that the girls have actually been planted at the estate by their teacher, Miss Bouton, to steal the new Gauguin. (It seems the "Gauguin" is actually a forgery, which the teacher—an art restorer—is seeking to replace with the original; the plot here gets a little too convoluted.)

Magnum takes his black pal, T.C. (Robert Moseley), into a rough section of Honolulu to search for the teacher, using (fake) clues the girls have given him. They get beat up by hoodlums and just make it back to the Ferrari in time to escape. By this point, Magnum realizes the clues are bogus and searches on his own for Miss Bouton. He finds her: a blond, twentyish, well-bred woman. But by then the girls have stolen the painting and replaced it with the *real* Gauguin. Higgins, confused and frustrated, threatens to call the police; Magnum talks him out of it.

When the teacher and her students return to their hotel room with the fake painting, however, they are kidnapped by a crooked art dealer. The crooked dealer hides the girls and holds them for ransom, asking, of course, for the real Gauguin. Higgins objects vehemently to trading it for the girls ("it's worth millions!"), but Magnum prevails and takes it to the kidnapper. The kidnapper gives him the girls' location, and just in the nick of time, Magnum rescues them. Magnum and T.C. then tail the crooked art dealer to the airport and cleverly replace the real Gauguin with the fake one, returning the authentic painting to Higgins. Back at the estate, the girls, Miss Bouton, Higgins, and Magnum all celebrate a happy Christmas. Magnum's "gift" to all, of course, is solving the crime and regaining the painting.

In a second episode, "Murder 101," Magnum displays not only his altruism but also his modesty. In this tale, Magnum is teaching an adult education class at a local community college titled "Beginning Private Investigation." He is a novice at teaching, and breaks his chalk on the blackboard several times. Further, because only five students have enrolled for the course, the college president is threatening to cancel it. However, determined to carry on, Magnum gets two of his pals, Rick and T.C., to sign up for the class, as well as a young woman, Stacey, whose fiancé, Ted Hazelet, is missing. The class chooses to find the young woman's missing fiancé as its class project. The class travels in one student's dilapidated van to a local bar where Ted was last sighted. There Magnum ends up being recognized as a P.I. by the bartender, has to buy several rounds of drinks for the patrons, and gets beat up by two strange men in the bar's men's room—not exactly a stellar showing for his students. The class next visits the motel where Ted had last stayed and searches his garbage for clues. (Magnum has to first purchase the garbage from the trashman.) They discover documents that suggest Ted may have been embezzling money from the bank where he and Stacey both worked.

Higgins provides some additional important clues to the case, and the class discovers that the vice president of the bank is laundering drug money. One evening, Magnum and Stacey break into the vice president's office and find him dead. Two U.S. Treasury agents immediately enter the office (the same two men who had beaten up Magnum in the bar) and question him and Stacey. Without their seeing him, Magnum manages to "lift" a safety deposit key near the dead man's body. Magnum and Stacey also realize at this point that the two Treasury agents are in on the scam. Magnum obtains important evidence from the safety deposit box and then sets up a "sting" of the two crooked Treasury agents. With the help of the class (including T.C. and Rick), the agents are tricked and arrested. Magnum's next course offering—Advanced Private Investigation—is packed with students, each eager to have their cases solved.

This episode, although lighthearted, contained some key archetypal themes. First, it teaches us that corruption—and criminal activity—can pervade even the federal government, a prevalent post-Watergate theme. Unlike the simple black-and-white world of Matt Dillon in *Gunsmoke,* public warriors during the 1980s must be willing to identify criminals *within* the government. Second, although Magnum solves the crime, he does so by organizing support *among* the common people (his students). This suggests a populist, communal approach to dealing with illicit behavior that again is quite different from the "leave it to the authorities" ideology found in, say, *Dragnet.* Because the authorities can no longer be trusted to do the right thing, ordinary citizens must be ready to organize themselves to defeat evil.

A third episode, "Novel Connection," features an actress borrowed from another popular detective series: Jessica Fletcher

(Angela Lansbury) of *Murder, She Wrote.*[3] The episode opens with Higgins bringing three of Robin Masters's women friends to the estate from the airport. Along the way, they are almost run off the road by a pickup truck. Once they arrive at the estate, one of the two women—a fortyish, attractive, divorcée named Mrs. Fulton—flirts heavily with Magnum. But Higgins and the other woman, Miss Cates, who is older and prissy, do not want Magnum to help them find the perpetrators; Miss Cates insists she knows an expert whom she will call, if need be.

Meanwhile, Rick and T.C. have gotten Magnum, who is perennially broke, to invest in a real estate deal. While flying by helicopter to check out their land, they spot the third of the three women, a young woman named Amy, driving off with a man following in pursuit. They are unable to intervene, however, and Amy becomes missing; Magnum is able to track Amy down to a hotel room where she is in hiding. (She was not kidnapped.) But he is observed by the same man who earlier had followed Amy; Magnum brings Amy back to estate.

Once they arrive there, he discovers that the expert Miss Cates has sent for is Jessica Fletcher, the famous mystery writer. Higgins and the four ladies have an elegant luncheon at the estate, excluding Magnum. (They seat him behind a tray table, where he is made to feel like an unruly child or big dog.) A handsome neighbor, whom Mrs. Fulton had been flirting with, arrives and invites them all over for a cocktail party that evening; but just then, a gunman appears at the window and shoots at the group. The mystery at this point is determining *who* is the target; all of the women have various reasons why they may be being attacked. Through following clues, Magnum is able to identify the shooter—a professional assassin named Paul Mayfield. The entire group goes to the cocktail party; Magnum and Jessica each have different theories as to who is the target. While at the party, Magnum locates Mayfield and pursues him; a gunfight occurs, and Mayfield is killed. Working together—albeit using different clues and styles of interpretation—Jessica and Magnum discover that Mrs. Fulton actually was the target. Her husband had recently died, leaving her an enormous company; the bank (another corrupt institution) was conspiring to kill her and seize the assets.

Somewhat analogously, the real estate scheme that Magnum had entered into with Rick and T.C. turns out to be worthless; Magnum, however, is unfazed. He does not care much about money anyhow. He lies back on his couch and reads a Jessica Fletcher novel. Magnum represents the "laid back" (pun intended) public warrior appropriate for the 1980s. He is moral, unmaterialistic, loyal, and easygoing. Very much like the Eddie Murphy/Axel Foley character in *Beverly Hills Cop,* he doesn't take authority—or himself—too seriously.

The Cosby Show

We close out the 1980s with two programs that echo the domestic settings of situation comedies decades earlier: *The Cosby Show* and *Roseanne.* Like their predecessors, *I Love Lucy* and *The Dick Van Dyke Show,* these two programs are set in the bosom of the American family. (Yet what remarkably different bosoms those are, depending upon whether we visit the Huxtables or the Connors!)

In the more traditional of the two shows, *The Cosby Show,* we see how things have changed since the 1960s days of Laura and Rob Petrie (Dick Van Dyke). First, Mom and Dad are different; *Mom works* (as a lawyer), and while Dad also works, he also gets more directly involved in raising his kids than he used to. Second, Mom and Dad are *African-American,* not WASP. But beyond these two monumental changes, many things remain the same. Each episode presents the family with a familiar problem (dating, grades, money) that must be acknowledged and dealt with.

The Huxtable family consists of the father, Heathcliff Huxtable (Bill Cosby); his wife, Claire; and their five children, Sondra, Vanessa, Denise, Rudy, and Theo. Cliff Huxtable works as an obstetrician; his wife is a lawyer. The family lives in a handsome town house in Philadelphia. In one episode, the teenaged, middle daughter, Denise, tells her dad that a girlfriend of hers has a "physical problem" and needs to talk to him in confidence about it; Cliff agrees to see the girl. It turns out that the young woman is not pregnant, as he suspected, but only has a bladder infection. However, the event concerns Cliff, because the young woman had waited four weeks before seeing him (possibly because she was worried she might have a venereal disease). Cliff tells Claire about the incident, and they worry that their own children might be similarly hesitant to confide in them.

Cliff and Claire call a family meeting in the living room and tell their children not to fear coming to them should a problem arise. The kids respond that they would probably seek out help from friends first, fearing their parents would be angry or disappointed in them. The family discusses different types of problems: sex, pregnancy, driving the car without permission, drinking. Daughter Denise tests their response by making up some examples, and the parents learn they actually are giving off "mixed signals"—*saying* they won't be upset, but actually *becoming* upset. Cliff and Claire come to recognize their own patterns of denial as parents, but remind the children: "We'll get angry, but still come to us [when you have a serious problem]. We love you and care for you more than anyone else." Later, up in their bedroom, Cliff and Claire recall how *they* skipped a church picnic once to go necking. Feeling guilty (twenty years later), they call up their own parents and tell them. The tale instructs us that even good mothers and good fathers are fallible and that it's sometimes very difficult to practice what you preach.

In another episode, the youngest daughter, Rudy (age seven), is reading a book to Cliff, who is sleeping on the couch. Theo, the sixteen-year-old son, comes in the door complaining about a very tough math test he just took from Mrs. Westlake, his teacher. Theo had studied for the test for several days, but feels he still failed it. Just then, Mrs. Westlake calls up and asks to speak to Cliff. Cliff asks her and her husband to dinner that evening, which panics Theo, who feels she will tell his dad he failed the math test. Theo has described Mrs. Westlake to his parents as a strict, mean monster who terrifies her students.

However, when Mrs. Westlake and her husband arrive at the Huxtables' door, they turn out to be a very attractive, friendly, and happy couple. Mrs. Westlake, in fact, is quite a beautiful and articulate woman from Brazil. Her family had immigrated to the United States, and she worked two jobs to put herself through college. (Thus, she serves as an excellent role model for other minorities to illustrate how hard work and an education can be used to achieve a

Archive Photos

The Cosby Show *expanded America's vision of the ideal family.*

successful career.) Theo, however, is still suspicious of her visit: Why does she want to see his father? Mrs. Westlake explains that she has just become pregnant and wants Dr. Huxtable to be her gynecologist; Cliff happily agrees.

While Cliff and Claire are in the kitchen preparing dessert, Mrs. Westlake calls Theo into the living room. She has put her hair up in a tight bun and put on her glasses, transforming herself back into the strict taskmaster Theo fears. Theo is sure she is going to show him his failed math test. But, miracle of miracles, she instead shows him his paper which bears a grade of 89. Just then, Cliff and Claire enter with dessert and coffee. Cliff sees the paper and feigns tears of joy—wiping his eyes.

After Mr. and Mrs. Westlake depart, Cliff and Claire tack Theo's excellent paper to his bedroom door and hug him. His dad tells him one big difference was Theo's strategy (this time) of preparing for the test throughout the week, rather than cramming the night before the exam: "Your head can only absorb so much material per day." He then invites Theo to join him for another piece of pie. Theo good-naturedly points to his father's expanding stomach area: "Yeah Dad, and I think your body has already absorbed enough food for one day too."

In a third episode, two types of issues are dealt with. First, Vanessa wants to wear her sister Denise's new sweater to a dance Friday night with her boyfriend. However, Denise does not want to lend it to her, since she has not yet worn the sweater herself. A second issue arises when Vanessa and her boyfriend Robert insist on studying together in the Huxtable's kitchen, preventing others from using the phone and, at the same time, not getting much real studying done. The next day, Friday, Vanessa shows brother Theo her history test grade—a D. Vanessa hides the test from her parents. She then sneaks into Denise's room and "borrows" the new sweater. When Vanessa returns from the dance, Denise angrily confronts her sister. They get into a shouting and shoving match and have to be physically separated by their parents; both are grounded and reprimanded.

The parents then go in to talk with Vanessa. They learn that she feels competitive with the other girls at school in terms of looking good and also feels pressure to keep Robert as her boyfriend. Vanessa shows them the D she made on the history test. Together, Vanessa, Cliff, and Claire go to talk with Robert, who has been waiting in the kitchen. They decide that Vanessa and Robert should take a two-week break from co-studying, challenging them to keep their grades up if they want to study together. With both issues resolved, the family is passing through the living room, when Martin Luther King's speech "I Have a Dream" appears on the screen. The entire group sits down and watches.

I have included this episode because it adds a very significant archetypal feature to what would be a standard, 1980s family situation comedy. *The Cosby Show* models healthy child-parent relationships for its audience. Cliff and Claire are not "perfect" parents (there are none), but they love their children and each other and try diligently to help them grow into productive, happy individuals. They are also a professional family, with both parents working at creative, demanding jobs. Thus, in many ways they evoke values that Americans respect. However, they are also an *African-American* professional family and, as such, serve as a highly visible set of archetypes for that cultural constituency. Further, given the frequent negative portrayal of black Americans by the news media, it is very culturally constructive to have the positive iconography of *The Cosby Show.*

Roseanne

We now switch to a different American family—the Connors of Lanford, Illinois. Like the Huxtables, the Connors must cope with issues regarding child rearing and family cohesion. However, unlike the Huxtables, they do so with substantially less money and substantially more sarcasm. The Connor household typifies blue-collar life in small-town America during the late 1980s. Dan Connor (John Goodman), a skilled worker, has (at this point in the series) lost his job running a bicycle shop. His wife, Roseanne (Roseanne Barr), has opened up a small restaurant with the help of her unmarried sister, Jackie, and her mother, in order to support the family. For most of the show's run, there were three children: Becky, the oldest, focused most of her attention on dating; Darlene is a brilliant, depressive middle child with liberal ideals and substantial writing talent who dreams of one day leaving Lanford and "getting a real life." D. J., the youngest for many years, is a lovable dolt, much like his father. The Connors, as we shall see, do not have the Huxtables' wealth, motivation, education, or class, yet they do have *soul.*

In one episode, Roseanne comes home from work at the restaurant to find Dan and Darlene sitting on the couch watching *The Price Is Right*—spending "quality time" with each other. Dan is unemployed, and there has been a bomb scare at Darlene's school. The next-door neighbor, Ty, and his daughter drop by and announce they are driving their Winnebago motor home to Branson, Missouri, to see country music concerts. Roseanne and Dan talk them into driving instead to Los Angeles and taking the Connor family along. On the trip the two families, attired in T-shirts, jeans, sneakers, and work caps, subsist on tuna sandwiches, bologna, soda, and hot cocoa: "This is just like home," Roseanne remarks sarcastically.

One evening, as Dan and Roseanne are driving the Winnebago, he looks out the window and muses about all the houses they are passing: "They're people just like us; I hope their little bike shops are doing well. . . . We're making money at your restaurant; let's have a baby." Roseanne doesn't say no, but does comment that they really do not have enough money to have a baby. However, she notes, if they do have another one, "I'm not gonna teach this one to talk!"

When they stop at a souvenir shop for gas, Roseanne calls home. There's a message that Dan got a job offer doing drywall construction; she tells him the good news: "The job even has medical benefits. Now we can afford to get an expensive illness. Maybe even have a baby." But instead Dan is angry: "I really needed something to look forward to. . . . People have spent their lives doing drywall, and nothing better came along for them. . . . I don't know what I want to do." Roseanne tells him she's behind him, whatever he decides. The Connor family's possibilities are much more tightly constricted than those of the Huxtables; their horizons much lower. Yet they still strive for family cohesion. Sometimes, however, economics come to dominate ideals.

In this next episode it is time for the annual Lanford Town Fair. Dan has gotten a part-time job manning a hot-tub sales booth, and Roseanne and Jackie are serving their "loose meat" sandwiches. Roseanne kids him that soon they'll have enough money "to diversify our portfolio beyond beer nuts." Hearing about the family's money, Darlene requests $300 so she and her boyfriend David can print and sell a thousand of their comic books. (The pair write and illustrate underground comics.) She doesn't get the money.

Darlene is a staunch vegetarian and criticizes David for eating a hamburger; he retorts to her: "Your family makes its living selling meat [at Roseanne's restaurant]. You are part of the giant meat industrial complex." Darlene realizes that David is right. The next morning when Roseanne and Jackie go to open their restaurant, they find graffiti of dead cows spray-painted in front of the door. Roseanne realizes immediately that Darlene did it and confronts her: "This is not a game, Darlene. You don't screw with the family business. We need the money. . . . We're too low on the food chain to mess with people; all there is left is animals."

To punish Darlene, Roseanne tells her she must serve loose

meat sandwiches at the fair—a task that is completely repugnant to Darlene. At the fair, Darlene reads a book and makes disgusting cannibal comments to any potential customers, scaring them off. Meanwhile, Dan mans his hot-tub booth; a young married man whose total family income is $15,000 comes by and wants to buy a hot tub. Dan tries to dissuade him from the purchase: "You really can't afford it." But the man insists: "If I don't get it from you, I can just buy it from someone else." Dan sells him the tub. Later, Roseanne comes by the booth; he tells her: "I have a hard time selling stuff to people who can't afford it." Roseanne admires him and takes off his clip-on tie. When Dan complains he doesn't have very many job skills, she tells him: "Hey, you are just as unskilled as the next guy."

Later, Roseanne and Jackie attend the school play about the founding of Lanford in which D. J. is appearing; Roseanne comments sarcastically to Jackie: "We definitely don't get to the theater often enough—don't you just love it when history comes alive!" Roseanne and Jackie join Darlene at the sandwich stand. A famous country singer, Loretta Lynn, comes by and asks for a meat sandwich. Roseanne is thrilled: "We're so proud to have you here," but Darlene tries to talk Loretta out of the sandwich. Loretta tells her, "I respect your views, but give me a big old meat sandwich anyway." Darlene tells Roseanne, "Well, at least I have convictions." Roseanne replies, "That's fine, but just shut up about 'em. We can't afford 'em."

The Connors and the Huxtables represent two very different archetypal visions of the American family. The Huxtables embody the American Dream—the belief that if one works hard, acts honestly, and perseveres, one can achieve any goal. This is a very admirable vision and one that has inspired many generations of Americans. However, as the Connors' life informs us, there is a dark side to this dream; not everyone will succeed in grabbing hold of the "golden ring" of success. Indeed, many American families in the late 1980s were struggling to get by, living as the Connors do, paycheck-to-paycheck. Still, even in the Connor family there is cohesion and love. Lives are lived very much in the present, because the future is a distant—and threatening—place. Cynicism is deflected with sarcasm, and the family carries on.

As we depart the decade, the Nielsen ratings show these two versions of America had huge and equal relevance to large segments of the populace. They were tied for first place during the 1989–1990 television season, each with a 23.1 rating. (This means that 23.1 percent of American homes with television were watching the shows.)

— EIGHT —

TELEVISION SHOWS IN THE 1990s

WELL, DEAR READER, welcome to the 1990s! Somehow, some way, we have found our way through four decades of television and are now about to embark on our final small-screen mythic adventure. Much social and political distance has been traversed, yet many of the archetypal forms we've encountered have remained constant. This will hold true for the 1990s, as well. Here we will encounter families, wise and elderly guides, heroes, epic struggles, and teeming communities, just as we have before; however, their location—and, especially, their gender—is markedly different from those of the earlier decades, particularly the 1950s and 1960s. A new world order has gradually evolved, and familiar archetypes have donned new garb and moved to new sites to accommodate these cultural shifts. Indeed, we might declare at this point that while the archetypal aspects of myth are immortal, residing forever in the human psyche, the *iconic representations,* that is, the specific forms these archetypes are assigned in a given tale, change and evolve in keeping with cultural values and beliefs.

Consider for just a moment the six television programs that dominated the 1990s: *Murphy Brown; Home Improvement; Murder, She Wrote; Seinfeld; ER;* and *Friends.* Conjure up a mental image of these shows and then compare it to the top shows of the 1950s: *I Love Lucy, Dragnet, Gunsmoke, Wagon Train,* and *Have Gun Will Travel.* Notice anything? Well, for starters women have now moved out of the house and into jobs, apartments, hospitals, and television stations. Second, as compared to the 1950s, the central focus of our most popular televised narratives has shifted from maintaining law and order to establishing a sense of community and belonging in urban, business settings. The new "home" of the "family" is now the office or apartment building, and the "family," in many cases, is a collection of men and women who share the same occupation (for example, medicine) or live in the same building (*Friends, Seinfeld*).

However, as we have already become well aware, the more things change, the more they stay the same. And so we begin our analysis with the most "traditional" of the six shows, *Home Improvement,* a family-centered situation comedy whose pedigree may be traced back as far as *I Love Lucy.*

Home Improvement

Tim "the Tool Man" Taylor (Tim Allen); his wife, Jill (Patricia Richardson); and their three teenaged sons live in a middle-class, white, suburban neighborhood in Middle America. Tim is the host of a local television show, *Tool Time,* which co-stars Al Borlin (Richard Karn). The fictional *Tool Time* show deals with *physical* home improvements (how to hang drywall) and serves as a metaphorical device for *Home Improvement,* the actual television show which addresses *emotional* relationships within the home (another type of "home improvement"). For example, in two of the episodes we will be discussing, the *Tool Time* show features engines; the accompanying *Home Improvement* scripts deal with the coming-of-age difficulties of the oldest Taylor son, Brad, who is having problems with his sexuality and automobile driving, both forms of "engine." As we shall see, also, the program gently spoofs old-style cultural notions of masculinity. Such notions as men being allied with machines, technology, and power are tweaked, as Tim is often shown to be more bark than bite in dealing not only with tools, but people.

In the first episode, "Salute to Engines Week, Part One," Tim and Al drive onto the *Tool Time* stage in a little yellow mini-car, announced by Heidi, the buxom, pretty *Tool Time* girl. (I warned you this show was somewhat retro.) Tim, dressed in a tie-and-suspenders outfit, shows the audience various types of engines. Then, over his co-host Al's strenuous objections, Tim takes a tiny car out of its casing and accidentally crushes it. (Al Borlin, as we shall see, is the much more authentic "tool man"; he wears jeans and a flannel work shirt and really does know about cars, engines, saws, and so on.)

The story then shifts to the Taylor household, where Jill has arrived home with back-to-school supplies for her sixteen-year-old son, Brad. Brad is there with his pretty, blond girlfriend, Angela. After Brad kisses Angela good-bye, Jill suggests that he "play the field" when school starts. He is too young for a serious relationship. (She fears the implications of his approaching sexual maturity.) Meanwhile, Tim and Al have been invited to bring their *Tool Time* engine show aboard the U.S.S. *Constitution*, a huge aircraft carrier. As usual, Al has a much deeper and more accurate knowledge of engines abroad the ship, than does Tim. Tim consistently overstates his knowledge and "screws up" by pressing levers, pushing buttons, or flipping switches that lead to humorous results aboard the craft.

Back at the house, Jill comes home to find Brad and Angela kissing on Brad's bed. Furious and frightened, she asks Brad "exactly how far have things gone?" but Brad refuses to discuss it with her: "It's none of your business. I'm not gonna talk to you about my sex life." Jill calls Tim, still aboard the carrier, and tells him: "I think Brad may be having sex." Tim mistakenly hits the wrong lever, again, setting the entire ship into top speed. When Tim arrives home, he learns that Jill has grounded Brad for a month and wants Tim to talk with Brad "about maturity, responsibility, and safety." To this Tim accurately replies, "The Navy will tell you I'm the last person who should be talking to *anybody* about *that.*" Tim makes a feeble effort by asking Brad, "Is there anything you'd like to talk to me about?" Brad replies, "Nope." Tim then says to himself, "Hey, that was easy."

However, Tim realizes that this "discussion" is not what Jill had in mind. And so he goes to talk with his next-door neighbor, Wilson, about the problem. Wilson is an extraordinary character to find on a situation-comedy and one whose presence makes my little archetypal heart leap for joy, for he is a manifestation of the wise old sage we have encountered elsewhere—in Yoda and Obi-Wan Kenobi of *Star Wars* and Seth Adams of *Wagon Train.* Among situation comedies, the closest we have come to this archetype is the character of the Fonz in *Happy Days.* In keeping with his spiritual guide role, Wilson's face and body are never fully revealed to the audience. Most often he is shown behind a high wooden fence, in profile, wearing a hat. From this obscured site, Wilson dispenses advice and counsel to Tim (and occasionally other family members), often citing poets, anthropologists, and other mystics in the process. In this instance, when Tim goes to seek Wilson's advice on Brad, he finds Wilson carefully tending to his yams. Wilson informs Tim that he belongs to the Tuber of the Month Club and that growing good tubers is a sign of family accomplishment in many cultures, for example, New Guinea. Indeed, Wilson notes, tuber-growing lore is deemed sacred knowledge, passed from father to son. Tim tells Wilson that he is afraid to talk to Brad about sexuality, "I just blew the whole thing." Wilson advises Tim to "just be yourself and speak from the heart." Tim thanks him and goes off to get Brad.

Tim takes Brad out to the garage to work with him on a hot rod (long a symbol of masculine potency). Tim constructs several analogies between cars and human sexuality, finally advising Brad that it is best to leave one's "car in the garage for a long time, and be sure that when you take it out of the garage, you use a car cover." Brad tells Tim that he is not yet having sex, but then asks Tim how old he was when he first had sex. Tim tells his son he was "a little older than you are now, but still way too young to know how much responsibility there was in having an intimate relationship with a girl." Tim advises Brad not to use sexuality to prove he is a man, but rather "be a man first, and then have sex."

A second episode, "Salute to Engines, Part Two," also begins with the *Tool Time* show. Tim and Al welcome three generations of the Al Unser car-racing family to the show: Al Unser, Sr., the famous NASCAR driver, introduces his son, Al Unser, Jr., and grandson, Al Unser, III. The youngest Unser, twelve, is learning to drive go-carts. The text then moves to parallel developments in the Taylor household, where Brad is nervously eating breakfast before Tim takes him for his driver's license test that morning. Tim tells Brad that he is expecting him to pass it on his first try: "It's a Taylor-man tradition." The pair return home successful; Brad has passed the test. A driver's license, Tim informs him, "is one of the most important documents you'll ever receive." That evening Brad sets out with his friends, driving the family car. Tim tells him to drive carefully and "no mooning of pedestrians while the car is in gear." Jill asks Brad to be sure and call her at eight o'clock to let her know everything is all right. Tim and Jill then go to a friend's house for dinner. While there, the two men discuss their own "first night out" with the car. The friend drag-raced at 110 miles an hour; Tim raced a freight train! Jill is appalled to hear this and becomes even more concerned as eight o'clock comes and passes with no phone call from her son. Finally, the phone rings. It is Brad; he has been in a minor accident—striking a telephone pole at a low speed. His parents are upset, but relieved it is not more serious.

Later, however, Brad confides to his two younger brothers that he actually hit a car and needs to borrow $200 from each of them to pay the driver. (He fears he will be grounded if Jill and Tim learn the truth.) Over the next few days, Brad has to drive his brothers on countless errands to help repay them. Then the attorney for the man whose car he hit calls, demanding even more money for the whiplash he claims to have suffered. Brad, like his father before him, decides to go see Wilson and seek his sage advice. This time, Wilson is in the backyard constructing a shrine from yak butter to celebrate the Buddhist prayer festival in Tibet. Brad tells Wilson the truth about the accident, and Wilson advises him to be honest with his parents: "Truth, like surgery, might hurt, but it cures."

Meanwhile, Jill and Tim are planning to take Brad out to dinner to celebrate his license. Tim tells Jill that his son is not to be taken "to some sissy salad bar. This boy needs red meat, a big steak, a baked potato smothered in sour cream." (Here is the cultural connection between women and vegetables and men and meat. This association has very ancient origins.) Brad blurts out the truth about the accident, the lawyer, and the whiplash; both Tim and Jill are very upset that he lied to them. They ground him for thirty days, which actually relieves Brad, who by now is tired of driving his brothers. Both these episodes deal with parenting relationships. Let's now examine a third that addresses the husband-wife relationship.

In this episode of *Home Improvement* Tim has just finished designing wooden cutouts for the Stump the Toolman booth he will be manning at the local fair. The male cutout shows a Mr. Atlas–type strongman physique, while the female cutout has blond hair, enormous breasts, and a curvaceous figure. Jill comments to him that both figures seem somewhat unrealistic, but Tim is not deterred. Later, Tim tells his three sons to "get your jockstraps on" and help him clean the basement. He instructs them to be careful not to throw away all his automobile magazines (which feature unclad women draped across the hood) because "that's your inheritance!"

The next day Jill, a journalist, returns home from interviewing a woman who had extensive plastic surgery to make herself more attractive after her marriage broke up. Tim comments to her that if the woman had had the surgery *before* her husband left her, she might still be married: "After all, not all men are as forgiving as I am . . . most women are like you; after having kids, they tend to spread out and let themselves go." Later, on the *Tool Time* show, Tim and Al describe to the audience how best to sand down a used table, getting rid of the "ugly knicks and marks it's gotten and make it look like new."

That evening, Tim helps his kids who are still cleaning up the basement. They decide to take a "babe break" and look at some of the women in the magazines—Miss Dual Exhaust 1984. Tim shows them photos of their mother in her younger years—a strikingly attractive woman. She is pictured with several of her former boyfriends, and his sons ask, "Why did Mom pick you out of all these good-looking guys?"

Later, Jill and a woman friend are in the living room discussing the article she is writing on plastic surgery. Jill shows her friend a computer imaging program on her PC that can alter various aspects of one's appearance. Using a photo image of herself, Jill enlarges her breasts to an enormous size; Tim walks by and comments that they "look great that way" and tries to operate the computer to make the breasts even larger. After the woman friend leaves, Jill sits Tim in front of the computer and shows him her ideal version of himself: It looks just as Tim does now. She tells him: "It's *you* I find sexy. Whatever changes you go through, I'll find sexy too." She shows him a possible future image of himself, bald and fat, and notes that she would still love him. She even constructs a fictional image of them as an extremely elderly couple (490 years old) and displays that to Tim. Tim has still not grasped what Jill is telling him, however. He responds by asking her "how much would a complete makeover on you cost?" Jill, exasperated, walks away.

Tim, seeking guidance and counsel, wanders to the backyard fence to consult with Wilson, the sage, who is smoking a salmon over his backyard barbecue. Tim confesses to Wilson that he really did prefer Jill in her younger body. Wilson explains to Tim that this is due to evolutionary traits that compel men to be instinctively drawn to "younger, more fertile women." Tim replies, "So it's just my instincts talking," and Wilson tells him, "Yes, but your *brain* should be able to overcome that." On *Tool Time,* Tim displays a beautiful, well-used, wood table to the audience. Al recommends sanding it down and refinishing it so it "will look like new again." But Tim advocates putting lemon oil on it, giving its patina a rich, deep sheen: "Now it's richer, warmer, more interesting." Tim takes the table home and presents it to Jill. She exclaims: "It's gorgeous!" He replies, "Just like you!"

Just as the first two episodes of *Home Improvement* dealt with the oncoming of puberty and male empowerment in the Taylor's oldest son, Brad, this last episode also resonates with deep, mythic themes. For not only does it address—as Wilson notes—the impulse of our species (and of all other species) toward reproduction and mating, it also touches upon deep psychological anxieties surrounding old age and death. Two of myth's basic functions are to assist societies in dealing with sociological (for example, mating and reproduction) and psychological (for example, death and dying) issues.

Social scientists have expended a good deal of research effort inquiring into human mating patterns, as Tim's adviser, Wilson, noted. And the current general consensus seems to be consistent with what was alluded to on *Home Improvement,* that is, that men tend to seek out young, fertile-looking mates, while women tend to select mates who appear to be responsible and good providers. This was true throughout much of civilized history, as men almost always had greater access to economic resources (for food, clothing, and shelter) than did women. Women, in essence, exchanged their physical beauty (at basis, reproductive fertility) for men's ability to support them and their children. The *Home Improvement* episode represents this cultural proposition in narrative form.

However, gender roles have evolved rapidly over the post–World War II era that our analysis has covered. And as we have already witnessed (*The Cosby Show, Roseanne*), women as well as men may serve as icons of family resource provision. (Indeed, in the Roseanne episodes we discussed, Roseanne was supporting the family completely, while her husband was unemployed.) Further, we are soon going to reach a television program in which a woman chooses to have a baby without marrying or in any way being supported by the child's father: *Murphy Brown.* This show, as we shall discuss at length, provoked tremendous cultural controversy *because* it challenged the basic archetypal pattern exhibited in *Home Improvement* (and *The Dick Van Dyke Show, Bewitched,* and *I Love Lucy*).

Let's now switch gears a bit and consider a second, deep-structure aspect of these three *Home Improvement* episodes: life and death. The first two episodes about Brad's ascension to manhood concern what are culturally regarded as treacherous, but very positive, rites of passage in modern human (especially male) life: sexuality and the control of technology (here represented by the automobile). Both passages have their dangers, (AIDS, pregnancy, car crashes, incarceration), but negotiating them successfully is required to become a fully functioning adult.

The third episode, on the other hand, taps our deepest anxieties about the inevitable end of life. Just as Jill is able to mockingly create a huge-breasted version of herself on the computer screen, she is also able to construct disturbing images of herself and Tim at a very advanced age (a fictive 490 years old), and the result is not a very pretty picture. (In fact, the audience is implicitly invited to do its own instinctive calculations and come to the unhappy conclusion that in 490 years all of us now watching the show will be dust.) Tim's response—always the Tool Man—is to run to technology for assistance: how much would a complete makeover cost? The deeper question he is posing is, Can we use our technology, our science, our knowledge to become immortal? How can we stave off old age and ultimately death itself? This we recognize as one of the deepest themes—and dreams—of myth: the ancient and ongoing desire of humans to find some means of living forever. Because in contemporary culture people have placed their faith in science, we turn to the products of science, that is, medical technology, for our salvation. This is no different from the mythic tales of earlier cultures who might have sought immortality by beseeching gods or drinking a magic potion. The myth—and the hope—is the same; only the icons have changed.

SEINFELD AND *FRIENDS*: TOWARD THE CONSTRUCTION OF WHITE URBAN COMMUNITY

While *Home Improvement* was set in the family home—as most situation comedies traditionally were—two other very popular television series developed a different archetypal construction of home and family. Descendants of 1970s programs such as *Laverne & Shirley* and *Three's Company*, these two new narratives featured same-age, mixed-gender collections of friends who live in the same area or building. These two shows are *Seinfeld* and *Friends*. Both shows reflected the demographic shifts in American society toward nontraditional, and especially single-person, households. This trend was particularly pronounced among twenty-somethings who had come to the big city (usually envisioned as New York) and begun living with roommates or on their own. Communities were constructed through a complex pattern of emotional, physical, and financial ties that resulted in clusters of mutually supportive individuals. Perhaps what these friendship clusters seem most to represent—in an archetypal sense—is a pack of *siblings*, surrogate brothers and sisters. Because of the brother-sister nature of the bonds being signified, incest taboos (preventing sexual liaisons among members of the cluster) usually (but not always!) were in place. Or as Elaine said to Jerry on *Seinfeld:* "Having sex can ruin a good friendship."

Seinfeld

In one episode of the enormously popular *Seinfeld,* the large, somewhat geeky character known as Kramer is having his portrait painted by Nina, a pretty woman who is Jerry Seinfeld's current girlfriend. While she is painting, Nina quizzes Kramer about Jerry's friendship with Elaine (Julia Louis-Dreyfuss), whom he used to date. Nina is somewhat jealous that Elaine and Jerry are still emotionally close. A few moments later, Jerry brings another friend, George (Jason Alexander) by to meet Nina. George feels pressured to buy one of Nina's artworks because he and Jerry are friends; he ends up leaving with one valued at $500 and promising to pay Nina "soon."

Nina's father, an accountant, has given her four tickets to a New York Yankees game. She and Jerry are unable to go, so Kramer, Elaine, and George attend the game. At the game, Elaine gets into a physical confrontation with several security guards because she is wearing a Baltimore Orioles baseball cap, while sitting right behind the Yankees dugout. During the melee, Kramer is struck on the head by a fly ball. When a photo of the incident appears in the *New York Times* sports section, Elaine panics, fearing her boss will see her. At Nina's studio, a wealthy, elderly couple is appraising Kramer's portrait. They cannot decide if he represents "existential angst" or "human debauchery." Jerry and Nina argue, and he decides to break up with her. Later, at Jerry's apartment, Kramer and George discover a handwritten note from Nina pleading to rekindle their relationship. The three discuss it, and Jerry decides to give her another chance.

A day or so goes by, and Nina and Jerry are at his apartment when Elaine, George, and Kramer pop in to see Jerry. Nina resents their casual entry into one another's lives and is envious of their friendship. After Nina leaves, the group sits down on Jerry's couch to watch television. They discover the text of Nina's letter was taken from Neil Simon's movie, *Chapter Two,* and decide she is a phony. At work, Elaine overhears her boss talking to a friend on the phone about "that crazy girl who wore a Baltimore cap to the Yankees game." (He does not realize it was Elaine.) Recalling that Elaine is from Baltimore, the boss asks her to accompany himself, his wife, and son to the *next* Yankees game—and to be sure to bring her Baltimore cap.

The elderly couple buys Nina's "Kramer" portrait for $5,000, and they hang it in their elegant dining room. They invite Kramer to dinner, where he regales them with tales of adventure (all fabricated). Jerry and George settle down on Jerry's couch to watch the Yankee game; a melee breaks out, as Elaine *again* gets into a tussle with the security guards.

What we are beginning to see the outlines of in the foregoing episode is an informal clique or community that is based upon hanging out together. Though having no formal or official status, this community is the strongest bond in these character's lives; and, indeed, Nina doesn't stand a chance in weaning Jerry away from his buddies. Just as commitment to the group outweighs romantic commitments to outsiders, the group itself can go on dates (the baseball game), fulfilling its members' needs for a social life outside the apartment. Sometimes the results of these buddy-dates are quite funny. In another episode, our four friends try to go to the movies.

Jerry, Elaine, George, and Kramer have decided to go see a mystery movie titled *Checkmate* at the local theater; George has gone to get tickets. Elaine arrives and stands with George in line, where they argue about movie plots. Kramer arrives, but is hungry, and goes across the street to get a hot dog. Suddenly, Elaine and George realize that they have been standing in the *wrong* ticket line; the show is now sold out. Meanwhile, Jerry has been trying to reach them in a cab to tell them he will be unable to attend the movie—he has gotten a last-minute comedy gig. Elaine and George go down the street to another theater showing *Checkmate.* Here they argue over who will pay for the tickets; the line starts. Kramer is still getting his hot dog, and Jerry has not arrived. Elaine goes in to save three seats, while George waits outside for Jerry and Kramer. The other moviegoers argue with Elaine about her saving three seats; George demands his $7.50 change from Elaine.

Kramer and George both describe each other (at different times) to the ticket clerk to see if the other has arrived. She claims to have seen neither of them. Elaine gives up the three saved seats, then leaves her own seat to go get popcorn. George returns to the theater, realizes he has lost his own ticket and gives the ticket taker

Jerry's ticket. He calls Elaine's name in the darkened theater and is yelled at by several patrons. Elaine becomes confused at the concession stand about her popcorn options: large, giant, and jumbo. Jerry finally arrives at the original theater, finds all of his friends gone, and spends several minutes hailing a second cab. The taxi driver has to stop for gasoline, causing Jerry to be late for his comedy gig.

Meanwhile, George, who has left the theater to look for Kramer and Jerry, loses yet another ticket stub. Returning to the theater, he must give up Kramer's ticket to the ticket taker. He decides instead to see the movie playing next door, *Rochelle, Rochelle,* an erotic film. Elaine returns to *Checkmate* with her popcorn only to find her seat taken (Kramer, having finally gotten his hot dog and breezing by the ticket taker with no ticket is sitting in it). Elaine complains to the usher and is told to go see *Rochelle, Rochelle,* which she does. She does not see George who is already there. Having missed his comedy gig, Jerry returns, once again, by cab to the theater; this time he decides to go see *Rochelle, Rochelle. Rochelle, Rochelle* is so hokey that Elaine begins complaining about it out loud. Jerry and George hear her voice and begin calling her name. The trio goes outside the theater, where they encounter Kramer; *Checkmate,* the movie *he* saw, just ended.

On the surface, this episode is a delightful social farce worthy of Molière. Yet a deeper look reveals a loosely knit group date. The characters attend to individual aspects of their lives—Jerry's comedy gig, Kramer's hot dog—yet keep themselves bound to one another by *intentions:* We *intended* to all go to see a particular movie together; it just didn't quite work out that way. However, the important point is that so long as the mutual intentions are present, the bond remains. This, in our harried post-modern world, is the essence of community.

We now turn to the famous Seinfeld "Orgasm" episode, which explores the sexual terrain between authentic and fraudulent sexual response and between lovers and friends. The story begins with George and Jerry discussing their intimate relationships with women; they are seated in a local coffee shop, which serves as their communal kitchen. George laments that he is uncertain if his girlfriend is having real orgasms, to which Jerry responds: "You just have to close your eyes and hope for the best." Elaine arrives and sits down with them. George declares that certainly when Elaine and Jerry were dating, *she* wasn't faking her orgasms. Elaine smiles coyly and then informs them that indeed she was faking; she *never* had an orgasm with Jerry. Jerry is crushed; he now wonders if *all* his girlfriends have been faking. Perhaps he has never caused a woman to have an orgasm.

Later, Kramer and Jerry discuss the issue in Jerry's apartment. Kramer is incredulous that Elaine could have been faking: "I used to hear her screaming from next door!" Still, he offers to give Jerry some pointers: "I know how to push those buttons." Kramer then confides to Jerry that he, Kramer, occasionally fakes orgasms. "If it's enough already and I want to get some sleep." That night, George goes out with his girlfriend, who becomes ecstatic over a delicious meal of risotto. George asks her, "After we have sex, do you feel like you do after the risotto?" In parallel, Elaine and Jerry are at the coffee shop where Elaine is polishing off a hot fudge sundae, moaning with delight. Jerry begs her to "give me another shot" (to cause her to have orgasm); "I know I could do it this time." But Elaine replies: "No, we're friends now; sex would ruin it."

Meanwhile, George and his girlfriend have gone to bed and George has become impotent. Frustrated, George exclaims: "It's Jerry's fault . . . he's made me so focused on sex." George goes to see Jerry to tell him of his impotence; Jerry assures him: "Don't worry; it happens to everybody." But then Jerry calls up an old girlfriend, Patty, and asks her if *she* had orgasms when they were together. Patty says yes; Jerry immediately calls up to tell Elaine, adding that he has called several of his old girlfriends and *they* all had orgasms. (Thus, it must be Elaine's fault.)

George has returned to Jerry's apartment from a fruit stand, where he has purchased some exotic fruits for Kramer. Instead of paying him cash, Kramer offers George a mango. George finds the mango delicious; he begins to feel the stirrings of an erection and rushes off to find his girlfriend: "I'm back, baby!" Elaine arrives at Jerry's apartment; they are still sore at one another over the orgasm issue. Elaine finally relents: "OK, let's go do it; I'll give you half an hour. . . . We have to have sex to save our friendship." When we see them again, they are lying in bed, frustrated; this time Jerry has been impotent. Hungry, Elaine suggests they sample some of the mango; Jerry's eyes perk up. They go to get the fruit. The episode ends.

What is particularly fascinating about this tale is the openness with which the mechanics of sexuality are discussed among the characters; they speak very matter-of-factly about the intimate details of their lives. Once again, this signifies the communal nature of their relationship with one another. Ironically, in a traditional family (as in *Home Improvement*) intimate sexual discussions are usually awkward and uncomfortable, probably because real children and real parents find discussing sexuality embarrassing. The ease with which such issues are discussed among the characters on *Seinfeld* also serves to signify just how strong their in-group commitment is. Surely if George were deeply in love with his girlfriend, he would not talk so openly with Jerry about the physical details of his relationship with her. It is *because* his relationship with the girlfriend is *less* compelling than his bond with Jerry, Elaine, and Kramer that such explicit discussions can occur. Similarly, Elaine's frank admission to Jerry that she never had orgasms when they were lovers is predicated upon the stronger bond they have toward each other as friends. The primacy of the *group* over any individual romantic linkages by group members is the most significant archetypal element of *Seinfeld.* We shall see a similar pattern in *Friends.*

Friends

Friends is an extension and gentilization[1] of *Seinfeld.* Here the community has been expanded to six—three men and three women—and the housing configuration has been somewhat consolidated and simplified. Two of the women, Rachel (Jennifer Aniston) and Monica (Courteney Cox), live together in an apartment. Across the hall from them live two of the men: Chandler (Matthew Perry), and Joey (Matt LeBlanc). Phoebe (Lisa Kudrow) lives on her own. And Ross lives on the Upper West Side. All the characters are in their twenties, attractive, and single; two of the six, Ross and Rachel, are romantically involved with each other—although still living apart. However, their relationship functions *within* the larger group to which they belong.

In one episode, Rachel meets a very handsome young man, Mark, who helps her get a terrific job as an assistant buyer for a fashionable New York department store. Ross is very suspicious of Mark's motives in helping Rachel and jealous of Mark's good looks. Ross offers to take Rachel to lunch her first day on the job, but she declines—Mark is already taking her to lunch. Ross confides his concerns to Chandler and Joey, who tell him to keep his eyes open; they, too, fear the worst. At the store Rachel and Mark work in the same office; Ross grows even more concerned when Mark, not Rachel, answers her phone.

Meanwhile, another group member, Monica, is having her own romantic involvements. She has met a handsome, intellectual Hispanic man, Julio, who works at the same diner where Rachel met Mark. She contrives to stay late with him at the diner; they kiss and make love. Afterward, Monica returns "home" to the apartment, bringing a love poem Julio has given her. The poem speaks of "an empty vase . . . a vessel so lovely with nothing inside." Monica shows it to Joey, Chandler, and Phoebe, who tell her it is insulting; they believe it means that she is vacuous and empty-headed. (A more Freudian reading would suggest that the "empty vessel" referred to is Monica's vagina.) Monica is offended that Julio could have insulted her in this way.

Ross, in an effort to fend off Mark's supposed advances upon Rachel, has sent her dozens of love tokens to decorate her work desk: flowers, candies, stuffed animals, cards, even a barber shop quartet. Rachel confronts him and, accurately, accuses him of territoriality and possessiveness: "You might as well have peed all around my desk." (This is the type of activity that *Home Improvement*'s Wilson would have diagnosed right away.)

Chandler and Joey warn Ross that he is now in really big trouble. Mark is sure to become Rachel's confidante—and from there—her lover. Ross bursts in unannounced at Rachel's office; he confronts Mark whom he has just seen kissing a girl he mistakenly believes to be Rachel. When the real Rachel appears, Ross is mortified and apologizes; analogously, Monica confronts Julio about the empty vase/empty head poem. He insists the poem is not about her, personally, but rather "all American women." Monica dumps him.

Later, the group has collected itself at a local café, where Chandler is busy showing a "naked woman" pen to Monica and Rachel. Ross joins them and apologizes to Rachel for his jealousy.

Rachel reassures him that there is no cause for concern; she and Mark are "just friends." Ross accepts this and then tells Rachel he is taking his son, Ben (from an earlier relationship), to a play-date with an attractive single woman and her son. The shoe is on the other foot now, and Rachel sulks. She copes by giving him a big wet kiss. As Ross leaves the café, Chandler tells Rachel: "Hey, that was cool. You just got him hot and sent him off to play with a great-looking babe." The group archetype in *Friends* and *Seinfeld* is that of a normative and advisory structure within which the individual functions. In this respect, it takes the place, iconically, of the family or small town that traditionally performed this role. It provides a sense of belonging, identity, and emotional security as well for these characters who have been removed from their parents and original communities and cast into the brave, new urban world.

Another episode of *Friends* provides us with some additional insights regarding the functioning of this new form of community. Ross, dressed in a tuxedo, arrives at Rachel and Monica's apartment. He is a paleontologist and is giving a speech that evening at a museum fund-raising benefit. Naturally, he has invited the entire group to accompany him. However, when he arrives at Monica and Rachel's, no one is yet dressed. Chandler and Joey are reading on the couch, Monica is absent, and Rachel has on her bathrobe; anxiously, he encourages them to begin dressing. Phoebe arrives. She *is* dressed and looks lovely. Ross encourages the others to use her as a role model.

Instead of heeding Ross, Chandler and Joey fight (like children) over who gets to sit in the big chair in the living room. In the course of their battle they manage to sling food on Phoebe's dress, ruining it. Monica arrives; she listens to the telephone answering machine and finds an "old" message from a former boyfriend, Richard. The group assures her it is, indeed, an old message, but Monica begins obsessing that it is "new" and Richard is trying to reach her. Against her friends' advice, she leaves a message on Richard's machine, then feels stupid and tries to erase it, ultimately replacing Richard's voice on his own machine with frantic mutterings of her own. Joey and Chandler continue to struggle over the chair, as Ross grows increasingly desperate about getting them dressed. Phoebe covers the food stain on her dress with a huge Christmas corsage (it is July), and

Rachel changes into four different outfits, finding each one unsuitable. Ross finally loses his temper and takes his anger out on Rachel, demanding she dress at once. Rachel, humiliated, refuses and puts on old clothes.

Joey's underwear has been stolen by Chandler, who has, however, finally managed to put on his own tuxedo. To retaliate, Joey puts on several of Chandler's clothes and *no* underwear; Chandler is disgusted. Ross tells them he does not want them to come to the gala; he wants only Rachel to come. He apologizes profusely to her, and she agrees to go. She emerges in a beautiful evening dress. Joey, Chandler, Monica, and Phoebe are dressed as well; they all get into a cab and head to the museum on time.

This tale is very funny and also very informative. The group resembles a collection of brothers and sisters of similar ages who are clustered together in a parentless vacuum. Here Ross is trying to be a benevolent father figure herding the unruly crew to a "grown-up" event. In rebellion, Chandler and Joey resort to juvenile behavior ("We don't want to grow up!"). Ross also has to negotiate the delicate line between fulfilling his professional obligations (attending the gala and giving a speech) and maintaining his romantic relationship with Rachel. Thus, the show is fulfilling the sociological and psychological functions of myth by providing instructions on assuming adult responsibilities and maintaining adult emotional relationships. It serves as a how-to manual for negotiating the very awkward transition from adolescence to adulthood. Interestingly, whereas this might have been an appropriate mythic topic for persons in their late teens at the beginning of the twentieth century, it is now deemed a good lesson for those in their twenties, as we approach the end of the twentieth century. As life spans have increased, so has the period of adolescence.

Murphy Brown, or The Compleat Woman

We turn now to a television program that extended the notion of community from the place of residence to the workplace and that presented an iconic female character of legendary proportions (at least according to former Vice President Dan Quayle). Of course, we are speaking of Murphy Brown.[2] I was fortunate to be able to get episodes of *Murphy Brown* from the 1992–1993 season when the show ranked number 4 in popularity and Murphy (Candace Bergen) had just given birth. Controversy had arisen that summer during the 1992 presidential campaign, when Vice President Dan Quayle criticized Murphy's pregnancy and childbirth out of wedlock. Responses that Murphy was not a "real" woman, but a fictional character, and that therefore Quayle was nuts, missed the point. Murphy was a very significant female icon embedded in a very popular mythic narrative. Therefore her actions, however fictive, *did* count. Popular television shows and motion pictures are cultural myths; as such, they are powerful and do have the ability to influence social and personal behavior.

Let's now take a look at three episodes from that period of the series and see what archetypal meanings were being purveyed, particularly with regard to the work community and women's roles within it.

In the first story, Murphy, a new mother dressed in navy blue pajamas and a T-shirt[3] is interviewing nannies to care for her son so that she can return to her career as a television investigative reporter. Elvin, a painter, who seems to be in semi-permanent residence at Murphy's house, is shown to be a better interviewer than Murphy. Finally, Murphy and Elvin settle on a nice, competent woman. Murphy laments having to leave her new baby—"My only child, all alone, helpless, with a total stranger"—with anyone and soon has scared off even the nanny with paranoid questions. Leaving the baby with Elvin for a short time, she comes in to work at the Washington, D.C., television studio that produces her news program *FYI*. She is disheveled, dressed in her pajamas, a baseball cap, and a trench coat. She tells her community of friends there—Corky, Jim, Frank, and Miles—that she feels overwhelmed and incompetent at motherhood. They give her conflicting advice. Jim, for instance, tells her to be happy she was not "stoned to death" for having an illegitimate child. After a short visit, Murphy returns home to breast-feed: "It's time for Bessy to get back to the barn."

That evening, Frank comes by to see Murphy and the baby. Murphy is still clothed in her pajamas and holds the baby stiffly and at a distance. Frank, who had many younger siblings, teaches her how to hold the baby closely and rock him. Murphy takes prodigious written notes on what Frank tells her. (Here Murphy is not only playing up her character's masculine side, but also acknowledging the incompetence *all* new mothers feel. Contrary to popular belief, women are not "born with" nurturing skills. They have to learn them.) The baby falls asleep in Murphy's arms. She thanks Frank and tells him, "I just might be able to do this."

The television network news comes on and a clip of Dan Quayle stating that Murphy Brown "glamorizes single motherhood" appears. Murphy stares at Frank incredulously: "Am I glamorous?! . . . I agonized over whether or not to have this baby."[4] A montage of the actual media debate generated by Quayle's comments is shown. Murphy goes into seclusion to hide from the press; she has become a victim of the very institution she represents.

Back at the *F.Y.I.* television studio, her friends are astonished at the flood of public commentary. Corky, a perky, conservative, Southern woman, comments that when she was growing up, she was taught that unmarried women having children was a very bad thing. But, she continues, she was also "taught that presidents never lie and that racial segregation was a good thing." The group discusses what a modern notion of "family values" might incorporate. At Murphy's house, the new mother is giddy from lack of sleep—"I have evolved into a higher being who no longer needs sleep"—and is struggling to focus on her child, instead of the controversy: "He's a baby, not a political statement."

Pulling herself together, Murphy comes into the studio professionally dressed and ready to make an on-camera statement. She talks about American values and the American family. She has gathered together a collection of seven or eight nontraditional families, many with single parents, and introduces them: "Families come in all shapes and sizes; they are based upon commitment and love." That night when her baby wakes, she comforts him gently, dancing to the rhythm of a Barry Manilow song.[5] She is learning to be flexible and to accommodate the baby into her life.

In the next episode, six weeks later, a new British nanny has been obtained for the baby. Murphy can still not bear to leave the baby alone with her, so she brings both baby and nanny into the office. The group there makes a tremendous fuss over the baby, ignoring Murphy. Murphy ensconces herself, the child, and the nanny in her office, promising to "immediately" come out to the group planning session. Three hours pass, and Miles, Corky, Jim, and Frank have grown impatient and hungry waiting for her to emerge. Finally, Murphy comes out; the nanny shortly follows her. She and Murphy fight, and the nanny resigns. Starving for lunch, the group, together with Murphy and son, head for their favorite local restaurant. Once there, Murphy has the owner, Phil, talk to all patrons and stop them from coughing, sneezing, and smoking. The group never does manage to get a food order in, much less get any work done. The baby begins crying, and Murphy sings Barry Manilow songs to quiet him.

Back at the office, Murphy tries to get the baby to nap, as everyone in the studio treads softly and talks in whispers; they still have made no progress in discussing story ideas. Just as the baby falls asleep, a loud new secretary arrives and awakens him. Corky, Frank, Miles, and Jim gather at an outside table, while Murphy attempts to communicate with them from a speaker phone in her office. At the end of the day, Murphy declares she has learned to "balance her career and motherhood," but promises to get a new nanny. She walks to the elevator to leave, suddenly pauses, and remembers the baby is still in her office. She retrieves him. . . .

Here we see the practical realities for women who are trying to be both mothers and professionals. Recall that one function of myth is to model just such social problems for us and to suggest ways in which they may be dealt with. In keeping with my earlier assertion that these programs are primarily about *groups as communities,* we see here the important role that group support plays for Murphy in coping with her first day back on the job. She could have been shunned and demeaned, or the narrative could have pretended that the baby came with her and everything was perfect and wonderful. Instead, the story line treads a balanced road between showing the very genuine discomforts (for all) when infants arrive at the workplace and, yet, the importance of trying to accommodate gracefully such efforts, because, in truth, there is no really good way to do this. (Having three children and an academic career, I sympathize with Murphy's situation.) Here we have an archetypal career woman/mother and her archetypal workplace community who show us how to succeed by muddling through. This is a pretty fair portrayal of life as it is, and probably should be, lived.

A third *Murphy Brown* episode is even more metaphorical in its story content. News anchor Jim Dial's forty-nine-year-old wife, Doris, has come to the studio to seek his opinion on fabric to recover his footstool at home. Murphy, Frank, Corky, and Miles are pleasant but dismissive to her. (After all, they have *real* jobs; she is a housewife.) When Jim, too, attempts to brush her off, Doris becomes angry. Her life is vacuous and empty, filled with stupid, insipid projects, such as recovering footstools. After she leaves, the group goes to their favorite restaurant and discusses the issue; Murphy encourages Jim to be supportive of Doris's desires to "add meaning to her life."

The following Monday, Jim happily reports to them that Doris has taken up topiary, and to encourage her quest toward selfhood, he has gotten her a set of stationery imprinted with the name Doris Dial, instead of Mrs. Jim Dial. Just then, Doris breezes into the studio and invites them all to come that evening to a local cabaret where she plans to sing. Her stage name will be Doris O'Rourke, her maiden name. (It seems that she had wanted to pursue a singing career prior to her marriage to Jim, thirty years ago. Now she is going to fulfill that dream.) Jim attempts to discourage her, but she ignores him: "Heat up a Lean Cuisine, dear. I'm going to be late."

That evening, the group troupes over to the cabaret. Doris comes on stage wearing a gorgeous blue-and-red evening dress. In a beautiful, beguiling voice she sings "Brother, can you spare a dime?" (This was a poignantly appropriate song choice, for it describes the lives of discarded Depression-era workers who had built America's economic power, only to be abandoned and forgotten when the factories shut down. Middle-aged housewives, past their prime and no longer attractive, represent just such a discarded population.)

During the song, Doris loosens up considerably, vamping the audience and even pressing Miles's head to her bosom. Jim demands that she leave with him and return home. When she refuses, he leaves. The next scene shows the group, plus Doris and minus Jim, at Murphy's house celebrating her performance. Doris is gleeful and exhilarated; the rest of the group is embarrassed and awkward. Murphy keeps trying to bring the party to a conclusion.

Jim appears at the front door and everyone, except Murphy and Doris, rushes out, eager to escape. Jim declares he has come to take Doris home and says he plans to forget "tonight's unfortunate incident." Doris is angry at him: "I have spent thirty years supporting you and your career; you couldn't support me for even one night." Jim confesses that he is afraid of Doris's newfound independence: "I'm afraid you won't want me or need me." Doris begins singing gently to him "Brother, can you spare a dime?" and kissing his face. Jim realizes Doris loves him, even in her new persona. He asks her: "May I take you home, Miss O'Rourke?"

This particular episode, and indeed, the *Murphy Brown* series in its entirety, presents archetypal role models for women in American culture. Perhaps even more specifically, it presents role models for "women of a certain age" in American culture—the forty-plus generation who were socialized prior to or just at the leading edge of the women's movement of the 1970s. Because television programs *do* serve as ideological influences, the stories they tell about how women (and men) can and should behave have significant cultural and personal impact.

Murder, She Wrote

Over the past forty years of television, we have watched women evolve archetypically from ditsy housewives (*I Love Lucy*) to competent, self-sufficient media professionals (*Murphy Brown*). The program perhaps the most remarkable in this respect, however, is one that remained in or near the top ten most popular television series from 1984 until 1995 and starred a woman well past her forties: *Murder, She Wrote* with Angela Lansbury.

What is especially striking about the enduring success of this show is that its hero, mystery book writer Jessica Fletcher, is not surrounded by a husband and family, does not work in an office or live in an apartment building full of interesting friends, and is certainly not a warrior-goddess or action hero archetype. Instead the series takes her from crime scene to crime scene, where she uses extraordinary mental powers of observation and deduction to identify the criminal. After much pondering about what or who Jessica

Fletcher actually was, in an archetypal sense, I suddenly realized that she is the female version of the wise old man/guide/seer archetype. She does not enforce law and order, as a warrior would do, rather she most often advises and counsels law enforcement officials—who invariably have identified the wrong culprit. Through her advisory capacity, she guides the authorities to the real criminal, often extracting a spontaneous confession in the process. Let's take a look at three episodes.

The first is set in Hollywood (almost every episode occurs in an exotic or glamorous locale), where a young, unemployed actor, Daryl, overhears two security guards and a movie executive, Carson, secretly discussing how to sell pirate copies of an upcoming film, *Cry of Destiny.* Jessica Fletcher is at the same studio, where she is discussing the motion picture rights to one of her novels with the studio president. He tells her that *Cry of Destiny* was the last film made by a famous director, Austin Young; it was never released after the director committed suicide some thirty years before. Another author, Fritz Randolph, is writing an exposé book about Austin Young's death, proposing that Young actually was murdered.

Daryl, the young actor, reports the conversation he overheard to a young woman, Elaine, who is the daughter of the studio president; but that night, the two crooked security men and Carson manage to sneak a copy off the studio lot. Also that evening, there is a gala screening of the film for the press and celebrities. Jessica attends, as does a former child star, Joan Kemp, who had a small role in *Cry of Destiny.* Joan meets Jessica at the screening and tells her how much she admired and cared for Austin Young. Fritz Randolph invites Jessica to come to his house the next morning, so he can show her the research he's completed for his exposé book. However, when Jessica arrives at Fritz's house, she finds him dead on the floor—a victim of wine and sleeping pills—just as was Austin Young. The police arrive and rule Fritz's death a suicide. Jessica, however, believes he was murdered. After all, Fritz's glasses are missing, there is no wine bottle, and some of his Austin Young negatives have been taken.

Later that day, Jessica discovers Carson retrieving Fritz's glasses from the studio screening room. He admits to her that Fritz died during the screening of the movie and that he took the body to

Fritz's house, but he denies any involvement in the murder. Remarkably, Elaine—the studio president's daughter—is arrested by the police for Fritz's death. They based this arrest upon the seating chart at the screening, which showed Fritz seated next to Elaine; sleeping pills were found under Fritz's chair. Jessica informs the police that Elaine was not sitting next to Fritz that evening, but to no avail. Jessica and Daryl go to Fritz's house to search for clues. While they are there, a deliveryman arrives with the missing photos; Jessica looks at them and deduces who the real murderer is.

Jessica has Daryl call Joan Kemp to an abandoned sound stage and ask her for $20,000 to destroy the photos; Joan looks at the photos and agrees to pay. Jessica then confronts Joan herself, noting that the photos show Joan, as a young teenager, emerging from Austin Young's trailer just before he was found dead. Joan confesses to both murders; apparently Fritz Randolph had threatened to blackmail her after discovering she had earlier killed Austin Young. The police arrive; they have found the sleeping pill bottle at Joan's house. She tells the police that she killed Young because she had been in love with him, but he was in love with someone else.

Another episode is set in San Francisco. Jessica is spending time at the offices of the *San Francisco Union* newspaper, where one of her novels is being serialized. While there, she discovers that one of her friends, an advice columnist named Loretta, is being sent hate mail. Further, the new owner of the paper, an Australian media mogul named Harry Mordechai, is trying to fire the long-time managing editor, John Graham, and turn the paper into a tabloid. We also meet a young, attractive woman reporter, Alexis, who has just won a journalism award for an outstanding series on the homeless in San Francisco, and a corrupt stock investment reporter, Max, who is plugging bogus stocks in order to reap profits. Loretta knows of Max's illicit activities and has warned him to stop.

Loretta is visited by a homeless woman named Nell, who tells her a secret about some missing documents belonging to a homeless activist who recently died. As Nell leaves, Alexis warns Loretta that she is not a very reliable source. Later, while Jessica and Loretta eat lunch in a nearby park, Nell comes by and tells Loretta that she "still can't find" the documents. Meanwhile, Mordechai talks with Alexis and hints to her that he may want to make her editor, replacing John. She is receptive to the idea. That evening, as Jessica and Loretta leave the building, a crazed man shoots at Loretta, wounding her. Using leads which Jessica provides, the police are able to apprehend the man; to help Loretta recuperate, John sends her to the newspaper's VIP suite at a nearby hotel.

That evening, John and Jessica go to visit Loretta at the hotel. There they find her murdered by a blow to the head. The police arrive and find a message: "John killed me" scratched by Loretta's ring onto the glass table surface. The police arrest John for her murder, despite Jessica's protestations that the message is false—Loretta's ring is turned inward on her hand, therefore, someone else used it to scratch the message to frame John. Back at the newspaper, Alexis tells Max she knows about his stock scams. She promises not to expose him, if he will support her becoming the new editor.

Jessica pieces together several diverse clues, including a manual typewriter, the time a hearing aid was delivered to Loretta's hotel suite, and information from Nell, the homeless woman, to identify the real murderer—Alexis. It seems that Alexis's award-winning homelessness series had been stolen from the dying activist and published as her own work; Loretta had discovered this through Nell. Fearing exposure as a fraud and desiring to become editor, Alexis had killed Loretta and framed John. Alexis admits this and is arrested by the police.

As is apparent from these two typical episodes, *Murder, She Wrote* is innovative not only in feminizing the iconic representation of the wise guide, but also in having female villains as well. Women in the series are depicted as having both good and bad qualities, which compel them to behave in constructive and destructive ways. Second, in several episodes, including these two, *Murder, She Wrote* greatly broadens the ages of the characters featured, especially in an older direction. In the episode recounted above, for instance, the publisher, editor, Loretta, Nell, and Jessica were all in their fifties or beyond. This stands in contrast to the other shows we have examined from the 1950s onward, which tend to concentrate their attention upon characters from their teens to mid-forties. (There are exceptions to this pattern—Seth Adams in *Wagon Train,* Granny Clampett in *The Beverly Hillbillies,* Endora in *Bewitched.*)

ER

We now turn our attention to a television series that in many respects weaves together the diverse strands of archetypal development observed during the 1990s: (1) the construction of community at the workplace, (2) events marking rites of passage, (3) the confrontation of moral and ethical issues, and (4) the balancing of public and private life. Further, the narrative is set at a crucial juncture of mythic struggle infrequently dealt with on television: life and death. I am speaking of *ER*.

Although there have been popular medical shows in the past—among them, *Ben Casey, Dr. Kildare, St. Elsewhere*—only one has previously been among the most popular shows of its decade, *Marcus Welby, M.D.,* which most unfortunately was not available for analysis. *ER* is the first medical show since the 1970–1971 season, when *Marcus Welby* was rated number 1, to reach the top spot.[6]

In the first episode we are examining, Dr. Peter Benton (Eric La Salle), a thirtyish black resident doctor, has spent the night examining a set of medical records from a clinical experiment in which he is participating. The experiment is being run by Dr. Vucelich, a very prominent senior heart surgeon, who has received a large government grant to conduct the study. Both Benton and Vucelich work at Cook County Hospital, a financially struggling, large, city-run hospital in Chicago. After looking at the medical charts, Benton becomes concerned that Vucelich is purposely excluding certain patients to improve the results of the study; this is scientifically and ethically improper. Later that morning, Benton talks to Vucelich about the questionable findings, but Vucelich arrogantly rebuffs him, reminding Benton of his higher status and financial importance to the hospital.

Two other young doctors who work in the emergency room (the ER), Dr. Mark Green (Anthony Edwards) and Dr. Susan Lewis (Sherry Stringfellow), ride in together on the train. A young medical student, John Carter (Noah Wyle), also on the train, sees them together and happily assumes they are now dating each other. (Both had recently ended relationships with other people.) When the trio arrives at County Hospital, each begins work on a variety of emergency cases: Green helps an elderly woman who has fallen and broken her leg, while Carter is assigned to care for a young, alcoholic man. Another resident pediatric doctor, Doug Ross (George Clooney), and a nurse gently kid Mark and Susan about their relationship. (This indicates how rapidly gossip spreads in a closed community. Mark and Susan are *not* dating, but have only spent an evening together as friends.)

Dr. Benton learns from the head nurse that Dr. Vucelich has removed him from several important surgeries scheduled for that day—an effort to damage Benton's career for "not going along" with Vucelich's faked data. A middle-aged man arrives by ambulance; all of his right-hand fingers have been cut off by a snowblower. Dr. Ross attends to him. A disheveled young woman, the girlfriend of the young alcoholic man, rushes in and leaps on his bed, embracing him.

Dr. Benton confides in Dr. Green about Dr. Vucelich's data and retaliatory actions. Mark tells Peter he must be certain that his charges against Vucelich are correct, for the grant money is vitally important to the hospital. Carter finds Benton and angrily tells him that Vucelich has now taken *him,* as well, off the experiment because he is Benton's medical student (the circle of retaliation widens).

An elderly, Jewish man, Mr. Rubidew, comes in to tell a physician's assistant that his beloved wife, who had recently been treated at the hospital, has died. He invites her to the funeral, and she promises to come. Five seven-year-old boys who were bitten by an angry llama at a children's petting zoo come in, and Dr. Ross begins treating them. It is the birthday of one of the boys; it is also Dr. Ross's birthday. The physician's assistant tells Carter about Mrs. Rubidew's funeral. (Carter had been one of the doctors attending her; he had initially given her husband an incorrect diagnosis of her condition. Now he is guilt-ridden over her death.) He tells the physician's assistant he is too busy to attend the funeral. We learn that the disheveled young woman has AIDS; she is afraid to tell her alcoholic boyfriend for fear he will abandon her. Susan strongly encourages her to tell him, so he can be tested for the disease. A variety of doctors and nurses comment to Mark and Susan that they are happy the two are now a couple! (Here the hospital is serving as small town.)

Dr. Ross's father, who abandoned him as a child, shows up and gives him a birthday card. But Doug is ambivalent about seeing him again. Doug learns that the father of the young birthday boy he is treating for animal bites did not even bother to come to the child's party; so Doug consoles him. Vucelich officially informs Benton that he—and Carter—are no longer participating in the experiment. Carter discovers the disheveled young woman with AIDS and her alcoholic boyfriend drinking and having sex in one of the examining rooms; he yells at them, disgusted. Susan angrily tells Carter that his job is to exhibit compassion, not rejection.

The story shifts from chaotic events at the hospital to Mrs. Rubidew's funeral; it is a dark, snowy winter's day in Chicago. About ten mourners, including the physician's assistant, participate in the ceremony. At the conclusion, Carter arrives; he apologizes to Mr. Rubidew. After the others have left, Carter removes the gloves from his hands and gently touches the woman's coffin.

Back at the hospital, a reformed prostitute with two young children learns from Dr. Green that she has cervical cancer. She must undergo a radical hysterectomy. A nurse volunteers to care for her children while she is recuperating from the surgery. That evening, Dr. Benton waits to see the head of the hospital to report Vucelich's unethical behavior; he loses his courage and leaves without saying anything. Angry at himself, he goes to see his brother-in-law, a car mechanic, and tells him what's happened. Benton is angry that his life is so full of "games, corruption, and falseness. . . . I always thought that when the time came, I'd be able to do the right thing . . . I couldn't." Mark is at Susan's apartment; he's given her a ride home on his new motorcycle. They mix drinks in the blender, sit on the couch, and discuss the rumors of their "torrid affair."

As can be seen from just this single story line, *ER* is an *active* show. There are several principal characters who interact within the hospital on an ongoing basis; further, the characters have lives outside the hospital as well. Some patients appear on a continuing basis over two or three episodes, while others are confined to one episode. This interweaving of public and private selves gives us a strong sense of who each character "is," especially what his or her strengths and weaknesses are as a human being. With the exception of the character of Vucelich—who represents the corruption of power—the other principals—Benton, Green, Lewis, and Carter—as well as the various nurses and attendants are genuinely heroic figures. They struggle daily in a very difficult working environment to save life and stave off death.

In the next episode, Dr. Green arrives at the hospital on his newly acquired motorcycle. At the age of thirty-two, he is recently divorced and balding. Confronting his own "crisis of declining youth," he is growing a goatee, wearing blue-tinted contact lenses, and riding a cycle. Vucelich's (faked) study has been a resounding success and recently been published in a major medical journal. Benton has complained widely to his peers about the fudged data, but has never had the courage to voice his concerns to the hospital board.

Dr. Lewis's alcoholic sister, Chloe, has returned to Chicago; earlier, Chloe had abandoned her infant daughter and run away to Los Angeles. Susan is seeking to adopt the baby, thus Chloe's return is very threatening to her. Validating Susan's worst fears, Chloe informs her that she wants the child back. A black grandfather and his teenaged grandson are brought into the emergency room; the grandson has injured his leg in a soccer game. Dr. Green identifies a malignant tumor on the injured leg. When Peter Benton goes back to some X rays that Dr. Ross had taken of the same leg four months earlier, he finds that the beginnings of the tumor are just barely visible. Benton angrily demands that Ross admit his mistake to the young man and his grandson; Dr. Green, noting that many competent doctors would not have detected the small growth, cautions Benton to stay out of it. The hospital legal counsel agrees with Green.

Concurrently, an agitated young lawyer has arrived at the ER complaining of wheezing; Carter, the medical intern, begins checking him over and discovers he is severely anemic. He asks the attorney to wait while additional tests are run. The attorney expresses frustration—he is up for promotion to partner and does not have time for tests. But he does wait, shoving some papers at Dr. Lewis to "fax to my office."

Drs. Mark Green and Doug Ross look at the young soccer player's X rays; Ross is very distraught that he did not see the tumor at its earliest stage. The young man will now probably lose his leg. Ross contacts an eminent oncologist (cancer surgeon) and offers to pay for the boy's care himself. (The family has no insurance.) Dr. Lewis receives a beeper signal from the day-care center at the hospital. She panics—believing Chloe has come to get the baby—grabs a security guard, and races to the nursery. Happily, the staff had beeped her to come witness the toddler taking her first steps. Susan cries: "That's my girl!"

Benton, despite being warned again by Green *not* to tell the boy's grandfather of the missed diagnosis, takes it upon himself to do so. The grandfather refuses to cooperate with Dr. Ross, ironically destroying the boy's opportunity to have his medical expenses covered. Thus, because of Benton's self-righteous actions two additional types of damage are incurred: (1) the boy's family faces $20,000 in medical fees, and (2) Ross's enormous guilt remains unassauged. Learning of this, Dr. Green yells angrily at Benton, "You didn't have the courage to bring down Vucelich and put your own career on the line. That's why you were so eager to be noble and bring down Ross's."

Carter learns that he has received a very desirable residency assignment; he abandons the anemic lawyer and runs off to a swank hotel with his girlfriend, where they spend the next three hours making love and drinking champagne. Carter returns to the hospital too drunk to assist on an emergency appendectomy and also learns that the lawyer's anemia was actually acute leukemia. The lawyer, his selfish urgency to get his work done for the partnership now reduced to triviality in light of this life-threatening illness, has been moved to intensive care. A young female gymnast is brought in with a broken neck; Ross and Benton almost come to blows over how best to treat her. Green orders Benton from the trauma room.

That evening after work, Green goes to a singles bar, complete with his goatee and blue contacts. As he is talking with one young woman, his contact pops out, landing on his goatee. Susan Lewis brings her baby home to her apartment; Chloe is waiting at her front door, demanding to see the baby. Susan struggles by her with the child and takes refuge inside. The episode closes with Susan rocking and feeding the baby.

One of the central messages of *ER* is that doctors are also human beings, subject to petty rivalries, insecurities, anger, frustration, fear, and pride just as the rest of us are. However, a very significant difference is that doctors—unlike the rest of us—*do* make life and death decisions on a daily basis; their work has much larger ramifications than ours does. Sometimes it is a responsibility that requires heroic behavior of mythic proportions. Let's consider a final episode.

Medical student Carter has just become a resident physician, passing over that symbolic bridge from student to practitioner. He arrives at the hospital in his new, white physician's coat and writes "Dr." Carter on his locker door. A passing nurse sees this simple ritual and calls out to him: "Dr. Carter, just try not to kill anyone!" He is put with a group of other new residents from medical schools across the country. The head of last year's intern group warns the new recruits: "Beware of Dr. Benton; he'll work you like a dog . . . he's from hell, the anti-Christ." It is the Fourth of July. A physician's assistant, Jeanie, who is a pretty young black woman, tells Peter Benton, her former lover, that she has tested positive for AIDS. He has not yet received his test results. Later, Benton meets with his new group of interns for breakfast; they are a bright, enthusiastic group. One of them, a black student from Louisiana., is particularly quick and motivated. Benton assigns Carter to the ER and the night shift.

Down at the ER, an older man having a heart attack is rushed in. Trying to insert an arterial catheter, Carter slips and nicks the man's lungs. Drs. Green and Lewis must rush in and save the patient. It is a humiliating failure for Carter—his first patient and he commits a serious error. Jeanie, the black female physician's assistant, goes to the AIDS section at the hospital; the ward there is full of sick and dying men, women, and children. She waits with the others for treatment. An HIV-positive man who was a medical technician at a nearby hospital sees her there and warns her *not* to let anyone in the hospital learn she is HIV-positive; he told his administrators and was forced out of work. He provides Jeanie with the name and address of a confidential treatment clinic. In his office at the hospital, Dr. Benton calls up the laboratory for the results of his own AIDS test; it is negative.

That evening much of the hospital staff takes the night off and regroups at a nearby park to celebrate the Fourth of July and play baseball. Benton joins his relatives and neighbors for a backyard barbecue. Dr. Carter is left virtually on his own at the hospital, covering the entire ER and the surgical wing; it is to be his rite of passage. At the baseball game, the Cook County Hospital team puts out a good effort, working well together and supporting each other's batting and fielding efforts. (The baseball game here is an metaphor for their daily work lives.) One of the nurses, Carol, sees an old boyfriend with his new lover; she is hurt. Doug Ross consoles her. They all stand in awe as the fireworks display explodes in the night sky.

Back at the hospital, Carter is up to his elbows (literally) in blood and trauma. Injury after injury bursts through the emergency room doors; he amazingly finds himself able to treat them. A violent drunk, covered with lacerations from a plate-glass window, comes in, and Carter must wrestle him to the gurney; an elderly alcoholic is brought in with a head wound. The nurses and Carter surround each patient, stanching the blood, closing up wounds, restarting hearts. At one point, deep in the night, Carter is overwhelmed. He screams out: "Somebody get a doctor!!" The nurses advise him firmly, "*You* are the doctor." He calms down, "I'm a doctor. I can do this." He successfully performs the same difficult procedure he had botched that morning.

Like an angel, the black male intern from Louisiana appears down the hall; he has come in two hours early to help Carter out. They work together stitching up the "plate-glass-window man." Carter sends out for donuts for the nurses to thank them for helping him. Dr. Green calls Carter outside to the parking lot—it is now the evening of July 5th—and presents him with a fiery sparkler: "You're gonna make it."

Jeanie talks to Dr. Benton again, asking him to please not tell anyone she is HIV-positive; he equivocates. He tells her he does not want her to assist him with any open-wound patients. Jeanie, crying, points out to him that it is easy to make such self-righteous pronouncements when you, yourself, are not HIV-positive. The episode ends. Jeanie's terrible predicament reminds us all that no one is immortal. Even those who seem to have God-like powers and the knowledge to save life are themselves vulnerable to death. To the extent that humans can rise above their own mortality, their own fears and self-doubts, and plunge in, time after time, up to their elbows in blood to save life, then we are heroes. *ER* instructs us that genuine heroism is born out of overcoming personal weaknesses, not out of unflinching courage. Those who have never flinched, who have never looked into the chasm of their own inadequacies and mortality, have never been truly tested.

— NINE —

MOTION PICTURES OF THE 1990s:

A Diversity of Heroes

WE HAVE ARRIVED at the 1990s, where a deluge of top-ranked films awaits us. To cope with what would otherwise be an unmanageable flood of archetypes and narratives, I have regrouped the collection into three sets of films, each with a different central theme.[1] This chapter is subtitled "A Diversity of Heroes" and includes motion pictures that both reinforce and challenge traditional notions of what a hero is. The four films we will examine are *Batman Returns, Home Alone, The Fugitive,* and *Forrest Gump.* The next chapter deals with male and female relationships and will discuss *Pretty Woman, Mrs. Doubtfire, Robin Hood, The Lion King,* and *Ghost.* The third, and final, portion of our 1990s trilogy looks at humans and technology and includes the films *Twister, Apollo 13, Independence Day, Jurassic Park,* and *Terminator 2.*

Joseph Campbell's remarkable book *The Hero with a Thousand Faces* recounts in splendid detail the structure of heroic quest as manifested across many cultures over the several millennia of human consciousness. In brief, the hero is called to depart on a quest or adventure; while on the adventure he is tested and tempted; he overcomes these obstacles to acquire a gift or treasure and then returns to his starting point in possession of the gift/treasure. I have purposely used the male pronoun here because most tales of heroic quest feature male protagonists. Indeed, women are often the *obstacles* the hero must overcome (a wicked witch) or the *gift/treasure* they acquire (the beautiful princess). We have been discussing the hero ever since Chapter 1, when we compared the signifying qualities of Rhett Butler, an icon of the rogue adventurer archetype, and Ashley Wilkes, an iconic representation of the chivalrous knight archetype. We have traced the evolution of the hero in American film through Moses, Dr. Zhivago, Ben Hur, Han Solo, Luke Skywalker, Superman, Indiana Jones, Batman, and Axel Foley.

As we have arrived now, finally, in the 1990s we are going to closely examine portrayals of heroes in four films which, with the exception of the *Batman* sequels, are atypical representations of the hero. First, we are going to remind ourselves what heroes "should" be like in American culture by studying *Batman Returns.* We are then going to compare this relatively traditional narrative to three that are nontraditional. One of these, *Home Alone,* is unusual in that it presents a prepubescent boy, Kevin, in a heroic quest. The next two, *The Fugitive* and *Forrest Gump,* are unusual in that their heroic figures are socially damaged at the outset of the narrative. *The Fugitive*'s quest begins with a good man unjustly labeled as evil whose quest is to restore his good name and avenge his wife's death. *Forrest Gump*'s protagonist begins and remains a mentally weakened figure who triumphs through emotional purity and happenstance more than by cleverness and physical strength.

Batman Returns (1992)

The second film in the *Batman* series is once again set in the nightmarish version of the urban world, Gotham City, found in several end-of-the-millennium films.[2] *Batman Returns* opens with a deformed baby (his hands and feet are black flippers) being born into a wealthy Gotham family on Christmas night. Horrified, his parents keep him in a cage, where he becomes angry and violent. A few Christmases hence, they wheel him to Central Park and dump the child, in his black basket stroller, into the river. It is a dark, snowy night. The child is carried in his basket boat (like Moses and Mowgli) down a series of darkened sewer tunnels into a hell-like womb until he enters a cold, dark, wet Netherworld under the city, populated by penguins. Having "died" to the human world, the Penguin (Danny DeVito) is reared by his bird family for thirty-three years, growing into an underworld criminal mastermind.

High in a dark corporate tower above ground, a second evil figure, corrupt businessman Max Schreck (Christopher Walken), plots to embezzle money from Gotham by building unneeded power plants. Thus, the text instructs us, evil is to be found in many locales. Max, like the Penguin, dresses almost entirely in black, our culture's symbol for evil and death. Max leaves the building to speak at the Christmas Eve tree-lighting ceremony in the streets below; his money has made him more powerful than the earnest mayor. But as Max distributes gifts to the cheering crowd, the Penguin's minions arrive from below ground, shooting spectators and destroying the festivities.

The Bat Signal is cast upward toward the dark sky over Gotham where it is seen by Bruce Wayne (Batman) who broods alone in his dark mansion. Bruce (Michael Keaton) transforms himself to Batman and roars to the rescue in the Batmobile. Batman scatters the Penguin's henchman and rescues Miss Kyle (Michele Pfeiffer), Max Schreck's mousy, timid, drab, spinsterish secretary. She is awestruck by his power. Batman accidentally drops one of his weapons, a stun-gun, and she clutches it, hiding it. Meanwhile, during the fracas, the Penguin has kidnapped Max and taken him below ground to his dark, damp grotto. Quite aware of Max's corruption, the Penguin views him as a kindred evil spirit and asks him to join forces to battle Batman. The Penguin tells Max that he longs to resurface (i.e., to ascend, reemerge) and rejoin the human race: "I want some self-respect; I want to find out my human name, learn who my parents are." Max agrees to help him.

Max returns to his office later that evening; Miss Kyle is there and has accidentally uncovered some secret files detailing Max's crooked dealings. Max cruelly pushes her from the window, attempting to kill her. Selena (Miss Kyle) falls into an alleyway and is nursed back to life by a host of alleycats. Here, she too has undergone a death of her "mousy," that is, victim, self and been reborn as a predator/cat. Selena returns to her apartment and destroys all vestiges of her former submissive self. She creates a skin-tight, black-vinyl costume for herself, complete with steel claws and a black whip: Catwoman is born.

The Penguin secretly kidnaps the mayor's infant son and then "rescues" the baby, presenting himself as a hero to the populace. Now viewed as a good guy, the Penguin searches the city's birth records and discovers his human name was Oswald Cobblepot. People view him as a tragic figure who has redeemed himself; Oswald decides to run for mayor. Selena, looking more vivacious and sensual than ever before, returns to work at Max Schreck's office, claiming amnesia. Here she encounters Bruce Wayne. The two are immediately attracted to each other, no doubt because they are both secretly creatures of the night.

In order to ensure his election as mayor, Oscar (Penguin) has his minions embark on a crime wave, discrediting both the present mayor and Batman. Catwoman fights the crime wave, but having a genuinely destructive side, she also wrecks department stores selling cosmetics and women's fashions (a rampant feminist!). She and Batman encounter each other and fight viciously, all the while their daytime personas (Selena and Bruce) are falling in love.

The Penguin and Catwoman begin working together to destroy Batman, attempting to disgrace him. However, the symbolism here is unclear. Even after several viewings, I was unable to completely comprehend Catwoman's motivation and meaning. I believe what the director and writers were striving for was to create a good and bad version of the destructive goddess archetype. The "good" version, Selena, shows women as tempting seductresses who devour men with their sexuality, like Scarlett O'Hara and Mrs. Robinson. The "bad" manifestations actively attempt to destroy men, as the beautiful evil fairy Maleficent does in *Sleeping Beauty.* This interpretation is supported by Penguin's observation to Catwoman: "You're Beauty and the Beast in one package."

Oscar/Penguin's mayoral hopes are dashed when Batman plays a tape of Oscar's violent musings to the populace. Oscar retreats once more to his dark grotto beneath the city: "I am not a human being; I am a cold-blooded animal." Reverting to his monster persona, the Penguin calls out his minions to "murder the firstborn sons of Gotham," recalling Pharaoh's terrible decree in *The Ten Commandments.* Angry at Max Scheck as well, because of his failed mayoral bid, the Penguin kidnaps him.

Batman manages to stymie the Penguin's baby-killers, saving the children of the city, and then pursues the Penguin into his grotto; Catwoman arrives, as well. In the underground grotto, Catwoman attempts to slay Max as revenge for his attempted murder of her. However, Batman tears off his own mask to reveal himself as Bruce Wayne in an attempt to convince Catwoman/ Selena not to exact personal revenge, but rather to let the justice system act on Max. Catwoman refuses. Max grabs a gun and kills her. In turn, Max is slain by the Penguin, who also dies; only Batman survives. As Batman returns to his lonely mansion on Christmas Eve, he sees a beautiful black cat by the snowy road. He carries it home, saying, "Merry Christmas, Good will toward men . . . and women."

This particular film appears to be a collection of archetypal images in search of a narrative. The most interesting character, the Penguin, is never developed in a way that lets us fully understand who he is. What this story line *should* have done was to omit the Max Schreck character, who is superfluous, and explore the intriguing terrain between humans and animals. All three principal characters—Batman, Catwoman, and Penguin—represent human-animal hybrids that have been rich images in myth since prehistory. Such mythic hybrids permit storytellers to artfully combine human and animal qualities, teaching us novel aspects of both species. The Penguin character would have been better represented as, say, a man-amphibian or man-reptile who dwells in dark, damp, cold conditions apart from light-loving, dry, warm-blooded "full" humans. Catwoman's character hinted at the tigress of the liberated female, able to both seduce and destroy less powerful males. Batman, a warm-blooded creature of the night, draws upon ancient European mythology of vampiric humans who emerged at night to consume the blood of their victims. Interestingly, in the Batman series of texts, this evil side is completely repressed and its power is used, instead, to provide potency to Batman's physical and mental prowess. Dracula, the vampire par excellence, also had a strong sexual presence, combining eroticism and death.

On a more Freudian level, we may also read Batman as a disguised representation of the young male's growth into mature, domesticated manhood. Boys of the ages thirteen through nineteen (and beyond) often like to imagine themselves as magnificent warriors, possessed of superhuman strength and powers, able to destroy frightening, larger enemies. Safe in this public warrior fantasy, more mundane responsibilities such as marriage, work, and child rearing can be comfortably kept at bay, sometimes indefinitely: "I don't have time to worry about the laundry or paying the bills; I have to go save the world." Thus, being a superhero is a socially acceptable escape from the unpleasant exigencies of adult life.

This subconscious theme is played out brilliantly in our next example of the hero in film during the 1990s: *Home Alone.*

Home Alone (1990)

It is Christmastime—that magical, mythical time of miracles. The McAllister family, consisting of Mom, Dad, and five children, are going with their uncle and his family (Mom, Dad, and five kids) to Paris for the holidays. Both families are gathered at the McAllister residence in Chicago, packing for the trip. A private security guard (Joe Pesci) checks in with Mr. McAllister to ascertain the length of their vacation, vowing to keep a careful watch on the house while the family is away.

The youngest child in the family, Kevin (Macauley Culkin), age nine, is ignored by his busy parents and harassed by his older siblings and cousins; one older brother points out an old man cleaning the snowy sidewalk outside and tells Kevin he is a murderer. Kevin argues with his mother, who sends him up to the third floor to sleep alone. Kevin makes a wish on the full moon: "I don't want to see any of those jerks again." A magical wind knocks a tree branch against the electric wire to the house, silencing the alarm clocks. The family oversleeps their early-morning trip to the airport. Chaos ensues; everyone except Kevin, still asleep on the third floor, boards the van to the airport and leaves for Paris. Kevin awakens to find his entire family gone, the house deserted. His wish has been granted.

Kevin is somewhat taken aback by his new magical powers, but soon recovers and begins dancing around the house engaging in all manner of forbidden activities: eating candy, making messes in the kitchen, raiding his brother's room, jumping on beds, and shooting toys with a BB gun. Suddenly, though, he realizes he is *alone;* he yells for his mother, but she is not there. On the plane to Paris, Mrs. McAllister does a mental count of her brood and realizes her smallest child is missing: Kevin. She feels enormously guilty. When the plane arrives in Paris, the parents make several futile attempts to contact Kevin, but the phone isn't working and no neighbors are home. The police, not realizing Kevin is very young, decline to assist.

Meanwhile, empty houses along Kevin's street, are being burglarized by the false security guard and an accomplice. When they arrive one evening at Kevin's house, however, he cleverly turns on all the lights and puts on loud music—creating the illusion of a crowded party; the burglars depart.

Kevin, still fearful of the old man down the street, hesitates to venture out of the house. (It functions as a protective womb.) However, he does begin exhibiting uncustomary maturity—brushing his teeth, showering, and slapping on his dad's aftershave: "I'm the man of the house." Discovering some money, Kevin finally ventures out to buy himself a new toothbrush, but again becomes frightened of the old man. Running back to the safety of his house, Kevin is almost hit by the burglars and their van. He recognizes one as the fake security guard and vows to protect his house. Once again, he sets up an elaborate party scene and scares them off.

Kevin subsists on delivery pizza and watching old movies in his parents' bed, the most secure area for him in their absence; he is lonely. The next day, however, he conquers his fear, ventures back out of the house, buys groceries (using coupons!), and washes his laundry. The burglars, however, have learned he is there alone and target his house. Meanwhile, Kevin's mother has been making her way back to her son. Since few return flights have vacancies, she has flown into Scranton, Pennsylvania, where she has gotten a ride with a polka band headed for Chicago.

Kevin ventures out of his house again to get a Christmas tree, which he carefully decorates. He stops by the church to hear Christmas carols, wishing—in this sacred place—for his family to return. The church is womblike, full of flickering candles and beautiful female singing voices; the old man is there, praying. Kevin, recognizing a fellow lonely soul, talks with him; he learns that the old man is estranged from his son and grandchildren, whom he misses very much. Kevin sagely advises him to overcome his fear and call up his son. Kevin then returns home and fortifies his house for the anticipated burglar attack: "This is my house. I have to defend it." With cleverness and courage, two cardinal heroic attributes, Kevin foils their invasion attempt. He has set up ice traps, hot irons, tacks, nails, and other booby traps all over the house. Kevin escapes and runs to a nearby empty house, but he is cornered there by the bandits. Suddenly, the old man appears and knocks out the burglars with a shovel; the police arrive and arrest the hoodlums for the several robberies they have committed.

It is how Christmas Eve; Kevin returns home, cleans up the house, and sets out cookies and milk for Santa Claus. The next morning, snow is falling. Kevin's mother is dropped off at the house by the polka band; she and Kevin warmly embrace. The door opens again and the rest of the family arrives, home from Paris. Kevin tells them he got groceries, brushed his teeth, and did the laundry; they are amazed at his self-sufficiency and maturity. Kevin, notably, displays remarkable modesty by not even mentioning his genuinely heroic exploits in foiling the burglars. As Kevin looks out the window, he sees his new friend, the old man, reunited with his family.

This simple, charming, and enormously popular tale shows us a more well-rounded hero than Batman. Kevin McAllister grows into manhood through two routes. One is the traditional, superhero route, which requires him to physically battle "bad guys" to protect his home and, by extension, his family's welfare. Kevin performs this route's requirements with cleverness and creativity. However, a second route is also made available to Kevin, and he conquers this one, as well. This is the route toward *civilization,* which requires, in American culture, concern about personal cleanliness, good nutrition, family cohesion, and neighborliness. Not coincidentally, these are typically seen as *female* traits and responsibilities. Kevin succeeds quite admirably in this venture as well; by story's end, he has not only vanquished the enemy, he has also grown up.

The Fugitive (1993)

Heroes such as Indiana Jones, Superman, Batman, Joe Friday, Paladin, and Matt Dillon often choose their challenges, setting off purposely on adventures or responding quickly when others seek their assistance. Other heroes, like Kevin McAllister, are forced into positions where they must either sink or swim, when the precipitating event happens unexpectedly. In the course of normal human life, this second, unplanned, course is most often what creates heroes of us. An accident or emergency occurs, and suddenly we are confronted with the necessity of responding to it using skills or resources we had never called on before. Perhaps the most difficult of these instances is the case in which a decent, normal person is going about his or her daily routine and suddenly is confronted with a tragic calamity that he or she cannot prevent. Even more horrible, our ordinary man or woman is then unjustly accused of causing the calamity and punished accordingly. Heroism then requires the person to right the wrong, which he or she did not cause, in order to merely regain his or her ordinary status. This is the subject matter of *The Fugitive,* a gripping narrative that deals with one man's attempt to correct an injustice he was innocent of causing.

Dr. Richard Kimble (Harrison Ford),[3] a prominent Chicago surgeon, has been unjustly accused, tried, and convicted of murdering his beautiful wife. In fact, Kimble returned home from an emergency hospital call to find his wife being attacked by a one-armed assailant. Kimble struggled with the assailant, but was knocked unconscious; and the assailant escaped. After his conviction, Kimble is loaded onto a prison bus with several others and transported to a maximum security prison. On the way, two prisoners stage an escape, causing the bus to crash onto train tracks. In his second act of selfless heroism,[4] Kimble risks his life carrying an injured guard off the bus before it is struck and demolished by a train. Kimble and another escapee free themselves from their shackles and begin running, separately, through the woods. Thus, in a very short interval of time, Richard Kimble's life has experienced dramatic downward shifts: from prominent, happily married surgeon, to distraught widower, to convicted murderer, to desperate fugitive. It is a frightening descent and a cautionary tale to all of us not to become too comfortable in the security of our daily lives.

A deputy U.S. marshal, Samuel Girard (Tommy Lee Jones), arrives at the scene of the train-bus crash and quickly deduces that Kimble is still alive; he vows to catch him and return him to prison. Girard is a frightening figure, obsessive, demanding, hard, and extremely intelligent. Yet we somehow feel he may ultimately be fair; he is surrounded by a diverse team of black women, blue-collar men, and young, ponytailed assistants. Can such an obvious promoter of multiculturalism be evil? No!

Richard resourcefully steals some work clothes from a pickup truck and then enters a local hospital, where he stitches up a wound on his side. He trims off his beard and eats a tray of hospital food. As he is leaving the hospital, the injured guard he saved is brought in; Kimble instructs the EMS personnel in how to care for the man and then takes off in an ambulance. The same wounded guard alerts authorities to Kimble's presence (injustice heaped upon injustice), and soon Girard is pursuing the ambulance in a helicopter. Richard seeks refuge in a viaduct, but is pursued on foot by Girard. At one point, Kimble has an opportunity to shoot Girard and escape, but does not do so. Girard pulls out a hidden gun and again pursues Kimble. Rather than be captured, Kimble jumps into a dam spillway, falling hundreds of feet into a river; Girard continues to search for him. Richard reaches a truck stop, where he dyes his hair black in an effort to disguise himself. He finally makes it back to Chicago, convinced his best hope of regaining his former life is to find the one-armed murderer. Girard's team, using their own resourcefulness, learns Kimble has returned to Chicago and begins searching for him.

Richard obtains some money from a doctor friend of his, Charles Nichols, which enables him to rent a small basement room. From this base, Kimble sneaks into his former hospital and, using a forged identity card, is able to obtain computer files of men with prosthetic arms in the Chicago area. Simultaneously, Girard begins questioning several of Richard's former medical associates, who consistently tell him that they believe Richard is innocent. A few days later, as Kimble is again searching the hospital records, a young black boy is brought into the emergency room. Kimble realizes he is seriously ill and wheels him up to the surgical wing, writing instructions for his care, a third heroic act. A woman doctor notices Kimble's actions (he is, after all, pretending to be only a hospital orderly) and becomes suspicious. Richard runs out, as she calls for the security guards.

Meanwhile, Girard has located Kimble's basement room and followed clues to the hospital. Arriving there, the woman doctor tells Girard about the "fake orderly who saved a boy's life." Girard realizes that Richard is attempting to locate the one-armed assailant through hospital records. He still, however, is intent upon recapturing Kimble. It is St. Patrick's Day. In his search to locate the assailant, Richard sneaks into the Cook County jail to see a one-armed prisoner; unfortunately, it is not the man who murdered his wife. On his departure, however, Girard spots Kimble and shoots at him; Richard narrowly escapes by blending into the St. Patrick's Day parade.

Richard finally locates the right one-armed man. He carefully enters the man's apartment, locating evidence of the man's involvement with several doctors and a pharmaceutical company scam. From this, Richard realizes he was framed for his wife's murder by several of his colleagues at the hospital to prevent his discovering falsified drug test results.[5] Kimble calls Girard's office and tells him of the documentation and then runs off to locate the man. Girard and his men arrive and find the incriminating evidence; they question the man, Sykes, and conclude he is guilty, but do not have enough material to make an arrest.

Richard calls Dr.Nichols, the friend who had earlier given him money, and tells him of the frame-up. Richard then goes to see a helpful woman doctor who assists him in locating those responsible for faking the drug test data. To his dismay, Richard realizes that one of those centrally involved is Nichols. He goes to a medical conference dinner where Nichols is speaking that evening to confront him, not realizing that Nichols has already sent Sykes to kill him. Sykes confronts Kimble on a subway train, killing a policeman. Richard manages to tie up Sykes, but is mistakenly identified as the killer of the policeman by the Chicago Police Department, another injustice. He escapes the subway and makes his way to the hotel at which the medical conference is under way. In the middle of Nichols's speech, Kimble confronts him. The two begin a fight, which moves to the roof of the hotel; they fall onto an elevator and continue their struggle, pursued now by Girard, who has arrived with his team. Girard yells to Richard: "I know you're innocent; Nichols and Sykes killed your wife. It's time to stop running." Nichols is captured; Girard escorts Kimble from the building and puts him in his own police car. Once in the car, Girard uncuffs Richard and comforts him; they drive off. The ordeal is over.

Through heroic efforts, Dr. Richard Kimble has avenged the slaying of his wife and gained back his earlier status in society. However, the tragic trials he has been through will have marked and probably damaged him, perhaps forever. Thus we learn that heroism is not necessarily rewarded with a perfect, or even happy, life.

We are now going to turn our attention to another unusual sort of hero; a man who begins life both mentally and physically weak, yet through good fortune and his own inner nobility and purity of character gains contentment.

Forrest Gump (1994)

The character Forrest Gump (Tom Hanks) is one we have met twice before, once on television, *Gomer Pyle,* and once in film, *Rain Man.* The archetypal figure he represents is an uncommon one in historical mythology, in general, and American mythology, in particular. Most protagonists of culturally popular tales are strong, intelligent, and powerful, as witness Superman, Batman, Han Solo, Ben Hur, and Rhett Butler. Kevin McAllister, of *Home Alone,* was an obvious exception to this rule, although he was remarkably clever and resourceful. But Forrest Gump, and his earlier incarnations, is an even larger exception, for he lacks intelligence, physical strength, and even physical beauty. What Forrest and Gomer Pyle and Raymond Babbitt do possess, however, is a simplicity and purity of the *spirit,*[6] which sets them apart from other men—and certainly from other heroes.

The narrative opens with a small feather floating across the sky and landing at the feet of a middle-aged, retarded man. He carefully places the feather (perhaps it is a gift from God, an angel's wing?) in his briefcase copy of *Curious George,* a children's book. The man introduces himself as Forrest Gump to the black nurse seated next to him and offers her a candy; both of them are waiting at a bus stop in a small, Southern town. The story then turns to Forrest's childhood, growing up in Greenbow, Alabama. His mother (Sally Field) supported them by running a boarding house (apparently, Forrest is illegitimate). The young Forrest has a twisted spine, which causes his legs to be weak, and must wear leg braces. He also has an I.Q. of only 75. To ensure his acceptance at public school, his mother has sex with the school superintendent.

Forrest's life, as we shall see, is marked by remarkable coincidences of historic import. The first occurs when a young rock 'n' roll singer, Elvis Presley, stops at the rooming house and adopts Forrest's twisted dance steps as his trademark. On his first day of school, Forrest meets a beautiful young girl, Jenny, who befriends him. Jenny's mother is dead; her father is an alcoholic who sexually abuses Jenny and her sisters. One day, a few years later, some bullies are harassing and chasing Forrest. Jenny tells Forrest to "run, run away!" As he runs, the heavy, steel braces fall from his legs and he runs like the wind; this is to be his lifelong gift.

Jenny and Forrest become fast friends, each sharing the other's problems. Forrest's swiftness carries him to a football scholarship at the University of Alabama, where he becomes a star runner. One day, he assists a young black woman who is historically integrating the University of Alabama over Governor George Wallace's objections. Forrest participates in history by chance, not by personal choice; he has little grasp of the significance of his actions. Jenny is attending a nearby women's college, and they continue their friendship. One day, Forrest "rescues" her from an amorous date, despite Jenny's objections. Jenny undresses in front of Forrest in her dorm room, embarrassing him; she apologizes. It is clear here that Forrest does not have a man's sense of sexuality, but rather that of an innocent child. Jenny, conversely, has a normal young woman's libido.

Forrest spends five years at the University of Alabama playing football, makes the all-America team, enlists in the Army, and is promptly sent to Vietnam. It is 1969, and the war is raging. In the Army, Forrest makes two close friends: Bubba Blue, a young, black shrimp fisherman from Alabama, and Lieutenant Dan, his commanding officer. Meanwhile, Jenny has been thrown out of college, for posing nude for *Playboy,* and becomes a folksinger and antiwar protester. A terrible battle involving Forrest's platoon in Vietnam destroys most of the group; Forrest heroically saves many men by carrying them to safety. However, despite Forrest's best efforts, Bubba dies. Lt. Dan is saved by Forrest, over his strenuous objections; his legs blown to bits, he wants to die "with honor" on the field of battle. Forrest is shot in the buttocks; both he and Dan are sent to recuperate at a Veterans Administration hospital.

While at the hospital, Forrest becomes a superb Ping-Pong player; Lt. Dan, however, is an angry, embittered amputee: "What am I gonna do now?" Forrest is awarded the Congressional Medal of Honor. In Washington, D.C., to accept his award, he reencounters Jenny, an antiwar demonstrator. Jenny, now at Berkeley (recall *The Graduate*), has become involved with a leftist student radical who is physically abusive to her. Forrest, in his army uniform, attacks him: "*I* would never hurt you, Jenny," Forrest tells her. They walk around Washington together, becoming reacquainted. At this point we recognize that Forrest and Jenny represent larger ideological metaphors for the generation that came of age during the 1960s: Forrest is the naive, true believer who patriotically followed orders and "did the right thing"; Jenny is the all-too-wise, abused child who both recognizes and is overpowered by the corruption of the adult world.

After his interlude with Jenny, Forrest continues to play Ping-Pong for the Army, traveling to China during Nixon's Ping-Pong diplomacy and appearing on the *Dick Cavett Show* with John Lennon. Outside a New York City television studio, he encounters Lt. Dan, now an angry, alcoholic paraplegic bound to a wheelchair and living in a flophouse. The pair spend Christmas together in New York, partying with two whores Dan knows. When one of the whores insults Forrest, calling him "stupid," Dan throws the prostitutes out. Concurrently, Jenny is shown in Los Angeles, drugged out, as she leaves her addicted boyfriend. It is the seventies.

Forrest's Ping-Pong team is feted by President Nixon in Washington and housed at the Watergate Hotel. That night, Forrest

Fotos International/Archive Photos

Tom Hanks as Forrest Gump reconfigures the wise man archetype.

notices lights on in a Watergate office and reports it to the police. The rest, as they say, is history. Nixon resigns as president, and Forrest is honorably discharged from the Army; he runs happily home to Alabama and his mother. Several companies seek him out as a Ping-Pong equipment endorser. With his endorsement money, Forrest goes to see Bubba Blue's family to pay his respects. Keeping his promise to Bubba made in 'Nam, Forrest buys a shrimp boat and takes up shrimping; he names the boat Jenny. Jenny, meanwhile, is at a Los Angeles disco, snorting cocaine; stoned and despondent, she climbs to the ledge of a building. She decides not to die, gets down from the ledge, and breaks down in tears.

Remarkably, Lt. Dan finds his way down to Alabama to become Forrest's first mate on the shrimp boat. They are not especially successful until a freak hurricane strikes the Gulf Coast, destroying all shrimping boats, save one—Forrest's. After that, as Forrest tells us, "Shrimping was easy." He and Dan become rich, naming their company Bubba Gump Shrimp; Forrest and Lt. Dan are featured on the front of *Fortune* magazine. An urgent phone call comes to Forrest's boat; his mother is quite ill. Forrest rushes home to find his mother dying of cancer. The woman to whom Forrest is telling his story begins to cry; Forrest tells her not to, that he invested his money from the shrimping business in computer stock, becoming a multimillionaire. He gave half the money to the Four Square Black Baptist Church and to Bubba Blue's family, since Bubba had inspired him to become a shrimper. He is now retired (at age thirty-five) and spends his days cutting the grass on the Greenbow High School football field. One day while Forrest is leading this idyllic existence, Jenny reappears, wearing a flowing white dress, like an angel. She stays with Forrest for a period of time, and they are happy together: "It was the happiest time of my life," says Forrest. They watch the 1976 Bicentennial fireworks together. Forrest asks Jenny to marry him: "I'm not a smart man, but I know what love is." Jenny declines, but late one rainy night she comes to Forrest's bed in a white gown and they make love. The next morning, she departs in a cab.

Forrest, despondent, sits alone on his porch for a long time. Then one day he puts on his Bubba Gump Shrimp hat and begins running across the country, twice. His beard and hair grow long, and he becomes a national sage and celebrity. One day, he decides he's run long enough and goes home to Alabama.

Forrest receives a letter from Jenny in Savannah, Georgia, asking him to come see her. She has straightened out her life and is working as a waitress; she has a young son named Forrest. Jenny gently tells Forrest, "You're his daddy." Forrest at first fears he's done something wrong, but Jenny reassures him and tells him that Forrest Jr. is "smart." He is indeed a very attractive, bright child. Jenny is ill with an unknown disease (AIDS); Forrest takes her and his son home to Greenbow. There they have a beautiful wedding in the backyard; Jenny, still looking like an angel, has garlands of flowers and leaves woven in her hair. Here we have a strong symbolic tie with the nurturant goddess of nature, signaling rebirth and renewal. Lt. Dan and his Vietnamese fiancé attend the service; Dan has now made peace with his violent past and, metaphorically, embraced those he had earlier attempted to destroy.

Jenny grows weaker and dies; Forrest buries her under their childhood tree. As Jenny requested, he bulldozes her abusive father's abandoned house to the ground. Forrest is an excellent parent to his son, reading to him, taking him fishing, playing Ping-Pong. He

places a letter on Jenny's grave: "I miss you, Jenny," which lies beneath a wonderfully archetypal Tree of Life. As he does so, a flock of birds, God's messengers and symbols of the nurturant goddess, fly past. At the close of the narrative, Forrest and his son wait for the school bus; he puts little Forrest aboard, telling him, "I love you." The white feather at his feet is picked up by the wind and carried aloft.

Forrest Gump wonderfully expands our comprehension of what a hero is. Much of Forrest's good fortune seems to occur as a result of happenstance: his fleet legs result, ironically, from his childhood metal braces; his college admission and graduation from his running ability; his Congressional Medal of Honor from his affection for his friends; his trip to China and early endorsement money from playing the game of Ping-Pong; his shrimping fortune from a fortuitous hurricane. And yet, we can also read these as the purposeful acts of a benevolent God who has chosen to bestow upon the simplest and purest among us God's worldly gifts: Blessed are the meek, for they shall inherit the earth; Blessed are the pure of heart, for they shall see God. Indeed, through one pure sexual act with an angel (Jenny), Forrest manages to bring forth a son, who is blessed with the intelligence and physical beauty he was lacking.

Forrest also serves as a sage to those who encounter him. His good intentions and purity of spirit help revive the jaded cynicism of Lt. Dan and Jenny, both of whom have been made much too aware of the injustices and corruption of everyday life.

Forrest's son and lifelong relationship with Jenny bring us to the close of this set of 1990s film narratives, for through them we are made suddenly aware of a gaping inadequacy in the heroes we have examined previously in this chapter: Batman, Kevin McAllister, and Dr. Richard Kimble were all encased in tales that did not permit them romantic involvement, marriage, and children. As we noted much earlier, in Chapter 2, when a hero leaves the public domain (Batman, Matt Dillon) and becomes "privatized" in a domestic, reproductive arrangement, his priorities change. No longer can he defend all of us; now he must attend primarily to his wife and (possible) children.[7]

We now turn to a set of motion pictures that examine this relationship directly. As we shall see, they are very different in tone from those we have discussed thus far.

— TEN —

MOTION PICTURES OF THE 1990s: Male and Female Relationships

WE ARE NOW GOING TO EXAMINE a very different manifestation of the hero using five motion pictures from the 1990s: *Ghost, Pretty Woman, Robin Hood, The Lion King,* and *Mrs. Doubtfire.* The heroes in these films concentrated their attentions upon a smaller set of human beings than, say, Batman or Moses. While some of them do try to save the world (Simba in *The Lion King* and Robin in *Robin Hood*), they do so as part of an effort to preserve their family and, especially, the women whom they love.[1] We have met such heroes before in earlier films; they were the princes in *Snow White* and *Sleeping Beauty*; Ben Hur; Yuri Zhivago; and Baron Von Trapp from *The Sound of Music.* What has changed dramatically, however, is the behavior and demeanor of the women they are sacrificing for. With one exception the women in these films are active and courageous themselves, not the passive princesses of the 1950s and 1960s.

Ghost (1990)

The most old-fashioned of the six films is also the most mystical and spiritual. *Ghost* pits the greedy materialism of Wall Street against the eternal power of true love. True love, of course, conquers all; even death and a friend's betrayal. The story opens with a young man, Sam Wheat (Patrick Swayze), his girlfriend Molly (Demi Moore), and a friend, Carl, bursting into an abandoned brownstone house they are renovating in New York City. Inside is a beautiful home, full of light (and spirits) that has been vacant for one hundred years. Molly finds an Indian head penny and keeps it as a good luck token. Carl, seeing only the financial windfall the house could represent, advises them to sell it and double their money. Instead, the couple transform the old house into a wonderful sunlit residence, complete with a pottery studio for Molly.

Both Carl and Sam work at an investment firm on Wall Street. Sam is Carl's superior. One day, Sam is in a time bind and gives Carl his financial PIN code to make a money transfer. That evening, Molly, unable to sleep, begins throwing a clay pot on her potter's wheel. Sam joins her, and they passionately make love to an old Righteous Brother's tune "Unchained Melody." The next day Sam finds several large money accounts are in serious disarray. Carl offers to help him sort them out and casually inquires what Sam and Molly are doing that evening. That night, as Sam and Molly walk home from seeing a play, they discuss getting married. Suddenly, a disheveled man leaps from the shadows and attacks Sam. In the struggle a shot is fired and Sam, mortally wounded, falls to the street; the assailant flees. Sam—in ghost form—returns from chasing the assailant to find Molly holding his lifeless body. White-light spirits (from heaven) come to get him, but he eludes them. His business on Earth is still unfinished; he must look after Molly.

In his invisible ghostly form, Sam attends his own funeral; he sees Molly being comforted by Carl. Back at his home, Sam finds himself unable to communicate his presence to anyone but the cat (a spirit animal, according to myth). While Molly is walking with Carl, one day, the man who killed Sam enters their house in search of something. Molly returns, with the intruder still there. Frantic to help her,

Sam frightens the cat, which scares off the intruder; Sam pursues him to the subway, and then to a run-down apartment in Brooklyn.

Nearby is the "office" of a spiritual advisor, Miss Oda Mae Brown (Whoopi Goldberg). Oda is a hoax who charges her (mostly black and Hispanic) clients money to contact their deceased relatives. Sam, however, *is* able to talk to her, terrifying Oda Mae, who has no idea where the strange voice is coming from. Sam tells Oda Mae she must help him protect Molly. Sam pesters her by singing until Oda Mae finally agrees to visit Molly. The next day, Oda Mae talks with Molly in a restaurant, telling her many details about her relationship with Sam to convince Molly that Sam *is* speaking through her. Molly, at first resistant, comes to believe what Oda Mae has told her. Later, when Carl comes to visit Molly she tells him of Oda Mae's visit. Carl acts skeptical and alarmed. Sam follows Carl to Willy Lopez's apartment, where he learns the awful truth—Carl arranged his murder, hoping to reap huge monetary profits by manipulating Sam's financial accounts. Sam, horrified, strikes out at Carl, but cannot touch him.

Molly goes to visit the police to report Willy Lopez, as Sam (through Oda Mae) had requested. While there, however, she learns that Willy Lopez has no criminal record; unfortunately, Oda Mae Brown does—as a con artist. Molly is crushed. Meanwhile, at the investment office Carl is busy rearranging funds and setting up a drug deal. He informs his criminal contacts he'll be putting funds in a fictitious "Rita Miller" account. Sam watches him.

Carl goes to see Molly; he's brought her some fruit. While Molly is not looking, he spills coffee on his shirt, so he can take it off; he tries, unsuccessfully, to seduce her. Sam lunges at Carl, but is able only to knock his own picture from the table. Sam runs back to the subway to talk to an unfriendly ghost he met there a few days earlier; this ghost has the power to move physical objects. Under his tutelage, Sam gains the same power. Sam goes to fetch Oda Mae, who now has become an extremely popular spiritual advisor; her office is jam-packed with clients *and* ghosts. One ghost jumps into Oda Mae's body, possessing her, so he can talk directly with his wife; when the ghost exits her body, he is exhausted. Suddenly, Willy Lopez shows up and begins terrorizing Oda Mae and her sisters; they narrowly escape.

Sam pleads with Oda Mae and gets her to help him foil Carl's drug scheme. With Sam's help, she opens up an account as Rita Miller and succeeds in withdrawing the $4 million Carl had deposited there. Sam then has Oda Mae give the entire amount to nuns who are running a homeless shelter (a good deed). Meanwhile, Carl has become frantic; his drug money gone, he fears violent retribution from the dealers. Sam types "murderer, murderer . . ." on Carl's computer screen. Carl, shouting at the unseen Sam, threatens to kill Molly and Oda Mae unless the money is returned. Sam rushes to tell Oda Mae that Willy and Carl are coming; while she escapes, Sam terrorizes the two men. Running away from Sam, Willy is struck by a cab and killed. His ghost is dragged by black specters to the underworld. Oda Mae and Sam rush to see Molly, telling her of Carl's money-laundering scheme and complicity in Sam's death. Molly, at first disbelieving, becomes convinced when Sam is able to levitate her lucky penny. Sam enters Oda Mae's body and dances, one last time, with Molly. Carl suddenly arrives at the door and lunges for Molly. Sam exits Oda Mae's body—as a ghost—in very weakened condition. Carl chases Molly and Oda Mae into an abandoned building. Slowly regaining his strength, Sam struggles with Carl; Carl falls against a window and is killed by a glass shard. The demons of hell come for his terrified ghost.

Sam calls out to Molly and, now, she is able to hear him. The spirits of heaven come for Sam. His work on Earth now completed, Sam kisses Molly and thanks Oda Mae. His countenance is infused with light and he ascends to heaven.

As can be readily seen, *Ghost* reinforces traditional Christian mythology regarding heaven and hell, the condemnation of worldly greed, and the inherent goodness of self-sacrifice. It also champions the eternal nature of true love. Further, its presents a narrative very much akin to that of traditional European fairy tales in which the hero/prince protects the safety of his beloved by engaging in physical combat with evil-doers; these are often monsters, but also may be evil people as well. Carl, the greedy, corrupt businessman, a 1980s evil icon, has sold his soul to the devil and must be kept from harming Molly. Sam devotes himself to this task, even postponing his already-earned trip to heaven to accomplish it. Notably, the story line allows both Willy Lopez and Carl to be killed by "natural" causes—a car crash and a window shard—to maintain Sam's purity. There is no blood on his hands, only noble intentions.

Molly is decidedly not a '90s (or even '80s or '70s) woman, however. Her character is very much that of the passive princess, a beautiful, feminine vessel[2] whom Sam must protect. Like Snow White and Sleeping Beauty, she is too gentle and naive to perceive the evil intentions in Carl's courting of her. This portrayal of the female character as defenseless and in need of male protection has dominated romantic mythology right up through Jane Austen. Some other of our 1990s films, however, show an evolutionary trend toward a more active role for the princess.

The Lion King (1994)

In 1994, Disney Studios released *The Lion King,* which became the highest grossing animated film in history ($350 million). The text follows the traditional mythic story line of hero-born-high, hero-falls-low, hero-sent-into-exile, hero-returns-triumphant pattern that we saw in *Ben Hur.* What is especially interesting, however, and may in part explain the film's tremendous success, is that *all* the characters are animals, not humans. Thus, the audience must read the story entirely in metaphorical form; that is, we "see" Simba not merely as a young lion, but as a young man who must return to claim his birthright after the tragic death of his father. Animal-character motion pictures have totemic or metaphorical qualities. They can present human truths in a disguised format that can invite viewer empathy more fully than if human actors and characters are used.[3]

At the opening of the narrative, we have every species of African animal gathering at Pride Rock, a large rocky outcropping above the African plain, to view a momentous occasion. Mufasa, the King of the Lions, and his wife Serafi have had a son, Simba, who is destined to eventually become the new ruler of all Africa, and all animal species. Rafiki, the wise, old shaman baboon, holds the young cub aloft for all to see; Rafiki puts a special water mark (holy baptism) upon the baby cub's forehead to signify his special status. All of the other animals cheer and bow before the cub.

Here in just this short sequence we have witnessed several significant mythic elements: the conclave of animal species (representing human races), the gathering at a high geographic spot (close to the gods), the declaration of royal (god-chosen) lineage, the reaffirmation of patriarchy (the king, after all, is a male, and so of course the future king must also be a male). Unfortunately, lurking in the background is King Mufasa's evil brother, Scar, who is plotting to do away with both father and son and ensconce himself as ruler. To this end, he has enlisted the help of the lions" natural enemies, the hyenas, a barbaric race of canine scavengers.

As Simba grows into a young cub, Mufasa shows him the extent of the kingdom, telling him he must not venture beyond its boundaries and must always respect the delicate balance of nature. Simba, still quite young, does not pay close attention. One day, the crafty Scar entices Simba and his play-buddy, a female cub named Nala, to a dangerous and forbidden place, the elephant graveyard. Zasu, their bird guardian, warns them against it, but they evade him. On the way to the graveyard, Simba and Nala wrestle each other; Nala wins. Once they arrive at the forbidden place, Scar's hyenas close in to kill them. Fortunately, Zasu has called Mufasa, who rescues the cubs. Mufasa reprimands Simba; telling him that he has a responsibility to become a good and wise king. Mufasa points to the night sky (heaven) and tells Simba that all the great lion kings of the past are residing there, looking over him; Simba can look to them for guidance.

Scar continues plotting; this time he tricks Simba into entering a narrow gorge. Scar's hyenas then cause a huge herd of wildebeasts to stampede through the gorge, trampling over Simba. Mufasa sees what is happening and dashes to save Simba, placing him safely upon some rocks. But Scar, seizing his chance, prevents Mufasa from escaping the thundering herd. Mufasa is trampled to death. Scar then tells Simba that he (Simba) caused Mufasa's death. Laden with guilt, Simba runs away. Scar sends a pack of hyenas to finish him off, but Simba leaps into a forest of thorns to escape them, indicating his innate resourcefulness and instinct to survive. Scar returns triumphantly to Pride Rock and declares himself king.

Just as Moses in *The Ten Commandments* and Ben Hur, Simba treks alone across a vast wasteland; the sun parches him and vultures stalk his steps. But, as with Moses, he awakens to find himself under a cool palm tree; he has been rescued from death by a muskrat and a warthog. Simba thanks them and tells them he is an outcast; they confide that they are, as well. They advise him to follow their philosophy of "hakuna matata": have no worries now, just do as you please. Thus, Simba joins up with a band of fellow outsiders. He puts his thoughts and responsibilities of being the Lion King behind him. Time passes, and Simba grows into a handsome young lion, the image of his father. One day a beautiful, athletic young lioness appears, who outfights him; of course, it is Nala. Suddenly, the two lions recognize each other. Nala tells Simba that Scar has declared himself king and he and his hyenas have ruined the kingdom. Everyone is starving; it is Simba's duty to return and set things right.

Simba, haunted by guilt, refuses to return. Campbell terms this "refusal of the call," the hero declines to accept a challenge. Rafiki, the wise old baboon sage, visits Simba and shows Simba his reflection in a pool of water, asking him: "Who are you?" Simba looks in the reflecting pool and sees his father's image. Rafiki tells him, "*You* are the one true king; you must return and take your place in the circle of life." This time, Simba responds to the call, returning with Nala and his two friends to Pride Rock. He finds the land in ruins; the delicate harmony of nature has been damaged by the rampaging hyenas.

Scar, the selfish despot, is in charge; he strikes Simba's mother, Serafi, for failing to find food. Simba emits an enormous roar and for a moment everyone mistakes him for Mustafa, his father. Scar, recovering his composure, orders his hyenas to throw Simba over a cliff; Scar glares down at him: "That's just how your father looked, just before I killed him!" Simba, summoning all his strength, leaps back atop the cliff, where he and the lionesses battle Scar and the hyenas. Lightning (signaling an epic struggle) ignites the dry grass, setting off a conflagration. Scar loses the battle and is ordered by Simba to leave Pride Rock forever; Scar pretends to obey, but instead turns and attacks Simba. In the struggle, Scar tumbles over a cliff and is devoured by his own hyenas. With the climactic death of the Pretender, a cleansing rain falls, quenching the fire and bringing new life to the land. The clouds part to reveal a wondrous starlit sky. Simba, his crown now valiantly earned, mounts Pride Rock and lets out an enormous roar: He is King! All of the lions shout with joy.

Simba rules the Pride Lands as a brave and wise king; the animals and lands, indeed, all of nature, flourish. Soon all of the animals gather again for another celebration, the birth of Simba and Nala's baby boy cub. Once again, Rafiki holds the king-to-be upward toward heaven as all look on; the circle of life continues.

Robin Hood: Prince of Thieves (1991)

We turn now to a live-action film with a story line remarkably similar to that of *The Lion King*. In one sense, *Robin Hood* is an older tale than *The Lion King*, harking back to twelfth-century England. But *Robin Hood*, like *The Lion King*, exhibits the same mythic structure of heroic quest described by Campbell; it is this common, ancient structure and plot line that lends these films, and so many others, their compelling familiarity to us. We know in advance where the story is going, but we still find the journey exhilarating. This historic tale is set in A.D. 1194; King Richard I (Coeur de Lion) has led the third crusade to Jerusalem to free the Holy City from the Muslim infidels. Many young English noblemen who followed him there were slaughtered or imprisoned and held for ransom. One of these men, Robin of Locksley (Kevin Costner), languishes in a filthy prison. He courageously offers himself in place of a weaker man to be punished for stealing food; but just when he is about to be punished, he overpowers the guards and frees several prisoners, including a black Muslim, Azim (Morgan Freeman). One of the English prisoners too weak to escape gives Robin a signet ring and asks him to look after his sister, Marianne; Robin promises to do so.

Azim leads Robin to safety and tells him it is Muslim custom for him to now remain with Robin until he, Azim, can save *his* life; reluctantly, Robin agrees. Four months later they set foot in England, where Robin kisses the soil of his countryland. (This gesture has its origins in the prehistoric worship of the earth as nurturant goddess.) Robin does not yet realize that his noble father, Lord Locksley, has been slain by the wicked Sheriff of Nottingham (Alan Rickman) in his absence, forfeiting the family's lands and titles. Robin had left England estranged from his father; now, sadly, there will be no possibility of making amends. As Robin and Azim approach Locksley Castle, they see the Sheriff's men chase a ten-year-old boy up a tree, attempting to kill him for poaching deer. Robin heroically battles six men and saves the boy. Upon arriving at Locksley Castle, Robin discovers his father dead and the house plundered; he gently buries his father and cares for his lone remaining servant, Duncan, who has been blinded by the Sheriff. Robin swears a blood oath to avenge his father's death, wearing around his neck a gold cross that was once his father's. This amulet symbolizes his fealty to Christianity.

In nearby Nottingham, the evil Sheriff is plotting with his aged sorceress advisor; he is a pagan or devil worshipper in league with black magic. Here we have the destructive goddess figure represented as a female witch; as Marija Gimbutas notes, this is a demeaned patriarchal representation of the early earth goddess. Christianity, a patriarchal religion, condemned as unholy the prehistoric, Druidic worship of (female) nature in England. The medieval concept of witches and witchcraft sprang from this ideological denunciation.

His own home in ruins, Robin ventures next to the home of his dead Crusader friend to look after his sister, Marianne, whom he had promised to protect. A servant permits Robin to enter the castle, which is run-down and largely deserted. He is challenged to a sword fight by a young warrior, who turns out to be the beautiful Marianne; Robin tells her of her brother's death. Marianne, a noble cousin of King Richard's, has been tending to the poor in the king's absence. She tells Robin that the Sheriff of Nottingham has been razing the countryside, destroying the nobility, and stealing from the citizenry; thus, he is closely akin to Carl in *Ghost* and, especially, to Scar in *The Lion King*.

Azim, using an early monocular, sees the Sheriff's men approaching Marianne's castle. So as not to endanger her by their presence, the pair rides off to nearby Sherwood Forest, a place supposedly haunted by spirits. They are courageous to enter it, for it represents the archetypal haunted forest or wilderness, a place of unknown danger. Once they enter the forest, Robin and Azim discover that it is indeed "haunted," but not by ghosts. Rather, impoverished people have gathered there to live off wild flora and fauna. The leader of these "outlaws," John Little, a huge man, challenges Robin to a fight, claiming possession of Robin's gold cross. Robin, after an exhausting struggle, emerges victorious; he discovers that the boy whose life he saved from the Sheriff's men is John's son. Robin urges the men to fight for their freedom from the Sheriff's despotism, but they are fearful.

That Sunday, Robin, dressed as a beggar, visits Marianne in church. She tells him the Sheriff is plotting more violence against the citizens. Robin then talks in secret with the bishop, a former family friend. However, the Sheriff abruptly enters, and Robin narrowly escapes, stealing the Sheriff's fine white horse and a bag of potatoes for his hungry friends; the Sheriff, meanwhile, is attempting to woo Marianne. He is a sinister fellow with black hair and beard, dressed all in black. The Sheriff gives Marianne a beautiful golden, bejeweled dagger (penis) as a gift; Marianne reluctantly accepts it.

Robin returns to the Sherwood Forest camp, giving bread to blind Duncan. He again urges the men to fight; they again decline. Azim takes Robin aside and warns him not to selfishly use these men to further his own aims. The Sheriff, however, begins burning the peasants' homes in order to subdue them and punish them for harboring Robin; homeless women and children flood into the forest. A young man, Will Scarlet, condemns Robin: "You have brought this misery upon us." He favors turning Robin in to the Sheriff. Will and Robin become involved in a fight, which Robin wins. He tells the group: "We must stop fighting among ourselves; we must act as free men." The people rally to Robin's call and begin training themselves in combat and constructing weapons. In essence, they come to form a people's army, a communal group committed to self-defense. Azim and Robin help instruct them in the arts of war. The group engages in guerrilla tactics to sustain their mission, robbing rich, corrupt sources and using the money to feed the hungry and dispossessed. The Sheriff is furious and vows to kill Robin and bring the rebels under control.

One day a fat friar rides through the forest with an armed escort. Robin Hood and his band kidnap him and discover an enormous convoy of gold belonging to the Sheriff. When the Sheriff learns of the theft, he kills his own cousin, who was head of the guard brigade; thus, he loves gold more than kin. Marianne and her maid ride into the forest in search of Robin; they come upon him bathing in a river, where Marianne is smitten with his naked image.

Robin conducts them on a tour of the forest village. The dispossessed peasants have constructed homes, have planted small crops, and are making their own utensils. In essence, they have created their own community within the safe confines of nature, away from the corrupt and dangerous larger culture.

Robin shows Marianne the huge gold cache they stole from the Sheriff, who had intended to use it to overthrow King Richard and place the corrupt Prince John, the King's brother, on the throne. (This story line very closely parallels that of Mustafa and Scar in *The Lion King*.) Marianne gives Robin the Sheriff's gold dagger to add to the cache.

Robin asks Marianne to stay for dinner at the camp. That night, there is dancing and music performed by the common folk. Robin tells her he has learned from this that "nobility is not a birth right; it is defined by one's actions." Thus, he has accepted the notion of democratic, rather than aristocratic, governance; true nobles are those who have exhibited exemplary human qualities, not (necessarily) those of a certain lineage.[4] That evening, Robin confides to Marianne his deep sorrow over his father's estrangement from him. It seems that when his mother died, Robin's father had begun seeing a nearby peasant woman; Robin, angered by this, demanded that his father stop the relationship. His father did so, but they were still angry at each other when Robin embarked on the crusade. Their conversation is interrupted by news that John Little's wife is having a difficult childbirth; Azim performs a cesarean section, saving the mother and her infant son. Marianne and Robin fall in love; she departs by boat the next morning.

The wicked Sheriff visits his witch/sorceress for advice on dealing with the peasant's revolt. She advises him to bring in the Celts, fierce Scottish tribes, to battle Robin Hood and for him to marry Marianne and father a (royal) child with her, placing himself near the throne. Marianne attempts to send word of this to Robin, but her maid is slain by the Sheriff's men; they then kidnap Marianne and bring her to Nottingham. Old, blind Duncan is tricked into riding into Sherwood Forest for help; he is followed by the Sheriff's Celtic and English forces, who use flaming arrows (fire of the destructive goddess) to burn the forest village to the ground. Azim and Robin fight valiantly, but to no avail. Will Scarlet and nine others are captured; many more are killed. The Sheriff forces Marianne to agree to marry him by threatening to slaughter the peasant children he has taken prisoner.

Will Scarlet is released by the Sheriff to betray Robin; when Will arrives at the secret camp, Robin asks him, "why do you hate me so?" Will replies: "Because our father loved you more than me . . . we are brothers. You ruined my life."[5] Robin is stunned, then happy, to learn he has a half brother. Will and Robin embrace and unite to fight together against the Sheriff. Robin, Will, John Little, John's wife, Friar Tuck, and Azim don various disguises to sneak into Nottingham, where some of the Sheriff's prisoners are to be hanged in the town square. Will is discovered by the Sheriff's men and sentenced to be beheaded. Robin uses remarkable archery to rescue Will and John Little's boy, again. Azim sets off a gunpowder explosion and rouses the townspeople to help.

The Sheriff and his sorceress take Marianne and the corrupt bishop to a high tower to perform the marriage ceremony; but Marianne actively resists him, as Azim and Robin attempt to break in and halt the marriage. Several archetypal outcomes then occur: (1) The corrupt bishop is pushed out a window by the good Friar Tuck; (2) The sorceress is slain by Azim; (3) The Sheriff attempts to slay Robin with the sword he stole from Robin's father, but instead Robin kills him with the gold dagger the Sheriff had originally given to Marianne.

A few days later, Robin and Marianne are married by Friar Tuck in a beautiful ceremony in the forest. Like Jenny in *Forrest Gump,* Marianne has leaves and flowers entwined in her hair, signaling her alignment with the nurturant goddess. Suddenly, good King Richard (Sean Connery) rides up, returned from the Crusades. He gives the bride away, as a flock of white doves flies skyward. Thus, the marriage is blessed by both royalty and the gods.

We now return briefly to discuss the slaying-pattern found in the movie, for it reveals an important archetypic pattern. First, the truly holy man, Friar Tuck, who had helped the rebel's just cause triumphs over the corrupt bishop, who was in the Sheriff's employ and debauched by worldly treasure. Second, the witch/sorceress who dabbles in black magic is appropriately destroyed by the heroic black warrior who dabbles in white magic, as exemplified by his mastery of ocular lenses, surgery, and gunpowder. Third, the Sheriff is unable to murder Robin with Robin's father's sword because its lineage causes it to serve the good; conversely, the gold dagger given by the Sheriff to Marianne and thence by Marianne to Robin to assist the worthy rebellion has been transformed from an instrument of ill to an instrument of good. Thus, appropriately, Robin employs it to slay the evil person who has wrought so much destruction in the land. Metaphorically, the Sheriff dies by his own hand.

The three films we've examined thus far in this chapter—*Ghost, The Lion King,* and *Robin Hood*—share in common the portrayal of the hero as the defender or protector of his beloved. I have also arranged them in ascending order from passivity to activity of the heroine. As we move from *Ghost* to *Robin Hood,* we find the heroine taking an increasingly assertive role in the narrative, both in terms of physical competence and establishing an independent identity. We now turn to two films that do not use physical conflict with an evil third party to provide the essential tension in the text, but rather which explore man-woman relations in terms of economic status. The first, *Pretty Woman,* has a Marxist subtext, while relying upon low-born princess/high-born prince tensions to propel it. The second, *Mrs. Doubtfire,* is remarkably modern not only in its exploration of late twentieth-century gender roles, but also in its unorthodox proposition that not all princes and princesses "live happily ever after."

Pretty Woman (1990)

The story opens at the swank hilltop residence of attorney Philip Stuckey (Jason Alexander), who is hosting a cocktail party in honor of his very wealthy client, Edward Lewis (Richard Gere), a leveraged-buyout businessman so iconic of the 1980s. Edward's girlfriend in New York is breaking up with him over the cell phone, because he is too busy making deals and money to pay attention to her. Frustrated, Edward leaves the party driving Philip's fancy grey Lotus, intending to go to the elite Beverly Wilshire Hotel.

Edward becomes lost in a tawdry area of Hollywood and stops to ask directions from a young, pretty prostitute, Vivienne (Julia

Roberts). She agrees to show him the way for $20. Vivienne is new to the world of prostitution, having come from a small town in Georgia to Los Angeles with her boyfriend. The boyfriend abandoned her, and after several menial jobs, she has turned to prostitution to earn money. Immediately, we note that Edward and Vivienne are a study in contrasts: male versus female, rich versus poor, elite versus common, well educated versus poorly educated, powerful versus unpowerful, well dressed versus cheaply dressed.

Vivienne drives the car to the hotel (she knows more about machinery than Edward does); Edward pays her and she waits for a bus to return to her street walking. Edward decides to hire her services for an hour for $100. They enter the elegant hotel, where Vivienne's out-of-place appearance causes the guests to gawk. Edward covers her with his coat. They go to his penthouse suite, which is the most expensive in the hotel. Vivienne likes the balcony with its wonderful view, but Edward is scared of heights.

Edward orders champagne as Vivienne exhibits her condoms. He decides to pay her $300 for the entire night, so they will not have to rush. At one point, Edward fears Vivienne is doing drugs in the bathroom, only to find her flossing her teeth, signaling her innate purity; he becomes fascinated by her easy laugh and naturalness. Vivienne undresses and performs fellatio on Edward; he then showers and returns to bed to find Vivienne asleep. Her hokey blond wig is off, and her long, auburn hair is spread across the pillow—symbolically, she is now revealed as a romantic princess. The next morning, Edward orders her an enormous breakfast, while he does business by phone. Vivienne comments to him that he "doesn't really build anything," he just sells businesses for money.

Philip Stuckey calls and tells Edward that a potential takeover candidate wants to have dinner with him; Edward needs to bring a date. Edward hires Vivienne for the rest of the week for $3,000 to be his "beck and call girl." Vivienne is ecstatic; she calls her friend, Kit, and leaves money for her at the hotel desk, demonstrating her innate generosity (a sign of nobility). Edward gives Vivienne money to buy a dress for dinner that evening and leaves for work.

Vivienne goes shopping on elegant Rodeo Drive, but is snubbed by the haughty saleswomen there. She returns to the hotel humiliated, where she encounters the manager who, after some discussion, kindly agrees to help her. He sends Vivienne to a gentle, helpful saleswoman who outfits her in a lovely dress; her transformation to externally visible princess status is under way. (The hotel manager and saleslady are Vivienne's guides/sages.) The manager then instructs Vivienne in the appropriate dining rituals. Edward returns to the hotel that evening to find his awkward "duck" transformed into a beautiful swan; Vivienne takes his arm and they go to dinner.

Vivienne's natural charm and naiveté are delightful at dinner, but the dinner guest, Mr. Morris, argues with Edward about Edward's planned takeover of his company. Back at their hotel penthouse, Vivienne and Edward discuss the evening. Edward prefers to keep his emotions in check and just to concentrate on winning and making money; Vivienne says she does the same when "turning tricks" as a prostitute. Edward goes downstairs. Later, Vivienne has a friendly elevator attendant take her to Edward; he has been playing piano in the ballroom for the hotel maintenance staff. We see from this that he too is beginning to be transformed

Fotos International/Archive Photos

Richard Gere and Julia Roberts portray modern versions of the prince and princess in Pretty Woman.

from a business machine into a caring human being. He and Vivienne make love on the piano.

The next day, Edward takes Vivienne shopping for clothes so that the salesclerks will not demean her. Edward tells the store staff he will give them "an obscene amount of money" to look after Vivienne; they, like prostitutes, rush forward to do so. Vivienne, now externally transformed into an elegant lady, takes her purchases back to the hotel. At this point, a Marxist would be screaming that this tale engulfs the viewer in false consciousness, that it teaches that money can buy happiness. However, hang on, because there is more tale to come.

The hotel manager happily notices the transformation Vivienne is undergoing. That evening, Vivienne and Edward enjoy an elegant dinner *en suite;* they then bathe together in the bathtub. This, of course, has symbolic implications beyond the sensual; both are being reborn into new personas. Edward tells Vivienne of his difficult childhood as the discarded son of a very wealthy man; he vowed revenge. As a man, he bought his father's company and then dismantled (dis-*membered*) it. Vivienne and Edward hold each other; they are comfortable.

The next day, Edward and Vivienne attend a polo match in Beverly Hills. Vivienne looks lovely and has retained her natural demeanor in contrast to the social-climbing attitude of many others there. Phil Stuckey is introduced to Vivienne by Edward; he becomes jealous of Vivienne's close relationship with Edward. She is drawing Edward toward love and humaneness, while Philip prefers Edward's former competitive, greedy self. Philip tells Edward he fears Vivienne may be an industrial spy hired by Mr. Morris to prevent their takeover. Edward laughs, then foolishly tells Philip, "She's not a spy; she's a hooker." Philip walks over to Vivienne and makes several crude, sexual remarks, touching her shoulder. Vivienne is crushed and deeply humiliated.

Edward and Vivienne return to the hotel; she is very angry and hurt. Vivienne gathers the few possessions she came with, as Edward struggles to overcome his pride and make amends. He puts the money he owes her on the bed; she ignores it and walks out. He follows her to the hallway: "I was stupid and cruel. . . . I don't want you to go." Vivienne returns to their room, where they make up and make love. She tells him of her impoverished childhood and ill-fated trip to Los Angeles. The next evening Edward takes Vivienne on a fairy-tale trip to the San Francisco Opera aboard his private jet. They have box seats among the social elite. Edward has borrowed some elegant ruby jewels for Vivienne to wear, and she looks like a princess. Even more significant, she responds to the opera as a true princess, with deep sensitivity and emotion: She is a "diamond in the rough"—a woman of genuine gentility born to a low status and a vulgar profession.

They arrive back at the hotel, where Vivienne convinces Edward to take the next day off and just enjoy being alive. She instructs him in all the common pleasures: walking barefoot in a park; getting close to the nurturant goddess, Nature; eating hot dogs; *not* using his cell phone. That night he falls asleep at peace with himself; she kisses him and they make love. Each has come a great social and emotional distance to find the other. It is the last day of their week together; Edward gently asks her to become his mistress because he cannot commit to marriage. She gently refuses his offer because being a mistress is still prostitution. They part as friends.

Edward goes to the business meeting at which he is supposed to take over Morris Industries, intending to make a handsome profit for himself and Philip Stuckey. However, Edward is now a changed man; he tells Mr. Morris he wishes to go into ship *building* with him, preserving all of the jobs that would have been lost. Morris, a dignified honorable father figure, tells Edward he "is proud of him." Thus, Edward becomes a worthy son and gains a worthy father. Edward walks outside on the fresh grass; he's become, in Marxist terms, "grounded in material reality"—a good place to be.

Philip, meanwhile, is consumed with anger. He storms over to the hotel where he finds Vivienne alone; he beats her and attempts to rape her. Edward rushes in (the heroic rescue) grabs Philip and tosses him out; their relationship is severed. Edward tends to Vivienne's bruises, but she still is leaving. She tells him she is very proud of his decision to work with Morris: "I think you have a lot of special gifts." The hotel manager has the limousine driver take Vivienne back to her apartment, a gesture of admiration and respect. Vivienne packs her bags to go to San Francisco, enroll in college, and start her life anew. She graciously gives Kit, her roommate, some money to return to school as well. "This is from the Edward Lewis scholarship fund." The hotel manager tells Edward, "It must be difficult to let go of something so beautiful." Edward decides not to let her go; he has the limousine driver take him to Vivienne's apartment, where, bearing flowers (symbols of the nurturant goddess) and playing operatic music, he climbs up the high tower (a fire escape) and asks her to marry him. They kiss; each has "rescued" the other.

Despite the fact that *Pretty Woman* is a modern text in which both the man and woman effect positive changes in each other, instead of the man merely rescuing the woman from physical danger, it does not attempt to peer into the future of Vivienne and Edward's relationship. Will our princess and prince continue to live happily ever after? Indeed, virtually all of the classic romantic films we have studied, from *Snow White* to *The Graduate* to *Robin Hood,* end at the protagonists' transition to marriage. Only one, *The Ten Commandments,* took us into the marriage, and, once there, we have Moses essentially abandoning his sexual and emotional commitments to his wife in order to commit himself entirely to God's work. *Mrs. Doubtfire,* to which we now turn, shows us one possible outcome to a long-term marriage that is rarely dealt with in the myths we've encountered thus far, but all too common in everyday life—divorce.

Mrs. Doubtfire (1993)

Daniel Hillard (Robin Williams) is a highly creative and comical actor; unfortunately, he is not a stable father figure or economic provider for his family. His wife, Miranda (Sally Field), is a level-headed, talented architect. One day Miranda arrives home from work to discover that Daniel has brought an entire petting zoo to their San Francisco town house to celebrate their twelve-year-old son's birthday party. The police have also arrived because of neighbors' complaints about noise. Miranda is furious to find the household in chaos; she tells Daniel that their fourteen-year marriage is over—she wants a divorce. At the court hearing, the judge looks askance at Daniel's spotty employment record and awards sole custody of the couple's three children to Miranda. Daniel is given three months to prove himself a capable father in order to be considered for joint custody. Daniel moves into a small, run-down apartment and gets a job at a local television station stacking and shipping videotapes. An old flame of Miranda's, Stuart Dunmeyer (Pierce Brosnan), asks her to design the interiors for a historic hotel he is remodeling. Stuart is charming and handsome and thus represents a threat to Daniel for both Miranda's and his children's affection.

To help keep himself in his family's life, Daniel creates an alternate persona for himself, Mrs. Doubtfire, a wonderful English nanny. Not recognizing who "she" is, Miranda hires Mrs. Doubtfire. Mrs. Doubtfire is a superb nanny—clean, disciplined, and efficient (everything Daniel wasn't). She organizes the children's homework, cleans the house, and prepares wonderful, nutritious meals. Daniel also continues to work at the television studio where he begins improvising a children's television show. While in his Mrs. Doubtfire persona, Daniel attempts to subtly slow Miranda's relationship with Stuart, advising her to be chaste and wear conservative clothes on dates.

One day, the oldest son walks into the bathroom unexpectedly and sees "Mrs. Doubtfire" peeing into the toilet standing up. Thus exposed (!), Daniel has no choice but to reveal his true identity to his two oldest children, who agree to help him try to win back Miranda. That evening, Miranda has a heart-to-heart talk with Mrs. Doubtfire, describing in detail why her marriage to Daniel didn't work out. (We are coming to realize that perhaps Miranda was right in ending it.) That weekend, Stuart invites the entire family, including Mrs. Doubtfire, to his private club for a swim. Stuart is attentive and genuinely cares for Miranda and the children; Mrs. Doubtfire, however, continues to sabotage his efforts.

Daniel's life is changing for the better; his apartment is now well kept and well furnished, and he has been developing a children's program in secret at the television station. The station director, Mr. Lundy, sees him performing by chance one day and invites Daniel to dinner to discuss putting the show on the air. That weekend it is Miranda's birthday, and Stuart has once again invited everyone to dinner. Daniel suddenly realizes it is the same evening as his dinner with Mr. Lundy; unable to cancel either, he must attend both. A hilarious charade occurs at the exclusive restaurant as Daniel/Doubtfire changes and rechanges his apparel,[6] attempting to have dinner in both personas. The effect is made more comical by his desperate drinking in an effort to remain calm. Ultimately, Mrs. Doubtfire's disguise is in tatters, and Daniel's secret identity is revealed to all.

A court hearing ensues in which Miranda is awarded full custody of the children and Daniel is remanded for a psychological evaluation. Soon, however, Miranda and the children begin to miss "Mrs. Doubtfire," who now is starring on Daniel's own successful children's television show. Miranda relents and permits Daniel as many visits with the children as they desire. Mrs. Doubtfire reads a letter from a divorced child on her television show advising the child that "there are all kinds of families; just because your mom and dad don't live together anymore doesn't mean they don't love *you.* They *do.* . . . Love is the tie that binds."

Mrs. Doubtfire does not present us with heroic archetypes per se, as the other films we've examined in this chapter have done. Rather, it performs the *sociological* function of myth by dealing with a very common social problem, divorce. For many families, almost half by today's statistics, there is no happy ending with mom, dad, and the children all living contented lives under one roof. *Mrs. Doubtfire* acknowledges this cultural reality and, instead, instructs its audience in how to cope with broken families in a mature and healing fashion. Even when the man and woman are no longer the heroic prince and princess they once were, they can still be good *parents.* That is the simple lesson here, and it is a wise one.

— ELEVEN —

MOTION PICTURES OF THE 1990s: The Love-Hate Relationship between Humans and Machines

DURING THE FIRST 99.9 PERCENT of human existence, there were no machines. Indeed, one of the most dramatic shifts in human culture occurred in the late 1800s with the advent of the industrial revolution. Societies around the world that had previously been based upon agrarian economies lurched radically in response to the massive population upheavals created by factory employment. People moved from outside to inside, off the open land and into huge buildings, away from nature and into technology. The mythic structures and archetypes that had served us well for millennia were challenged to adapt to this new world order. Were machines heroes or villains, saviors or monsters, good or evil? We have already seen some strong hints of our culture's interpretation of technology in the *Star Wars* trilogy. There, writer and director George Lucas presented us with unmistakable images of the evil side of the machine. The Galactic Empire and Darth Vader made vividly clear to us that technology could be used to serve despotic ends, that it could dehumanize, that it stood in masculine opposition to female Nature.

In this chapter we examine five motion pictures of the 1990s that in various ways explore the controversial terrain between people and technology. In some of these narratives technology is portrayed as valuable and useful—necessary to the survival of our species. In others, however, machines are depicted as our natural enemies, our greatest threat, the entities against whose dominance we must remain ever vigilant. The films are *Twister, Apollo 13, Independence Day, Jurassic Park,* and *Terminator 2.*

Twister (1996)

Our story opens with a flashback to 1976. An extremely powerful tornado is bearing down upon a Midwestern farm family; with only seconds to spare, the mother, father, daughter, and pet dog rush to their storm cellar. But the storm is so strong that the father, trying to keep the cellar door shut, is picked up and carried away. Shifting forward twenty years, the young farm girl has grown into an attractive woman scientist who investigates tornadoes; Jo[1] (Helen Hunt) is the leader of a band of techno-nerd storm chasers who comb the Midwestern plains attempting to study tornado activity. On this particular day, her ex-husband, Bill (Bill Paxton), and his fiancé, Melissa (Jamie Geertz), have driven out in Bill's new, red pickup truck to have Jo sign off on the divorce papers. Bill has decided to quit storm chasing, settle down, and work as a television weatherman.

When they arrive, Jo stalls on signing the papers and instead distracts Bill by showing him the new tornado tracking device they hope to test. Called Dorothy, after the *Wizard of Oz* heroine, this contraption sends metal discs into the tornado's air flow, permitting its movement to be tracked by computer. The device is intended to provide advance warning of tornado activity, saving human lives. Suddenly, a tornado call comes in to the team, and they all jump into a mismatched jumble of vehicles to pursue it. Bill, still waiting for Jo to sign the paper, takes Melissa and follows behind.

On the road, they encounter a sinister-looking caravan of very expensive, hi-tech vans led by a corporate-sponsored scientist, named Jonah, who is also chasing the storms, hoping to earn a monetary profit. This is in contrast to Jo's team who are public-sponsored, welfare-of-the-people types.[2] In symbolic marking, Jonas's group is outfitted all in black (bad, evil), whereas Jo, Bill, and the others are in casual, worn, common-man apparel and vehicles. Jonas, an egotist as well as a mercenary, also corrupts himself by doing television interviews and bragging about *his* new technology for tracking storms, a rip-off of Jo's machine.

Bill promises Jo he will help her track storms over the next day or so, so that Jonas will not beat her. Bill carefully feels the dirt and wind to instinctively read nature and determine the storm's position; Jonas, by contrast, has no natural instincts and is completely dependent upon his hi-tech gear. A tornado is spotted on the horizon. Jo, Bill, and Melissa jump into Bill's truck to pursue it. We glimpse the tornado; it is a visual incarnation of the destructive goddess, a violent, uncontrollable tube of wind that rips up everything in its path. Jo, and Bill become trapped in a gully under a bridge, narrowly escaping death. Back in Bill's truck, Bill, Jo, and Melissa pursue two other storms, again following Bill's natural instincts. An airborne cow flies by, and their truck is spun around. The tornado vanishes as abruptly as it appeared; Bill and Jo embrace, excited by the sexuality of destruction.

The entire troupe then drives to Jo's aunt's house for breakfast. The aunt is a farmer and sculptor who constructs melodious wind chimes. Everyone chows down on steak, eggs, potatoes, and lemonade—traditional, hearty, *real* food. A call comes in that yet another tornado has been spotted, and they all rush out of the house in chase. Once again, Bill's instincts prove superior to Jonas's technology for tracking the storm. As an airborne boat flies by, Bill and Jo struggle to position Dorothy so "she" will be picked up by the storm and carried aloft, just as the girl Dorothy was on her trip to Oz. This twister is a half-mile wide and roars like a wild beast: it is the monster. Bill and Jo, stimulated by the raw, sensual energy around them, begin to fall in love again. Melissa senses this and realizes she is an outsider in their world.

The group stops at a small motel/drive-in theater for the night.

It is dark, but the wind begins to pick up ominously. Bill and Jo sense an oncoming tornado and courageously herd those around them into a nearby shelter as a huge storm passes by. Jo's aunt is watching television that same evening, when her wind sculptures begin to blow gently; the huge tornado is heading her way. By the time Jo and her team arrive, the little town in which her aunt lives has been decimated. The aunt's house lies in ruins; they rush in to rescue her and her pet golden retriever. Bill, Jo, and the group quickly refill the Dorothy machine in an effort to track this terrible storm. Bill and Jo succeed in placing the machine near the funnel, but it malfunctions. They are almost killed when a tanker truck is nearly dropped on them, exploding in flames. We have a classic iconic scene here of their truck going, unscathed, through the inferno.

Jonas and his crew have been tracking the same storm, but ignoring Bill's warnings, they drive directly into its path. Jonas is killed, a victim of his own technological hubris and the violent destructive goddess of nature. The same storm begins pursuing Bill and Jo again; they drive into a cornfield to escape it, finally abandoning their truck and running on foot to a farm. Magically, the storm closes in on the truck and carries it aloft, together with the Dorothy machine. Data begin feeding into the National Weather Service computers tracking the path of the storm; their heroism has been rewarded and lives will now be saved. The storm continues to pursue Bill and Jo, however. They run through a barn and finally seek refuge in a small pump house. Using leather straps, they tie themselves to pipes which are anchored deeply in the ground; symbolically they are anchoring themselves to Mother Earth, to escape her own destructive force.

The extraordinary storm passes and the sun shines down; a farm family with a mother, father, daughter, and dog emerge safely from their storm cellar, echoing Jo's childhood. Bill and Jo agree to work together on their tornado project; they are about to kiss when their team shows up. They kiss anyway.

Twister instructs us to respect the awesome powers of nature as the destructive goddess. Bill and Jo, our two intrepid storm chasers, have no illusions or intentions of controlling the natural force of tornadoes. Instead, their goal is to provide fragile humanity with sufficient warning to take shelter from their deadly power. Marija

Gimbutas very cogently observes that death and life are inextricably bound up together within nature. The nurturant goddess creates and procreates; the destructive goddess destroys and ends. Technology, in this narrative, is seen as less powerful than nature; it can provide humans with (some) safety, but not control or dominance; nature is depicted as the superior force. We will see the same kind of human-technology-nature relationship in our next film as well.

Apollo 13 (1995)

Of the many motion pictures we are discussing, *Apollo 13* is the only one based largely upon historic characters. The narrative begins with the 1969 moon landing of Neil Armstrong, as documented on television by America's contemporaneous sage/wise man Walter Cronkite. Looking upon these events from his middle-class, suburban household in Houston, Texas, astronaut Jim Lovell (Tom Hanks) declares to his wife: "I want to do that. I want to walk on the moon." The national mood at that time was one of technological dominance; we felt invincible, able to leave Mother Earth at our whim and venture, as in *Star Trek,* "where no man [has] ever gone before," to the far reaches of space.

Lovell gets his chance when he is chosen to replace Alan Shepherd as the commander of the Apollo 13 moon mission. He and his two-man team practice rigorously for their upcoming journey. At the back of their minds, however, is the knowledge that technology can, and does, fail; three other astronauts had burned to death when their escape hatch jammed shut during a training exercise. But this fear cannot be shown publicly; Lovell, his wife, and the families of the other astronauts are expected to make public relations appearances portraying themselves as heroes/warriors, the men who conquered Space (Nature writ large).

As the launch date approaches, one of the team members; Ken Mattingly (Gary Sinise), is exposed to measles and taken off the mission. In his place comes Jim Swaggart (Kevin Bacon) as pilot while Fred Hayes (Bill Paxton) continues as the third member. The morning of April 11, 1970, at Cape Kennedy, Florida, the astronauts are being prepped for takeoff. Jim Lovell's wife, Marilyn, drops her wedding ring down the shower drain; it is a bad omen. The astronauts don their white, sterile, plastic suits and are sprayed with cleansing gases, all part of the ritual purification for their voyage to the Unknown. Here, space represents the wilderness—that unknown, uncontrollable, dangerous natural place, where only the very brave or very foolish venture, the rest of us choosing to remain safely at home in the secure village. The Mission Control director (Ed Harris) is sent his "lucky" white vest by his wife, a quaint superstitious token to appease the gods for daring tread upon their domain. The entire mission control staff is white, male, and dressed in white shirts and dark ties; these are the high priests of technology assembled in their temple.

The astronauts are loaded aboard an enormous rocket and sent skyward in a huge ball of fire. Clearly, this is man's attempt to usurp godlike powers, a male phallic thrust into heaven. Awestruck wives and citizens watch the rocket lift skyward and disappear. The launch is successful; Lovell, the cool-headed commander, calmly deploys the booster rocket. One engine misfires, another omen, but the flight continues. Aboard the ship, the crew continues its technological maneuvers, then turns to human necessities: peeing into plastic tubes and spewing the urine into space. They broadcast pop music ("Spirit in the Sky") from space. Back on Earth, the mission (the thirteenth) is viewed as so humdrum that the television networks decline to broadcast it. Mission Control has emptied out, and only a skeleton crew remains. Suddenly, during a routine maneuver, an explosion occurs on board; Lovell calls to mission control: "Houston, we have a problem." Oxygen, that precious, life-supporting bit of Earth that sustains their lives, is venting into space. Without it, they will soon die.

The technicians at Houston are confused. There has been a quadruple systems failure; something unheard of. Chain-smoking, the Mission Control director tries to calm his staff: "Let's work the problem." Reluctantly, they realize they must abandon all hope of a lunar landing, the mission goal, in order to save the crew. Oxygen continues to escape the spacecraft; to survive, the crew takes shelter on the lunar landing module (LM) and cuts electric power usage to the bare minimum. Television, that godlike gauge of cultural importance, continues to turn a blind eye to their plight; the technocrats do not want to acknowledge their failure at this stage. Abruptly, however, reporters catch wind of the emergency; a special television bulletin appears that the astronauts are in serious jeopardy. Marilyn Lovell must tell her son "something broke on daddy's ship."

At Mission Control in Houston, the engineers begin crafting a survival plan. The spaceship is guided carefully around the moon, and gravitational pull, a power of nature, is used to move it partially toward Earth. Here the scientists are working *with* natural forces, rather than challenging them. Mattingly, the astronaut left behind, is called in to help the technicians comprehend what went wrong with the spacecraft and how to salvage it. He sets himself to the task of devising a rescue plan for his colleagues. Everyone works together using the crude instruments of the era—blackboards, slide rules, batteries, tape, pencils. It is a celebration of self-reliance, resourcefulness, and Yankee ingenuity.

The three men in space are barely surviving; their quarters are below freezing, lightless, and soundless. They are adrift in a vast, vacant ocean in a very small metal can; how frail and fragile our species looks in such emptiness. Inevitably, anger, fear, and recriminations arise. As death becomes increasingly probable, television news crews bombard NASA for information. With noted irony, the mission that was too boring to cover has now become an international focus of macabre attention. Cronkite tells America, "They may be in real trouble." The crew, justifiably angry at the continuous monitoring of their human activities, rip off their biomedical devices. They have been reduced to eating frozen hot dogs from plastic bags and scraping ice from their windows. Technological hubris has cost them dearly; now they just hope to return alive. Using intelligence and creativity, they navigate their reentry, using Earth as the "fixed point." This has obvious symbolism; Earth is their ultimate homing device.

Mission Control and Mattingly have calculated their reentry as precisely as humanly possible; but they all fear that it is not good enough. Television turns its awful gaze toward the sky and the fearful families of the crew on the ground. Cronkite tells us "the whole world is watching, waiting." Congress asks the nation to pray to God for the safe return of the three men. In their tiny craft, the astronauts prepare themselves for their uncertain future; they may or may not survive reentry. As Cronkite notes, their damaged ship may catch fire in the Earth's atmosphere; their torn parachutes may not open. Only God knows what will become of them. Jim Lovell embraces Fred Hayes, who has pneumonia, warming and cheering him. Below the sky, military ships and helicopters prepare to locate the craft when it strikes the ocean; it is April 17, 1970.

Reentry is an Earth-bound ball of fire, a gift from the gods to the Earth. Are the humans inside still alive? Television's eye and Walter Cronkite's sonorous voice guide the American public. There is a long silence; then parachutes come into view. Jim Lovell's voice is heard: "The ship is secure; this is Apollo 13 signing off." The tiny metal island bobs in the sea of life. On board the rescue vessel, the three men pray, thanking God for their safe return and "the thousands of people who worked to bring us home."

There are two themes that propel *Apollo 13* and make it such a memorable film. The first is an affirmation of the dominance of natural forces over human intelligence. The film compellingly demonstrates the price of technological hubris (excessive pride) and complacency in the face of the much, much greater forces of space. We are puny, tiny, fragile specks of life held by gravity to our maternal sphere. We venture forth from it at great risk. Somewhat paradoxically, however, the text also celebrates human resourcefulness and ingenuity. It tells us that we are a scrappy, tough, terrier-like species. Even in dire situations, we will try to eke out survival, patch together a scheme to stay alive. That, after all, is one of the great purposes of myth: to simultaneously create a sense of awe for those forces larger than ourselves, yet give us sufficient pride-in-species to slog through disaster after disaster and somehow see survival as a triumph. That same lesson is taught in *Independence Day.*

Independence Day (1996)

We now come to a film that is something of a mythic masterpiece of Americana—*Independence Day.* I knew this was going to be archetypically juicy when I first saw the television commercials for it in the spring of 1996. They showed enormous dark shadows slowly and systematically gliding over our most sacred national shrines: the Washington Monument, the Statue of Liberty, the Empire State Building, the White House. Immediately, one realized that the American way of life was under threat. The movie itself is a fantastic smorgasbord of iconic images drawn from the past fifty years of moviemaking; indeed, it is one of the richest *intertextual* narratives that I have ever seen—drawing bits and pieces from countless science fiction films, John Wayne westerns, World War II propaganda movies, and contemporary, hi-tech motion pictures based on computer wizardry.

Just as *Apollo 13* warned us about the hazards of overconfidence and complacency regarding the technological requirements of venturing into outer space (the last frontier, the last unknown), *Independence Day* warns us that monsters, which are capable of devouring us, may dwell in that wilderness. Indeed, our little planet Earth may be akin to the little island of Amity in *Jaws,* a tiny bit of civilization and safety floating in a hostile, shark-infested sea. The story opens with shots of the American moon landing in July 1969, just as *Apollo 13* did. Astronauts leave behind an American flag and small plaque to mark our venturing into space. In 1996 a shadow passes across the plaque and the entire moon as an enormous alien craft makes its way toward Earth. The spacecraft's presence is detected by a secret government installation in New Mexico: "It's the real thing, a signal from outer space." Military commanders are called to Washington, D.C., to discuss the situation; the secretary of defense calls the president (Bill Pullman), who is watching CNN with his ten-year-old daughter.

In New York City, David (Jeff Goldblum), a Jewish MIT-dropout, notices that the cable television service he works for is beginning to experience satellite interference. In the background, the 1951 sci-fi film classic *The Day the Earth Stood Still* plays on the monitor. It is July 2. U.S. military tracking stations send data to Washington indicating that several "objects" (spacecraft) have separated from the large object ("mother ship") and are encircling Earth. Television reception is being disrupted worldwide; in the Iraqi dessert and on the Russian steppes peasants are panicking at the sight of "burning clouds in the sky." These scenes are quite reminiscent of Spielberg's *Close Encounters* images: archetypically they signal the arrival of the gods.

An AWAC plane sent to investigate one of the spacecrafts is incinerated; the gods have the power of fire and death. David, who has been monitoring the signal, notices that it is shortening with each cycle. He deduces that when the signal stops, the aliens may attack. The alien craft have positioned themselves above key cities: New York, Washington, D.C., Los Angeles, Paris, Moscow, Tokyo, London. People gawk skyward, confused and fearful. The American president addresses the country, telling the populace, "We are not alone in the universe . . . we must assume that these beings have peaceful intentions."

At a suburban house in Los Angeles, a young black boy awakens his mother, Jasmine, and his mother's boyfriend to see the awesome spectacle outside. The boyfriend, Steve Hiller, an Air Force pilot (Will Smith) is called to El Toro Air Force Base as a potential defensive maneuver. Meanwhile, David and his father (Judd Hirsch) begin driving from New York to Washington to warn David's ex-fiancé, the president's press secretary, of the possible impending attack. People begin fleeing the cities; there is mass panic as roads are jammed with cars and desperate people. The president contacts his wife, who is presenting a speech in Los Angeles, and tells her to leave at once. An alcoholic crop duster in Arizona, who was once abducted by aliens, begins warning his neighbors that the Day of Reckoning is coming.

By the time David and his father reach the White House, only twenty-eight minutes remain until the signal's end. The president, realizing David's prediction is very likely correct, orders all remaining personnel to leave immediately. The president, his daughter, chief of staff, secretary of defense, press secretary, David, and his father rush aboard Air Force One, just as the alien craft open to reveal their enormous, laserlike weapons. Explosive balls of fire engulf the world's cities; the wrath of the gods has come in wind and fire. The White House and Capitol are consumed in flames; Air Force One narrowly escapes destruction. The morning of July 3 finds the world's population centers decimated; there are millions of casualties; human civilization lies in ruins.

Out on the borders of Los Angeles, Jasmine and her young son have narrowly survived by taking shelter in a traffic tunnel. Jasmine displays great courage and resourcefulness, locating a working truck and using it to gather up survivors. Remarkably, she comes across the president's wife, badly injured in a helicopter crash, and cares for her, taking everyone to El Toro Military Base, where she hopes her boyfriend will be. Unknown to Jasmine, Hiller's squadron has been sent to attack the alien ships; but their most sophisticated missiles are no match for the aliens' superior technology. El Toro base is destroyed, together with most of the fighter squadron. Hiller, the lone survivor, is pursued through desert canyons by an alien fighter aircraft. Cleverly, he causes the alien ship to crash by ejecting his parachute. Hiller locates the alien craft on foot and screams at its ugly, reptile/amphibian occupant: "Who's the man? Welcome to Earth." Hiller punches the alien in the chin (just like John Wayne) and begins dragging it to the top-secret military base that first detected the alien craft. Hiller is assisted by a convoy of the crop duster's friends who are driving across the desert in their trucks and RVs. The president lands at the same base, which is called Area 51; here secret research is being conducted on similar aliens who crash-landed forty years earlier. The chief scientist, Dr. Okun, a long-haired mad-scientist figure, takes the president, David, and others to see the remains of the earlier aliens. Area 51 also houses an intact alien fighter craft from the 1940s crash.

We learn that the aliens are physically fragile, like humans, but technologically much more advanced. Thus they are not gods, after all, but rather mortal creatures, like ourselves. They are predatory, however, and intend to exterminate the human species and take over Earth. Hiller arrives at Area 51 with his alien corpse and the caravan of refugees. As the scientists attempt to dissect the alien, it attacks them, killing Dr. Okun; a brave sergeant shoots and kills the creature. Hiller, again demonstrating initiative and courage, flies a helicopter to the remains of El Toro Air Base in search of Jasmine and her son; he finds them, and the First Lady as well, and brings them to Area 51.

David, meanwhile, has had a keen insight into how to penetrate the alien defenses. A software virus must be planted in the computer of the mother ship; once implanted, the virus will cause the force field protecting the alien ships to fail, permitting human aircraft to destroy them with nuclear weapons. Hiller volunteers to fly the alien craft to the mother ship so that David can implant the virus. Once the plan is developed, the surviving military personnel around the world are notified to be ready for attack; all nations overlook their petty rivalries and, for the survival of the species, vow to work together. Every available pilot, including the alcoholic, alien-abducted crop duster, is rallied for the effort; he is thrilled: "It's time for some payback!"

Dawn comes; it is the Fourth of July. The American flag wafts in the breeze. The president addresses his motley group of warriors: "We are fighting for our freedom. . . . The world will not go quietly; we are going to survive!" A cheer goes up. David and Steve Hiller climb aboard their craft after saying good-bye to their womenfolk; their task is to save the world, every hero's dream. The children of the crop duster proudly watch him climb into his plane. As David and Steve set off for their rendezvous with the alien mother ship, Steve declares: "I've been waiting for this my whole life."

David and Steve fly their alien craft into outer space and then into "the belly of the beast"—the mother ship—where David successfully uploads the computer virus. Back on Earth, the president orders the planet's remaining warriors into the air. The president's daughter and Jasmine and her son talk and hold on to a golden retriever; the future of the world is at stake.

After a fierce battle in the sky, the human forces have many of their missiles disabled by the alien technology. Ultimately, only one armed aircraft remains aloft, that piloted by the crop duster. With a

Twentieth Century Fox

Humans learn to work together to overcome a dangerous evil in Independance Day.

photo of his children resting before him on the dashboard, the pilot flies into the mother ship's weapon system; a cataclysmic explosion occurs. The pilot's life is gone, but his children, and all other human children, are safe. David and Steve, trapped in the mother craft, prepare to die, but at the last moment, their small ship breaks free. Steve yells triumphantly, "Elvis [Presley] has left the building!" Around the world people of all nations and races celebrate their triumph; the president embraces his daughter. Steve and David crash into the desert; they walk, heroes, out of the fiery conflagration. "Happy Fourth of July." (Again we see that walking through flames is a popular iconic image!)

Independence Day is an archetypal amalgam containing bits and pieces of many types of myth. It represents an inversion of the typical heroic quest myth in that the heroic figures within it—the president, David, Steve Hiller, Jasmine, the crop duster pilot—do not venture forth into an unknown land per se, but rather are charged with *repelling* hostile alien forces that have invaded their territory, Earth. Thus, this is one of very few top-50 motion pictures that offers a *defensive* tale. The nearest analog we have to this mythic pattern is *Jaws,* in which a frightening creature comes to terrorize Amity Island and three warriors—the sheriff, the hunter, and the scientist—are sent into the unknown (the ocean), to defeat it. In *Independence Day,* David and Steve venture into the unknown to destroy the mother ship, but much of the action and heroism takes place on the ground or in the air of Earth. Perhaps an even closer textual analog is *Ghostbusters,* in which New York is invaded by evil spirits and the three intrepid heroes must use unusual technology to eliminate them.

Independence Day offers us some interesting insights into American cultural fears in the late twentieth century. Viewing it in connection with *Apollo 13,* we are able to more clearly see our anxiety regarding technology. On the one hand, we recognize that technology may lure us into danger, taking us places where we are unable to survive, putting us into a helpless little tin can launched into space, unable to return. We fear we may overstep our boundaries and incur the wrath of the gods for intruding upon their domain. Better to be safe than sorry, stay on the ground and enjoy our lives. On the other hand, what if evil beings come to harm us?

How will we defend ourselves? Mythically, we thank God for the nuclear bomb, computer software, communications satellites, and jet fighter planes. Otherwise, how would we ward off these vicious foes? Thus, we also fear *not* having advanced technology. We will see these same anxieties played upon in our last two films, *Jurassic Park* and *Terminator 2*.

But before we turn to those texts, let's take a closer look at the evil archetype in *Independence Day*. Very clearly, the movie's continual reference to the "mother ship" gives us a clue that this force represents the destructive goddess. In essence, the enormous alien ship is a flying womb, filled with millions of offspring that she carries from solar system to solar system as her aggressive brood consumes planetary resources. This time, Earth is her target, and we must defend ourselves or perish. The filmmakers have depicted the alien creatures in ways that make them especially distasteful to us; they appear to be reptilian or amphibian in body type, both scaly and slimy, with an insectlike mandible and hood. They have claws, gnashing teeth, cartilage appendages, rasping tails, and shell-like carapaces. These are clearly very different alien images from the benign cuteness of E.T. or the ethereal fragility of the space visitors in *Close Encounters*. Indeed, the director seems to have pretty much adopted James Cameron's iconic vision from *Alien* and *Aliens*. Thus, our visual representation of something as ugly or beautiful is closely tied to our cognitive notion of whether it is good or evil. And now, on to some other ugly, bad reptilian creatures.

Jurassic Park (1993)

We now come to another Steven Spielberg film, this one populated by monsters even more horrific than the great white shark of *Jaws*. Dinosaurs have been fascinating to humans ever since paleontologists began unearthing their remains and informing us about their enormous size and predatory nature. We of the late twentieth century still seem impelled by some atavistic urge to put ourselves into direct confrontation with them; to test our mettle against these enormous predators.

Spielberg's tale begins with a British "great white hunter" (*very* similar in appearance to Indiana Jones) helping a group of workers unload a violent, unseen beast into a metal cage on a remote island off Costa Rica. It is night. Suddenly, the monster roars and devours one of the workers; we see its yellow, reptilian eye through a slat in the cage. A lawyer in an expensive suit arrives on the island; we learn that a wealthy developer is building a dinosaur theme park there, to be populated by living dinosaurs.

Meanwhile, in the Badlands of the United States, a paleontologist, Dr. Grant (Sam Neill), and his team are excavating dinosaur fossils. A woman paleobotanist, Dr. Sadler (Laura Dern), is assisting him. The dinosaur park developer flies in by helicopter to see them. Without telling them what project he has in mind, the developer promises to finance their fossil expedition for three more years if they will assist him; they eagerly agree. Meanwhile, back in Costa Rica, a fat, corrupt computer programmer for the dinosaur park (Jurassic Park) agrees to sell dinosaur embryos to a crooked scientist who works for a biogenetics corporation.

The developer brings Drs. Grant and Sadler, together with a mathematician and the lawyer, to see the park. They land in a pristine, dense jungle: the primordial forest of myth, where nature reigns supreme. Driving across open grasslands, they encounter some of the developer's handiwork: enormous, leaf-eating dinosaurs re-created from DNA trapped inside amber. The lawyer is ecstatic: "We're going to make a fortune!" The scientists are awestruck. The group arrives at Jurassic Park to find a large lobby arrayed with fossils, the centerpiece of which is an intact skeleton of a Tyrannosaurus rex, the king of dinosaurs and a magnificent monster.

The group is taken on an educational tour, which explains how dinosaur DNA is retrieved from amber and then inserted into frog eggs, where it hatches. The tour guide informs them that the resulting dinosaurs are all genetically programmed to be female, so that no matings can occur; that is, humans are in complete control of the animals" lives and reproductive capacity. (We recognize this as tampering with Mother Nature and know that she is not to be contained by man!) The mathematician senses this as well, warning them: "Life finds a way [to continue itself]." The group is taken to see an ox being fed to raptors, a particularly vicious dinosaur predator.

That evening, the group muses about the meaning of Jurassic Park. The mathematician is quite critical of this "abuse of scientific power." He notes that dinosaurs became extinct originally because nature willed it to be so. Now man is interfering with this natural design, in effect, playing God by manipulating life. We have overstepped our bounds in doing so and soon must suffer the consequences, he warns. The developer's grandchildren—a boy of ten and a girl of thirteen—have arrived at the park; he puts them and the rest of the group in an automated, jeep-driven ride through the park to test it. The boy attempts to make friends with Dr. Grant, but Grant feels awkward and ill-at-ease around children. He fears parenting and fatherhood. We learn that a hurricane is approaching the island. [Beware, the destructive goddess is on the way.]

The tour enters the dinosaur section of the park through immense wooden gates, reminiscent of *King Kong,* and surely, there *are* monsters lurking on the other side. The trip quickly becomes an exercise in frustration, however, because no dinosaurs are visible. The mathematician, in particular, complains bitterly about the "lack of dinosaurs on my dinosaur tour." A mini-rebellion occurs and the entire group abandons the jeeps, scales the fence, and goes in search of dinosaurs. They find a sick triceratops and Dr. Sadler stays to examine her. The storm sets in; heavy rain begins falling; everyone, except Sadler, returns to the cars to escape the rain. Meanwhile, the corrupt computer expert purposely crashes the entire electrical system, so he can sneak out several dinosaur embryos to take to the illicit purchaser. This compromises the security of the whole park, as the dinosaurs are controlled by electrical fences. The computer expert then accidentally crashes his jeep in the heavy rain. He is attacked and killed by small dinosaurs and drops the embryos; they are covered with fertile mud.

The tour group is now sitting in jeeps in the dark, thanks to the computer crash. A loud thumping is heard; the Tyrannosaurus rex arrives, and it is very hungry. It begins attacking the jeeps; the lawyer dashes out and runs for a nearby outhouse, where he is promptly gobbled up.[3] The mathematician and Dr. Grant rescue the two children, whom the lawyer had abandoned. Grant and the two children are knocked over a steep embankment by the creature; heroically, Grant brings the boy, Timmy, out of a damaged tree and shelters the two children in a tall tree "nest" through the night; he is learning to be a parent. The white hunter and Dr. Sadler arrive in a jeep at the accident site and find the mathematician there with a broken leg. They are searching for Grant and the children, when a T. rex arrives; they barely escape.

The next morning, Grant and the children set off for the main building; along the way, they find a clutch of recently hatched dinosaur eggs. As the mathematician predicted, nature has found a way to reproduce herself; the dinosaurs are no longer under human dominion. Grant and the children also encounter a "flock" of small dinosaurs running from a T. rex. Grant explains that dinosaurs probably evolved into birds; thus they are not truly extinct. In order to restart the computer system, Dr. Sadler and the white hunter must go to an unprotected building some distance from the compound. Sadler enters the building as the hunter stands guard. She succeeds in restoring power—that is, man's technology is revitalized— but is attacked by vicious raptors. She escapes, but the raptors attack and kill the white hunter. In secret, they follow her back to the compound.

Fotos International/Archive Photos

Humans tamper with nature and pay the price in Jurassic Park.

Dr. Grant and the children have also arrived back there after narrowly escaping electrocution when the power was restored. Grant has proven himself a sensitive, courageous caretaker; he leaves the children to eat their dinner while he looks after Dr. Sadler's injured leg. While he is gone, the raptors sneak into the building and terrorize the children, almost devouring them in the kitchen (a touch of irony). In the knick of time, Drs. Sadler and Grant return and rescue the children. The girl uses her computer skills to close off a room in the compound to save their group, but the wily raptors break through a window and continue their pursuit. The group escapes through the ceiling, landing upon the T. rex skeleton, just as a *live* T. rex crashes in the door. Happily, the T. rex and raptors then begin attacking one another, permitting the developer, the mathematician, Grant, Sadler, and the two children to flee to a helicopter—the last bit of functional technology left on the island. They pile in and take off for the mainland, leaving behind the dinosaurs in their own primeval forest; nature prevails.

Jurassic Park provides a contrary view of technology from that advanced in *Independence Day.* Here we are given a cautionary tale informing us of the awful consequences when humans adopt godlike powers and begin creating life. In many ways, *Jurassic Park* follows the same story line as Mary Shelley's classic *Frankenstein:* human scientists use their skills to construct a life form that then becomes monstrous and acts to destroy human life. Dr. Frankenstein employed cadavers and electricity to construct his monster; the scientists in Jurassic Park utilize DNA to accomplish the same end. In both cases, the monsters soon roam out of control and destroy their makers. We are thus warned by these stories that the creation of life properly belongs to God/Nature. It is beyond human authority to dabble in it: when humans make life, death soon follows.

Terminator 2: Judgment Day (1991)

We now turn to our final film, *Terminator 2.* Archetypically, this is a very powerful film. It combines many strands of cultural meaning touched upon over the course of the 1990s—the nature of heroism, including unusual or atypical heroes; male-female relationships;

and the complex sociology of humans and machines. In this vein, *Terminator 2* confronts us with three atypical heroes: a woman/mother, a twelve-year-old boy, and a cyborg. It shows us a male-female relationship between a woman and a male machine, and it posits that humans' construction of living machines will lead to our destruction.

The narrative opens by telling us that on August 29, 1997, three billion humans were killed in a thermonuclear holocaust started by supercomputers that had gained the power of conscious thought. From that time forward, the surviving humans were hunted and killed by the machines; some of the hunter-machines were androids having metallic skeletons covered with living tissue. The leader of the remaining humans in their battle to survive is a man named John Connor; the machines realize his power and have vowed to kill him as a child, before the nuclear holocaust. To accomplish this, they have sent a very advanced hunting machine—an android composed entirely of liquid metal alloy—back to the year 1991 to kill the young John Connor. Fortunately, John Connor has anticipated this move (in A.D. 2029) and sent back his own android machine to protect his young self. These hunting androids are called Terminators.

It is night; the witching, black magic time. Electrical charges surge in a deserted parking lot. A large, muscular, naked man appears in a ball of light (Arnold Schwarzeneggar). He walks into a nearby biker bar and asks for clothes and a motorcycle. The bikers begin fighting with him, but soon discover he has superhuman strength. Dressed in outlaw biker clothes, the terminator emerges from the bar and rides off with a Harley cycle and a shotgun. As we shall soon see, *this* terminator is the good guy, so we are being treated to an ironic depiction of the evil warrior archetype. Soon after, an electrical disturbance occurs again; a police officer goes to investigate, only to find a molten metal man (Robert Patrick) standing before him. This advanced terminator "absorbs" the policeman and takes his gun and patrol car. Once again we are teased with an ironic icon, for this terminator is the bad guy.

Both terminators set off in search of John Connor. John is a boy of thirteen or fourteen presently living with foster parents; his father was killed by an earlier terminator prior to his birth.

His mother, Sarah Connor (Linda Hamilton), is viewed as a dangerous psychotic by the authorities because she keeps warning them of the impending nuclear holocaust; therefore, she has been institutionalized in a mental hospital. While there, she has been keeping herself in warrior condition and has already made several escape attempts.

The policeman-terminator arrives at John's foster home and learns he has just left. John and a friend have stolen a credit card and used it to get money for the video game arcade; thus, we learn that he is a "wild" kid and not well behaved. The policeman-terminator arrives at the arcade intending to kill John. Just as he has John trapped in a corridor, however, the biker-terminator appears and the two machine warriors fight violently. John runs to his motorbike and drives off, pursued on foot by the policeman-terminator. The biker-terminator also pursues him on his motorcycle.

John, believing both are attempting to kill him, tries to elude them. The P-terminator commandeers a tractor-trailer truck and almost runs John down. At the last moment, the B-terminator reaches him, carrying him off on his Harley. When the truck explodes in a huge fireball, the metallic terminator walks out of the flames unscathed and resumes his identity as the policeman. (Please note, this is the *fifth* time we have witnessed the walks-through-fire-and-lives iconic image in our film set.) John and the B-terminator pull off the road and talk. John comes to realize that this terminator is there to help him. John calls his foster parents to warn them of the other terminator, but it is too late; they have already been murdered. John realizes also that his mother Sarah's seemingly insane ramblings about terminators and nuclear war were accurate; he hurries to go get her.

Unfortunately, the P-terminator has already arrived at the hospital and is stalking Sarah; Sarah, however, has prepared for him and already broken out of her cell. She is remarkably resourceful. John and the B-terminator find her, but at first she is terrified; the only previous terminator she has seen killed her lover and almost killed her thirteen years earlier. Moments later, however, the P-terminator appears and begins attacking her. Like John, she suddenly realizes that the terminator with John is her protector, not hunter. The trio escapes from the building with the evil terminator in close pursuit. They speed off in a car, but the evil terminator latches on with his metal claws; they wrest him off and escape.

Sarah reprimands John for coming for her: "You cannot risk your life for me. You *have* to survive; all humanity is depending on you." Thus, she displays the noble character of self-sacrifice. Sarah, John, and the good terminator take refuge in a closed gas station, where Sarah tends to the terminator's flesh wounds. The terminator, who does not need sleep, keeps guard over them during the night; he tells them that although he is a machine, he is able to learn from people; that is, he is capable of becoming more human. In the morning, the trio steals a car and drives to a secret weapons cache Sarah has hidden in the desert. The good terminator tells Sarah that the scientist responsible for creating the destructive super computers is named Miles Dyson. Indirectly, his invention will lead to the thermonuclear war and the destruction of human civilization. Sarah speaks Spanish fluently with the Chicano friends who have been guarding the weapons for her; she also drinks tequila from the bottle and puts on all-black commando gear. She is clearly an Amazon archetype, a female warrior. John and the good termi-

Zade Rosenthal/Fotos

Finally, the great goddess arrives! Sarah Conner saves the world in Terminator 2.

nator are becoming buddies, a father-son pairing; they trade jokes, assemble weapons, and fix a broken truck together. Sarah, watching them interact, realizes that the terminator is a good father figure for John: always responsive to his needs, willing to die to protect him, and able to teach him how to fight.

Sarah has a horrible dream about the future nuclear holocaust; when she awakens, she vows not to let it happen. Without telling John or the terminator, she dresses in warrior gear, arms herself with laser-equipped rifles, and sets off to kill Miles Dyson. (This is the first and only instance we have among the top-50 films in which a woman-warrior sets off to save the world.) Sarah reaches Dyson's house and is aiming her rifle at him when his son's radio-controlled car jostles Dyson's chair, saving his life. There is ample irony here as Dyson is saved by a machine, the toy car. Sarah enters Dyson's house, terrifying him, his wife, and son, but she is unable to shoot him. This is morally appropriate because Dyson has committed no crime; he merely is doing science that will be used to evil purposes by others. The terminator and John, realizing where Sarah has gone, rush to Dyson's house. Once there, they explain to Dyson what will become of the computer he is now designing, that it will lead to world destruction. Sarah yells at him: "All you men know how to create is death and destruction. We [women] create Life." This strongly feminist sentiment is one worthy of the nurturant goddess.

Together, Dyson, Sarah, John, and the terminator break into Cyberdine Laboratories that night to destroy the equipment and notes Dyson had made. Unbeknownst to them, the P-terminator has followed their trail. At Cyberdine, John cleverly uses a computer game to crack the entry code, demonstrating once again his early mastery of machines. Sarah and the terminator wire the laboratory with explosives, and the terminator also fends off the scores of police who arrive outside the building. Sarah, John, and the terminator escape the building, as Dyson, mortally wounded, holds the detonator until they reach safety. He then heroically blows up himself and his work. (This act of self-sacrifice was essential for the story line, as Dyson's survival would have permitted the knowledge residing in his mind to be used to reconstruct the dangerous technology.)

As Sarah, John, and the terminator are leaving the scene in a stolen truck, the metallic P-terminator rides up. Seeing the trio, he steals a *police* helicopter (he consistently uses the resources of goodness for evil purposes) and pursues them. When the helicopter crashes, he walks away unscathed and commandeers a huge tanker truck. Symbolizing their less-powerful status, John, Sarah, and the B-terminator are being chased at high speeds in a little "house repair" truck by the P-terminator in his hi-tech, metallic "big rig." They all arrive at a metal foundry (highly appropriate, for here machines are constructed from molten metal), and the two trucks crash. The metallic terminator is shattered, but soon re-forms himself, chasing John, Sarah, and the good terminator into the foundry.

At this point, Sarah and the good terminator are both injured but committed to using their lives to save John's; the good terminator puts himself between the P-terminator and Sarah and John. A horrific, violent struggle ensues in which the valiant terminator is torn limb from limb. As a final ironic gesture, the evil P-terminator crushes the good terminator's right arm in a machine, using a machine to destroy a machine. He then sets off after John and Sarah, who are running through the foundry. Sarah courageously shoots the evil terminator with grenades, but cannot stop him. He impales Sarah's shoulder and is about to kill her when suddenly the good terminator slices him from behind—having dragged himself in pursuit. This time, the P-terminator crushes him with a metal beam and stabs his back with a metal rod. The good terminator appears dead . . . , but slowly a red light appears in his microprocessor brain. He pulls the spear from his own back. (Now *this* is heroic commitment!)

Imitating Sarah's voice, the evil terminator calls to John; John responds, but Sarah comes up behind the evil terminator and shoots him with the grenade gun. The evil terminator merely absorbs the grenades into his metallic self. Finally, the good terminator arrives and, using an enormous shotgun, blasts the evil terminator into a vat of molten metal. Unable to absorb this much additional substance, the evil terminator dissolves—destroyed.

The trio gazes over the edge at the vat of molten metal; they toss in a computer chip and machine part remaining from Dyson's work. Sarah now must lower the good terminator into the molten metal, destroying him at his own request, for his machine parts could be used to lead to the same nuclear holocaust. John is distraught—his only true father figure must die to ensure his survival; they embrace tearfully, the terminator now having become fully human and possessing genuine emotions. The heroic terminator disappears into the fiery cauldron and departs as the noblest of men; he gives a final thumbs-up sign as his microchip fades out. John and Sarah drive alone down a darkened highway toward a new future.

Terminator 2 is a remarkable tale in several respects. In my view, it represents the most progressive development of archetypes of the top-50 motion pictures. Let's take a look at the four primary characters and consider why this is so. First, we are presented with a distinctive contracts between the good and evil terminator characters. With wonderful irony, James Cameron has presented us with the good terminator as an outlaw biker and the evil terminator as a straight-arrow policeman. By inverting the usual cultural meanings of these two figures, the text asks us to take a closer, more thoughtful look at what constitutes good and what constitutes evil. Evil, we are instructed, is a heartless, soulless, coldly rational killing machine—the liquid metal terminator. This machine, although *appearing* human, has no human feelings or parts. As a result it/he can never be transformed, or "won over," to our side; he/it can never learn to care for others. Indeed, all life forms to this terminator are weak and inferior beings, while he is a perfect, supreme *machine.*

In contrast, the good terminator, our bad-to-the-bone renegade biker, has human elements. As an android, he lives within a human skin, and, the story informs us, this human exterior eventually transforms him into a caring, feeling being. He is a *humane* vision of Dr. Frankenstein's monster, a beast refashioned into a father-protector. Indeed, the biker-terminator becomes—over the course of the film—a genuinely magnificent warrior. We weep at his self-imposed execution because he takes with him the noblest aspirations of our kind: the willful sacrifice of oneself to preserve the greater good.

As we turn to the young John Conner, we see in him the emergence of a truly American-style warrior-messiah. His future task is literally "to save the world," but he must first grow into an individual worthy of that task. As we see him develop over the course of this narrative, he matures from an out-of-control, selfish street kid to a caring, thoughtful young man, capable of undertaking not only courageous tasks, but of engaging in sensitive moral decision making as well. We sense that he will continue on this path, combining the two aspects American culture seeks in its saviors: moral purity and physical valor.

Finally, let us close this chapter by considering what we have in the character of Sarah Conner. Sarah Conner is the first female figure we have encountered in the top-50 motion pictures who embodies fully the great goddess archetype, as described by Gimbutas. Note here that I did not put the modifiers "destructive" or "nurturant" in front of "goddess," for Sarah Conner is both, just as Marija Gimbutas proposed the earliest humans envisioned her: "the one Great Goddess with her core functions—life giving, death-wielding, regeneration and renewal." The character of Sarah Conner is all these things. In specific aspects, she also represents the good mother, protecting and nurturing her child, putting his needs before her own survival. She is also a courageous and valiant warrior, an Amazon who competently employs all the usually male destructive technology: guns, bombs, fists, cars, trucks, grenades. In her most essential form, we recognize Sarah Conner as nature, herself: life-giving, life-destroying—all with the aim of preserving life itself. Thus in Sarah we have come, at the end of the millennium, full circle to the archetypic origins of our species, combining all the diverse elements of the female into one figure.

— TWELVE —

SAILING INTO THE NEW MILLENNIUM

THE MILLENNIUM IS HERE. The human species has been weaving mythic narratives for more than seven thousand years now, and directors James Cameron and George Lucas, both gifted modern storytellers, have recently completed two of the most expensive narratives ever to be put on film—the magnificent *Titanic* and *Episode I* of the epic *Star Wars* series. As we shall see, *Titanic* and *Star Wars* are both worthy vessels with which to summarize the voyage on which we have come and to carry us into the mythic future. For as this chapter's title suggests, in myth, as in life, the more things change, the more they remain the same. And if we have learned anything about myth at all, it is that even as specific icons change, archetypes and the textual structures in which they are embedded endure.

Titanic (1997)

Like many epic myths we have examined—*Gone with the Wind, Dr. Zhivago, Ben Hur, The Ten Commandments*—*Titanic* makes use of a historical event to construct a larger lesson about life, death, and morality. In this case, James Cameron's script weaves archetypal patterns of rich and poor, male and female, purity and corruption into the actual sinking of the largest steam-powered vessel ever constructed, the *Titanic.*

The story opens in the present day. A modern, hi-tech salvage project is under way in the North Atlantic; it has been funded by business entrepreneurs seeking to locate a remarkable deep-blue gem believed to have sunk with the Titanic. The crew brings to the surface an ancient safe; however, once forced open, it reveals only a charcoal drawing of a beautiful young woman, dated April 14, 1912, the day the *Titanic* went down. As the drawing is broadcast via television, an old woman, Rose Calvert, recognizes herself, eighty-four years ago. She and her granddaughter, Lizzy, are flown to the salvage ship in the hope that she will be able to locate the diamond.

Rose looks at the videos they have taken of the once great ship, and cries. Memories of her time aboard come flooding back. As Rose recounts her tale the story shifts back to 1912 and Southampton, England, where the passengers are boarding *Titanic* for her maiden voyage. Rose (Kate Winslet), herself a virgin, is boarding the ship with her mother and fiancé, Cal Hockley (Billy Zane). They are all of American birth; the generation of the Gilded Age, when the industrial revolution had made millionaires of a small portion of Americans, transforming them into nouveau royalty. Rose is in deep depression. The marriage is an arranged one to a man she does not love, undertaken to shore up her mother's shambled finances. As they board the vessel, Cal declares, "Even God cannot sink this ship." Of course, when *we* hear this, we know better; not only history informs us otherwise, but also a multitude of our myths (e.g., *Star Wars, Terminator 2*) bear testimony to the supremacy of God over human technology.

In a smoky bar on the shore, a young blond and handsome American man, Jack Dawson (Leonardo DiCaprio) is winning third class tickets for himself and his Italian friend, Fabrizio, aboard the *Titanic.* Jack is a commoner from Minnesota; orphaned, he has made his own way in the world. As the ship sets sail, we are given a full view of its enormous structure—a man-made iron island, powered by huge steam engines. *Titanic* signifies the dominance of the new machine age; man is challenge to God and nature for the supremacy of the Earth.

Cal and Rose are settled into an enormous, elegant suite. Rose's affection for abstract art and cigarettes are used to signal her nonconformity. Rose's attempts to become independent are supported by an older female passenger, Molly Brown, but vigorously resisted by Rose's mother and fiancé.

The ship's vertically arranged decks provide a wonderful metaphor for the social hierarchy on board. The third-class passengers—mostly working-class Irish, but also Hungarian, Italian, Swedish and Polish, represent the "teeming masses" speaking a multitude of languages, roughly clad, smoking their cigarettes and drinking their dark beer. The first-class passengers are elegantly attired, impeccably groomed, imbibe champagne and dine on caviar and lamb. Jack views Rose above him from his third-class vantage point. They gaze at each other across the great social divide, but Cal soon fetches her back.

That night Rose again runs off, this time attempting suicide by climbing over the railing; Jack valiantly risks his own life to pull her back to safety. Cal callously attempts to pay him, but when Rose objects to the vulgarity of his offer, Cal invites Jack to dinner the next evening, intending to humiliate him. Later that night Cal presents Rose with a beautiful blue diamond necklace, the Heart of the Sea.

We learn that Jack has been a drifter since becoming an orphan at fourteen. He has developed into a remarkably resourceful young man—courageous, intelligent, and handsome; the stuff of which princes and heroes are made. Rose's mother is deeply threatened by Rose's friendship with Jack, fearing her daughter's marketability is being tampered with. Prior to dinner that evening, Molly Brown, the nurturant goddess/fairy godmother figure, takes Jack under her wing, dressing him in her son's evening wear and instructing him on the dining rituals of the upper class. Jack is a quick study and is so transformed by his new apparel that he is immediately taken as a gentleman. (Recall this same transformation scene figured prominently in *Pretty Woman;* both Vivienne and Jack are earthy aristocrats, "diamonds in the rough," that show their true brilliance and heroic qualities once they are cleaned up and polished a bit).

At the elegant dinner, Cal and Rose's mother assault Jack with demeaning barbs, but his innate nobility shines through. Jack passes Rose a note asking her to join him; she does so, and they venture into steerage for a wild, raw, Celtic party, full of drinking, dancing, and raucous laughter. Here Cameron, the director, draws a clear distinction between the sedate, confining rituals of the upper class, with their stiff clothes and manners, versus the naturalness, looseness, and spontaneity of the "earthy" lower class; even their beer is dark and their music self-made versus the upper-class orchestra. Unfortunately, Cal's manservant discovers Rose's whereabouts and reports her brazen activities back to his master. The next morning as Cal and Rose dine, Cal berates her and smashes the breakfast table. Rose's mother then binds her tightly into her corset, symbolizing her attempts to control Rose's behavior and body.

Titanic is sailing full speed into icy waters; but believing the ship to be an invincible island of human handiwork, all aboard are oblivious to the peril. Jack contacts Rose but, subdued by Cal and her mother, she tells him she can no longer see him. Later, at a banal lunch with her mother's friends, Rose realizes the suffocation of her own life and runs to find Jack. They kiss and she spreads her arms like wings out toward the wind: "I'm flying." She has broken free of her social chains and now can become her own person. Rose brings Jack back to her suite, takes off her clothes, and puts on the necklace. Jack, enraptured, sketches her beautifully and dates the picture: April 14, 1912.

To escape Cal's servant, Rose and Jack run through steerage, into the engine room, and finally into the storage area of the ship. Here they find an exquisite automobile; they make love in the back seat, having now decided to spend their lives together. Cal and his servant discover Jack's drawing and contrive to frame him for robbery. Suddenly, jagged edges of ice tear into the ship's right hull; frigid seawater floods the engine room. Once again, the text instructs us, nature has proven herself more mighty than man.

Cal, oblivious to these larger events, reports his contrived "theft" to the ship's officers demanding Jack be arrested. When Jack and Rose return to her suite to warn Cal and her mother of the danger, Cal has Jack handcuffed and taken below to the brig. He then violently slaps Rose, calling her a slut.

The ship's architect informs the captain that the unsinkable *Titanic* will indeed sink; with the nearest ship over four hours away, the loss of life will be catastrophic. The crew begins organizing the passengers, attempting to get women and children to board the lifeboats, but the process is slow and confused. First-class women and children are given priority, all "less worthy" steerage passengers being locked into the now flooding lower levels of the ship. Warning flares are sent up (to plead with the gods?) as the ship founders lower in the water. Jack is beaten and left to die by Cal's servant. However, Rose refuses to play the role of the weak woman. Sensing Jack's fate, she struggles out of a lifeboat and runs to save him. Risking her own life, Rose finds Jack and frees him. In doing so, she frees herself, also, from the social role of passive princess—here the princess rescues the prince.

Cal finds Rose with Jack and puts his coat around her, urging her to board a boat; Jack pressures Rose to board the lifeboat as well. Rose, however, sensing Jack's certain doom, again struggles out of the lifeboat and back onto the sinking *Titanic.* She has cast her fate with him come hell or high water, and both, as we know, are on their way. Seeing Jack and Rose reunited proves too much for Cal. He grabs a gun and begins shooting at them. The pair runs through the deserted, flooding hallways, narrowly escaping drowning. Cal grabs a crying, abandoned girl and uses her to gain entry to a lifeboat. Jack and Rose rush to the back railing, where they cling as the *Titanic* breaks apart, upending itself. The last of the great ship disappears under the waves (nature's inevitable triumph over technology), leaving hundreds of thrashing, freezing humans on the surface. Jack rescues Rose and they swim to a large piece of floating debris. Alas, the raft is only big enough for one, so Jack pushes Rose atop it. The sole returning lifeboat finds hundreds of dead, frozen people bobbing about the surface. Rose, after first letting the boat pass by, signals them and is rescued.

The *Carpathia,* another passenger ship, arrives soon after and rescues the survivors. Cal searches for Rose, but she hides herself by wearing an inexpensive woolen scarf; she now has transformed herself into a commoner. Upon her arrival in New York City, Rose changes her last name from deWitt to Dawson, in essence, marrying herself to Jack's memory. Back in the present, she tells her rapt listeners, "Jack saved me in every way a person can be saved."

That evening as the sun is setting, 101-year-old Rose, in a flowing white nightgown (evocative of both a wedding and funeral dress), walks to the back of the salvage ship as it hovers above the sunken *Titanic.* In her bare feet she climbs up on the railing and tosses an object into the sea; it is, of course the long-lost blue diamond necklace; she has placed it at rest with her beloved Jack. That night Rose, warm in her bed with photographs of her full, wide life surrounding her, dies in her sleep. She dreams of herself and Jack aboard the Titanic; they are young and vigorous. Jack takes her hand as all on board applaud. At long last, they are now together for eternity.

Why was *Titanic* so compelling a tale, not only in America, but worldwide?

Following Lévi-Strauss's structuralism we can identify three sets of bipolar oppositions within *Titanic* that are central to its meaning. Perhaps the most significant pairing is that of the two virgin vessels featured: Rose deWitt and the *Titanic.* At the tale's opening, both are embarking on their maiden voyages: Rose as the virginal passive princess on her way to be wed; the *Titanic* as a maiden vessel making her first voyage and carrying a microcosm of human society in her iron womb. Rose's name implicitly suggests her innate meaning and ultimate fate. Over the course of the trip, she abandons her high-born status and becomes an "earthy" commoner, capable of surviving the natural disaster that occurs. The female vessel *Titanic,* however, is entirely removed from nature. Constructed of iron, powered by man-made fire in her huge engines, she cannot float when her womb is pierced by ice. Thus, like Rose, *Titanic* also descends and is engulfed in nature. (In essence, both Rose and *Titanic* go *downward* to a more natural status).

There are also two princes in this story. The true prince, of course is the low-born, and much more natural, Jack Dawson. The false prince is the high-born, and technology/capitalism-allied, Cal Hockley. The story provides two types of death for them, which are quite instructive. Cal survives the death of the *Titanic,* but learns

Fotos International/Archive Photos

Lovers Rose and Jack aboard the Titanic*—we've come a great distance since* Snow White.

no lessons from it. Rose informs us that in 1929 Cal takes his own life with the death of capitalism: that is, the stock market crash.

Jack Dawson, conversely, makes the ultimate sacrifice of the true prince by giving up his own life to save that of Rose. He does so, the narrative states, so that Rose can have a "wide full life and lots of babies," in essence, so that Rose can express her nature (and Nature) to its fullest. Although our storyteller, director James Cameron, does subtly hint that Rose may have borne Jack's child by pairing her strongly with her blond granddaughter, the mythic structure of *Titanic* would be stronger if this had been made explicit. One of the most compelling elements of romantic myth is the sacrifice of life by the warrior/father to perpetuate the life of his children. Indeed, the entire mythology of patriotism is premised upon the death of men/fathers to preserve the life of children and women. Thus, Jack's great sacrifice would be most fully meaningful, if we were assured his seed, safe inside Rose's womb, survived and prospered.[1]

Finally, we must consider the story's two sage/mother figures, Molly Brown and Mrs. deWitt. Mrs. deWitt, Rose's mother, represents both a false guide and the destructive goddess. Through Mrs. deWitt's comments, we learn that Rose is the child of a loveless marriage, one undertaken and perpetuated for money. Essentially, Mrs. deWitt sold herself (or was sold by her parents) into a life of upper-class domestic slavery to a dissolute man from a "good," that is, wealthy, family. In turn, Mrs. deWitt, now destitute except for her beautiful virginal daughter, is selling Rose into the same domestic prostitution in order to ensure her own financial security. As the *Titanic* voyages from the old world (Europe) to the new (America), Rose decides to break free of this unhappy form of bondage and become her own person.

Assisting both Rose and Jack in this effort is the character of Molly Brown, a woman who, despite being rich, retains her earthiness and honesty. She recognizes the inherent nobility within Jack and helps guide him through a potentially destructive encounter with the "sharks" (as she describes them) of the upper class. Further, she recognizes the naturalness within Rose and provides herself as a role model. Unlike the other wealthy women aboard the *Titanic* who are all traveling in the company of, and under the control of, men, Molly is unaccompanied, quite capable of taking care of herself.

THE LOVE STORY: *Titanic* has three additional thematic elements that help us to see both the continuity and evolution of myth. First, we are reminded that love stories are immortal. They have been with us always, and unless our species loses its emotional impulses entirely, they will remain part of our heritage forever. In many ways, the story of Jack and Rose follows the most traditional of patterns—the prince rescues the princess from many perils. However, in this telling, the prince perishes in the effort; while the princess, freed from restrictive social boundaries, grows into a full and complete woman.

If we explore this theme a bit further, we can view in it the evolution of women's roles in American culture over the course of the twentieth century. As several of our early films (*Snow White, Sleeping Beauty, The Ten Commandments, Ben Hur*) informed us, women originally were confined to the domestic sphere. Although a prince may have risked his life to save his princess, it was to salvage her for a life of domestic bliss as his wife, living happily ever after. And usually it was during this lengthy "happily ever after" period that the princess-*cum*-wife sacrificed her talents, ambitions, and aspirations in the caretaker role, serving as a support person to further her prince's career.

Titanic turns this traditional formula on its head by having Jack sacrifice his life for Rose's career—as an actress, explorer, horse rider, and mountain climber. It is little wonder that American women have been the repeat audience for this film (some seeing it four, five, and six times); it is the first we have encountered in our lengthy analysis in which the *princess's* aspirations were given preference in the text.

THE INHERENT NOBILITY OF COMMONERS: We also see in *Titanic* the American cultural impulse toward grounding nobility among the common folk. Although we have already discussed the notion of high birth versus low birth for heroes and heroines, it is worth noting again here that Americans have an abiding love for the underdog. As a culture, we find great satisfaction in thumbing our nose at the titled aristocracy, searching for character flaws among the well bred, and cheering the impoverished prince who rises to the challenge. Thus the populist values on display in *Titanic* resonate strongly with American audiences.

Somewhat more subtle than Jack's diamond-in-the-rough status as the true prince is Rose's social journey from royal princess to "people's princess," which eerily echoes the untimely death in mid-1997 of England's Princess Diana. Despite our common-man liberatory posture, Americans still delight in feminine and female embodiments of royalty. The most sought-after virgins are always high-born, pure vessels—the means to an improved lineage for our impoverished, but bright and ambitious, prince. Although Rose journeys downward socially over the course of the narrative in order to display her strength of will and motivation to live, we never lose sight of the fact that she is more elegant and refined than the everyday girl next door. She is the ideal princess for us, meeting our two subconscious sets of mythic criteria: well bred yet able to throw a good right hook.

Third, we are reminded that the industrial age has had a profound impact upon America's social structure and storytelling. The late 1800s and early 1900s continue to be seen as a watershed era in American (and world) history. Indeed, from the first film we discussed, 1939's *Gone with the Wind,* to 1997's *Titanic,* the advent of mass mechanization reconstituted our culture's sense of itself and its relationship to nature and the divine. *Titanic,* the ship, represents the industrial revolution's faith in technology and science as the means to bring nature under human control. At the outset of the twentieth century, American culture was infused with a sense of mechanistic mission, a technological eminent domain that gave birth to construction projects such as the building of the *Titanic.* Cameron illustrates this attitude well at the outset of the film. The *Titanic* is depicted as enormous and enormously important—an iron-clad monument to human industry—and hubris. However, once the ship strikes the iceberg—encounters the greater power of nature—the camera pulls back to reveal, suddenly and ominously, its diminutive size relative to the vastness of the ocean. Just as the *Titanic* is revealed to be but a small speck in the hugeness of the sea, so are we humans revealed to be but infinitely small dots in an increasingly vast natural universe.

We come to understand our humble role in the order of things—a sentiment Joseph Campbell would surely have appreciated. At its most sublime level, *Titanic* is a myth appropriate for closing one millennium and opening another. It presents us with a cautionary tale of birth and death—and rebirth. For we have all been aboard the *Titanic* for a century or so now; we have ridden science and technology from one era into another. And although they do not appear to be taking us under, neither do they seem to be the passages to human perfection and control over our destinies that we had hoped. We, like Rose, are bobbing at the surface of cataclysmic change. The continuing strength of myth, I believe, will be one of those sturdy rafts that safely bears us home.

Star Wars: Episode I—The Phantom Menace (1999)

In 1999, George Lucas presented us with the origin story for his *Star Wars* series. An origin story is a myth that tells how things came to be as they are. For example, the book of Genesis in the Bible tells how God created the world over a six-day period. In *Episode I,* Lucas presents us with a fully formed universe already populated with several species spread across many galaxies and operating under countervailing forces of good and evil. Just as in the original *Star Wars* trilogy, these are characters readily recognizable to American eyes—public warriors, crooked politicians, beautiful princesses, and child messiahs.

The story opens with a classic mythic format—cataclysmic change is threatening human society. The forces of evil, this time embodied in the greedy Trade Federation, are threatening the smaller and weaker segments of society. Two Jedi knights, the public warriors of Lucas's universe, have been sent as emissaries of peace to the Trade Federation headquarters, but soon find that the evildoers have no desire to compromise. Lucas's conceptualization of the Jedi knights is a wonderful compendium of several American cultural ideals—they are allied with God or the Good, but—in deference to American desires for physical combat—are also athletic and proficient with weapons, most notably the light saber (God's holy fire). The Jedi knights dress in biblical earth-tone robes and have a biblical mien. In essence, they are angels with an attitude. In contrast with them, Lucas provides two evil figures: a red-shrouded politician who directs the villainous Sith population and his warrior-minion, Darth Maul, who is modeled after American conceptions of the devil and is dressed in red and black with yellow eyes and a horned head.

The target of evil is also familiar to us, given our acquired grasp of American mythological symbolism; it is the small, verdant planet of Naboo, which is headed by the beautiful, young and virginal Queen Amidala. At basis, Naboo and Amidala represent nature, goodness, and the female principle. As such they are ideal prey for the technological, evil, maleness of the Trade Federation.

After escaping the initial attempt of the Trade Federation soldiers to murder them, the two Jedi knights, QuiOn Jim and Obi-Wan Kenobi, encounter an interesting being on Naboo. His name is Jar Jar Binks, and he is a remarkable hybrid creation by Lucas. Jar Jar combines positive cultural meanings drawn from dogs, horses, and Rastafarian Jamaicans. (My sense here is that Jar Jar and his species, the Gungans, are meant to evoke the purity, simplicity, and spontaneity of nature; thus, they make an appropriate opposition to the mental, mechanical, hierarchical, competitive content of Lucas's vision of evil.) Jar Jar and the Gungans live in a wondrous undersea city that evokes childhood images of forest fairies and gnomes. The two Jedi knights attempt to convince the Gungans to assist the Naboo humans' efforts to repel the invaders. But the Gungans are noncommittal; the Nabooines, it seems, have always treated them as lesser beings, second-class citizens of the planet.

The evil invaders capture Queen Amidala, but she is heroically rescued by the two Jedi knights and Jar Jar. A helpful machine, the robot R2-D2, is introduced, who assists the humans with technological problems. The group escapes to the planet Tattooine—a criminal outpost operated by the outlaw Hutts. Tattoine is immediately recognizable to us as Dodge City, minus Matt Dillon. It is a dry, dusty western town populated by all manner (and species) of outlaw, riffraff, ne'er-do-wells, crooks, and bad guys. Here they encounter a young, blond-haired slave, named Anakin Skywalker. As we immediately detect, of course, Anakin has a special destiny. He is a Golden Child, a princeling, a young messiah. We learn that his mother bore him immaculately and that he has special gifts of foreseeing and technological wizardry.

Anakin's mother is a Madonna-like character—she has dark hair and a kind, beatific face, and wears grey, rough robes. She recognizes that her son has a special purpose and that these Jedi knights were sent (no doubt by his divine father) to fetch him. However, Anakin must first prove his worthiness. He accomplishes this by building and racing a hot rod, here termed a "pod," against a larger, stronger foe, Sepulbaba, a criminal modeled after Massala in *Ben Hur.* Just as with Charlton Heston's heroic character in *Ben Hur,* it is Anakin's divinely guided fate to emerge victorious from the race. His mother encourages his quest, telling him: "You have brought hope to those who had none."[2] Thus, Anakin wins his freedom and proves his inherent worth; he prepares to leave Tatooine with the Jedi knights to fulfill his destiny. His mother, like those of Moses, Ben Hur, and Jesus, lets him go, knowing he has been called to a larger task.

Just at their moment of departure, however, Darth Maul appears, dressed in red and black and riding a "black cycle"; Darth carries a red light saber. QuiOn Jim tricks him, and the troupe speeds off to Curisal—a completely urbanized and politicized planet. It resembles the mythic Metropolis, a futuristic version of New York City where the universe's governing senate is housed. All manner of life forms, political agendas, and varieties of moral position are present here. Curisal represents the distillation of the good and bad social elements of culture. Within the august senate's chambers, Queen Amidala is being betrayed by one of her closest advisors—Senator Palpatine, the secret leader of the evil Sith brotherhood.

In the same city is located the Jedi knight council (the racially and zoologically diverse conclave of Good Angels).[3] QuiOn Jim presents Anakin to the council. They recognize his special gifts and sense the Force within him, yet they sense deep character flaws as well. Perhaps, they suggest, he will use his divine powers in tragic ways. Like Satan in Milton's *Paradise Lost,* he may grow to challenge God and have to be cast forcibly from heaven. QuiOn Jim rejects the council's judgment and takes Anakin on as his apprentice; Obi-Wan Kenobi is elevated in rank to a full Jedi knight.

Palpatine, in league with the Trade Federation, makes his move on Naboo, sending in thousands of mechanized, insectlike troops. The Gungans courageously commit themselves to battle and together with the Naboo humans engage the invaders in combat. Lucas depicts the battle as a classic struggle between nature/good and technology/evil. The Gungans emerge from their lakes and forests mounted on animals. (This battle is symbolically equivalent to that between the Ewoks and Darth Vader's evil forces in *Return of the Jedi.*) Also echoing that earlier film, this story presents a classic duel between the two Jedi knights and Darth Maul. Lucas clothes the knights in white, Darth Maul in black. QuiOn Jim is slain (the dying god motif of martyrdom), and Obi-Wan Kenobi proves his worth as a knight by slaying Darth Maul alone and avenging the death of his mentor/father.

Anakin displays his courage and giftedness as well, using a fighter plane and explosives to blow up the Trade Federation command post. With their military brain destroyed, the robotic storm troopers collapse. Tatooine is saved. At the close of the battle QuiOn Jim's spirit speaks to Obi-Wan, instructing him to guide Anakin to knighthood. QuiOn believes that Anakin is indeed the Chosen One who will bring harmony to the universe. QuiOn's mortal remains are burned atop a funeral pyre; this frees his spirit to join the Force. A victory celebration ensues during which all Naboo's various species are united in cooperative friendship. Peace and goodness have been restored—at least for the present.

As you, the astute reader, have no doubt already discerned, *Star Wars: Episode I* is a classic mythic tale of heroic quest; it carries traces from not only the three "later" *Star Wars* episodes, but also from the Christian story of Jesus' immaculate birth, as well as the many Sumerian, Greek, and Roman myths of the special child marked for a special destiny. As human culture now embarks on its next millennium of existence on our small planet, Earth, it is perhaps worth taking note of how little our stories have changed since we first became conscious beings. Our present project has reviewed the tales told through motion pictures and television shows over the past sixty or so years—a tiny droplet in the flow of human mythmaking. Yet in this droplet we have glimpsed the archetypes, story structures, hopes, anxieties, wishes, fears, and longings that are inscribed on our species. Every myth we view in a darkened theater or watch on the television set has embedded within it the echoes of our human memory—a memory that stretches deep into the past and will be carried forward as long as there are storytellers to speak and an audience to listen.

NOTES

CHAPTER 1

1. Others in our analysis include *Sleeping Beauty, The Lion King, The Jungle Book,* and *101 Dalmatians.*
2. Indeed, perhaps the primary indicator of myth's centrality to human culture is its longevity.
3. Translated into other terms, Snow White = white (good) female magic; the wicked Queen = black (evil) female magic.
4. Significantly, seven is a mystical number and pigs are female symbols, according to Gimbutas (1989).
5. Wind, hail, thunder, lightning, and rain are all mythically linked to powers of the destructive goddess.
6. Each culture has its own story, internally believed to be *the* story, of how the world began.
7. And in a puritanical American vein, clearly discourages inebriation.

8. Thus Ashley and Melanie are literally of the same "blood." This tendency toward inbreeding may also be suggestive of the progressive weakening often ascribed to aristocratic lineages.
9. Tara means "land" in Gaelic. The Southern plantations represent castles in a mythic sense.
10. It is interesting to note here that the Wilkes home, symbolizing the true aristocracy, was completely demolished, whereas the O'Hara home was simply stripped of its "pretensions." It was as if, recognizing one of their own kind, the Yankees simply reduced the O'Hara house to make it resemble a factory worker's dwelling.
11. Significantly, the term "material" springs from the Latin root *mater* ("mother"). Scarlett is a thoroughly material woman, loving both land and wealth.

CHAPTER 2

1. An iconic image is an archetype that has been translated into the imagery of a given culture. For example, the warrior archetype becomes a samurai in Japan and a western sheriff in America.
2. Instead of just riding up and kissing her as in *Snow White.*
3. Although it is not made explicit in the film, Nefertiri is Ramses' sister. To preserve the purity of the royal lineage, pharaohs mated with their sisters.
4. A consistent pattern in biblical myths is a patriarchal preference for male children. Women are merely the vessels that perpetuate the lineage.
5. Recall the use of the mystical number seven in *Snow White.*
6. "Hebrew" springs from *habiru,* which in Arabic means "wanderer."
7. See, for example, the Gilgamesh epic from about 2500 B.C.
8. This is directly parallel to Moses' journey through the Sinai desert.
9. Even more remarkably in this film, her head is covered with black bull horns, resembling (as Gimbutas notes) the female uterus.
10. James Bond is also an excellent example of a public warrior.
11. This episode was directed by John Ford, renowned director of several John Wayne westerns. Ward Bond, the wagon master in *Wagon Train,* was a protégé of Ford's.

12. In a wonderful bit of intertextuality, the Count declares that he is descended from *Ben Hur*! The motion picture was released earlier that same year (1959).
13. Belle Watson is a similar figure in *Gone with the Wind.*
14. In syndication.
15. Significantly, Lucy most often wears *slacks* in the show, not dresses, indicating her largely asexual status.

CHAPTER 3

1. As before, all four of these characters are unmarried, leaving them free as warriors to safeguard the public at large.
2. Up until now, Billy had told everyone he was accused of stealing *one* horse.
3. As an aside here, we might want to consider why, in both shows, prejudice against the *Chinese* was chosen to illustrate this point. Although historically accurate—the Chinese were a very abused ethnic minority in the American West—it is perhaps also true that defending a black or Hispanic man would have proven too politically controversial to be addressed during the 1950s and early 1960s. Indeed, we will have to wait until the 1970s before anti-black and anti-Hispanic prejudice is addressed by a new type of character to appear on American television screens—Archie Bunker.
4. I suspect that both may be imitating the *I Love Lucy* show in this respect. Recall that Ricky Ricardo's show business career provided ample fodder for exciting show plots.
5. They can also take on animal forms. In the opening credits, Samantha is shown in cartoon form turning herself into a cat.
6. Symbolically, of course, this represents Samantha's (female equals cat) control over him (man equals dog).
7. The park setting is a nice touch here, for it reminds us of the inevitable cycle of life: birth, death, rebirth.
8. Griffith is originally from Mt. Holly, North Carolina.
9. The character of Lenny in John Steinbeck's *Of Mice and Men* is based upon the same basic archetype.

10. It is also perhaps seen as “slow” and “backward,” which amounts to the same thing.
11. Analogously, Endora, Samantha’s witch mother, was much better at using magic than Samantha was; she, like Granny, had much more experience in these ancient female arts.
12. As witness its very successful, live action return in 1996.
13. The PETA people should consider using Cruella as their poster woman.
14. This is virtually the only instance I encountered where vultures were used as friendly beings; in almost all other instances they were associated with destruction and death.
15. A Freudian interpretation of this scene is that Mowgli has now reached puberty and his desire to mate and procreate outweighs his desire to remain a boy. Confronted with a choice between playmates and a wife, he chooses the wife.
16. *Dr. Zhivago* won six Academy Awards in 1965, including the one for Best Picture.
17. Mediating texts or archetypes contain elements of two bipolar positions. For example, mediating between urban and rural is suburban, between masculine and feminine is androgynous, between rich and poor is middle class.
18. *Dr. Zhivago* is the first text we have encountered thus far that uses a nonlinear time sequence. This, too, marks it as a modern film.
19. Recall that Nefertiri and Ramses were also ruling-class brother and sister. The inbreeding of the upper class, which gives rise to its destruction, is featured in both these films.
20. Recall that the “good” aristocrats, Melanie Hamilton and Ashley Wilkes, were unable to successfully navigate the New South in *Gone with the Wind.*
21. “Plastics” here signifies the falseness and inauthenticity of his parents’ life.

CHAPTER 4

1. The ultimate denouement occurs at the end of *Godfather II,* a sequel; Michael has his only remaining brother, Fredo, shot. He then sits brooding, alone, in his study.

2. Here he is an archetypal male warrior seeking a pure female vessel to bear his children. *The Godfather* is one of the few films we have examined which explicitly deals with the notion of perpetuating a lineage.
3. The analogy to the United States' involvement in Vietnam is also clear: We had to destroy the country in order to "save" it.
4. Which features the song "When You Wish Upon a Star."
5. This may be due at least in part to Joseph Campbell's serving in an advisory capacity to the film's writer and director, George Lucas.
6. This is the 1970s; by now women are working outside the home and active in nondomestic roles. Remember Lois Lane, Chris McNeil, and Princess Leia!
7. In one example, Danny must race his car against a rival gang leader's. In a scene reminiscent of *Ben Hur*'s chariot race, Danny's white car outruns his rival's black, spike-wheeled car.

CHAPTER 5

1. *All in the Family* was truly a phenomenon in television programming, remaining number 1 from October 1971, when it debuted, until April 1976.
2. Could this be Garry's hometown?
3. *Three's Company* was rated number 2 in the 1979–1980 season, after *60 Minutes,* which is not a series.

CHAPTER 6

1. It is interesting here that *flowers*—a pre-Christian female symbol—are used to signal spiritual life and death. In our culture, female-nature-spirituality are all symbolically linked in opposition to male-technology-science.
2. An aside here: While there are probably historic or contemporary societies whose myths uphold maintenance of the status quo and the firm rule of law and order, ours is not one of them. Almost always our heroes are the rebels, the revolutionaries, and the underdogs. Americans love a come-from-behind victory.

3. Bellock challenges him, saying, "Go ahead, blow it back to God. You and I are simply passing through history. This *is* history."
4. This was a disturbing finale to me. It would have been much more mythically meaningful for Spielberg to have Jones transport the ark back to a secret location in the Holy Land.
5. It is my intuitive belief that the Indiana Jones character was based upon George Lucas's and Steven Spielberg's friendship with Sarah Lawrence College's brilliant scholar of archaeological mythology, Joseph Campbell—the very same Joseph Campbell whose research informs this present work. Lucas came to know, and deeply admire, Campbell while developing his *Star Wars* trilogy. I believe he based his initial conceptualization of Indiana Jones on what Campbell "might have been like," if he had been able to act upon his fantasies.
6. Unfortunately, Spielberg has made the interior golden.
7. Note that no overt mention is made of the fact that Indiana and Henry have now become immortal; to do so would lessen the purity of the film's central message, which is about true love and self-sacrifice.
8. Recall that *both* Henry and Indiana bedded Elsa.
9. Recall the ancient association between women and music.
10. This is the first African-American actor to star in a top-50 motion picture. The year is 1987.
11. Except for Kryptonite.
12. The African-American actor in *Ghostbusters* was certainly a positive step, but he still did not play the main role.

CHAPTER 7

1. I am heartbroken that I was unable to obtain videotapes of *Dynasty,* a comparable series that featured Joan Collins as the destructive goddess Alexis Carrington Colby.
2. Don Johnson in *Miami Vice* represented this same iconic imagery.
3. Borrowing characters from other shows is not uncommon on television and is termed "intertextuality." It is done to transfer the archetypal meaning of the character into a new setting. In the present instance, the crime-solving styles of Magnum and Jessica

Fletcher are compared. Similarly, "spin-off" series take a character whose archetypal meaning has been established on one series and then place that character in his or her own narrative.

CHAPTER 8

1. *Seinfeld* had an overriding Jewish sensibility; *Friends* does not.
2. Before we launch into a discussion of *Murphy Brown,* we need to spend a moment or two pondering her *name.* Quite intriguingly, many androgynous female heroes from 1980 onward have been assigned ambiguous or masculine names. Consider, for example, Ripley (Sigourney Weaver) in the *Aliens* motion picture trilogy and J. C. Wyatt (Diane Keaton) in *Baby Boom.* This is done as a cultural signal that these women, like Murphy Brown, possess both masculine and feminine qualities.
3. It is also worth noting that Murphy often wears masculine clothing: pants suits at work, pajamas at home. This plays as irony against Candace Bergen's ravishingly beautiful blondness.
4. Murphy became pregnant during the previous season after a short relationship. She was faced with the decision to either get an abortion or give birth.
5. Murphy prefers Motown music; the baby likes Manilow.
6. *ER* first reached number 1 during the 1995–1996 season and continued at number 1 during the 1996–1999 time period.

CHAPTER 9

1. I'm not completely happy with this grouping, as many of the films cut across the themes, but we'll try to make the best of it.
2. *Strange Days* starring Ralph Fiennes is another.
3. Harrison Ford has appeared in more top-50 films than any other actor.
4. His first was attempting to rescue his wife.
5. Recall the allegations of data falsification in the television series *ER.*

6. In this they greatly resemble Tiny Tim in Charles Dickens's *A Christmas Carol.*
7. Yes, I do mean to be using the male pronoun here. None of these films features a female champion. We shall have to wait until the end of Chapter 11 to encounter one.

CHAPTER 10

1. To steal a line from the Duke of Windsor.
2. Even her pot-making marks her as female.
3. I don't fully understand the psychological mechanisms that permit this to occur. It could be that the use of nonhuman signifiers permits us to make full use of the power of the metaphorical imagery, rather than focusing upon a specific human character.
4. This story line is a bit more progressive than that in *The Lion King.*
5. Unknown to Robin, his father had had a son with the peasant woman he was seeing.
6. Remember *Tootsie*!

CHAPTER 11

1. Here again is the masculine-androgynous name for the woman protagonist, as in *Murphy Brown.*
2. Thus, here the conflict is not between technology and humans, but rather between for-profit and for-people uses of technology.
3. There is ample archetypal irony here: The predatory lawyer is devoured by a *real* predator, the T. rex.

CHAPTER 12

1. Mel Gibson's movie *Braveheart* altered factual history to fulfill this mythic need. In the film, William Wallace impregnates the wife of the future King of England. Thus, even though Wallace perished attempting to free Scotland from English rule, fictively

his son becomes King of England, placing Scottish progeny upon the throne.

2. Once again we see the underdog theme, so beloved by Americans, played out.
3. Symbolically, this is *not* the best location for the Jedi knights; their physical proximity to the tumult of human politics could taint them. Lucas would have done better to set them on a distant nature-based planet.

REFERENCES

Boas, Franz (1911). *The Mind of Primitive Man.* New York: Macmillan.

Campbell, Joseph (1968). *The Hero with a Thousand Faces.* Princeton, New Jersey: Princeton University Press.

______ (1970). "Mythological themes in creative literature and art." In *Myths, Dreams, and Religion,* J. Campbell (ed.). New York: E.P. Dutton.

______ (1973). *Creative Mythology: The Masks of God.* New York: Penguin Books.

Chase, Richard (1949). *Quest for Myth.* Baton Rouge, LA: Louisana State University Press.

Denzin, Norman K. (1991). *Hollywood Shot by Shot.* New York: Aldine de Gruyter.

Durkheim, Emile (1961). *The Elementary Forms of Religious Life,* trans. by Joseph Ward Swain. New York: Collier Books.

Freud, Sigmund (1946). *Totem and Taboo.* New York: Vintage Press.

______ (1953). The *Interpretation of Dreams* (Standard Edition IV), trans. by James Strachey. London: The Hogarth Press.

Gimbutas, Marija (1989). *The Language of the Goddess.* London: Mouton de Gruyter.

Hopper, Stanley R. (1970). "Myth, dream, and imagination." In *Myths, Dreams and Religion,* J. Campbell (ed.), 21–39. New York: E.P. Dutton.

Hyman, Stanley Edgar (1965). "The ritual view of the myth and the mythic." In *Myth: A Symposium,* T. A. Sebeok (ed.), 136–53. Bloomington: Indiana University Press.

Jung, Carl G. (1958). *Psychology and Religion.* New York and London: Hogarth.

______ (1967). *Symbols of Transformation* (Collected Works of Carl Jung), trans. by R. F. C. Hull. New York and London: Hogarth.

______ (1968). *Man and His Symbols.* New York: Dell Books.

Kirk, G. S. (1970). *Myth: Its Meaning and Functions in Ancient and Other Cultures.* Cambridge: Cambridge University Press.

Leach, Edmund R. (1967). "Genesis as myth." In *Myth and Cosmos,* J. Middleton (ed.), 1–14. Garden City, NY: The Natural History Press.

Lévi-Strauss, Claude (1965). "The structural study of myth." In *Myth: A Symposium,* T. A. Sebeok (ed.), 81–106. Bloomington: Indiana University Press.

______ (1967). "Four Winnebago myths: A structural sketch." In *Myth and Cosmos,* J. Middleton (ed.), 15–26. Garden City, NY: The Natural History Press.

______ (1969). *The Raw and the Cooked.* New York: Harper and Row.

______ (1978). *Myth and Meaning.* New York: Schocken Books.

Littleton, C. Scott (1982). *The New Comparative Mythology.* Berkeley University of California Press.

Lowry, Shirley Park (1982). *Familiar Mysteries: The Truth in Myth.* Oxford: Oxford University Press.

Malinowski, Bronislaw (1926). *Myth in Primitive Psychology.* London: Allwin.

Middleton, John (ed.) (1967). *Myths and Cosmos.* Garden City, NY: The Natural History Press.

Sebeok, Thomas A. (ed.) (1965). *Myth: A Symposium.* Bloomington: Indiana University Press.

Watts, Alan W. (1953). *Myths and Ritual in Christianity.* London: Allwin.

Wheelwright, Philip (1965). "The semantic approach to myth." In *Myth: A Symposium,* T. A. Sebeok (ed.), 154–68. Bloomington: Indiana University Press.